Ky, We've been to page 252 and perhaps others as well, but I am still hungry for adventures with you. To great food, and always better company!

Love,
James

FOOD
JOURNEYS
of a
LIFETIME

500

Extraordinary Places to Eat Around the Globe

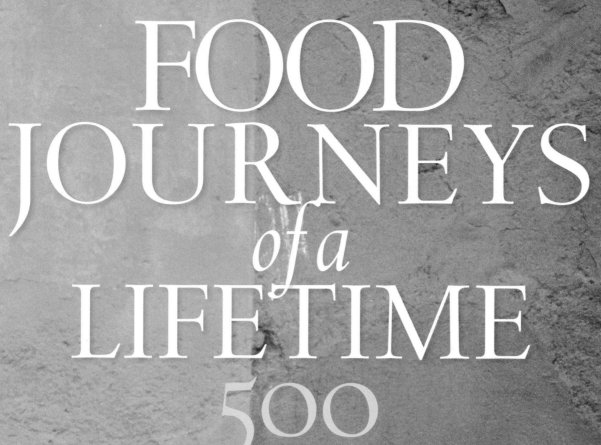

FOOD
JOURNEYS
of a
LIFETIME

500
Extraordinary Places to Eat
Around the Globe

INTRODUCTION BY KEITH BELLOWS
EDITOR-IN-CHIEF, NATIONAL GEOGRAPHIC TRAVELER MAGAZINE

NATIONAL GEOGRAPHIC
WASHINGTON, D.C.

CONTENTS

Previous pages: Delivering freshly baked bread in Mexico City.
Opposite: In the kitchens of Vienna's Hotel Sacher, a pastry chef
ladles chocolate onto the hotel's opulent signature cake, the *sachertorte*.

THE TASTE OF TRAVEL

t is 4 a.m. and I'm with a friend in Tokyo at the world's largest wholesale fish market, Tsukiji. Saws whine as huge tuna are carved up. Buckets brim with octopus, sea urchins, salmon, and creatures bizarre enough to appear in a science documentary. We slip into Daiwa Sushi, the city's oldest sushi counter.

My companion begins ordering in a flood of Japanese. The dishes come in rapid succession: Indian Ocean tuna, mackerel, freshwater eel, oysters, flounder. Suddenly, a single shrimp is set before each of us. I do a double take. Each is undulating, clearly alive. My friend downs his with a grin. After watching mine squirm for 30 seconds, I swallow it without gagging.

This little adventure in eating is part of what makes travel so exhilarating. Invariably, when I think of a place, I recall a memorable experience—either because of the food I've eaten or the people I shared it with. I've had lamb's cheeks sitting cross-legged on the floor of a Bedouin tent in Jordan; dined on fresh-caught piranha in the Amazon; eaten sweet shrimp while dangling my legs over azure Thai waters; and lived off baguettes, cheese, and salami while backpacking through France.

A meal abroad is more than an intake of calories; it's an exercise in cultural immersion. What people eat, when they eat, where and how they source the food, what gastronomic rituals they observe—all offer telling insights to a place and its people.

This book celebrates the unique relationship between food and travel, between place and the plate. It is endlessly fascinating, offering up a cultural and culinary smorgasbord that can enrich your travels, surprise your palate, and even enliven the meals you serve at home. It truly delivers the taste of travel.

Keith Bellows
Editor-in-Chief, National Geographic Traveler magazine

Opposite: With views that seem to come straight from a Canaletto painting, the ultra-luxurious Dogaressa Suite of Venice's Hotel Cipriani offers dining paradise.

SPECIALTIES & INGREDIENTS

1

For those who love good food, the chance to sample local specialties is one of the greatest joys of travel, and there is no better way to appreciate the heart and soul of a place and its people than to share their harvests, the hard-won catches of their fishermen, the delicacies fashioned by their bakers, and the treasured recipes showing these ingredients at their best.

The journeys that follow take you to some of the world's most enticing landscapes, such as the ancient olive groves of Greece, the rose-red cherry orchards of rural Michigan, and rocky coves on the Massachusetts coast, where the Atlantic tide nurtures clams and oysters to be savored in their raw, briny state, or simmered, or fried. Chili-aficionados can follow a fiery odyssey into the heart of Mexico, exploring the nuances of smokiness and sweetness in spectacular dishes devised by Mexican cooks. There are urban adventures, too, such as the disciplined frenzy of Tokyo's Tsukiji Fish Market, where perfect specimens of tuna are auctioned daily to the master sushi-makers of Japan—a formidable breed of culinary artists.

No food is as evocative of its source of origin than the wonderful array of seafood that is harvested from the world's shorelines and coastal waters, whether simply cooked or combined with other ingredients.

Piles of wooden lobster traps are a common sight on the wharves of New Brunswick's coastal towns.

CANADA

LOBSTERS AND OYSTERS

Sample some of the Atlantic's tastiest
seafood along New Brunswick's eastern shore.

If you are searching for just-off-the-boat seafood, there is no better place to start than Shediac, northeast of the city of Moncton, where you can join a cruise to learn about lobstering as you feast on whole steamed lobster. North of Shediac, a series of seaside villages provides the opportunity to sample lobster stews and bisques, pastas with lobster sauce, and lobster rolls made with moist chunks of meat mixed with a touch of mayonnaise. Beausoleil oysters are harvested just offshore, and in Bouctouche and Shippagan they are on the menu either steamed, grilled, sautéed, or in thick, hearty chowders, while near the Acadian community of Caraquet you can savor the buttery-sweet Caraquet oysters from nearby Chaleur Bay. Heading back south, cross to Prince Edward Island (PEI) via the Confederation Bridge for a taste of Malpeque Bay oysters—an oversized bivalve with a sweet, mild flavor harvested from the eponymous bay on the island's northwestern shore. In Hope River, in central PEI, look out for St. Ann's Church, where you may see a sign announcing a lobster supper.

When to Go Fresh seafood is available year-round. Summer and fall—the seasons when most attractions are open—have the best weather.

Planning Fly into the Greater Moncton International Airport and rent a car. Stay at least a week to eat your fill of lobsters and oysters and visit landmark sights, such as New Brunswick's Hopewell Rocks and Fundy National Park, and PEI's Charlottetown and the house in Cavendish that inspired L.M. Montgomery's *Anne of Green Gables*.

Websites www.tourismnewbrunswick.ca, www.peiplay.com, www.lobstertales.ca, www.lobstersuppers.com

Seafood Festivals

■ Shediac, which bills itself as the Lobster Capital of the World, has held an annual **Lobster Festival**, featuring lobster-eating contests and lobster dinners, every July since 1949.

■ Plan your itinerary around the **Atlantic Seafood Festival** held in Moncton in August. The festival combines celebrity-chef demonstrations, wine and food tastings, and culinary competitions with musical entertainment. Competitors vie for the title of fastest oyster-shucker or top chef for the best seafood chowder.

■ The **Prince Edward Island International Shellfish Festival** in Charlottetown features three different oyster-shucking competitions pitting the world's best shuckers against each other. The September event also includes championships for best potato seafood chowder and best cream chowder, as well as shellfish cooking demonstrations presented by the Culinary Institute of Canada.

Fresh lobster is a regular fixture on many of the area's menus.

VERMONT

MAPLE SYRUP

As winter draws to a close, visit Vermont
to find yourself in maple heaven.

A cloud of steam envelops visitors as they push open the door to a Vermont sugarhouse where sap from the local "sugarbush" (stand of maples) is boiling down in large metal pans known as evaporators. The sugarmaker raises a dipper of the amber liquid and watches as it drips back into the evaporator to test whether it "aprons" (drips off the end of the dipper in sheets)—an indication that the sap has reduced to a syrup and is ready for pouring off. It is a scene repeated in sugarhouses across Vermont from late February through early April, when a succession of freezing nights followed by warm days causes the sap to run. To tap the trees, holes are drilled through the sapwood (outer tree trunk) at a slightly upward angle and fitted with spouts or taps. The sap flows out through the tapholes and is collected either in buckets hung on the taps or via plastic tubing. Purchase a gallon of maple syrup and a handful of maple-sugar cakes, or head to a sugar-on-snow party at one of the local town festivals or sugarhouse open house weekends. At these, hot syrup is dribbled over a dish of fresh snow and hardens in lacy patterns as it cools. Scoop up the maple with a popsicle stick and take a lick. You can cut the sweetness with a bite of a sour dill pickle.

When to Go The sugaring season, though weather-dependent, traditionally begins around Town Meeting Day, the first Tuesday of March, and extends into April. The annual Vermont Maple Open House Weekend, when a number of sugarhouses open their doors to the public, is held the first weekend of spring.

Planning Many sugarhouses welcome visitors during the season, but call ahead to make sure they are boiling that day, and dress for the cold. Sugar-on-snow parties are held each year as part of early spring festivals and are listed in the local press or on the Vermont Maple Sugar Makers' Association website.

Websites www.vermontmaple.org, www.travel-vermont.com

Maple Products

Maple syrup is best known as a topping for pancakes and waffles—but that's just the beginning. The sweet, thick liquid is added as a flavoring to everything from meats to desserts, including even vodka. And, like the early Native Americans, many sugarmakers make **maple** or **Indian sugar** by boiling syrup until most of the water has evaporated, leaving a crumbly, granular sugar.

Syrup boiled down to a thick consistency can be pressed into molds and hardened to make small candies known as **sugar cakes. Maple cream** or **maple butter**, used as a spread for toast and muffins, is another Vermont favorite. The sweet cream results from boiling the syrup, cooling it rapidly, and stirring until it is smooth.

Each bucket is hung on the sugar maple on a spout through which sap flows when conditions are ideal for the sap run.

FOOD FACTORIES & MUSEUMS

Many people have a passion for food and drink, and some have opened museums dedicated to their favorite. Many factories are also open to visitors. Most offer samples.

❶ Ben & Jerry's, Waterbury, Vermont

Watch as giant machines mix and stir the basic ingredients, add chunks and swirls of fruit, caramel, or nuts, and fill the 1-pint containers with finished ice cream, which heads for the spiral hardener and the final freezing. Then taste-test the flavors of the day. Before leaving, you can wander the Flavor Graveyard, where a selection of the less successful flavors are memorialized.

Planning The factory is open daily except major holidays. The tour lasts 30 minutes, with free samples at the end. The site also includes a picnic area and shop. www.benjerry.com

❷ World of Coca-Cola, Atlanta, Georgia

Through a glass tunnel you can watch a bottling plant, decelerated for easier comprehension, and then taste some 60 global Coca-Cola products. The site also has advertisements from 1905 onward and a Pop Culture gallery. While most exhibits are solidly promotional, one covers 1985's doomed "New Coke" launch.

Planning Self-guided tours last 1.5–2 hours. www.worldofcocacola.com

❸ Mount Horeb Mustard Museum, Wisconsin

Founded in 1986, the museum houses a collection of 5,000 mustards from around the world, together with memorabilia such as antique mustard pots and old advertisements, and displays explaining how mustard is made. In the shop you can sample many of the featured mustards and buy your favorites.

Planning The museum, which began in Mount Horeb, is now located in Middleton and is open daily except major holidays. www.mustardweb.com

❹ Shin-Yokohama Raumen Museum, Japan

This lively museum-cum-historical theme park celebrates everything to do with raumen, the popular Japanese noodle and broth dish. Displays include one on the history of noodle-making and collections of raumen-related utensils and dishes, while the lower floors house a re-creation of Tokyo streets in 1958—the year that instant noodles were created—with shops, bars, and raumen restaurants each featuring dishes from different parts of Japan.

Planning Close to JR Shin-Yokohama station, 15-45 minutes from central Tokyo, depending on the transport you use. www.raumen.co.jp

❺ Museum of Bread Culture, Ulm, Germany

Covering bread's 6,000-year-old impact on human history, this museum features no actual bread, but rather the tools used to make it. It includes a gallery of bread artworks by Picasso and others, and has exhibits celebrating bread's religious significance.

Planning Open daily, the museum is in the 16th-century Salzstadel in Ulm's old city. A local specialty is *Ulmer zuckerbrot* (sugar bread). www.museum-brotkultur.de

❻ Pick Salami and Szeged Paprika Museum, Hungary

The city of Szeged in southeast Hungary is a leading producer of salami and paprika. The Pick company opened its salami factory here in 1869, and paprika has been produced in the city since the mid-18th century. The Pick factory houses a museum explaining the history and manufacture of both.

Planning The museum is open afternoons, Tuesdays through Saturdays, except public holidays and Christmas. For guided tours in English, reserve a week ahead. www.pickmuzeum.hu

❼ Museo del Peperoncino, Maierà, Italy

So vital is Calabria's chili (*peperoncino*) that it appears even in desserts like *crostata del diavolo* (devil's tart). The museum in Maierà's ducal palace was founded by Calabria's chili society and displays paintings and examples of around 150 chili varieties.

Planning The museum is open seasonally: check ahead. To reach Maierà, take a Naples-Diamante train (2.5-3.5 hours), then a bus or taxi. September sees Diamante's Peperoncino Festival. www.aptcosenza.it

❽ Alimentarium, Vevey, Switzerland

Vevey hosts food-giant Nestlé's global headquarters. Overlooking Lake Geneva, the Alimentarium covers Nestlé's history since 1867 but also has sections on cooking, eating, the history of food production, the senses and food, and the digestion process.

Planning The museum is open Tuesdays to Sundays, and has a special section for kids. Book ahead for English-language guided tours. Vevey is an hour by train from Geneva. www.alimentarium.ch

❾ Museum of Cocoa and Chocolate, Brussels, Belgium

This fun-sized museum offers plentiful chances to taste—and sniff—chocolate and to trace various stages in its production. Explore chocolate's history from its origins in Aztec culture to more recent developments, such as the invention of praline in Belgium in the 20th century and even cocoa's cosmetic uses.

Planning A 17th-century building off Brussels's Grand Place hosts the museum. It is open Tuesdays to Sundays, and daily in July and August, except on public holidays. www.mucc.be

❿ Bramah's Museum of Tea and Coffee, London, England

London has long majored in tea-trading, while its 17th-century coffeehouses were important wheeling-and-dealing locations for the city's insurance and commodity brokers. Bramah's explains London's role in the history of tea and coffee and has a tearoom serving cream teas—a pot of tea and scones spread with thick cream and jam.

Planning Open daily except December 25-26. www.teaandcoffeemuseum.co.uk

Right: The bottles travel a circuitous route as they are filled, checked, and capped in the bottling plant at World of Coca-Cola.

A yacht swings gently at anchor, with one of Cape Ann's six lighthouses poking up on a headland beyond.

MASSACHUSETTS

Ipswich Clams

The mudflats and estuaries of the Massachusetts coast provide the main ingredient for some iconic seafood dishes.

Along Massachusetts Route 133 from Gloucester to Essex and Ipswich at low tide, the briny smell of the intertidal flats hangs in the air, mingling with the distinctive aroma of fried seafood. Where the road merges with Route 1-A, continue north toward Newburyport. Known locally as Clam Shack Alley, this stretch of road is a mecca for clam-lovers. Long lines snake out of the Clam Box of Ipswich, J.T. Farnham's, and other popular eateries. Regulars and first-time customers crowd into wooden booths at Woodman's of Essex, home of the original fried clam: cooked-to-order, crunchy-crisp clam bellies to be dunked into tangy, homemade tartar sauce. The iconic Ipswich soft-shell clam is hand-harvested from the clam flats of the Great Marsh, a diverse environment of salt marshes and estuaries stretching from Cape Ann north into New Hampshire. Along this coast, you can sample a traditional New England clambake, where clams and sides of corn on the cob, mussels, lobsters, sausages, and potatoes are steamed on a layer of wet seaweed over heated stones.

When to Go Most clam shacks are open from spring through late fall, closing for the season around the end of October.

Planning Expect long waits in summer, especially on weekends and holidays. Some places allow you to place a takeout order in advance, so call and ask before you go. Or dine mid-afternoon, after the lunchtime rush, or on a weekday evening.

Websites www.massvacation.com, www.ipswichma.com/clambox, www.woodmans.com

Portuguese Steamed Clams

The addition of Portuguese sausage during cooking gives the clams a spicy piquancy.

Serves 4
4 lb/1.8 kg steamers
Kosher salt or sea salt
1 cup/5 oz/150 g cornmeal
  (polenta)
Portuguese hard sausage, cut
  into chunks
Unsalted butter, melted

Rinse the clams well until you stop seeing sand. Sort through the clams and discard any with broken or cracked shells. Tap any open clams sharply and discard them if they do not close. Your aim is to throw out clams that have died; eating them can cause food poisoning.

Fill a clean sink or large pan with cold water. Add the salt (2 tbsp/1 oz/50 g salt to 1 gal/4L water) and cornmeal and stir. Add the clams and let stand for an hour or two. Rinse again.

Put the clams in the cooking pot with 2 cups/16 fl oz/475 ml water. Add the sausage. Cover and cook for 5-10 minutes until the clams open. Transfer the clams to serving plates. Pour the clam water (liquor) through a mesh or tea strainer into a pitcher.

Serve bowls of clams with liquor in one small dish, melted butter in another. Peel off the dark membrane over the neck before dipping and eating the clams. Dip first in liquor to rinse off any remaining sand, then in the butter. Discard any clams that have not opened. Real New Englanders drink the liquor at the end of the meal.

MICHIGAN

CHERRIES IN TRAVERSE CITY

Immerse yourself in all aspects of cherry cuisine
in the self-proclaimed Cherry Capital of the World.

The pastoral back roads of Leelanau Peninsula, on the west side of Lake Michigan's Grand Traverse Bay, are surrounded by miles of cherry orchards. If you travel the route in July, when the trees are dense with fat clusters of ruby red fruit, you will come across farm stands, their wooden counters groaning from the weight of heaped baskets of just-picked, tart, Montmorency cherries, cherry-filled pies standing 3 inches (7.5 centimeters) high, and jars of chunky cherry preserves. At some of the farms you can pick your own fruit. While here, you could also visit one of more than a dozen wineries in this bucolic countryside—reminiscent of Tuscany—to sample cherry wine, before reaching Traverse City. Cherries have been an integral part of this northern Michigan city's economy and cuisine for more than 150 years, giving rise to an industry whose roots go back to 1852, when a Presbyterian missionary planted the first orchard on nearby Old Mission Peninsula. Inventive chefs at local restaurants showcase cherries in season with such creations as whitefish in cherry sauce, cherry chicken soup, and cherry pulled pork. Locally produced cherry products fill the shelves at area shops, with cherry pies, dried cherries, cherry jams, and chocolate-covered cherries sharing shelf-space with the more unusual cherry Dijon mustard, cherry barbecue sauce, cherry salsa, cherry tea, and cherry-blueberry popcorn.

When to Go July through August for the sour cherry harvest, a few weeks earlier for sweet cherries, and May to see the cherry trees in bloom. The National Cherry Festival is held in the first full week of July.

Planning Allow a week to explore the region fully. Cherry Capital Airport is approximately ten minutes from downtown Traverse City. To travel around the peninsulas and visit the cherry orchards and wineries you need to rent a car. If you are visiting during the eight-day National Cherry Festival in July, make your hotel reservations early to avoid disappointment.

Websites www.visittraversecity.com, www.cherryfestival.org

National Cherry Festival

Nearly 75 percent of the world's tart cherries—the type used for pies, cakes, jams, jellies, and preserves—and 20 percent of the world's sweet cherries are produced in orchards along Grand Traverse Bay, a fact celebrated with the National Cherry Festival held annually in Traverse City.

Marvel at the many foods on sale made with cherries, including specialty foods, such as cherry bratwurst and hamburgers made with added ground cherries and topped with zippy cherry mustard.

Cherry-lovers vie for top honors in the **Sweet Treats Cherry Recipe Contest** and compete in cherry-pie eating and cherry-pit spitting contests.

Clusters of fruit ripen in the cherry orchards around Grand Traverse Bay.

CALIFORNIA'S ARTISAN CHEESES

The lush farmlands of northern California provide
the perfect setting for a tour of specialty cheese-makers.

Calidornia claims the greatest number of artisan cheese-producers in the U.S., but there's one small niche north of San Francisco's Golden Gate that is making a special name for itself. Tucked among the rolling grasslands and misty mountains of the North Bay (essentially Marin and Sonoma Counties), small farms have been producing specialty cheeses since the early 1980s. That's when Laura Chenel, who originated creamy, sumptuous American chèvre using the milk of her beloved goats on her Sonoma farm, was discovered by chef Alice Waters of Chez Panisse fame. Since then, artisan North Bay cheese-makers have earned national and international reputations, and their cheeses—which include soft, creamy bries, earthy California crottins, and soft, light-textured chèvre—are sold in some of the nation's most exclusive restaurants and shops as well as in local farmers' markets. Head out on the region's gloriously rural, untrafficked roads to tour the farms and see how the cheeses are made. Most farms also offer cheese tastings. Along the way, you can purchase your favorites for the epitome of a gourmet picnic—and don't forget that you are in the nation's most celebrated wine country as well.

When to Go The four-day California Artisan Cheese Festival takes place in March in Petaluma, 32 miles (51 km) north of San Francisco. Otherwise, plan for the scenery: the wild mustard flowers bloom in February; the vineyards are in full leaf May through August (though the region can be hot then, and weekend crowds considerable); September through October is harvest time, while fall colors ignite in November.

Planning Base yourself in chic Healdsburg or historic Sonoma with its Spanish-colonial town plaza. Sonoma is 20 miles (32 km) north of San Francisco; Healdsburg is 50 miles (80 km) farther on. Sonoma County Farm Trails provide good visitor information.

Websites www.marinfrenchcheese.com, www.redwoodhill.com, www.bodegaartisancheese.com, www.cowgirlcreamery.com, www.laurachenel.com, www.artisancheesefestival.com, www.farmtrails.org

Cheese-makers

■ Founded in 1865, **Marin French Cheese** in Petaluma, Sonoma County, specializes in soft-ripening cheese, such as brie, camembert, and schloss, plus new offerings such as triple-cream and goat-milk brie.

■ The family-run **Redwood Hill Farm** in Sebastopol, Sonoma County, produces award-winning, small-batch goat cheeses, such as their musky crottin (only sold fresh).

■ **Cowgirl Creamery** at Point Reyes Station in Marin County and at Petaluma produces buttery, triple-cream Mount Tam and a slew of organic cheeses.

■ **Bodega Artisan Cheese** in Sonoma County produces a sour-cream-like crema, ideal for strawberry dipping, and offers tours and cheese samplings.

A wide range of artisan cheeses from California (and the rest of the world) are on sale at the Ferry Building Marketplace in San Francisco.

Long bundles of dried peppers adorn the markets in Mexico's towns and villages.

MEXICO

In Search of the Hottest Chili

Native to the Americas, chili pepper is a signature flavor in several of Mexico's regional cuisines, some hotter than others.

The best place to set out on the chili trail is Mexico City, at the heart of the country, and the best way to taste chilies is in the wide variety of salsas served in the city's *taquerías*, each with its own distinctive recipe for adding heat to tacos. From the capital, travel south for increasingly piquant flavors. The pickled *chipotles* of Puebla can be sampled in the markets, and are an essential ingredient in the *cemita*, a huge meat, cheese, and avocado sandwich served on a crusty sesame roll, sold in small eateries where it is the only menu item. Farther south, the seductive, smoky flavor of Oaxaca's *pasilla oaxaqueña*, cured on wooden racks over fire pits, is best tasted in the regional *mole negro* sauce, featured in restaurants on the city's central plaza. From here, the chili aficionado can travel to the Yucatán, where the *habanero*, ranking highest on the Scoville scale used to measure capsaicin, or "chili heat factor," is used in fiery salsas. Try habanero salsa with the regional specialty, *cochinita pibil* (marinated roast pork). Other fresh hot chilies include the *chilaca*, *jalepeño*, and *serrano*. The dried versions are found most frequently in the states of Puebla, Oaxaca, Veracruz, and Chiapas. Fresh and dried chilies are stuffed to make *chiles rellenos*, filled with a variety of ingredients including meat, cheese, beans, and seafood.

When to go To taste regional cooking that includes fiery habaneros, visit the Yucatán in fall or winter, avoiding the intense heat of the spring and summer months. For the best *chiles en nogada*, visit Puebla in central Mexico during the two weeks preceding and following Independence Day, September 16.

Planning In Mexico you can sample a variety of chili salsas and condiments in the local markets. In central Mexico, try *chipotles en escabeche* (pickled dried jalapeños), which go well with roasted meat or poultry.

Websites www.travelyucatan.com, www.visitmexico.com

Chiles en Nogada

Considered by Mexicans to be the **culinary emblem** of their country, *chiles en nogada* (chilies in walnut sauce) was created at the time of Independence from Spain in the early 19th century. Its colors represent those of the Mexican flag: **poblano chiles** for the green, **nogada**–walnut cream sauce–for the white, and **pomegranate seeds** for the red.

The large, medium-hot, green chili poblano is roasted, seeded, peeled, and filled with chopped meat and the seasonal fruit of late summer in central Mexico– apples, pears, peaches–plus raisins, almonds, citron, and spices. It is served bathed in the nogada sauce and garnished with the seeds.

Families have their own generations-old recipes for this labor-intensive delicacy, and it is usually prepared as a group effort. It is offered in restaurants throughout the country in August and September, when all the ingredients that go into it are freshest.

Chiles en Nogada is the national dish of Mexico.

GREAT NATIONAL DISHES

Most countries have a favorite or national dish. Popular with residents and forming part of a country's identity, they are an essential experience for visitors.

❶ Hamburgers, USA

Although the origins of the hamburger are disputed, there is no argument over the popularity of this classic dish. Toppings and accompaniments vary from region to region, but for an original version visit Louis' Lunch in New Haven, Connecticut, which has been serving hamburgers since 1900 and claims to be the oldest hamburger restaurant in the U.S.

Planning Louis' Lunch is open most days for lunch, and some days until the early hours of the morning. www.louislunch.com

❷ Ackee and saltfish, Jamaica

Despite ackee's unhappy origins as slave food, Jamaicans have reclaimed it as part of their national dish. A nutritious fruit with a buttery-nutty flavor, ackee resembles scrambled egg when boiled. Jamaicans sauté the boiled ackee with saltfish (salt-cured cod), onions, and tomatoes. Sometimes the dish is served atop bammy (deep-fried cassava cakes) with fried plantains.

Planning Jake's, Treasure Beach, is renowned for ackee and saltfish and also offers cooking classes. www.visitjamaica.com

❸ Coo-coo and flying fish, Barbados

A polenta-like cornmeal and okra porridge, coo-coo pairs perfectly with flying fish—once abundant but now overfished and scarce—which is either steamed with lime juice, spices, and vegetables or fried and served with a spicy sauce.

Planning The Flying Fish restaurant overlooking St. Lawrence Bay claims to be the Bajan national dish's home. www.visitbarbados.org

❹ *Bulgogi*, Korea

Beef bulgogi (fire meat) is a dish of thinly sliced, prime cuts of meat marinated in a mixture of soy sauce, sesame oil, garlic, onions, ginger, sugar, and wine, and then grilled. It is often eaten wrapped in lettuce or spinach leaves and accompanied by *kimchi* (fermented vegetable pickle). Many Korean restaurants have miniature barbecues embedded in tables where diners grill the meat themselves.

Planning Seoul's upmarket Byeokje Galbi chain is a bulgogi sensation. www.visitkorea.or.kr

❺ *Kibbeh*, Lebanon/Syria

Dining well Levantine-style often means sticking to the delicious *mezes* (appetizers). Kibbeh, a versatile confection of ground lamb, bulgar, and various seasonings, is a core component of mezes. It is often fried in torpedo or patty shapes, baked, boiled, or stuffed, but is tastiest raw.

Planning Aleppans in northern Syria are kibbeh's greatest innovators, flavoring it with ingredients like pomegranate or cherry juice. www.destinationlebanon.gov.lb, www.syriatourism.org

❻ Goulash, Hungary

Gulyás—Magyar for "herdsman"—became a national dish in the late 1800s, when Hungarians sought symbols of national identity to distinguish themselves from their partners in the Austro-Hungarian Empire. A filling stew of beef, vegetables, red onions, and spices, goulash gets its flavor from the use of slow-cooked beef shin, or similar richly flavored cuts, and paprika.

Planning For a lighter version, sample *gulyásleves* (goulash soup). www.hungarytourism.hu

❼ Wiener schnitzel, Austria

Made with the finest ingredients and served fresh, this simple dish of pounded veal cutlets breaded and lightly fried is Austria's food ambassador, despite the dish's Italian origins. Austrians typically eat Wiener schnitzel garnished with parsley and lemon slices, alongside potato salad.

Planning Vienna's leading Wiener schnitzel purveyor, Figlmüller, has two outlets within a few blocks of Stephansplatz (St Stephen's Square). Expect gigantic helpings. www.austria.info

❽ *Pot-au-feu*, France

Originally a rustic dish that was stewed continuously all winter and topped up as needed, pot-au-feu (pot-in-the-fire) is a warming, fragrant dish of stewing steak, root vegetables, and spices. Traditionally, cooks sieve the broth and serve it separately from the meat.

Planning In downtown Paris, Le Pot au Feu at 59 Boulevard Pasteur (Métro: Pasteur) specializes in its namesake. www.franceguide.com

❾ Roast beef and Yorkshire pudding, England

Despite England's increasingly cosmopolitan cuisine, this dish remains a much-loved Sunday lunch—and national symbol. Named for England's eponymous county, Yorkshire—or batter—puddings originally served as fillers before the main course for those who could afford little beef. Today, the two are usually eaten together alongside gravy-soaked roast potatoes, vegetables, and horseradish sauce.

Planning Try the traditional British restaurant, London's Rules, founded 1798, or country pubs. www.enjoyengland.com

❿ Irish stew, Ireland

Originally a thick broth of slow-boiled mutton with onions, potatoes, and parsley, Irish stew nowadays often incorporates other vegetables, such as carrots, and many cooks brown the mutton first. It is a staple of Irish pubs worldwide.

Planning One place in Dublin to enjoy Irish stew and other traditional fare is Shebeen Chic, in George's Street. www.discoverireland.com

Right: Koreans traditionally cook bulgogi over a tabletop grill.

JAPAN

Tsukiji Market Sushi

Take a tour of Tokyo's famous fish
market and sample the freshest sushi.

Five o'clock in the morning along the Tokyo waterfront and the Tsukiji Fish Market is already at fever pitch, workers whisking seafood around in wooden handcarts and electrified *ta-rays* that look like futuristic golf carts. The market's inner sanctum is a warehouse where the world's best tuna is auctioned each morning to professional buyers under contract to the leading fishmongers and restaurants around Tokyo. A label on each fish identifies its point of origin—Somalia, Tahiti, Ireland. The action is frenzied, the auctioneer standing on a wooden box as the buyers shout their bids. Many of the tuna wind up in Tsukiji's warren of 1,500 stalls, where around 450 types of seafood are sold on any given day, including the ingredients that go into Tokyo's prized sushi. Most of the stalls have been family run since the 1920s, when Tsukiji was established, and many of them specialize in a particular type of seafood—*tako* (octopus), *ika* (squid), *unagi* (freshwater eel), *hamachi* (yellowtail tuna), and so on. Sushi was originally created as a way to preserve seafood in salt and rice in the era before refrigeration, and there are now hundreds of types ranging from ancient *narezushi* (salted, fermented fish layered with rice and left for six months before eating) to modern forms like the California roll that includes avocado and imitation crabmeat.

When to Go There is no particular season for sushi in Japan, and Tsukiji Fish Market is open year-round. Tuna auctions take place 5:30-7 a.m.; the market winds down by early afternoon.

Planning Sushi is available in eateries around the edge of Tsukiji, and even at the crack of dawn the locals would not consider eating it without a bottle of Japanese beer or potent sake. One of the more authentic market cafés is Ryuzushi, where patrons sit along a bar while the chef makes the sushi in front of them. Three hours is plenty of time to witness the tuna auction, wander through the market, and grab a bite to eat. The busy streets around the market are lined with shops and stalls selling culinary accessories, including sushi and sashimi dishes, soy-sauce holders, wooden cutting boards, chopsticks, and wonderful hand-crafted knives.

Websites www.jnto.go.jp, www.tsukiji-market.or.jp/tukiji_e.htm

Wasabi and Other Condiments

Sashimi and sushi comprise many of the same seafoods. But while sashimi is generally eaten solo, sushi is always bundled together with a bite-sized portion of white rice. They also share several popular condiments, including **soy sauce**, **wasabi** (mustard), and *gari* (pickled ginger). Although purists declare that wasabi and soy sauce should never be mixed prior to their arrival in your mouth, even in Japan it is common to blend them into a dipping sauce that dilutes the fiery green mustard.

Wasabi is made from the thick roots of a leafy green plant called *Wasabia japonica*. In olden days, a **sharkskin grater** was used to produce the flakes that were ground into a mustard paste.

Although wasabi complements the taste of sushi and sashimi, it may also contain compounds that kill the microbes and parasites found in raw fish.

Indigenous to the Japanese archipelago, wasabi once flourished along mountain streams, but is nowadays more commonly farmed. Demand is such that Japan must now import wasabi from China, Taiwan, and even as far away as New Zealand.

Opposite: A market worker chooses a prime specimen from bins of octopus. Above: A perfect plate of sashimi

WHITE SILVER TIP TEA

The palest, most delicately flavored of
all teas can be found in Fujian province.

The Fujian Mountains in southeast China are the Champagne of white tea regions. Tea is a great deal like wine: The *terroir* and the variety are as important as they are for grapes. The best teas are found in mountain regions where the tea plant is indigenous and thrives. The air is clean and the environment untouched, which is rare in modern China. The finest type of white tea is called *bai hao yin zhen*, or silver tip, and it comes from bushes grown on tea farms high in the mountains of Fujian. The tea is picked in the spring, when the new leaves are mature but still tightly furled in needle-like buds. Moving imperceptibly through the terraces, experienced pickers carefully pinch out the delicate green, silver-tipped buds, picking them in the early mornings just as the buds are about to open. At lunchtime everyone returns to the farm for a lunch of boiled eggs in a sugary soup. Then the tea buds are laid out on flat bamboo trays, and, talking softly, the workers sift through the buds and painstakingly remove extraneous leaves and twigs. The silver tips are laid out to dry on huge bamboo racks positioned to catch the best of the soft afternoon sun. At this time of day, roofs and terraces on the farm are covered in tea.

When to Go White silver tip tea is picked at the beginning of spring–late March/early April. It is harvested only in the early mornings.

Planning The best silver tips come from the gardens around Fuding, 185 miles (298 km) north of the provincial capital, Fuzhou. The journey takes a good three hours by road. There is a wonderful tea market in Fuding, where the local farmers gather with their baskets of leaves, and many interesting tea shops. It may be possible to visit the tea gardens, but they are not set up for tourists. To visit them, you should hire a guide through a hotel in Fuzhou or arrange a tailor-made tour through a good travel operator. You are unlikely to find anyone who speaks English in Fuding, so take a Mandarin-speaker–or even better, someone who speaks the local dialects, especially if you plan to venture off the beaten track.

Websites www.rareteacompany.com, www.chinadiscover.net

White Tea

All teas–white, green, and black–come from the leaves and buds of the **Camellia sinensis** bush. Differences in plant variety, terrain, growing conditions, and processing create the different types of tea.

Exceptionally pure and natural, **white silver tips** undergo the least processing of any type of tea, and retain higher levels of antioxidants.

White tea is always drunk **without accompaniment**–it is so light and delicate that it would be overpowered by the strong flavors of the local food. When they have finished a cup of tea, the locals often leave the silver tips in the cup and continue adding hot water to make additional cups.

Pickers select buds that are on the verge of opening.

Plump, ripe, succulent figs can be found on sale at market and roadside stalls throughout Turkey.

SPECIALTIES & INGREDIENTS

OUTSTANDING MARKETS ⋅ SEASONAL DELIGHTS ⋅ IN THE KITCHEN ⋅ FAVORITE STREET FOODS ⋅ GREAT FOOD TOWNS ⋅ ULTIMATE LUXURIES ⋅ THE BEST WINE, BEER, & MORE ⋅ JUST DESSERTS

Fig Desserts

While dried figs are often eaten in Turkey as a snack, they are more commonly used in desserts such as *incir tatlisi*—the dried figs are poached in syrup before being filled with walnuts and are served with cream and a sprinkling of chopped walnuts or pistachios.

Dried figs are also added to **baklava**, a layered pastry filled with honey and chopped pistachios or walnuts, or stewed with spices to make **compotes**, which are then topped with *kaymak*, or Turkish clotted cream, a thick, rich cream made by heating cream to evaporate some of the liquid.

Asure (wheat pudding, or the Pudding of Noah), one of the oldest and most traditional desserts in Turkey, also calls for dried figs in addition to about 15 other ingredients, including *dövme* (dehusked wheat), chickpeas, rice, white beans, apricots, and raisins. It is traditionally served during the month following Kurban Bayrami, the Islamic Feast of Sacrifice, and symbolizes the pudding made by Noah after the ark landed on Mount Ararat, using food left from the journey.

TURKEY

Fig Harvest

Southwest Turkey has the perfect climate and soil for growing a fruit that local people regard as sacred.

At the first blush of daybreak, fig-growers gather to harvest the plump fruit grown on the fertile plains of Aydin province in southwest Turkey, the center of Turkey's dried-fig production. The annual *incir harmanı* (fig harvest) requires many hands, and family members and friends assemble in the coolness of the morning to collect ripened figs that have fallen to the hard-packed earth overnight. Women clad in *salvar* (loose trousers), their colorful headscarves a bright contrast to the smooth gray trunks of the 15- to 30-foot (4.5–9 meter) tall fig trees, spread buckets of sweet, honeyed figs on mats and racks in orchard clearings so that they can dry under the Mediterranean sun. All work halts for the midday meal, which consists of a seemingly endless procession of dishes set out on makeshift tables under the spreading branches of sun-dappled trees. A *meze* (appetizer) of *cacık* (thick yogurt and cucumber seasoned with fresh dill and garlic) is followed by *çöp sis* (lamb kebabs) and *baba gannus* (mashed eggplant dip) served with *pide* (Turkish flatbread). Glasses of *ayran*, a yogurt drink, cool the palate and provide a nice accompaniment to the *incir tatlisi* (walnut-stuffed dried figs) that cap off the meal.

When to Go Figs are harvested in late August through September, with many towns holding an annual festival in September to celebrate the harvest.

Planning The Aydin Turizm Bus Company operates buses from Istanbul's Büyük Otogar (main bus terminal) to the city of Aydin, where you can rent a car or hire a local taxi to see the fig orchards. Plan to stay for a few days to explore the area.

Website www.tourismturkey.org

SPECIALTIES & INGREDIENTS

OUTSTANDING MARKETS   SEASONAL DELIGHTS   IN THE KITCHEN   FAVORITE STREET FOODS   GREAT FOOD TOWNS   ULTIMATE LUXURIES   THE BEST WINE, BEER, & MORE   JUST DESSERTS

GREECE

OLIVE HARVEST

Visit Crete during the olive harvest, and sample some
of the best products in the birthplace of olive farming.

It is a cold October morning on the island of Crete. As the sun breaks through gray skies, the stillness is broken as women from the village of Kato Zakros lay nets under the trees in their local olive grove. This is the first stage of the olive harvest, an activity that takes place all over Crete and mainland Greece between now and February, depending on the variety of olive and whether it is picked unripe and green or left to ripen and turn purple or black. Crete is one of the biggest olive-growing areas in the country. Indeed, it was on this lovely island that olive cultivation is said to have originated more than 4,000 years ago. Although most harvesting is now done mechanically, using a flail, there are many places where families and villages use the traditional method—the nets are sometimes left down for weeks to allow the olives to drop naturally, but mostly nature is given a helping hand and the trees are shaken or prodded with a long stick to help them yield more fruit. Then the delicate and crucial work begins of separating the olives from the silvery green leaves without crushing the precious fruit, which is carefully piled into baskets or sacks for transportation to the local olive press, or *eliotriveia*, where it is transformed into the liquid gold that is olive oil. The highest-quality oil is Extra Virgin, followed by Virgin. Both come from the first pressing without any refining with hot water or chemicals. Plain olive oil is a refined oil with a little Extra Virgin or Virgin oil added to improve its flavor and color.

When to Go From October through February.

Planning Allow at least a week to see this beautiful island, the center of Minoan civilization. The Cretan diet—and especially its olive oil—is said to be the healthiest in the world, so take time to enjoy it. Once the harvest is in, you can visit some of the local olive presses to see how the oil is produced.

Websites www.explorecrete.com, www.creteonthe.net, www.cookingincrete.com

Greek Olives

During its most productive years, each tree produces an annual average of 132 lb (60 kg) of olives. Crete produces many varieties, including the **koroneiki**, **throumbolia**, and **tsounati**, which are used mainly to make olive oil.

Olive varieties from other parts of Greece are cured in brine and served as table olives. The **kalamata** is a large, almond-shaped black olive with a rich, fruity flavor and meatlike texture, produced in the region of Messinia in the western Peloponnese.

The round or oval **konservolia** is the best-known variety of table olive in Greece.

The **halkidiki** (or **chalkidiki**) is a large, pale green olive from the Halkidiki region of northern Greece. It has a peppery, slightly sharp flavor and because it is large it is often stuffed with fillings such as cheese or dried tomatoes.

The **megaritiki** is a small olive cultivated in the Attica region in southeastern Greece. It is dry-salted to produce a naturally wrinkled olive.

Opposite: Workers harvest olives the old-fashioned way. Above: The picked olives are ready for processing.

SAN DANIELE HAM

Natural sea salt and the fresh mountain air of northeastern
Italy contribute to the fine flavor of this cured, aged ham.

Mention the words "Italian ham," or "prosciutto," and the town of Parma comes instantly to mind. But there is another Italian town whose name is synonymous with a ham that, many consider, far surpasses Parma's in texture and flavor. The town is San Daniele, in the gentle countryside of Friuli-Venezia Giulia, and the ham is *prosciutto di San Daniele del Friuli*—a delicate, rose-pink meat with a sublimely sweet flavor. San Daniele ham undergoes the same stages of seasoning, pressing, and aging as other Protected Designation of Origin (PDO) hams, and as with those hams, only natural sea salt is used. Unusually, the pig's trotter is included in the pressing, giving the ham its distinctive guitar shape. After pressing, the hams are aged in naturally ventilated rooms for up to 18 months to remove the saltiness. The unique flavor is attributed to the pigs themselves (they must come from one of ten designated regions) and the ideal maturing conditions offered by the combination of natural salt, humidity, and mountain air in the town itself. Positioned where the Adriatic Sea meets the Alps, it seems that San Daniele del Friuli was especially created for ham-making. Try the results for yourself in one of the town's many *prosciuttifici*, or curing houses, where you can sample the ham—sliced paper thin, wrapped around *grissini* (crisp Italian breadsticks) or on its own with a glass of local Friuliano wine. You will be converted.

When to Go June, if you want to visit the annual ham fair. Otherwise spring and fall are best.

Planning You may want to take some time to explore Udine, the historic capital of the area, and sample the local *musetto* sausage and *frico*—a melted cheese accompanied with herbs and spices. The nearby medieval town of Cividale del Friuli is very picturesque. If you are planning a longer trip, the beautiful towns of Treviso, Verona, and Venice are not far.

Websites www.discoverfriuli.com, www.deliciousitaly.com, www.prosciuttosandaniele.it

San Daniele Ham

■ Visit the **Aria di Festa**, San Daniele's annual four-day ham fair held at the end of June. You can enjoy tastings, concerts, and visits to traditional prosciuttifici.

■ There are many *salumerie*, or delicatessens, on the town's main square where you can buy and taste the ham. If you buy a whole ham, look for the San Daniele PDO logo (DOP in Italy).

■ **La Casa del Prosciutto** on the main square is a small, family-run curing house where you can see the different stages of the process; there is a café where you can try out the ham, on its own or with local cheeses.

■ Another family company, **Prosciutti Coradazzi**, on the outskirts of the town, offers tastings and short tours of their production center.

San Daniele hams are air-dried. The quality of the air is essential to the success of the process—too warm or dry and the hams will be ruined.

Modena's balsamic vinegar is traditionally aged for 12 years; bottles marked *extravecchio* are 25 years old or more.

SPECIALTIES & INGREDIENTS

OUTSTANDING MARKETS   SEASONAL DELIGHTS   IN THE KITCHEN   FAVORITE STREET FOODS   GREAT FOOD TOWNS   ULTIMATE LUXURIES   THE BEST WINE, BEER, & MORE   JUST DESSERTS

Balsamic Vinegar

True traditional balsamic vinegar can be identified by the unique, 3.4 fl oz (100 ml), orb-shaped, glass container designed by the famous car designer, Giorgetto Giugiaro. The vinegar comes in two ages: 12–25 years old (identified by a red cap) and more than 25 years old, or *extravecchio* (identified by a gold cap).

A series of barrels made from different types of wood, including juniper, cherry, oak, and chestnut, each diminishing in size, hold progressively more concentrated forms of the original **cooked grape must** (traditionally made from local *trebbiano* or *lambrusco* grapes).

The tradition of making balsamic vinegar at home has become increasingly popular during recent years, and many couples request a set of barrels as a wedding gift—a present that will last the family a lifetime.

ITALY

BALSAMIC VINEGAR OF MODENA

The complex, sweet-sour flavor of balsamic vinegar features widely in the traditional cuisine of Italy's Emilia-Romagna region.

Walk into almost any building in the *centro storico*, or historic center, of Modena in northern Italy, and your senses will be seduced by the heady aroma of the town's most famous export, balsamic vinegar. On the top story of many a Modenese building, families still make their own vinegar, patiently waiting at least 12 years from grape to first drop of the dark, unctuous, sweet yet sour, authentic *Aceto Balsamico Tradizionale di Modena* (traditional balsamic vinegar of Modena). Any tour of Modena should start at its gastronomical heart—the *mercato coperto*, or covered market. Here you will find a wealth of local produce, ranging from wheels of Parmigiano-Reggiano cheese to handmade tortellini, ready to be served in chicken broth—another specialty of the town. Try Schiavone, a tiny bar in the corner of the market, for a *panino* (lightly toasted sandwich) filled with smoked goose breast, Parmesan shavings, and traditional balsamic vinegar, all washed down with a glass of local, Lambrusco wine. For a sit-down meal, Trattoria Ermes is hosted by the genial Ermes himself. All the traditionally Modenese dishes are freshly prepared by his wife, including *scaloppine all'aceto balsamico* (veal escalopes in balsamic vinegar), wild strawberries drizzled with balsamic vinegar, and the strangely delightful ice cream with—no surprise here—balsamic vinegar.

The region's grapes are the main ingredient in balsamic vinegar.

When to Go Any time of year. Events relating to balsamic vinegar take place in and around Modena during fall, including Open Vinegar Lofts at the end of September and a Festival of Taste in October.

Planning Modena is an excellent base for discovering the Emilia-Romagna region, with Parma, Bologna, Ferrara, and Ravenna nearby. The tourist information center organizes balsamic vinegar tasting tours.

Websites www.acetaiadigiorgio.it, turismo.comune.modena.it

Cows grazing the alpine meadows of the Piedmont region produce high-quality milk for the region's cheeses.

ITALY

Piedmont's Cheeses

Tucked away in the northwest corner of Italy is a beautiful region of mountains, lakes, rolling hills, and a rich cuisine.

Located between the Alps and the Apennines, Piedmont is a land of mountain pastures, lush valleys, and vineyard-clad hillsides; of quiet mountain villages housing crumbling castles and ancient churches, and modern, industrial cities, such as the regional capital, Turin, that offer glamorous fashion and food shopping. Dining ranges from bustling trattorias and baroque-ceilinged wine bars to modern, minimalist, innovative restaurants. Any eatery worth its salt will present a remarkably varied cheeseboard providing fresh-curd or gently oozing, mold-ripened cheeses, briny, crumbly, "grating" ones, and the smooth tang of the finest blues, all produced within Piedmont and including cow's-, goat's-, and sheep's-milk cheeses, and some that are a blend of all three. No fewer than six of Piedmont's cheeses boast the Protected Designation of Origin (PDO; DOP in Italy) marque; many other cheeses are unique to a single valley or two—too scarce to boast a DOP but well worth seeking out. You might encounter them in a city deli, a wine bar, or the local market; or arm yourself with a map and meander along the valleys to remote artisan producers. Lovers of cheese should visit the biennial cheese festival in Bra, when the streets of this small town near Turin offer an endless feast for eyes, nose, and palate.

When to Go Bra's biennial cheese festival is organized by the Slow Food Association and takes place in late September. Late October is the best time to visit if you also want to sample the region's white truffles.

Planning You need a few days and a car to explore the mountain roads, hilltop villages, and local cheeses around Piedmont. The Piedmontese Tourist Authority (Regione Piemonte) publish a booklet of walking tours in Turin, cheese guides, and a map detailing gastronomic hot spots. If you are visiting during the cheese festival, book accommodations well in advance.

Website www.slowfood.com

Piedmont Cheeseboard

Toma del Maccagno is an alpine cheese from the towns of Biella and Vercelli. Sold in varying degrees of maturity, it ranges from subtly mild to tangy.

Robiola di Roccaverano DOP is a small, soft, ivory-colored cheese (check that only raw goat milk has been used).

Castelmagno DOP is produced in only three communes in the province of Cuneo.

Murazzano DOP is made from Alta Langa ewe's milk and sold soft and subtle at seven days old or mature, firm, and tangy after two months.

ITALY

ORANGES FROM MOUNT ETNA

Eastern Sicily produces the jewel-colored blood orange,
or *arancia rossa di Sicilia*, one of the island's most prized fruits.

Visit Catania, in southeast Sicily, in spring and you will catch the unmistakable scent of the *zagara*, or orange blossom, drifting from groves that blanket the lower slopes of Mount Etna. The location is no accident as the ash spewed out by Europe's highest active volcano makes the best fertilizer on earth. Pistachio, lemon, and peach trees also mix with vines here, but it is the thousands of orange trees, with their jewel-like fruit and glossy leaves, that have a special story, for the naturally rich soil, changes in temperature (hot days and cold nights), and quality of light at the mountain's base have combined to create one of nature's greatest miracles: the blood orange, or *arancia rossa*, characterized by a deep-red, juicy flesh and a raspberry-sweet taste. The oranges have a higher-than-average vitamin C content, while their coloring comes from an antioxidant called anthocyanin, which also has remarkable health-giving properties. The arancia rossa comes in three main types: the Sanguinello is a full-blood orange with red skin and flesh, and is sweet and tender; the Moro, the most acidic, is small and has deep crimson flesh; and the Tarocco has orange skin and slightly red flesh. Seedless, and with the sweetest flavor, the Tarocco is said to have the highest vitamin C content of any orange in the world and is Sicily's most popular table orange. Try the oranges the Sicilian way, in a salad with fennel and olives, or enjoy their exquisite flavor in a health-packed juice that is guaranteed to revive even the most tired of taste buds.

When to Go Any time of year, though you may want to avoid the heat of the summer months, especially if you are planning a walk on Mount Etna. If you want to see the orange harvest, December and January are best.

Planning Allow at least a week to see the region's highlights: Catania, Etna, and the beautiful ancient town of Syracuse. If you are planning to walk on Mount Etna, be sure to take proper walking shoes. The small town of Lentini is known for orange cultivation.

Websites www.mountetna.net, www.globusjourneys.com

Sicilian Orange Salad 'Nzalata d'Aranci

This salad is sometimes made without the olives, sometimes with a sliced onion instead of fennel, and sometimes very simply with just oranges and a scattering of pepper, oil, and parsley.

Serves 4 as an appetizer
4 Sicilian blood oranges
1 fennel bulb
2 tbsp olive oil
Black pepper and sea salt
12 black olives

Peel the oranges, being careful to remove all of the pith. Save any juice and pour into a large, shallow serving bowl. Slice the oranges and arrange in overlapping circles in the bowl; pour over any more juice. Slice the fennel very thinly and scatter it over the oranges. Drizzle with olive oil, season well with black pepper and salt, and garnish with olives.

Mount Etna's oranges look like regular oranges on the outside, but inside they have crimson to deep-red flesh.

WESTPHALIAN PUMPERNICKEL

Pumpernickel originated in northwest Germany, a land of ancient forests and medieval towns.

The origins of the name "pumpernickel" may be debated, but no one can argue with the delicious taste and texture of this typical Westphalian sourdough bread. Westphalia, part of the state of North Rhine-Westphalia, is a region of small towns with half-timbered houses and moated castles nestling among lush pastures and dark woods. From Münster, a bustling university town in the north of the region, eastwards to the town of Detmold in the Teutoburger forest, local foods are highly valued. Westphalian pumpernickel is made the same way it has been for centuries—baked slowly in a steam-filled oven at around 212–230°F (100–110°C) for 24 hours, giving the crustless bread its characteristic sweetness, dark color, and texture. No sweeteners or coloring agents are added. Germany's oldest pumpernickel bakery, Haverlands, founded in 1570 in the medieval city of Soest, is still in business, selling pumpernickel that has been made in the same way for twelve generations—using only rye, water, and a slice of old pumpernickel to start the fermentation. The process can be seen at the Bread Museum, part of the Westfalen Culinarium in the town of Nieheim (south of Detmold). Pumpernickel is best eaten plain with a little butter, but it goes well with almost any cheese—layered sandwiches with cream cheese are a German staple. The sweet, crustless bread is even used in desserts, soaked in kirsch and topped with cherry compote and whipped cream.

When to Go The best time is spring and summer, but in winter local menus offer a large choice of game dishes and you may also get a taste of a local pre-Lent carnival (*Fasching*) in February.

Planning Train travel between cities is reasonably fast, easy, and reliable. For trips into the countryside it is best to rent a car. The *NRW kulinarisch/Gourmet NRW* logo indicates selected pubs and restaurants that offer regional specialties, from boar-blood pudding to quark, raspberry, and pumpernickel desserts.

Websites www.nrw-tourism.com, www.hist-stadt.nrw.de, www.bahn.de, www.westfalen-culinarium.de

Westphalian Treats

■ Westphalian **ham** is also referred to as *Knochenschinken* (bone ham) because it is produced with the bone left in. The meat is dry-cured, then smoked. The best-quality hams come from acorn-fattened pigs.

■ *Altbier* (old beer), a type of ale, is the traditional beer of Westphalia and is still produced at the Pinkus Müller brewery in Münster, Germany's oldest certified organic brewery. The Westfalen Culinarium's Museum of Beer and Schnapps produces bock beer (a strong, dark, malty beer) and holds brewing classes.

■ Try *Tecklenburger Hosenknopf*, which is a soft, camembert-like goat cheese, or *Nieheimer*, a sour-milk cheese flavored with caraway, produced at the Westfalen Culinarium's Cheese Museum.

Loaves of pumpernickel are displayed with other local breads.

Fresh salmon from one of Scotland's many famous rivers is a regular on many menus.

SCOTLAND

WILD SCOTLAND

A surfeit of produce from the country's rivers, lochs, moors, forests, and coastline has given rise to a distinctive cuisine.

At times, the mountains and moors of Scotland can seem the wildest and most desolate places on Earth—if you cross Rannoch Moor when the fall mists lie suffocatingly low, or when rain drives like shards of glass and the purple tops of the mountains merge seamlessly into an unforgiving sky; but on a bright, breezy day in early summer, sun-lit lochs form a glassy contrast to sandy bays, and waves of grass give way to still stretches of purple heather. Small wonder that the flavors of foraged foods, fish, seafood, and game also range from the soft and gentle to the wild and near-savage. Scottish game, both furred and feathered, is justly famous, as are its wild mushrooms and berries, and its trout, salmon, and seafood. Visitors can go wild camping, hiking, and wildlife spotting; or foraging, fishing, and shooting; or follow a route that takes in country inns, city restaurants, or Highland hotels adept at presenting game, fish, and forage dishes in traditional or novel combinations. There can be no better way to feel closer to, and curiously content with, wild nature after a day's hike through a wet wilderness than by relaxing beside a welcoming log fire followed by a warming meal composed of produce that carries the taste of heather, bracken, and brine.

When to Go September is when the Highlands are at their most gentle. October is best for seekers of culinary drama as grouse, partridge, pheasant, red deer, wild mushrooms, elderberries, and native oysters are all on the menu. Food festivals take place mainly in September and October.

Planning Camping and foraging codes, guides to seasonal wildlife spotting and wild food sampling, and three-star restaurant trails are available via a number of Scottish websites.

Websites www.wild-scotland.org.uk, www.snh.org.uk, www.foodtourismscotland.com, www.visitscotland.com

Scotland's Wild Larder

The most popular and delicious fungi are the **chanterelles** and **ceps** of autumn.

Langoustines caught In West Coast lochs have a fresh, sweet flavor and firm, juicy texture. They are best from April through November. Scotland's native **oysters** are meatier and pricier than their Atlantic cousins. They are available when there is an "r" in the name of the month.

Venison may be red deer, roe, fallow, or Sika. Flavor and tenderness vary according to source, age, sex, and length of hanging; availability varies within the shooting season.

Scotland offers a range of **game birds**. Whether your preference is for the milder pheasant and partridge or gamier grouse, check that the source is wild, not farmed.

PLACES TO CATCH YOUR SUPPER

No fish tastes better than one you have caught yourself. Many fisheries maintain a no-kill policy, but if you can, cook your catch over a campfire, or ask if your hotel or a local restaurant will cook it for you.

❶ Gaspé Peninsula, Quebec, Canada

Southern Quebec's Atlantic salmon rivers, from the mighty Matapedia to the gemlike Bonaventure, compete for top billing and center stage, with the Grand Cascapedia, Petit Cascapedia, Matane, and Sainte Anne as the best supporting members of a star-studded cast.

Planning Mid-June to mid-September are viable fishing months on the Gaspé. Camp Bonaventure offers gourmet dining and reserved pools. www.campbonaventure.com

❷ Princess Royal Island, B.C., Canada

In the pristine Great Bear Rainforest, accessed by float plane, northern British Columbia's remote Princess Royal Island offers Pacific salmon angling, together with hiking, climbing, and kayaking, and wildlife ranging from the Kermode, or Spirit, Bear to the rain-forest wolf and the orca whale.

Planning Best between June and September. King Pacific Lodge offers 17 comfortable guest rooms. www.kingpacificlodge.com

❸ Penobscot River, Maine

Beneath 5,280-ft (1,610 m) Mount Katahdin, Maine's highest peak, the West Branch of the Penobscot River, with its deep pools, rapids, and broiling water, holds hefty landlocked salmon and brook trout. The Ripogenus Dam releases cold water into the river throughout the summer, which produces consistent fishing conditions all season.

Planning The second week of July is good for the mayfly hatch, when fish feed avidly. Baxter State Park hires out cabins at Daicey and Kidney Ponds. www.flyfishinginmaine.com, www.baxterstateparkauthority.com

❹ Beaverkill River, Catskill Mountains, New York

The junction of the Beaverkill River and Willowemoc Creek at the town of Roscoe is a fabled meeting point and the birthplace of American dry-fly fishing. The no-kill section downstream from Junction Pool is stacked with big brown trout.

Planning Early May through mid-June offers the best temperatures and flows. The Roscoe Motel provides simple lodging within casting distance of the Beaverkill. www.catskillflyfishing.com, www.roscoemotel.com.

❺ Madison River, Montana

From the Bighorn to the Big Blackfoot, the Missouri, the Beaverhead, and the most beautiful of them all, the wide and serpentine Madison, Montana's mountains beget, above all, rivers. The Madison offers hard-fighting rainbow, brown, and cutthroat trout amid spectacular scenery.

Planning July and September are the best times for fishing the Madison. Ennis is the hub and the Beartooth Flyfishing Lodge in nearby Cameron is the place to stay. www.beartoothflyfishing.com

❻ Río Grande, Patagonia, Argentina

At the windblown southernmost tip of South America, the Río Grande on the Isla Grande de Tierra del Fuego is filled with sea-run brown trout (brown trout that spend three years at sea after spawning in the river) weighing 10–30 lb (4.5–13.5 kg). Rainbow and brown trout are also available in nearby rivers.

Planning December to May is the prime Patagonian fishing season. The Toon Ken Lodge pampers a half a dozen anglers at a time. www.flyfishingpatagonia.com, www.toonken.com

❼ New Zealand

The wide valleys and spaces of New Zealand are crisscrossed with the waterways of every angler's dreams, brimming with mammoth wild brown and rainbow trout. Sight fishing—walking the riverbank and casting to specific fish that you spot along the way—in the region's pellucid streams may be the best in the world.

Planning New Zealand's fishing season runs from October through April. www.flyfishingnz.co.nz, www.nzfishing.com

❽ Kupa River, Croatia

In northern Croatia's mountainous Gorski Kotar region, the Kupa River forms the border with the Republic of Slovenia. Flowing through a spectacular landscape of unspoiled wooded mountains, the river harbors magnificent brown trout and grayling in its crystalline waters.

Planning May and June are the best months to fish the Kupa. Mislav Kupic is a fishing guide who can arrange everything. www.kupa-flyfishing.com.

❾ Narcea River, Asturias, Spain

Northwest Spain's Narcea River offers the chance to fish for Atlantic salmon, sea trout, and trout all in a single day on this deep, fast-flowing river that plunges over waterfalls and through ravines in the emerald hills of Asturias.

Planning Mid-late June is the Narcea's best fortnight. Hotel La Fuente in Cornellana is the traditional clubhouse for salmon anglers from around the world. www.flyfishingspain.co.uk, www.cti.es/la_fuente/

❿ Moy River, County Mayo, Ireland

The Moy River is western Ireland's best salmon stream, flowing through rolling farmland, with the Ox Mountains always in view, down to the Atlantic at Ballina. The many upstream tributaries and lakes also offer myriad trout opportunities, and the estuary offers seatrout fishing.

Planning June and September are the best months on the Moy. The Ice House Hotel & Spa in Ballina, overlooking the Moy estuary, is the finest place in County Mayo. www.northwestfisheries.ie, www.icehousehotel.ie

Right: Montana's Madison River combines dramatic scenery and world-renowned trout fishing.

FLAVORS OF THE SEA

Along Brittany's Atlantic coast, intricately scalloped
with bays, inlets, and islands, the oyster reigns supreme.

The cold French coastal waters from the city of Brest south to the Guérande salt flats near the resort of La Baule-Escoublac yield a remarkable variety of oysters, and one of the best places to sample them is around the Golfe du Morbihan. South of the city of Vannes, the *Route de l'Huître* (Oyster Trail) begins at the town of Sarzeau and runs along the Rhuys peninsula to the Port-Navalo headland. Scanning the island-studded gulf waters, you can see the slanted posts that mark 1,200 acres (485 hectares) of oyster beds, now farmed, where natural oyster banks once thrived. The oysters on local menus are usually listed simply as *huîtres du golfe*, but occasionally *huîtres boudeuse* ("sulky" oysters) are available. Gathered after three to five years, these small, plump oysters have a flavor that is rich with aromas of the sea. The gulf is also home to Belon oysters. These flat, round mollusks with firm meat and a nutty finish are moved from deep-water nurseries in Quiberon Bay to oyster beds in the Belon River estuary near the city of Pont-Aven, where saltwater flows in with the tide and the Belons take on their distinctive flavor. Farther down the coast, *paludiers* (salt-rakers) can be seen on Guérande's salt flats on warm summer days, harvesting *fleur de sel* by skimming a fine crust of crystals off the base layer of coarser gray sea salt. Fleur de sel is a table salt and adds a final touch to a meal, while the sea salt lying below it is the chef's choice for cooking.

When to Go October to April is prime time for the widest selection of oysters, while all over France it is traditional to eat Breton oysters around New Year. Through December and January, two- to three-year-old *huîtres sauvages* (wild oysters) are collected at 165-ft (50 m) depths and may appear on menus.

Planning Allow a weekend for the Golfe du Morbihan, with time to ramble along harbors, past blue Breton trawlers pulled ashore and sailboats being fitted for sea journeys. Add a week if you also want to sample crêpes, explore Guérande's salt flats, and taste wines in the Muscadet vineyards above the Loire estuary.

Websites www.brittanytourism.com, www.golfedumorbihan.fr

Other Breton Fare

■ Try a hot **crepe** or a buckwheat **galette** artfully folded around a savory filling of Breton ham. And, just as the locals do, sip a bowl of refreshing, slightly alcoholic **cider**.

■ Watch for posters in harbor stores and bars announcing a ***Fest Noz***—a local music session that may include local foods as well—and stop in for a bracing ***chouchen***, Breton mead made with honey and yeast.

■ Near Vannes, stop in the city of Theix at the brewery, **Brasserie Mor Braz**, for a sample of beer made with seawater—lending a hint of marine aroma.

■ Sharpen your sweet tooth with **salted-butter** *carmels* (caramels) or a ***niniche*** (a long, thin caramel lollipop) from Quiberon.

Muscadet, a fruity, but dry, white wine is the popular choice of drink with a plate of fresh oysters along the coast of Brittany.

Paris abounds with traditional *boulangeries*, where you can buy baguettes, croissants, and a variety of pastries.

FRANCE

Best Baguette in Paris

Parisian bakers compete to produce the crustiest, softest, most delicious baguette of the year.

As iconic as a black beret or the Eiffel Tower in evoking French culture, the baguette (literally, a wand), has been a Parisian staple since the 1920s. Each baker uses the simplest ingredients: flour, salt, and water mixed with natural leavening, but the way in which he or she gently kneads the dough and the time the loaves spend in the traditional wood-fired oven are closely guarded secrets. It is this individuality in approach that results in 12 judges being shut away in a room to sniff, prod, taste, and chew samples of 140 loaves in a blind tasting to find the Best Baguette in Paris. The winning baker is awarded a cash prize and a 12-month contract to provide bread for the president's table at the Élysée Palace. No machine-mixed, pre-frozen, or underbaked loaves need apply. The prize is open to all Paris bakers who produce additive-free baguettes made by hand, and competition is stiff. As you buy a loaf in one of Paris's many *boulangeries* (bakeries), you be the judge: Is the 27-inch (70 centimeter) long, golden crust blister-free? Are the slashes across the top of the loaf evenly and harmoniously spaced? Then break off an end and catch the aroma of wheat with a hint of hazelnuts. And before you bite, take a moment to admire the honeycombed crumbs, plump and pearly, in your hand.

When to Go There are no seasonal limits. The annual Best Baguette winner is announced in the early spring.
Planning Avoid buying baguettes late in the afternoon, when long lines form at the best bakeries. Watch for labels: *baguette classique* is a classic white loaf, while the *baguette traditionelle* is made by hand using unbleached flour and no additives.
Websites gridskipper.com/59453/pariss-baguettes-dor, www.dupainetdesidees.com

Baguettes and Bakers

■ 2009 **Best Baguette** winner is Franck Tombarel of **Le Grenier de Félix** in the 15th *arrondissement* of Paris.

■ In mid-May, don't miss the **Fête du Pain** (bread festival), which takes place in front of Notre-Dame Cathedral. Bakers demonstrate their craft, and competitors shape their entries in the master baguette competition. There are hands-on workshops for children.

■ Not all bakers make baguettes. The famed **Poilâne bakery**, with shops in the 6th and 15th arrondissements (and one in London's Belgravia), is best known for its sourdough *boule*, a round, crusty loaf.

■ Bread-history lovers should visit **Du Pain et Des Idées**, master baker Christophe Vasseur's corner shop at 34 rue Yves Toudic in the 10th arrondissement, which is full of copper molds and antique baking tools. The fancifully painted ceiling is a listed historic monument.

CHEESE TOURS OF FRANCE

Airy mountain slopes, fertile pastures, and damp caves provide ideal conditions for the rich range of cheeses produced in France, and for which the country is world famous.

❶ *Camembert*, Normandy

This noble cow's-milk cheese is worth the search. Just a handful of Normandy's artisan producers remain. In the village of Camembert, visit the Durand farm whose daily production of 450 camemberts takes four weeks of shaping, salting, and aging before going to market. On Saturdays, Nadia Durand offers selection tips at the nearby village of Le Sap's brick market hall.

Planning Normandy's lush pastures and medieval villages are a day trip from Paris. www.normandie-tourisme.fr

❷ *Brie*, Seine-et-Marne region

The soft, cow's-milk cheeses of the brie family have been made in pasturelands between Meaux and Melun, east of Paris, since Charlemagne's time. In Coulommiers, the market hub of the area, the annual spring Cheese Fair is perfect for getting to know the brie range—either for nibbling or to garnish spring soups.

Planning Coulommiers is 30 miles (50 km) from Paris. Arrive at the Foire aux Fromages (Cheese Fair) in time to catch the opening parade of cheese brotherhoods in brie-shaped hats. www.tourism77.co.uk

❸ *Chaource* and *Époisses*, Champagne/Burgundy

Sample creamy cow's-milk cheeses in central France, rambling from southern Champagne through the rustic byways of northern Burgundy. Begin in the town of Chaource, tasting its eponymous smooth cheese with a tangy edge. Then continue south into Chablis vineyards, and on to the village of Époisses for a tour of the Berthaut farm and *fromagerie*, where époisses cheese is made.

Planning Approach Chaource from Troyes, southeast of Paris. Avallon offers a central base. www.burgundytoday.com/gourmet-traveller

❹ *Chèvre*, Loire Valley

South of the Loire River, discover a variety of goat's-milk cheeses. From the truncated pyramid-shaped cheese named after the town of Valençay, to small round Selles-sur-Cher and the Sainte-Maure de Touraine log varieties with a supporting central straw, all are made between the towns of Chinon and Vierzon. A dusting of fine ash conserves flavor and protects the chèvre from insects as it cures.

Planning Spring into early summer are the best seasons for tasting chèvre. Loches, a medieval city 27 miles (44 km) east of Valençay, is an ideal base for touring the area. www.loches-tourainecotesud.com

❺ *Comté*, Jura region

Even before Roman times, cow's-milk cheeses of the Jura's alpine meadows were renowned. Cheese-makers carry on their traditions in a collaboration between farms, dairy cooperatives, and *affineurs* (aging specialists). The result: rich flavors with a nutty finish. Visit dairies in the towns of Pontarlier or Arbois to see the process.

Planning Comté is an any-season cheese. www.lesroutesducomte.com

❻ *Maroilles*, Picardie region

Among the pungent cheeses of northern France, look for cow's-milk Maroilles, a brick-toned, perfect square. The aroma may be strong, but the taste is mild, surprisingly rich, with hints of citrus aromas. Maroilles are made in three sizes. For advice, try Phillipe Olivier's cheese shop at 3 rue du Curé St-Etienne in the city of Lille.

Planning About an hour by TGV train from Paris Charles de Gaulle, Lille is a summer weekend getaway. The huge Wazemmes Market, open on Sunday mornings, is one of France's largest. www.lilletourism.com

❼ *Roquefort*, Aveyron region

Roquefort cheese is matured in caves around the village of Roquefort-sur-Soulzon—the sole area allowed to make Appellation d'Origine Contrôlée (AOC) Roquefort, using only French sheep's milk. The variation in color from cream to ivory, and the blue to green-gray pinholes with which the cheese is riddled, distinguish each maker's style.

Planning Drive north from Montpellier to Roquefort in the fall for colorful vistas of hardwoods. Use Millau as a base. www.ot-millau.fr

❽ *Cantal*, Cantal Mountains, Auvergne region

Made year-round, Cantal cheese continues an Auvergne tradition dating back 2,000 years. Salers is Cantal's farm-made cousin. It is produced by a few cheese-makers who still live in summer *burons* (stone huts) to make the cheese immediately after milking their red Salers cows on mountain slopes. Look for the red metal tag on the stone-like crust of a Salers, assuring a farm-produced cheese.

Planning Visit Salers and Cantal country in June or September. This is steep terrain, so bring sturdy shoes. www.fromages-aoc-auvergne.com

❾ *Ossau-Iraty*, French Pyrénées

This firm, fragrant mountain cheese from the western Pyrénées is made of sheep's milk. Visit Fromagerie Agerria in the town of St.-Martin Arberoue, and add a dab of black cherry jam from Itxassou to a plate of Basque cheeses during the June cherry fete.

Planning Stay in the village of St.-Étienne de Baïgorry in summer, when sheep graze in mountain pastures: cheese-makers open their doors in late July. www.terre-basque.com, www.bearn-basquecountry.com

❿ *Vacherin du Haut-Doubs*, Franche-Comté region

This winter treasure is held together with a *sangle*, a wide band of spruce. Inside its velvety, golden crust, the mature cow's-milk cheese is so runny that it is often served with a spoon. For details on cheeses of the Haut-Doubs area, visit the Rochat brothers' cheese shop in the village of Charbonnières-les-Sapins.

Planning Settle into an alpine bed and breakfast or a hotel on the canal in the town of Ornans and dine in a mountain inn to taste vacherin ladled over hot fingerling potatoes. www.france-voyage.com

Right: The display within a traditional French *fromagerie* can only hint at the wealth of variety of the country's regional cheeses.

La Mancha's Saffron Harvest

An ancient Spanish tradition, the timing
of the saffron harvest in La Mancha is crucial.

It is a late-October morning outside the town of Almagro in Castile-La Mancha, central Spain. As the first streaks of light appear on the horizon, time is running out for the workers bending to pick the purple crocus flowers that blanket the fields here for just two weeks each year. This is the annual saffron harvest, and each six-petaled flower must be picked before it opens—and before sunrise—so that the heat does not dry out its precious contents. For inside each bloom lie three delicate, blood-red stigmas that, when dried, produce the sweetly pungent spice that is saffron, or *azafrán*—the defining ingredient of Spain's classic paella, amongst other dishes. The ten-day harvest can be seen in many nearby villages, such as Barrax, San Pedro, and Consuegra. It also takes place in the northeastern province of Aragon. But it is the windmill-dotted region of La Mancha, the fabled land of Don Quixote, that is said to produce the very best saffron, with a Protected Designation of Origin (PDO) classification to prove it. Those fortunate enough to time a visit well might take part in the harvest—some tour operators can arrange this. Then join generations of families for the *monda*, in which the stigmas are stripped from the petals before being dried in the oven. And, best of all, savor the spice itself in exquisite, saffron-infused fish and seafood dishes, paella, and other delicacies from the local cuisine.

When to Go The saffron harvest takes place in the last two weeks of October, though it may sometimes spill over into November. An annual saffron festival is held in the village of Consuegra at the end of October.

Planning Visit the cheese-making factory in the nearby village of Tembleque, and sample the sublime Manchego cheeses produced from the milk of locally reared sheep. Explore the area's vineyards and visit Valdepeñas—the "city of wines"—one of Spain's main wine-making centers. You can sample its wines in one of the many *bodegas* (shops) that offer wine tastings.

Websites www.atasteofspain.com, www.euroadventures.net, www.cellartours.com

Saffron Facts

■ More than 60,000 flowers need to be harvested to produce 1 lb (450 grams) of dry saffron. It is one of the most expensive spices in the world.

■ Saffron powder is often adulterated with the addition of turmeric. Buy threads instead—the redder the better.

■ Stored in a cool place, in an airtight container, saffron threads will keep for as long as two to three years.

■ To use saffron, steep a few threads in hot water for at least 20 minutes, then use the soaked threads and liquid in your recipe.

The saffron harvest is dependent on the climate. It begins as soon as the first flowers emerge from the earth and lasts up to ten days.

SPECIALTIES & INGREDIENTS

OUTSTANDING MARKETS SEASONAL DELIGHTS IN THE KITCHEN FAVORITE STREET FOODS GREAT FOOD TOWNS ULTIMATE LUXURIES THE BEST WINE, BEER, & MORE JUST DESSERTS

Rows of ibérico hams hang alongside other traditional, regional cured foods in a typical Spanish *charcutería*.

SPAIN

Jamón Ibérico

Lovers of this revered ham will find some of the country's finest producers in the southwestern regions of Spain.

You see them in every traditional bar and restaurant in Spain—haunches of ham hanging from the ceiling, confirming their status as the nation's favorite snack food. In Spain, ham, or *jamón*, is an integral part of life and the choice of varieties can seem overwhelming. But for most food lovers there is only one contender: *jamón ibérico*, the finest and most aristocratic of them all. Characterized by its rich, red flesh marbled with translucent fat, jamón ibérico has an earthy, nutty flavor that is the by-product of the black-footed Iberian pig's diet of plump acorns, or *bellotas*. It is produced in many parts of Spain, but the best is said to come from the regions of Extremadura and Andalusia, where, alongside buttercup-strewn fields and olive groves, specially maintained forests of holm oak and cork shed the acorns that are the pigs' favorite food. The *montanera*, or fattening-up period, lasts for about four months. The hams are seasoned and cured by traditional methods, then aged for nine to 36 months depending on the quality of the ham, producing a distinctly flavored meat that is rich in monounsaturated fat. To find jamón ibérico at its source, visit the tiny village of Montánchez in Extremadura. Explore the narrow alleyways with their many *charcuterías* (delicatessens), where you can sample this crown jewel of hams—thinly sliced from a *tabla* (board)—with the local pitarra wine or a glass of chilled sherry.

When to Go Visit Extremadura or Andalusia in spring or fall to avoid extreme temperatures.
Planning If going to Extremadura, allow time to visit Montánchez and the other nearby ham-producing villages of Monesterio, Calera de León, Cabeza la Vaca, Segura de León, and Jerez de los Caballeros, where there is a ham fair in May. If buying, look for a label that says *Dehesa de Extremadura* (Plains of Extremadura). Allow an extra day to visit the town of Jabugo in Andalusia. The town is not very picturesque, but its jamón ibérico is said by many to be the best in Spain.
Websites www.atasteofspain.com, www.infohub.com

Ham Varieties

Spain's acclaimed ham accounts for only around six percent of the country's ham production and is made according to strict Protected Designation of Origin (PDO, DOC in Spain) regulations. It is always made from the **ibérico pig**, but there are several varieties.

The three main types, defined according to the pig's diet, and in ascending order of quality (though all are excellent), are: **jamón ibérico de pienso** (fed on grain only), **jamón ibérico de recebo** (fed on acorns and grains), and **jamón ibérico de bellota** (fed only on acorns). Bellota is the finest. Anything sold as *paletilla* comes from the foreleg and is therefore not strictly ham, though it has a good flavor.

If you are cutting from a whole ham, slice as thinly as possible and do so just before serving to retain the moisture.

Coffee bushes produce berries that are bright red when ripe. In the center of each berry is a pair of blue-green beans.

ETHIOPIA

The Home of Coffee

Coffee has been grown in the highland forests of southwest Ethiopia for at least a thousand years.

The ancient province of Kaffa in southwest Ethiopia is the proud birthplace and namesake of coffee. Legend has it that a young boy, Kaldi, was alerted to the energizing properties of coffee beans when his goats started to leap and dance after eating them. A road trip to a coffee plantation in this densely forested area provides a fascinating insight into the origins of the bean loved all over the world. Much of the area's coffee is grown in remote forest plantations, the bushes shaded by fine, tall trees alive with brightly colored birds and black-and-white colobus monkeys. Plantations also grow papaya, ginger, cardamom, and mango. The Ethiopian coffee ceremony is central to daily life on the plantations and around the country. The person conducting the ceremony, often a young woman, roasts the green beans over a charcoal burner and then grinds them by hand, adding her own choice of spices. She then brews the coffee in a long-necked clay pot, or *jebena*. Popcorn and roasted barley are the traditional accompaniments, and sweet grasses and flowers are scattered on the floor. It is polite to drink at least three cups, which will be small but strong.

When to Go Avoid June to September, when heavy rains can make the roads hazardous.

Planning Tepi, a large town in southern Ethiopia, is a good base for exploring the big plantations: the Coffee Plantation Guesthouse on the Tepi plantation is clean, friendly, and peaceful. The oldest and largest forest plantation is at the town of Bebeka. A loop through the region, taking in Jimma (Kaffa's capital), Tepi, and the town of Bedele, would be a real adventure–allow at least ten days and expect basic conditions. Then enjoy the creature comforts and excellent restaurants of Addis Ababa for a few days.

Websites www.ethiopianquadrants.com, www.highergroundstrading.com/fair-trade-tours.html

Ethiopian Dishes

■ *Injera*–a large fermented pancake with a distinctively sour taste that is used as a shared plate–is the staple food.

■ *Doro wat* is a rich chicken stew made with hard-boiled eggs and sweet onions caramelized in butter for several hours. It is served on special occasions.

■ Warming, substantial, and served in a clay pot, **shiro**–ground chickpea sauce with garlic, tomatoes, and rosemary–is everyday food for millions and no less delicious for that.

■ **Beef** is popular in a spicy or mild stew (*kai* or *alicha wat*); fried in bite-sized pieces with chili and onions (*tibs*); or as ground fillet steak (*kitfo*) with spiced butter and sharp white cheese.

SPECIALTIES & INGREDIENTS

OUTSTANDING MARKETS   SEASONAL DELIGHTS   IN THE KITCHEN   FAVORITE STREET FOODS   GREAT FOOD TOWNS   ULTIMATE LUXURIES   THE BEST WINE, BEER, & MORE   JUST DESSERTS

RÉUNION/MADAGASCAR

VANILLA

In 1841, a 12-year-old slave boy single-handedly discovered how to make vanilla available to the world.

The boy was one Edmond Albius, and he had perfected a simple way to artificially pollinate vanilla flowers on the tropical island of Réunion. This made commercial cultivation possible for the first time and spurred a vanilla boom on the islands of the western Indian Ocean. More than 160 years later, vanilla is a culinary icon (and major export earner) in Réunion, Madagascar, and the Comoros archipelago. The aromatic plant with thin, dark pods is now also attracting tourists as vanilla plantations have thrown open their gates to curious visitors. "The temperature and humidity of these islands are ideal for growing vanilla," says François Mayer, manager of Réunion's Coopérative de Vanille. "Réunion doesn't produce an awful lot of vanilla compared to places like Madagascar and the Comoros, but we like to think that we grow the best. And the savoir faire, the know-how, comes from Réunion and spread from here to the rest of the world." At the Coopérative de Vanille, a working plantation near the village of Bras-Panon on Réunion, you can see historical exhibits and vanilla-processing demonstrations. While most of the vanilla produced on these islands is exported to Europe, the islanders do keep some for themselves. Among typical dishes that you come across in Réunion's Creole restaurants are chicken or duck à la vanille, as well as incredibly tasty vanilla ice cream, crepes, and rum punch.

When to Go The vanilla growing season lasts from June to December. Toward the end of this period, the pods are cut, collected in baskets from the fields, and taken to the plantation factories for drying.

Planning Anyone wishing to visit the vanilla-producing regions of Réunion, Madagascar, and the Comoros will need two weeks; two or three days will suffice if you narrow the quest to just one island destination. The best restaurants are found in Antananarivo (Madagascar) and St.-Denis (Réunion); St.-Denis is also the best place for buying local cookbooks with vanilla recipes and various forms of vanilla that can be used for cooking at home.

Websites www.la-reunion-tourisme.com, www.air-mad.com

Vanilla Sugar

This vanilla-spiked sugar adds a hit of vanilla to all your recipes. It is delicious sprinkled on strawberries or your morning porridge.

2¹⁄₄ cups/1 lb/450 g sugar
2 vanilla beans (pods)

Pour the sugar into an airtight cannister. Using a sharp knife, slice each pod in half lengthwise. Scrape out the seeds and put them into the sugar. Stir to mix. Poke the pods into the sugar, making sure they are completely covered, and seal the cannister.

After two days, the sugar will take on a vanilla scent and flavor. Use as you would regular sugar.

Vanilla sugar keeps for months. As you use it up, top up with more sugar until the beans lose their scent.

Following the harvest, vanilla pods are dried in the sun for three to four weeks. They are then sorted into different grades according to size and quality.

OUTSTANDING MARKETS

Nothing could be less like a routine dash to the supermarket than these life-enhancing journeys to the places where dedicated cooks seek out their ingredients, luxurious emporia where gourmets find their favorite delicacies, vibrant markets displaying produce harvested just minutes away, and sprawling urban bazaars that lie on the crossroads of ancient trade routes.

No matter where in the world you are, there are delights to sample. In New York City, acquaint yourself with the soul-pleasures of authentic pastrami sandwiches, pickled lox, or fresh bagels or bialys. In Moscow, enter the palatial premises of Yeliseyevsky for the type of caviar that graced the pre-revolutionary tables of the Tsars. Perch on a stool at one of the snack bars in Barcelona's beloved La Boqueria market to sample intensely savory seafood stews or giant potato omelets. Be dazzled by the colors and perfumes of sun-warmed tropical fruits on the market-boats that ply canals in Thailand. Whatever your destination, carry a roomy shopping basket and come hungry—these feasts are not just for the eyes.

Heaps of chilis, avocado pears, and cherimoyas are among the luscious fruits and vegetables on sale in the local markets of Mexico's towns and villages, providing the basic ingredients for a sophisticated and at times fiery cuisine.

One of New York's best-loved foodie destinations, Zabar's draws big crowds with its smoked fish, coffee, cheeses, gourmet groceries, and much more.

NEW YORK DELIS

In a city of great delis, the Lower
East Side is home to some of the best.

New York City's Lower East Side, a downtown neighborhood between Houston and Grand Streets, could be mistaken for another trendy spot overrun with hipsters and boutiques. But the narrow, crowded streets and old tenement buildings speak of an era when millions of East European Jewish immigrants settled here and, desperate for a taste of home, established culinary traditions that live on today. A stroll reveals the area's rich roots. Katz's, a delicatessen founded in 1888, is a favorite for old-timers; its massive sandwiches stuffed with thick, hand-cut slabs of pastrami or brisket and its crisp-edged potato latkes make a memorable meal. Appetizing stores, which sell dairy and fish, were once as common as delis on the Lower East Side. Today, only Russ & Daughters remains. A tiny shop, it offers a dozen kinds of smoked and cured salmon and a range of cream cheeses, as well as Old World staples, such as herring fillets and pickled lox topped with ribbons of sweet onions. Several blocks south, brick-colored barrels clustered along the sidewalk signal Guss' Pickles. Garlicky full sours and extra-hot spicy pickles are among the best; munch on a few while the current owners regale you with the story of their business. If you are still hungry, Zabar's, the appetizing counter turned renowned food emporium on the Upper West Side, is worth a trip uptown for its selection of traditional and gourmet products.

When to Go Katz's Delicatessen and Russ & Daughters Appetizers are open seven days a week during normal business hours; weekends are especially busy. Guss' Pickles is closed on Saturdays. If possible, avoid peak travel season to New York City over holidays, such as Christmas.

Planning To soak up the history of the Lower East Side, visit the Tenement Museum, which recreates immigrant life at the turn of the 20th century in a series of restored apartments.

Websites www.tenement.org, www.katzdeli.com, www.russanddaughters.com, www.zabar's.com

Appetizing Stores

Cream cheeses, smoked and cured fish, caviar, dried fruits, and nuts are just a few of the tasty offerings you will find at appetizing stores, which sprang up in New York City in the late 19th century. Kosher dietary laws dictate that meat and dairy products cannot be sold or eaten together, so stores such as **Russ & Daughters** tout classic fish and dairy pairings, such as lox and cream cheese, and pickled herring in cream sauce.

Appetizing foods include a range of **sweet and salty options** to accompany fresh bagels and bialys. Though the food once represented typical immigrant fare, today it is regarded as a rare treat. What has not changed are the interactions between customers and counter-men, many of whom have been slicing salmon while swapping news with regulars for more than 20 years.

CALIFORNIA

FERRY BUILDING MARKETPLACE

The Marketplace and weekly farmers' market provide
the finest seasonal produce and local specialties.

In San Francisco's flagship Ferry Building on the Bay, a foodie's paradise has taken reign. Walk through its doors into the vaulted, skylit nave, where a line of archways down each side create storefronts for northern California's finest food vendors, whose stalls spill over with bins of fresh mushrooms and bunches of sunflowers, delectable pastries, and coffee stands. One of the first shops is Cowgirl Creamery, a purveyor of earthy artisan cheeses. Next door, just try ignoring the aroma of Steve Sullivan's legendary Acme Bread, where breads made from organic flour and handpicked grains are baked daily in the hearth oven. Down the way, indulge in an extravagant snack of caviar and champagne at Tsar Nicoulai Caviar, a caviar café run by pioneers of domestic sturgeon-farming. Further on down the aisle, at Recchiuti Confections, pick among seductive, handmade, jewel-like creations—signature truffles, *fleur de sel* caramels, and *pâtés de fruits*. Nearby, sip tea the Chinese way at Imperial Tea Court, an emporium of exclusive teas. Here, too, you'll find some of San Francisco's most celebrated restaurants and cafés, chief among them The Slanted Door, serving modern Vietnamese cuisine using ingredients culled from Bay Area farms; and Mijita, a *cocina Mexicana*, or Mexican kitchen, known for its Oaxacan chicken tamales and Baja-style fish tacos.

When to Go The Marketplace is open daily; the farmers' market takes place Tuesdays and Saturdays (plus Thursdays and Sundays seasonally), with Saturday mornings being its epicurean peak.

Planning The Marketplace is located along the Embarcadero at the foot of Market Street. The farmers' market takes place in front and at the rear of the building. San Francisco City Guides offers free walking tours of Ferry Building. Two hotels have food tours of Ferry Building Marketplace—the Four Seasons Hotel San Francisco and W Hotel San Francisco; both tours end with a gourmet feast.

Websites www.ferrybuildingmarketplace.com, www.slanteddoor.com, www.mijitasf.com, www.sfcityguides.org, www.fourseasons.com, www.whotels.com

Ferry Plaza Farmers' Market

On Tuesdays and Saturdays, a rambling farmers' market pops up outside the Marketplace, providing a showcase for **organic, in-season fare**: heirloom tomatoes, pungent herbs, flowers, local wine, honey, olive oil—and hard-to-find provisions, such as nettles, as well as free-range eggs in tints of mint and baby blue.

Free samples will ensure that you don't need to buy lunch. But if you do still have an appetite, grab some local cheese, fresh-baked bread, and local wine and stake out one of the plein air tables behind the Ferry Building, with spectacular bayfront views. Life doesn't get much better than this! Or maybe it does: Go to heaven with an oyster po-boy from the **Hayes Street Grill** stand (ask for it on a baguette).

Bins filled with colorful displays of fresh local fruit are among the many attractions that draw residents and visitors to the Ferry Building Marketplace.

HISTORIC FOOD SHOPS

In a world increasingly dominated by chains, a few august institutions
rail magnificently against unwelcome progress.

❶ Yeliseyevsky, Moscow, Russia

Few places better symbolize Moscow's transformation into a consumer's paradise than this 18th-century mansion, which opened in 1907 as Moscow's grandest food hall and has now been palatially restored after communist-era neglect. Vodka and caviar are obvious buys, but Yeliseyevsky trots the globe with reassuringly expensive goodies to satisfy the most discerning tastes.

Planning Open 24 hours, Yeliseyevsky is at 14 Ulitsa Tverskaya. www.smartmoscow.com

❷ KaDeWe, Berlin, Germany

Founded in 1907, continental Europe's largest department store survived near-destruction during the 20th century, but now its vast food hall has an overwhelming array of German and international food and drink delicacies, including an American section, many miniature restaurants, and a winter garden. As it is Germany, the sausage selection sizzles.

Planning KaDeWe is downtown at 21-24 Tauentzienstrasse. www.kadewe.de

❸ Dallmayr, Munich, Germany

Behind a magnificent historic facade, Swiss fruit brandies, cold-plucked chicken from Lower Bavaria, pasta prepared in front of your eyes, first-flush Darjeeling, Beaujolais walnut salami, more than 100 types of bread, freshly roasted coffee stored in hand-painted vases, and more than 150 cheese varieties are among the treats at this venerable delicatessen, started as a grocer in 1700.

Planning Dallmayr is downtown at 14-15 Dienerstrasse. www.dallmayr.de

❹ Antico Pizzicheria de Miccoli, Siena, Italy

In an ideal world, every town—if not street—would have an Italian deli like this tiny temple to Tuscan fare. Dating from 1889, the shop brims with hams, salamis, sausages, cheese, huge bags of porcini, truffles, and bottles of olive oil.

Planning Miccoli is at 93-95 Via di Città. There are some seats inside for diners. Another fine deli on the same street is Antica Drogheria Manganelli, founded in 1879. www.sienaonline.com

❺ Fauchon, Paris, France

For the finest champagne, caviar, truffles, chocolates, lobster, or any other luxury food, Fauchon represents uncompromising quality, opulence, and indulgence. Founded in 1886, it is considered Paris's top grocery. Its fuchsia-and-black signature colors feature in everything from the gorgeous packaging to some of the world's most eye-catching window displays.

Planning Closed Sundays and holidays, Fauchon is at 24-30 Place de la Madeleine. Nearby Hédiard is another historic food shop. www.parisinfo.com

❻ Maille, Paris, France

The French take mustard seriously. Few companies know it better than Maille, which established its first Paris store in 1747. This small, wood-lined shop—along with another in Dijon—dispenses potent varieties unavailable elsewhere. Around 30 prepackaged flavors, including blue cheese, cassis, and mango, join three house mustards drawn from taps into stoneware pots, their recipes unchanged since founder Antoine Maille's lifetime.

Planning Closed Sundays, Maille is at 6 Place de la Madeleine, a few steps from Fauchon. You can sample the three house mustards before buying. Maille also has a store in Dijon. www.maille.com

❼ Voisin, Lyon, France

A vision of chocolate statuary—especially at Easter, when ducks, swans, and other creatures burst out of chocolate eggs—Lyon's Voisin chain, founded in 1897, specializes in *coussins de Lyon* (chocolate-and-marzipan cushions flavored with curaçao).

Planning Voisin has several outlets throughout Lyon. www.chocolat-voisin.com

❽ Paxton & Whitfield, London, England

At its best, British cheese rivals any in the world. In London's courtly St. James's, Paxton's has purveyed cheese to the gentry since 1797, gaining a string of royal warrants. Churchill said a gentleman would buy his cheese nowhere else. For a taste of England's finest, try the best-selling Montgomery cheddar.

Planning Paxton's is at 93 Jermyn Street. It also has outlets in Bath and Stratford-upon-Avon. www.paxtonandwhitfield.co.uk

❾ Brick Lane Beigel Bake, London, England

Although Brick Lane was once a vibrant Jewish neighborhood, Bangladeshis have now largely replaced them in this part of London's East End. This cheap takeout is a rare throwback, dispensing chewy bagels filled with salt beef or smoked salmon round the clock to a line of celebrities and clubbers.

Planning Beigel Bake is at 159 Brick Lane. It is not kosher. www.jewisheastend.com

❿ Ye Olde Pork Pie Shoppe, Melton Mowbray, England

Melton Mowbray pork pies use uncured pork and have a slightly irregular shape with bowed sides. In 2008, manufacturers gained European Commission approval to protect the brand alongside Champagne and Stilton. This old-fashioned shop, which has been in business since 1851, is the last remaining town-center producer of authentic Melton Mowbray pies.

Planning Pork-pie-making demonstrations and classes are available. www.porkpie.co.uk

Right: Restored to its pre-Revolutionary, art nouveau splendor, the Yeliseyevsky food store in Moscow sells delicacies from around the world.

GRANVILLE ISLAND MARKET

Granville Island's passion for local produce makes this
multicultural market in central Vancouver unmissable.

Over the last 30 years, Granville Island has been transformed from a hazardous sandbar in False Creek into one of Vancouver's biggest attractions. "It's a temple of food," says Jérôme Dudancourt of Oyama Sausage Co., busy serving a stream of customers with sausages and fragrant hams in a variety that, like Granville Island Market as a whole, reflects Vancouver's ethnic complexity and cosmopolitan tastes, and its preference for locally sourced, organic, and traditionally made products. "We use traditional French, Italian, Spanish, German, Dutch, and British recipes but we adapt them to this century," he says. A similar approach is taken at nearby Edible British Columbia, promoting jelly made from locally grown lavender, coffee roasted on nearby Salt Spring Island, homemade Thai curries, and much more. Cheeses at Dussa's include local sage Derby, and soft, rich Salt Spring Island goat's cheese. Other stalls are piled with the freshest salmon, scallops, and crabs from the same ocean that laps the market building. Vancouver's large Chinese population dominates the fruit and vegetable stalls, and also sells everything from Indian curry and Italian ice cream to fish and chips, which can be consumed at water-view tables while watching for herons and harbor seals. Even simple grocery shopping is out-of-the-ordinary here.

When to Go Open year-round, the market attracts a mixture of local shoppers and visitors, so it is busiest in the summer. Vancouver's best season is the fall, with warm, dry days and cool evenings, and the leaves changing color along the tree-lined streets.

Planning The Public Market is open seven days a week, February through December; it is closed on Mondays in January. Various stalls offering breakfast open early, when there is plenty of water-view seating and a chance to see the market gradually come alive. Market tours are run Tuesday, Thursday, and Saturday at 8:30 a.m. and must be booked in advance. Part of the market's pleasure is reaching it onboard one of the 12-seat False Creek ferries, which depart from several points around the inlet and offer a water-level view of the city.

Websites www.granvilleisland.com, www.edible-britishcolumbia.com, www.granvilleislandferries.bc.ca

Market Food

■ For a unique local product buy the **syrup of British Columbian birch trees**. The yield per tree is only about 10 per cent of that of the maple, but the flavor is richer and more complex, and works well in marinades for local salmon.

■ One of the longest-standing vendors is **Lee's Donuts**, and the warm, sweet smell of the freshly baked rings and doughnut holes (powdered or glazed) pervades the market. A special pumpkin spice doughnut baked only around Halloween attracts long lines of customers.

■ Edible BC offers a three-hour, **chef-led tour** of the market that is often sold out. It includes tastings of ingredients and discussions of their best use. Even residents who take the tour find that they learn something new about what is on sale.

Artisan bakers are among the array of specialist vendors in the market, where the senses are bombarded with mouthwatering sights, smells, and colors.

Artfully arranged piles of flawless fresh produce are typical of local markets all over the state of Puebla.

MEXICO

The Markets of Puebla

Explore the city where indigenous cooking traditions and Old World ingredients combined to produce modern Mexican gastronomy.

Seventy miles (112 kilometers) southeast of Mexico City, at the foot of the great volcano Popocatépetl, lies the city of Puebla. Built by the Spaniards, this showplace of baroque architecture is surrounded by much older Indian towns. The inevitable culinary commingling of the two cultures is nowhere more evident than in Puebla's markets. The aroma of spicy stews being cooked in clay pots over wood fires is joined by the scent of flowers from fields outside the city. To the clapping of women patting out corn tortillas, a sound called "the heartbeat of Mexico," is added the cry of the vendor, who hawks everything from regional candies to hand-carved wooden spoons. Wend your way through aisles lined with stacks of fruits and vegetables, basketsful of aromatic spices, piles of bright green chilies and dried red ones. Stop to try the blue corn quesadillas filled with squash blossoms, wild mushrooms, and local cheese. Quench your thirst with an *Agua de Jamaica*, a refreshing hibiscus flower punch. Get herbal remedies, candles, and amulets from the *hierbero* (herbalist) and cooking advice from the *pollera*, whose freshly plucked chickens sit on an intricately embroidered cloth. Then carry your purchases home in a handwoven market bag.

When to Go A temperate climate makes Puebla a year-round destination. During the Day of the Dead (*Dia de los Muertos*) on November 1-2, markets are filled with the best produce of the harvest season, as well as candy skulls and adornments for family altars.

Planning One of the oldest and best *tianguis* (indigenous street market) is held on Sundays and Wednesdays in the pre-Hispanic town of Cholula, 7.5 miles (12 km) west of Puebla. At this market, go to the Las Cazuelas stall to buy excellent mole and *pipián* pastes to take home. These are also sold at the very traditional Mercado del Carmen in downtown Puebla, located on 21 Oriente Street. While there, try the *cemitas*, crunchy sesame-topped rolls filled with meat, Oaxaca cheese, avocados, and chipotle chilies.

Websites www.advantagemexico.com, www.planetware.com, www.mexconnect.com

Demystifying Mole

Mole (pronounced moh-lay) is a rich, dark, sweet, and spicy sauce, the product of Spanish-indigenous culinary fusion.

Mole poblano (mole with turkey or chicken) was probably invented in the 16th century in Puebla's Santa Rosa convent. Native chilies and chocolate were ground with cinnamon, cloves, and allspice to create a sauce with sophisticated layers of flavor.

Not all mole contains chocolate. Seed-based mole is called *pipián*—green when made with pumpkin seeds and fresh chilies, red when made with sesame seeds and dried chilies.

Squash blossoms are used in tacos, soups, and crepes.

The vibrant colors of the Christmas market in Cusco's Plaza de Armas adds to the holiday atmosphere.

PERU

Cusco's Christmas Market

The local Andean people begin their Christmas
celebrations with a large market in the center of Cusco.

One of the largest markets in the Andes, Santuranticuy unfolds in Cusco's main square and the surrounding streets on Christmas Eve as thousands of Peruvians gather to do their yuletide shopping and soak up the holiday atmosphere. Santuranticuy literally means "selling of saints"—a reference to the fact that the market once specialized in nativity scenes. But over the years all sorts of items have been added to the makeshift stalls, from indigenous arts and crafts to traditional Andean foods. One of the more visible dishes is *cuy* (guinea pig), slowly roasted on rolling barbecues and served with a spicy chili sauce. Other market edibles include barbecued corn on the cob, tamales (a meat filling wrapped in banana leaves), *rocoto relleno* (stuffed peppers), and *anticuchos* (beef hearts). Santuranticuy's trademark beverage is *ponche de leche*, a potent hot toddy made from milk and pisco brandy. As Peruvian families have their big holiday dinner on Christmas Eve, many of the restaurants around the plaza and elsewhere in central Cusco serve special meals that center around stuffed turkey, roast pork, and half a dozen different types of potato. Among the restaurants that serve a traditional Peruvian holiday dinner are Pachapapa on the Plazoleto San Blas, the MAP Café inside the Museo de Arte Precolombino, and the Inka Grill on the main plaza.

When to Go Arrive in Cusco a few days before Christmas in order to have time for all the Inca and Spanish colonial sights. Although the yuletide season is technically summer south of the Equator, the highland climate means that Cusco temperatures can range from 20 to 70ºF (-7 to 21ºC) on any given day.

Planning If your stomach is at all sensitive to exotic foods, stick to eating in the better restaurants in central Cusco. Reservations are highly recommended for Christmas Eve dinner. If you visit the cathedral, admire the painting of "The Last Supper" by Marcos Zapata perched high above the nave, in which cuy (guinea pig) features among the dishes spread before Jesus and his apostles.

Websites www.perutourism.com/info/cusco.htm, www.cusco-peru.org

The Potato

Peru's most popular foodstuff is the humble potato, which originated thousands of years ago in the highlands around Lake Titicaca. While scientists attribute the potato to plant evolution, the ancient Inca believed that it was a gift from the gods, one of the crops that supreme being Viracocha bestowed upon his devotees so that they would never go hungry.

Nowadays, the variety is astounding—around 5,000 different types of potato are either cultivated or grow wild in Peru. They come in all colors—brown, purple, red, white, and yellow. And while almost always roasted or baked, they are rarely served plain. Peruvians garnish their potatoes with cheese, garlic, onions, fried eggs, lime juice, and dozens of other items that complement their flavor.

SALCEDO MARKET

Sample the different cuisines of the Philippines' 81 provinces at Manila's weekly community market.

The Philippines boasts a regionally diverse cuisine influenced by centuries of Chinese, Malay, Spanish, and American trade and colonization. There is no better place to get acquainted with its varied flavors than at Salcedo Community Market, a Saturdays-only collection of more than 130 stalls selling fresh and prepared food in the heart of downtown Manila. Arrive ravenous and follow the lead of locals, who alternate on-the-hoof grazing with sit-down feasts at shared picnic tables. Sweet tooths might start with *piaya*—griddled flat cakes oozing muscovado sugar—from the central island of Negros, accompanied by a cup of hot chocolate made with local cacao; chili fanatics will want to sample the spicy Bicolano preparation of fresh crab bathed in chili-hot coconut milk. There are deep-fried, rice-flour empanada from the northern province of Ilocos, stuffed with garlicky pork sausage, green papaya, and an egg; and diminutive, delicate empanada filled with crab meat from the nearby gourmet province of Pampanga. Join the lines in front of grills piled with boneless milkfish stuffed with tomatoes, red onion, and cilantro mixed with soy sauce; or deep-fryers sizzling with *ukoy*—crisp shrimp and sweet-potato fritters. Not to be missed is *lato*, a briny seaweed resembling miniature bunches of grapes that marries well with a dressing of coconut vinegar. *Pasalubong*, or edible souvenirs, include smoked tuna belly and truffle-like *pastillas* made from the milk of water buffalo.

When to Go December through March are relatively cooler, drier months. Avoid the wet, flood-prone monsoon season (June–October). The market is open year-round on Saturdays, 7 a.m. to 2 p.m.

Planning The market is held in Jaime Velasquez Park, Makati City (Manila Central Business District).

Websites www.philtourism.gov.ph, kulinarya.net

Salcedo's Alternative Market

Salcedo's alter ego is a boisterous **morning market** (6 a.m.–1 p.m.) held on Sundays on the grounds of the Philippines Lung Center in Quezon City, about 20 minutes from downtown Manila.

Expect twice as many booths, four times the number of patrons, and an exhaustive selection of fresh produce, meats, fish, and well-priced Philippine crafts. Provincial specialties include Negrenese **lumpiang ubod** (soft spring rolls filled with batons of fresh palm heart), **bibingka** (cheese-crowned puffy rice-flour pancakes cooked in clay pans set over charcoal), and cups of **barako**, a super-caffeinated variety of coffee grown in the southern Luzon province of Batangas.

The Saturday market is a meeting place for the whole community and provides visitors with a chance to try delicious delicacies from the country's many regions.

Lunch vendors selling cooked foods mix with others selling fresh produce in Thailand's traditional floating markets.

DAMNOEN SADUAK

Experience the colors and flavors of
Thailand's busiest floating market.

Laden with green papaya and orchid garlands, a sampan glides across the water in the early dawn, leaving barely a ripple on the silky waters of the *klong* (canal). A dog barks, a bird calls, as housewives venture one by one onto the canal-side pontoons to bargain for supplies with the vendor in the boat. Minutes later, a whole flotilla is paddling along the labyrinth of waterways toward the market klong. Located about 60 miles (100 kilometers) west of Bangkok, Damnoen Saduak is the meeting place of locals, visitors in search of tasty food, and country women peddling wares from their orchards and gardens. Exotic fruits abound, and luscious vegetables burst with vitamins. There are pea aubergines and yard-long beans, lotus roots, bamboo shoots, water spinach, giant radish, baby corn, and much more. Soon, floating kitchens fill the air with fragrance and smoke as stir-fries sizzle in the woks. Try a takeout meal wrapped in banana leaves, or join the locals feasting on spicy soup and noodles, satay, or rice flavored with fish balls, tofu, or shrimps. Expect tangy accents of lemongrass and coriander, lime, ginger, tamarind, and plenty of coconut milk in whatever you sample.

When to Go November to March for pleasant temperatures and generally dry weather.

Planning The market operates daily between 8 and 11 a.m. For a genuine experience, set off for Damnoen Saduak as early as you can, before the tour groups arrive and souvenir stalls hog the limelight. Take the first bus (at 6 a.m.) to Damnoen Saduak from Bangkok Southern Bus Terminal, a journey of 2.5 hours. On arrival, pick up a sampan or long-tail boat (sit at the back for the best views but expect to get wet). Eat food piping hot, peel your own fruit, and go easy on chilies.

Websites www.amazing-thailand.com/FandD.html, www.bangkok.com, www.thailand-huahin.com

Thai Cucumber Salad

This salad provides a refreshing counterpoint to satay or spicy meat dishes.

Serves 4
1 cup/8 fl oz/225 ml vinegar
1/4 tsp sea salt
2 tbsp sugar
2 cucumbers
2 shallots, finely chopped
1 red bird chili, seeded and
 sliced into thin rings
1/2 red bell pepper, diced
1 tbsp chopped cilantro (fresh
 coriander)
2 tbsp chopped peanuts

Put vinegar, salt, and sugar into a small saucepan. Simmer over medium heat until the sugar and salt dissolve and the sauce thickens slightly. Let cool.

 Wash the cucumbers, then cut them into quarters lengthwise. Slice them thinly and place in a serving bowl along with the shallots and peppers.

 Just before serving, pour the sauce over the salad and mix. Garnish with chopped cilantro and peanuts.

RAMADAN MARKETS

Break the fast with some of the best Malay food
in Kuala Lumpur's impromptu Ramadan street markets.

Come Ramadan, Kuala Lumpur, Malaysia's largest city, is transformed into a street-food mecca as dozens of markets catering to fasting Muslims spring up in parking lots, along alleys, and at curbsides. Each afternoon around half-past three, hundreds of vendors—some seasoned catering professionals and others gifted home cooks—heap tables with pyramids of *popiah* (soft spring rolls filled with chili-sauce-seasoned jicama and carrot), rainbow-hued *kuih talam* (unctuous coconut-milk-based sweets), and tubs of *bubur*, a soulful meat and rice porridge scented with cloves, cinnamon, nutmeg, and peppery laksa leaf. Clouds of smoke wreathe sellers of *ayam percik* (barbecued chicken doused with chili-coconut sauce), *satar* (skewered banana-leaf-wrapped packets of seasoned fish paste), and *ikan bakar*—meaty stingray, whole snapper, or mackerel doused with fiery *sambal* (chili sauce) and grilled on a banana leaf—as others labor over hillocks of wide rice noodles snapping and sizzling on enormous griddles. By half-past six the crowds are thick and spirits high in anticipation of *buka puasa* (breaking the fast). Thirty minutes later it is all over, and the visitor is left to decide which of Kuala Lumpur's other Ramadan markets to visit the next day.

When to Go Ramadan markets are open in Kuala Lumpur (and all over Malaysia) every afternoon of the ninth month of the Islamic lunar calendar, which begins each year approximately ten days earlier than in the previous year. They begin around 4 p.m. and finish up shortly after the fast is broken.

Planning The number, size, and location of markets vary year to year; detailed market lists are searchable on the websites of Malaysia's major English-language newspapers, the *New Straits Times* and *The Star*, and can be obtained from Kuala Lumpur City Hall (DBKL). Wait to dive into your purchases until the call from nearby mosques marks dusk and the end of the fast (or until you have returned to your hotel). Most vendors supply plastic forks and spoons and napkins on request. Women should avoid wearing revealing clothing, such as tank tops, short-shorts, and miniskirts.

Websites nst.com.my, thestar.com.my

What to Order

It is said that the best Malay food Is found in private homes. So Ramadan markets—where many vendors are also homemakers—offer an unrivaled opportunity to sample authentic Malay home-style dishes.

■ *Kerabu* are salads made from anything, from perky wild fern tips to shredded green mango, dressed with coconut milk, chili, fish sauce, and lime juice.

■ *Dalca* is a comforting mélange of coconut milk, chili, and turmeric-stewed vegetables and lentils.

■ *Rendang* consists of chicken or beef simmered to tenderness with lemongrass, galangal, chilies, coconut milk, and warm spices, such as cloves, nutmeg, and mace.

Neatly arranged piles of skewered snacks tempt hungry customers at the end of a day's fasting.

INDIA

Old Delhi's Chandni Chowk

This lively market in Delhi's "Old City" is a
must for anyone seeking traditional Indian fare.

Chandni Chowk, "the moonlit avenue," is a bustling thoroughfare running through the heart of medieval Old Delhi. Built by Mogul emperor, Shah Jahan, it has operated as one of the city's busiest and most colorful market areas since the 17th century. Lined with stallholders who sell everything from calculators to caged birds, the avenue and its many ancillary back streets are also home to thousands of different types of traditional Indian foods. Look out for *chaat* (salty street snacks), like *vada*, a kind of savory doughnut made from spiced lentils or potatoes dipped in gram flour; or sample *pani puri*, a crisp puff of hollow bread filled with curry. The area also houses some of India's oldest *halwais*, or candy stores, where the recipes have been passed down through generations of store owners for hundreds of years. Sticky *jalebis* made from a piped squiggle of dough, fried golden in ghee and drizzled with syrup, are a local specialty. Order a *namkeen lassi* (a salty yogurt drink) to cool the heat of any chili-spiked nibbles you have eaten, and push past the crush of people, goats, trishaws, and bullock carts to spend some time browsing the market stalls for clothes, jewelry, and souvenirs. Once done with shopping, take some time to explore the historical mansions lining the side streets, or to visit the rich variety of holy shrines that surround the area. No trip would be complete without seeing the Jama Masjid—India's largest mosque—and the Red Fort, both nearby.

When to Go Chandni Chowk is open year-round, from 10 a.m. to 4 p.m. Many stalls close on Sundays. Try to avoid the area on national and religious holidays, when it can become overcrowded.

Planning One of the best ways to experience Chandni Chowk—bustle, smells, sounds, and all—is from the back of a trishaw. You will find hundreds for hire at the Red Fort, across the street from the market. Ask your driver to recommend food stalls; the stalls tend to move around and change frequently, so local knowledge is invaluable.

Website www.ghantewala.com

Local Specialties

■ In the walled city just to the south of Chandni Chowk are several Jain temples, including the **Lal Mandir**. Many Jains, who are strict vegetarians, live here, and the local restaurants produce some of the finest vegetarian food in the city.

■ Look out for **Paratha Wali Gali**, a little lane leading off Chandni Chowk. Most of the shops here specialize in *parathas*—flatbreads, often topped with, and folded around, delicately spiced fillings.

■ **Giani's Ice Cream** on Fatehpur Chowk, near the Red Fort, is famous for *rabri falooda*, an ice-cold concoction of noodles and nuts in thick, sweetened, cardamom-scented milk.

■ To try *chaat*, the savory snacks that are Delhi's favorite street food, drop in at the hole-in-the-wall **Shree Balaji Chaat Bhandar** (shop no. 1462, Chandni Chowk), **Lala Babu Chaat Bhandar** (no. 1421), or **Natraj Café** (no. 1396).

Opposite: A rare quiet moment on Chandni Chowk. Above: The market is also a busy thoroughfare.

OLD-FASHIONED CANDY STORES

Relive childhood pleasures as you take a retro-chic journey to shops lined
with sherbet dips, flying saucers, and candy cigarettes.

❶ Orne's Candy Store, Boothbay Harbor, Maine

Little changed since 1885, this timber-lined store in a rustic fishing village delights visitors with old-fashioned saltwater taffy, truffles, and hand-dipped chocolates displayed in old glass-and-wood cases. But fudge is its most famous product: flavors include penuche (brown sugar with walnuts), maple pecan, and peanut butter.

Planning Orne's is open daily from Mother's Day through mid-October. Inaccessible by public transport, Boothbay Harbor is 58 miles (93 km) from Portland, Maine. www.ornescandystore.com

❷ Economy Candy, New York City

Mainline nostalgia at this unreconstructed penny-candy store chockablock with hard-to-find American and European treats, such as candy necklaces and cigarettes, and Squirrel Nut Zippers. Run since 1937 by the same family, the store's many fans consider it to be New York's best candy store.

Planning Open daily, Economy Candy is at 108 Rivington Street on Manhattan's Lower East Side. Avoid weekends, when crowds impede browsing. www.economycandy.com

❸ Ghantewala Halwai, Delhi, India

Since 1790, seven generations of the Jain family have dispensed seasonally inspired candies to emperors, presidents, prime ministers, and lesser mortals in the frantic Chandni Chowk district. India's oldest *halwai* (traditional candy store) enjoys renown for its *sohan halwa*, made from dried fruits, sprouts, and sugar.

Planning Ghantewala is open 8 a.m.–9 p.m. It is located near the Gurdwara Sisganj Sahib, the shrine built in memory of the Sikh martyr, Guru Tegh Bahadur. www.ghantewala.com

❹ Ali Muhiddin Hacı Bekir, Istanbul, Turkey

In 1777, Hacı Bekir set up shop in Istanbul with a training in confectionary and a recipe for *rahat lokum*, the soft, sweet, pink, jelly-like cubes that were named Turkish Delight by a 19th-century English traveler. Nowadays, apple, ginger, and cinnamon are among the flavors on sale beside the traditional rosewater Turkish Delight in this gloriously restored Ottoman throwback, which is still owned by the Hacı Bekir family.

Planning Hacı Bekir is at Hamidiye Caddesi 83, Eminönü. www.hacibekir.com.tr

❺ A La Mere de Famille, Paris, France

Founded in 1761 in Montmartre, Paris's oldest and most venerable confectioner's offers hundreds of French regional specialties, such as *calissons* (iced candied fruits) and *berlingots* (twisted sugar ribbons) from Provence, set out on wooden counters beneath chandeliers. The cash register looks little younger than the shop.

Planning The store is at 35 Rue du Faubourg Montmartre. www.parisinfo.com

❻ Confiserie Temmerman, Ghent, Belgium

A visual throwback to the 1800s, Temmerman has an odd specialty: *cuberdons*, nose-shaped candies filled with raspberry jam. Many customers also prize the shop for its salt licorice.

Planning Temmerman is at 79 Kraanlei. www.visitflanders.co.uk

❼ The Oldest Sweet Shop in England, Pateley Bridge, North Yorkshire, England

Most self-respecting English main streets once had a sweetshop (candy store); this blissful town caressed by some of England's loveliest countryside still does. Lined with neat rows of glass jars filled with old-fashioned goodies, such as butterscotch gums, humbugs, and aniseed balls, this sweetshop dating from 1827 is a hop, skip, and leap down memory lane.

Planning The store is open Wed to Sun and on public holidays. Pateley Bridge is 55 minutes by bus (number 24) from Harrogate. www.oldestsweetshop.co.uk

❽ Mrs Kibble's Olde Sweet Shoppe, London, England

In a tiny outlet lined with jars of more than 180 types of candy, mostly boiled (hard), Mrs Kibble dispenses friendly service and old-fashioned goodies, such as sherbet dip, sugar mice, and the best-selling rhubarb and custard.

Planning Open daily, Mrs Kibble's is at 57A Brewer Street, Soho, and St. Christopher's Place, off Oxford Street. www.visitlondon.com

❾ *Turrón* factory, Jijona, Spain

Comprising toasted almonds, sugar, honey, and egg whites, *turrón* is a type of candy resembling halvah. It is especially popular at Christmas. For centuries it has fed the economy of the ancient Alicante town of Jijona (Xixona in Valencian). This factory, with a museum attached, is a fascinating place to observe turron's production, and the shop sells acclaimed brands, such as El Lobo and 1880.

Planning The museum is open most days of the year and is outside Jijona, 18 miles (29 km) north of Alicante. www.museodelturron.com

❿ La Violeta, Madrid, Spain

In a quarter bursting with old-fashioned independent stores, this is perhaps the quirkiest. Behind its original wood facade this tiny shop has, since 1915, been selling violet products, especially *violetas* (candies made of violet essence), a Madrid specialty. Other novelties include candied natural violets, violet marmalade, jelly, and tea.

Planning La Violeta is at 6 Plaza de Canalejas, near Puerta del Sol. www.turismomadrid.es

Right: The allure of shelf after shelf of candies in every shape, size, and color never fades.

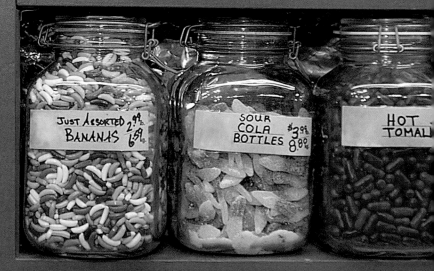

The Deli Hall is a good place to shop and people-watch.

QUEEN VICTORIA MARKET

Drop in for coffee or spend the whole day exploring
this vast market in one of the world's great food cities.

Food is important in Melbourne and this large market, housed in a series of old buildings on the northwestern edge of downtown since 1878, is heaven on Earth for foodies—and anyone who enjoys a good pie, croissant, baklava, chocolates, bratwurst, sashimi ... Melburnians are sophisticated when it comes to culinary matters because their city, more than any other in Australia, has been built on the arrival of successive waves of immigrants. Greeks, Chinese, Croats, Vietnamese, Italians, Indians, Lebanese, and others have arrived in large numbers, each bringing their own unique cuisine. These varied culinary traditions, combined with the availability of local fresh produce, have created a robust tradition of excellent food, and where better to sample this glorious legacy than in the halls and open sheds of the venerable Queen Vic? Within are high-quality (but competitively priced) delicatessens, their stalls groaning under the weight of fresh local produce: delectable cheese, wine, luscious fruits and vegetables, and a weight-watcher's nightmare of doughy delights too numerous to list. It is a great place for lunch, or a snack at any time of day, or even just to wander around—take in the aromas and capture the essence of one of the world's great food cities.

When to Go The market is open Tuesday and Thursday–Sunday. The hours vary according to the day of the week. Closed on public holidays.

Planning One of the pleasures of Melbourne is its compact size, and although the market is on the edge of the city center, it is within easy walking distance of Melbourne Central Station. The site is spread across several buildings and open sheds; the main food area is situated in the block between Elizabeth Street and Queen Street. Tours of the market are available; they last two hours and must be booked in advance.

Website www.qvm.com.au

Market Favorites

■ Many people's favorite part of the market—and without doubt the most aromatic—is the **Deli Hall** (sometimes called the Dairy Produce Hall) with 17 delicatessens and specialty stalls devoted to bread, olive oil, cheese, wine, pasta, and coffee.

■ The **Food Court** is a modern addition to the market and a great place to enjoy a quick snack or more substantial meal. Takeout food is also available.

■ The **Meat Hall** is the place to find top-quality butchers and fishmongers.

■ The **Elizabeth Street Shops** is a delightful 19th-century parade housing several gourmet cafés and specialist merchants.

TURKEY

BALIK PAZARI, ISTANBUL

Istanbul's covered fish market has a reputation for selling the best fish and shellfish available in Turkey.

At Balık Pazarı, literally "fish bazaar," near Çiçek Pasajı, or Flower Passage, in Istanbul's lively Beyoğlu district, uniform rows of silvery mackerel lie head to tail on beds of shaved ice, like soldiers in parade formation. Flat, pinkish flounder from the Aegean Sea hang from heavy metal hooks at the back of stalls displaying a wealth of the sea's seasonal bounty: such as *palamut* (bonito) and *lüfer* (bluefish) from the Bosporus and fist-sized octopuses from the blue waters of Bodrum, where the Aegean meets the Mediterranean. "Nice *levrek* (sea bass) today," a mustachioed *balıkçı* (fishmonger) calls out as he unloads another crate of the Mediterranean fish—a signature dish of Turkey when baked whole in a thick crust of salt. Muslim women dressed in *tesettür*, the traditional headscarf and long, lightweight topcoat, young children in tow, carefully examine the day's catch, as do chefs from the city's most prestigious restaurants. The tantalizing aroma of mussels sizzling in kettles of olive oil lure customers, who inspect the wide assortment of mezes, or appetizers, available to sample and buy. Visitors to the market will also find a colorful mélange of fresh-produce vendors, *dükkân* (small grocers), and *meyhane*—traditional Turkish tavernas for drinking raki (anise-flavored aperitif) and other alcoholic beverages with tapas-style mezes.

When to Go Year-round, although the weather is generally more pleasant in spring and fall.

Planning The market is open daily from dawn to dusk and is generally less crowded during prayer time. Allow an hour or so to wander through the market, longer if you plan to eat at one of the meyhanes in Balık Pazarı or on Nevizade Street, an adjacent side street where restaurants stay open later.

Websites www.tourismturkey.org, www.turkeytravelplanner.com

Dining Like a Turk

An evening at a **meyhane** is one of drinking—usually rakı—and eating, starting with a number of different **mezes** shared by the table. Your waiter will bring out several dishes, each plate with enough food for two or three people (more if everyone just wants to sample). The meal starts with cold, typically vegetarian, mezes, such as cheese, yogurt dishes, or pureed dips served with **pide** (Turkish flat bread), and sometimes shrimp, octopus, or other seafood. Hot mezes are next—fried calamari, sautéed lambs' livers, or **börek** (meat, cheese, or spinach-filled pastry)—followed by an **entrée** of grilled meat, chicken, or fish, ordered individually. Dessert is often a selection of **baklava**, *kadayıf* (pastry), and seasonal fruits, served with **Turkish coffee**.

The wondrous displays of fish at Balık Pazarı draw local shoppers, visitors, and the city's top chefs.

CHRISTMAS FAIR IN PRAGUE

Every winter, the Czech capital plays host to some of Europe's most atmospheric Christmas markets.

P rague, with its Gothic architecture and ice-clear winter light, provides the ideal backdrop for traditional festive cheer. In the Old Town Square, between the looming cathedral and the astronomical clock, stalls are set out throughout the month of December, arranged around a huge Christmas tree and a wooden nativity scene, complete with real animals for visitors to stroke. Other squares in the town also host Christmas markets, and at each one are rows of homely wooden stalls with pitched roofs. Traders sell all manner of glass, wood, and straw decorations and Czech handicrafts, such as puppets, birch boxes, and glassware. Every so often, you will come across seasonal local delicacies, many prepared in front of you. Buy a cup of hot, mulled wine to warm yourself as you browse, or sample the sweet Czech honey liqueur (*medovina*), and nibble on gingerbread, almond cakes, and *trdlo* (grilled rings of sweet bread dipped in ground almonds and sugar). Local meat snacks include spit-roast pig and grilled sausages, roast chestnuts, and grilled corn. Look for food gifts, like elaborately decorated gingerbread houses, sugared almonds, molded marzipan, and spiced cookies. Prague at this time of year is a city straight out of a winter fairy tale.

Christmas Entertainment

There is a stage in the Old Town Square that hosts performances by **choirs** and **instrumental groups** from around the world throughout December. Particularly charming are the children who come from schools all over the Czech Republic to perform **carols and dances** here, beautifully dressed in traditional costume. The markets are at their best in the evening.

When to Go Prague's Christmas markets run daily from 9 a.m. to 7 p.m., from the Saturday four weeks before Christmas Eve until the start of January.

Planning The two largest markets, with about 80 stalls each, are at the Old Town Square and Wenceslas Square, but smaller Christmas markets can also be found at Havelske Trziste and Námestí Republiky. All these markets are within ten minutes' walk of each other. Try to find a hotel in the old town, a good central location from which you will be able to stroll to almost all the city's main sights.

Websites www.prague.net, www.pragueexperience.com

Prague's markets are lit with thousands of tiny lights, shimmering against the backdrop of some of the city's most beautiful buildings.

Locals head to the Rialto fish market early in the day, when the catch is at its freshest and the choice at its richest.

ITALY

RIALTO FISH MARKET

The colorful, bustling food markets of Venice are just a short walk from the Rialto Bridge on the Grand Canal.

As gulls hover in the air and motorboats chug across the water, you might be forgiven for thinking you were at the seaside. But this is the famous Rialto fish market—a covered, colonnaded marketplace in Venice, one of the world's most beautiful cities. Market day at the Pescaria, as it is known, begins just before 7 a.m., when the fish is unloaded from small motorboats on the side canals. Glistening fresh and still smelling of salt, the fish tumble onto the tables in an unending stream. Every fish and crustacean you can think of is here, along with more unusual varieties: black eels writhing in buckets, purple octopus, or *moscardini*, and special Venetian favorites, such as cuttlefish, *canocche* (a cross between a shrimp and a crab), and *schie*, tiny shrimp from the lagoon that are eaten grilled or fried. Fish has been sold here for more than 500 years, and locals still come to do their daily shopping. There is an old plaque on one of the walls giving required fish measurements. And, like the tides of the lagoon itself, the market constantly fluctuates, filling and emptying by the minute. The noise can be deafening as the stallholders shout out to their customers while deftly filleting fish on makeshift tables. By noon, the crowd has grown into a seething mass. And then, just an hour later, it is all over: the stalls are empty, the tables and people have gone, and all that is left are the seagulls swooping down to pick up the scraps.

When to Go Tuesday to Saturday, from 7 a.m. to 1 p.m. Arrive early to avoid the crowds. Avoid the summer in Venice generally, to escape both the crowds and the heat.

Planning An hour at the market is probably long enough, though you may also want to see the adjoining fruit and vegetable market, the Erberia. Venice and its environs will keep you busy for at least a week.

Websites www.yourfriendinvenice.com, www.deliciousitaly.com, www.venicevenetogourmet.com

Buying and Eating Fish

■ Visit the adjoining stalls in the **Campo delle Beccarie** selling salted fish (salting fish has long been a tradition in the lagoon), canned and smoked fish, and bottles of cuttlefish ink.

■ No visit to the Rialto is complete without lunch at the nearby **Trattoria alla Madonna**—Venice's best-known fish restaurant. The seafood risotto is one of the finest in the city.

■ Sample fish *cicheti* (snacks) in a *bacaro* (wine bar) or one of the many bars in the area. **Nazaria**, **Bancogiro**, and **Al Pesador** near the Rialto Bridge are all good for snacks as well as full meals. Be sure to try the classic Venetian favorites: *seppie al nero* (cuttlefish in its ink), *sarde al soar* (sardines marinated in onions and white-wine vinegar), and *baccala mantecata* (creamed cod).

STREET MARKETS

Scruffy and chaotic or orderly and refined, the world's street markets offer fresh, local—and often cheap—seasonal produce, alongside a slice of local life.

❶ St. Lawrence, Toronto, Canada

This farmers' market emporium has operated since 1803, when it cohabited with Toronto's city hall. Redeveloped between the 1970s and 1990s after long neglect, the area's mix of homes and businesses showcases urban regeneration. More than 120 retailers dispense everything from seafood to coffee.

Planning The market is in Toronto's old town; Saturday is market day. www.stlawrencemarket.com

❷ Union Square Greenmarket, New York City

Once a Manhattan focal point, by the 1970s Union Square had become a junkie hangout. Barry Benepe founded a farmers' market in 1976, aiding struggling Hudson Valley farmers and reintroducing New Yorkers to seasonal food in one stroke. The market's variety in this now revitalized area bewilders many supermarket shoppers.

Planning Flanking East 17th Street and Broadway, the market is open on Monday, Wednesday, Friday, and Saturday, year-round. www.cenyc.org

❸ Castries Market, St. Lucia

Opened in 1894 and still occupying the original orange-roofed building, this market in St. Lucia's capital is the island's largest and loudest. Stock up on island spices (star anise, mace, cinnamon); breadfruit, bananas, and other tropical fruits; condiments like hot-pepper sauce; hot food, including rotis; or the fishermen's catch.

Planning Next to Jeremie and Peynier Streets, the market is open daily (except Sundays), but is best on Saturdays. www.castriescitycouncil.org

❹ Ver-o-Peso, Belém, Brazil

Noisy and chaotic, yet irresistibly atmospheric, with parallel rows of fishmongers selling odd-looking specimens, this vast riverfront emporium hugs Bélem's Ver-o-Peso docks, where the boats land their Amazonian catch. Alongside the original neo-Gothic market building, imported from England in 1899, a marquee shelters stalls vending dizzying varieties of fruits and hot food.

Planning Visit early in the morning when fishermen unload their catch. Belém has a riverboat station and international airport but no railroad. www.paraturismo.pa.gov.br

❺ Mercado Central, Santiago, Chile

Under a wrought-iron, art nouveau canopy dating from 1872, this animated fish market groans with an extraordinary shoal of sea creatures, from barnacles to giant squid, many unlabeled, untranslatable, or unknown outside Chile. Marvel at the fishmongers' speed and skill. If the thought of identifying and preparing the fish is too much, onsite restaurants offer local dishes like *paila marina* (Chilean bouillabaisse).

Planning The market is two blocks north of Santo Domingo church. Beware scalpers and slippery surfaces. www.allsantiago.com

❻ Kreta Ayer Wet Market, Singapore

Like most things Singaporean, this Chinatown market is spotlessly clean, its floor hosed down regularly for hygiene, hence the term "wet market." But in variety the food is anything but sterile: offerings range from turtles, frogs, eels, and snakes (often still alive) to medicinal, dried animal parts. The upstairs food center offers local breakfast fare, like spicy noodle soup.

Planning Visit around 6 a.m. to beat the crowds. The market closes around 1 p.m. www.visitsingapore.com

❼ Kauppatori, Helsinki, Finland

For a taste of the Arctic, hit this fiesta of traditional Finnish fare. Star buys include moose, reindeer, and bear salami; chocolate infused with salted licorice; and salmon and herring delicacies.

Planning The open-air market is situated on Helsinki's South Harbor. www.hel2.fi/tourism

❽ La Vucciria, Palermo, Italy

In a gritty part of Palermo, and reflecting Sicily's heady ethnic brew, the boisterous atmosphere of La Vucciria is more Middle Eastern than European. Musicians bang drums and sing Arabian-infused ballads, the smell of barbecued sausages and kebabs permeates the air. The name comes from the French *boucherie* (butchers' market) but expect everything from fish to fruits.

Planning La Vucciria is off Piazza San Domenico. Take a local guide. www.aapit.pa.it

❾ Cours Saleya, Nice, France

This pretty flower-and-food market is so crowded that fellow-shoppers jostle you as you shop. Among the essentials of Niçois cooking are indelicate animal parts like lambs' testicles, and pigs' ears and heads, alongside more internationally acceptable ingredients. Lined with cafés and seafood restaurants, the market has a different atmosphere on summer nights, when it becomes a covered eating area.

Planning Cours Saleya lies between the sea and the old town and runs Tuesday to Sunday, mornings only. www.nicetourisme.com

❿ Borough Market, London, England

London's oldest food market—here for more than 250 years—is wholesale most of the week, but Thursdays through Saturdays it delights foodies with its cornucopia of fine foods from independent suppliers throughout the U.K. and beyond, from the choicest olive oils and cheeses to ostrich burgers and wild-boar sausages.

Planning In good weather, take a picnic into the gardens of Southwark Cathedral, next to the market. www.boroughmarket.org.uk

Right: A market vendor at Castries Market, St. Lucia, waits for customers, her stall laden with typical West Indian fruits, vegetables, and spices.

Little has changed in the Campo dei Fiori, and vendors continue to ply their trade as they have done for almost 150 years.

ITALY

CAMPO DEI FIORI

For a truly authentic Italian market experience, nothing beats a stroll through the oldest street market in Rome.

Situated in the historic center of Italy's capital, the Campo dei Fiori was once nothing more than a grassy field (its name means, literally, "field of flowers"). Now, the piazza is paved with cobblestones and has been the site of a bustling flower and food market since the 1860s. All the vibrancy of the city of Rome is reflected here, not just in the brightly colored flower stalls, but in glorious displays of fruits, herbs, and vegetables spilling out from suspended antique baskets or arranged in neat rows on the stalls. As well as the standard Mediterranean fare, at different times of the year you can find yellow radicchio with purple-blushed leaves, small, firm zucchinis in flower, long-stemmed artichokes, *puntarelle* (a jagged-leaved salad plant), white currants, white cherries, and the delicate *fragole di Nemi*—tiny, sweet strawberries that grow wild in the region. The colors are dazzling and the whole experience is a sensory feast, as the air fills with the voices of stallholders advertising their wares and the heady aroma of fresh spices wafting from the stalls. Many kinds of meat, bread, fish, and cheese are also sold here, along with everyday household items. And there is plenty of room to wander at will until lunchtime. Things start to wind down after 2 p.m., and by 3:30 the market is cleared up in readiness for the piazza's other function—as a center for the thriving nightlife that fills the surrounding bars and restaurants. Until then, it's time to sit down in a café, order an espresso or an aperitif, and partake in that favorite Italian pastime of people-watching.

When to Go From 7 a.m. to 2 p.m., Monday to Saturday. Spring and summer are the best seasons for seeing the market at its liveliest. Avoid Saturdays, when it can become overcrowded.

Planning Allow one to two hours for your visit, though you may want to spend a whole day exploring the area around the piazza in general. There are many local buildings, such as the Palazzo Farnese, to admire, as well as a number of churches and museums.

Websites www.rome.info, www.enjoyrome.com, www.conviviorome.com

Roman artichokes
Carciofi alla Romana

Serve hot or at room temperature.

Serves 4
4 globe artichokes
1 lemon, cut in half
2 tbsp fresh mint, chopped
2 cloves garlic, finely chopped
1/2 cup/4 fl oz/125 ml olive oil

Mix mint and garlic in a bowl with 1 tbsp of oil. Snap off artichokes' dark green, outer leaves, rubbing exposed edges with lemon to prevent discoloration. Cut 1 in (2.5 cm) off the top of each one, and use a spoon to scoop out any fuzzy parts. Peel the stalks.

Spoon herb mixture into each artichoke and place, stalk ends up, in a pot. They should fit tightly. Add salt and water to the oil to make 1 cup (8 fl oz/225 ml) of liquid and add to pan. Cover and simmer for 1 hour until tender.

NIGHT MARKETS, DORDOGNE

The Dordogne's night markets are popular community events with everyone from grandparents to babies in prams turning out.

Visit any number of the Dordogne's medieval villages in the evenings during July and August, and you will find one of France's cherished local food markets in full swing. With the roads through the village closed, the central squares of Creysse, Issigeac, and Eymet, to name just a few, fill with local residents and visitors walking from stall to stall, choosing their meal for the evening from vendors hard at work with portable stoves, barbecues, and paella pans. Oysters, mussels, shrimp, *bulots*, (whelks), *magret de canard* (duck breast) served with garlic potatoes, paella, round steak, freshly baked bread, *charcroute* (sauerkraut), barbecued eels, and grilled whitebait are just some of the local fare on offer, as well as strawberries, crepes, ice cream, and, of course, a choice of wines from several local estates. Order what you fancy and join the throngs at the tables that have been put out in the square. Everyone is welcome to buy, sit, eat, and drink, wherever they like. If you are lucky, a band will strike up later on and spectators will get up to dance—husbands with wives, grannies with grandchildren, mothers with sons, friends with friends—as the music flits from a traditional French line dance, through waltzes and foxtrots, to rock and roll.

When to Go Night markets are held in countless villages throughout the region during the months of July and August. Each village hosts a market on a different night of the week, usually starting at 7 p.m. Festivities begin to wind down around 11 p.m.

Planning Bergerac offers a good base for a week's vacation, with several villages within 20 miles (32 km). Night markets are small, local affairs, and tables are set out on a first-come, first-served basis, so try to arrive early to secure a good place. Alternatively, you can buy food to take away.

Websites www.northofthedordogne.com, www.pays-de-bergerac.com

Five Popular Markets

■ **Creysse**, just to the east of Bergerac, holds night markets on Saturdays, overlooking the Dordogne River.

■ Further east, **Cadouin's** markets are on Mondays, held beneath the town's renowned Cistercian Abbey.

■ The wine-producing town of **Monbazillac**, south of Bergerac, holds a market in the château grounds every Sunday.

■ In **Eymet**, further south, the night markets are on Tuesdays.

■ **Issigeac**, to the southeast of Bergerac, hosts a night market every Thursday.

A familiar night market scene as festivities get underway in the 14th-century town of Sarlat, 45 miles (72 km) east of Bergerac.

SPAIN

Mercat de la Boqueria

Just off Barcelona's main promenade, Las Ramblas,
is the entrance to a temple to gastronomy.

The Mercat St. Josep, popularly known as La Boqueria, is the living heart of the city and one of Europe's most famous markets. For the first-time visitor it is an unforgettable experience: the colors, noise, bustle, and scale of the market are overwhelming. More than 30,000 different types of food are sold here, from local specialties, such as *pimientos de padrón* (small green peppers), *bacalao* (dried salt cod), and *fuet* salami, to exotic fare, such as ostrich and emu eggs. Meat and charcuterie, fish and shellfish, nuts, fresh and dried fruits and vegetables, chocolates, flowers, breads, cheeses—everything is here. And the quality is excellent—many of the city's Michelin-starred chefs buy their produce here. But the real treasures of La Boqueria are the numerous *kioskos*, or tiny eating places. Kioskos are the birthplace of the *cuina de mercat* (market cooking), and their food is not only top-quality (they use fresh ingredients from the market) but cheap. Diners sit on stools at U-shaped counters around tiny kitchen areas and watch Catalan delicacies being turned out at top speed. Local favorites include El Pinotxo, El Quim, and the Bar Boqueria, but there are others. You can breakfast, lunch, or snack your way through the day here on mouthwatering tapas, such as clams steamed in wine, garbanzos and blood sausage, tender baby squid sautéed in garlic and olive oil with eggs—or the ubiquitous Catalonian staple, *pa amb tomàquet* (tomato-rubbed toast)—washed down with a glass of chilled cava.

When to Go Any time of year, but spring is best if you want to avoid the summer heat and crowds. The market is open Monday to Saturday, 8 a.m. to 8 p.m.

Planning Give yourself plenty of time to see the stalls (one to two hours at least) and enjoy a snack or meal. La Boqueria is in the heart of Barcelona's old quarter, or *Barri Gòtic*, with numerous backstreets to explore. There are plenty of *granjas*, or milk bars, outside the market where you can have coffee, or ultra-thick hot chocolate, with pastries. Try Escriba, in a lovely art deco building on Las Ramblas itself.

Websites www.boqueria.info, www.viator.com, www.traveltoe.com, www.saboroso.com

Tomato-rubbed toast
Pa amb tomàquet

Grilled bread with tomatoes is the signature dish of Barcelona. It is served alone or as a first course. Anchovies, roasted vegetables, or salami, ham, or other cured meats can be served with it.

Serves 2
*2 large slices day-old sourdough
    or other rustic bread
1 clove garlic (optional)
1 ripe tomato
Olive oil
Sea salt*

Toast the bread until it is a deep golden brown. If you are using garlic, cut a peeled clove in half and rub it over the bread to flavor it. Discard the garlic.
    Cut the tomato in half and rub the cut half against the bread. If the bread is slightly stale and well toasted, it will act as a grater against the tomato. As you rub, the bread will become slightly soggy and you will be left with the tomato skin, which you should discard.
    Drizzle the top of the bread with olive oil and sprinkle with sea salt. Repeat with the second slice of bread.

Opposite and above: An abundance of food is on offer at Barcelona's historic La Boqueria market.

Fortnum and Mason's food halls are spread over two elegant floors at the famous shop on London's Piccadilly.

ENGLAND

LONDON'S FOOD HALLS

Several of London's high-end department stores are home to world-class food halls.

In England's thriving capital gastronomes can browse among caviar and truffles to their hearts' content. One of the smaller food halls in the city is on the ground floor of Selfridges & Co., on busy Oxford Street. Here you can find unusual groceries alongside a handful of great places to eat, including a traditional London pie shop, an outlet selling English bangers (sausages), and an Italian gelateria. For a more traditional experience, head to Fortnum and Mason on Piccadilly, where old-fashioned curiosities, such as vintage marmalades, rose and violet creams, mustard recipes dating back to the Tudors, and relishes like piccalilli and pickled walnuts are stacked high—and have been for 300 years, since the founding of the store in 1707. Perhaps the most opulent of all is the sprawling series of halls, each the size of a ballroom, at Harrods, Knightsbridge. Built in 1902, the halls retain many of their original features. Look out for the display of fresh seafood next to the oyster bar, where the fish is presented in blocks of color, much like an artist's palette; and don't miss the cavernous room full of tempting artisanal chocolates. It is all about choice—where else can you find 15 different kinds of butter? Don't be shy to ask to sample a sliver of cheese or charcuterie before choosing one of the hundreds on offer, and make sure you take plenty of time to explore what must be one of the greatest temples to food in the world.

When to Go These stores become crowded just before Christmas and during the January sales. Food halls, bars, and restaurants may operate different opening times to the rest of the store. Check websites for details.

Planning You cannot eat your purchases in-store—if you get hungry, visit one of the restaurants. You can dress casually, but these stores may not admit customers carrying backpacks or large luggage items.

Websites www.selfridges.com, www.fortnumandmason.com, www.harrods.com

Taking a Break

■ At Selfridges & Co., try the **Moët Bar** above the Chanel Boutique for classy nibbles, a glass of champagne, and a bit of celebrity spotting (it's a favorite gathering place for fashionistas).

■ Once you have filled your basket with goodies at Fortnum and Mason, visit **St. James Restaurant** upstairs for afternoon tea.

■ Try the **Ladurée tearoom**, the **charcuterie bar**, **oyster bar**, **sushi bar**, or **tapas bar** at Harrods—you can find them in the food hall alongside several other eateries.

Fortnum and Mason's tea

KHAN EL-KHALILI

Cairo's burgeoning, labyrinthine market lies
at the heart of the city's old Islamic quarter.

At times the *muezzin's* call to prayer drowns out the cacophony of voices haggling over prices and the blare of Arabic music at Khan el-Khalili, Cairo's famous 14th-century grand souk. Passing shops selling gold, silver, papyrus art, textiles, perfume, and syrup-soaked sweets, head to the section where spices are sold. Large, open sacks and baskets overflow with golden saffron, fire-red curry, sweet nutmeg, red and green peppercorns, and dozens of other exotic, aromatic spices. Strings of dried sweet peppers and eggplant hang in shop doorways. Solemn men in *gallabéyahs* hurry to the al-Hussein Mosque in the Khan as you pause at one of the market's street-food vendors to order *ful mudammas*, Egypt's national dish of garlicky mashed fava beans served with *eish masri* (Egyptian pita bread). After shopping, you can relax at El-Fishawi Café, a 200-year-old *qahwah* (coffee shop) on al-Badistan, where smoking a *shisha* (water pipe) and drinking hot *shay bi-nana* (mint tea) is de rigueur. Locals also drink *karkady*, tea made from the dried, dark-red petals of the hibiscus flower and drunk cold. If you order coffee, expect it to be *ahwa turki*—a strong Turkish coffee served in a tiny porcelain cup. Drink it slowly, with small sips, to allow the coffee grounds to sink to the bottom. And be firm about how much sugar you want—the Egyptians like their coffee sweet!

When to Go Cairo is hot and dry all year, although the weather is generally milder from November through April.

Planning The shops open around 10 or 11 a.m. daily, except Sunday. They close during the Friday prayer hour at noon (1 p.m. during daylight saving time). For the best prices, shop where the Egyptians do, in the area beyond Midan el-Hussein north of al-Badistan, and be prepared to haggle.

Websites www.touregypt.net/khan.htm, www.egypt.travel

Fava Beans
Ful Mudammas

This Egyptian staple is often eaten for breakfast with slices of hard-boiled egg.

Serves 2
1 cup dried fava (broad) beans
1 onion, finely chopped
$^1/_2$ cup/4 fl oz/125 ml olive oil
2 cloves garlic, chopped
Juice of 1 lemon
$^1/_4$ tsp ground cumin
Salt and pepper

Cover the beans with water and soak overnight. Drain. Cover with fresh water, add the onion, and simmer until tender (about 1 hour). Drain the beans, put them in a bowl, and stir in olive oil, garlic, lemon juice, cumin, and salt and pepper to taste, partially mashing some of the beans. Serve at room temperature with pita bread, chopped parsley, lemon wedges, and more olive oil.

Copious quantities of aromatic, culinary spices fill the air with the heady aromas of North Africa and the Middle East.

SEASONAL DELIGHTS

F or those with a passion for truly great food, the most valuable resource is not a cookbook but a calendar. Seasonality is the key to food's perfection, and each moment in the turning year brings its own opportunities for gastronomic exploration and experiment.

In the fall, farm stands beckon from the rural roadsides of northern Connecticut with arrays of orange pumpkins, rosy apples, and jugs of golden cider. Across the Atlantic, foragers in France and northern Italy slip into the forests to hunt for truffles and wild mushrooms, whose aromas perfume the seasonal specials that appear briefly on local menus. Next, winter sharpens the appetite for robust dumplings designed to counter the sharp winds coming off the Austrian Alps.

Yet soon enough, the earth warms up again, sending up the green, springtime shoots of wild leeks, or ramps, in the Appalachians, and the sea yields up the soft-shell crabs of Maryland's Chesapeake Bay. Finally, the sun melts the mists over the British Isles in time for that quintessential summer pleasure—a bowl of local strawberries and cream.

Each September, wine villages all over the Burgundy region of France celebrate the *vendanges*, or grape harvest, when the year's crop is brought in from the vineyards ready to be turned into some of the finest wines in the world.

APPLES AND PUMPKINS

The primarily rural region of northwest Connecticut promises a delightful harvest treat come fall.

The fall landscape unfolds like a painter's canvas in northwestern Connecticut's Litchfield Hills. Covered bridges, century-old farmhouses, and red dairy barns loom large against a tapestry of rich harvest colors—fiery salsa reds, vibrant oranges, and shimmering Midas-touched golds. The explosion of fall color comes not only from the changing foliage but also from the ripening fruits of the season. At numerous local farm stands, the reds and yellows of McIntosh, Macoun, and Honeycrisp apples blend with the orange of pumpkins for carving jack-o'-lanterns and making into pies. Delight in the aromatic smells of cinnamon and nutmeg that waft out of the open doorways of on-site bakeries at pick-your-own orchards. Watch apples being crushed into sweet cider in cider-mill apple presses as you munch on hot apple-cider doughnuts. Sample all manner of pumpkin butters, apple jellies, and other harvest treats. After a fall hike up Mount Tom for panoramic views of three states (Massachusetts, Connecticut, and New York) or through the shaded forests of Kent Falls State Park, dine at a harvest supper at a local church or town hall, where hams glazed with apple jelly, potatoes mashed with creamery-fresh butter, and thick slices of chewy homemade bread spread with sweet fruit preserves crowd the serving table. Before diving in, remember to save some room for generous helpings of apple cobbler and pumpkin pie.

When to Go Mid to late October, when the fall colors are at their peak.

Planning Room reservations are strongly recommended, especially for weekend travel during fall foliage season, and should be booked well in advance. Many inns and B&Bs have a two-night required minimum stay, although you should stay at least three or four days to enjoy the beauty of the area.

Websites www.litchfieldhills.com, www.ctvisit.com

Apple Varieties

Northwestern Connecticut's apple season extends from late August through October, though not all varieties ripen at the same time. Visit the orchards early in the season and you will find **Paula Red** and **Tydeman**. **McIntosh** and **Gala** ripen next, with **Red** and **Golden Delicious** and **Idared** ready for picking at the tail end of the season.

Bear in mind that some varieties are better suited for eating fresh, others for baking. For munching, try **Honeycrisp**, **Gala**, **McIntosh**, **Macoun**, or **Red** and **Golden Delicious** varieties. The best apples for pies include **Crispin**, **Jonagold**, and **Winesap**. Tart apples, such as **Cortland**, **Empire**, **Northern Spy**, **Rome**, and **Granny Smith** can also be used for baking, but you should add extra sugar.

A familiar sight at many farm stands in the region, rows of harvested pumpkins await their fate as carved wonders.

The beautiful Mendocino Coast is a popular destination for mushroom-lovers during the wild mushroom season.

CALIFORNIA

Mushroom Picking

In the fall, California's tourist season makes way
for the serious business of foraging for fungi.

The initial rains of winter are met with great anticipation by food enthusiasts in northern California; that is because the first big storms that sweep in from the Pacific mark the beginning of the wild mushroom season. From November to April, a succession of wild fungi appears in the forests of the coastal mountains and on the western slopes of the Sierra Nevada. Some people hunt them obsessively; others merely wait for them to show up on the menu of their favorite restaurants. California's wild fungi fall into two categories—fall and spring. Fall mushrooms include various species of the *Boletus* genus (sponge fungi collectively known as porcini in Italy); the pallid and subtly flavored oyster mushroom; nutty, fluted chanterelles; and, perhaps the most prized, matsutakes, an intensely aromatic mushroom that sells for more than $100 a pound (500 grams) in Japan. Spring is primarily devoted to the search for succulent, meaty morels. Wild mushrooms are best prepared simply—included in risotto, sautéed in some butter or olive oil, or simmered in a soup or broth. And now for the obligatory warning: if you are inexperienced, do not hunt wild mushrooms on your own. Secure an experienced forager as a guide for your initial trips, and concentrate on looking for three or four easily identified species.

When to Go The mushroom-picking season typically runs from October through May; the best foraging is from November through April.

Planning Visitors should concentrate on the Sonoma and Mendocino Coast, where mushrooms, good restaurants, and comfortable lodgings are all available. The Mycological Society of San Francisco sponsors regular forays led by experienced mycologists throughout the season. Plan at least a week for exploration.

Websites www.mssf.org, www.mykoweb.com, theforagerpress.com

Chanterelles

These popular mushrooms are usually abundant throughout northern California's coniferous forests from October through December. They are ubiquitous, easy to identify, and have a rich, complex flavor with overtones of peaches and walnuts.

White and **Pacific golden chanterelles** are the most common types, with similar flavors and aromas.

The **false chanterelle** has an orange color not typically associated with chanterelles, and finer gills; it is edible, but inferior in flavor to true chanterelles.

And beware jack-o'-lantern mushrooms—they are easy to confuse with chanterelles. Darker than chanterelles and with different gill structures, they can make you sick and should be avoided.

KITCHEN GARDENS

From spectacular botanical gardens to walled kitchen gardens, what better way to enjoy local, seasonal produce than from the source?

❶ Patrenella's, Houston, Texas

In a house owned since 1938 by the Patrenella family, this restaurant serves up Sicilian specialties, using fresh, organic herbs and vegetables from its garden. It was originally the family home, and eating here still feels like being the house guest of friends with impeccable cooking—and gardening—skills.

Planning At 813 Jackson Hill, Patrenella's closes Sundays and Mondays. www.patrenellas.net

❷ Chez Panisse, Berkeley, California

Besotted with local, seasonal ingredients after visiting France, in 1971, chef Alice Waters created this influential restaurant, birthplace of "California cuisine." Fusing French recipes and California produce, menus change daily depending on what is freshest. Nowadays, it is two venues in one: fixed-menu, dinner-only restaurant downstairs; à la carte café upstairs.

Planning It is open daily except Sundays. Restaurant reservations are compulsory. www.chezpanisse.com

❸ Flik, Warsaw, Poland

Overlooking Morskie Oko Park, stylish Flik offers supremely airy summer dining, cozy wicker armchairs, and romantic candlelit alleys. The plant-filled indoor dining area doubles as an art gallery. While the menu is international, regulars recommend *pierogi* (Polish ravioli with various fillings) and the delicious desserts, including chocolate cake with sour cherries.

Planning Flik's at 43 Ulica Puławska. www.flik.com.pl/kartadan

❹ De Kas, Amsterdam, the Netherlands

Dining in a greenhouse may sound like a year-round climatic conundrum, but this one has air-conditioning and heating. Focusing on the freshest ingredients, De Kas grows organic vegetables and herbs in a greenhouse and nursery next door, while local eco-friendly farms supply the meat. The continental prix-fixe menu changes daily. Enjoy daytime vistas, nighttime romance—and decor by modish interior designer, Piet Boon.

Planning In Frankendael Park, De Kas opens daily except Saturday lunchtimes and Sundays. www.restaurantdekas.nl

❺ L'atelier de Jean-Luc Rabanel, Arles, France

After gaining the first-ever Michelin star for an all-organic restaurant at La Chassagnette, near Arles, chef Jean-Luc Rabanel opened an atelier (workshop) and biodynamic farm, where he harvests rare edible plants at their peak. Changed daily, the tasting menu features around a dozen courses.

Planning Open Wednesdays through Sundays, the atelier is at 7 Rue des Carmes. Reservations are necessary. www.rabanel.com

❻ Château de la Bourdaisière, Loire Valley, France

In 1991, Princes Philippe-Maurice and Louis-Albert de Broglie bought this 16th-century Renaissance château and converted it into an upscale B&B. They also laid out a walled *potager*—kitchen garden—in its 135-acre (55 hectares) woodland park with some 550 varieties of red, white, green, and yellow tomatoes. There is a popular two-day tomato festival every September.

Planning The nearby town of Montlouis-sur-Loire is around two hours from Paris by train. www.chateaubourdaisiere.com

❼ Tangerine Dream Café, London, England

The Worshipful Society of Apothecaries founded the Chelsea Physic Garden in 1673 to educate apprentices about medicinal plants. Nowadays, the exquisite 3.5-acre (1.4 hectare) walled retreat nurtures around 5,000 plant varieties, some tropical, in a snug riverside microclimate. Its café refreshes visitors with lunches, and teas with scones and cakes.

Planning At 66 Royal Hospital Road (tube: Sloane Square), the café opens Sundays, Wednesdays through Fridays, and public holidays, April through October and some winter dates. www.chelseaphysicgarden.co.uk

❽ Petersham Nurseries, London, England

In overcrowded London, few places offer swankier garden dining than this riverside nursery on glorious Richmond Hill, run by voguish chef, Skye Gingell. Despite the rustic setting inside three restored Victorian glasshouses, the café's achingly hip menu attracts sophisticated foodies. Menus change weekly.

Planning Take the tube to Richmond, then the Number 65 Bus. The restaurant opens for lunch only, Tuesdays through Sundays. Reservations are necessary. www.petershamnurseries.com

❾ Longueville House, Mallow, Ireland

A Georgian manor overlooking County Cork's Blackwater Valley, Longueville's 500-acre (202 hectare) wooded estate provides almost all its restaurant's produce, from smoked salmon to lamb. Expect French and modern Irish dishes when dining in the manor's splendid restaurant or the intimate glass-and-iron greenhouse.

Planning 3 miles (5 km) from Mallow station (two to three hours from Dublin), the restaurant opens for dinner. www.longuevillehouse.ie

❿ Silvertree, Cape Town, South Africa

The magnificent 1,305-acre (528 hectare) Kirstenbosch National Botanical Garden on Table Mountain makes a blissful restaurant setting. In summer, diners toast sunset over glasses of local Sauvignon Blanc; in winter, a log fire toasts them. The international menu has local twists.

Planning Open 8:30 a.m.–10 p.m. daily. www.kirstenboschrestaurant.com

Right: Woven blinds cast dappled shade over the tables in a seductive, sunny corner of London's Petersham Nurseries.

Ramps are traditionally harvested in spring, when the bulbs are at their most tender.

WEST VIRGINIA

RAMPS

Considered a specialty by some, scallion-like
ramps grow wild in U.S. and Canadian woodlands.

Ramps—also known as wild leeks and, more officially, *Allium tricoccum*—are the first edible signs of spring. Celebrated in the Appalachian region and spreading north to Canada, these potently nutritious plants are rich in vitamins C and A: for many centuries native Americans have used them to make tonics, and Southerners used to use them as a cure for scurvy. Rural areas are dotted with festivals that celebrate the appearance of the ramps, which can be found in markets, fancy restaurants, and the hearts and palates of the seasonal eater. In the wild, they grow in woodlands, especially those on hillsides. Look for clumps of the broad, smooth, bright green leaves. If you tear a leaf, it should give off a smell like an onion. Using a shovel, extract the whole plant from the soil, gently lifting it by its roots. Ramps have a very strong smell when picked, so take just a few plants at a time. Clean off the mud in cold water, and strip the bulb of its outer membrane down to the milky white, purple-edged flesh. Every part that is left is good for eating. The leaves are tender and have a slightly sweet flavor, while the bulb is pungent. Used raw or cooked in place of garlic and onion, ramps add a special accent to salads, scrambled eggs, bean dishes, and pasta.

Ways to Eat Ramps

Devotees find these delicate bulbs addictive. Most closely described as a cross between onion and garlic with a hint of white truffle, theirs is a unique flavor with a multitude of uses.

Slice or grate them raw into salads or sandwiches.

Cooked, ramps can be eaten on their own—simply sauté with extra-virgin olive oil and a tiny crush of sea salt. A potato gratin with the sautéed ramps and a hefty shredding of aged strong Cheddar is another happy marriage of flavor, as is a generous helping of pasta, ramps, and wild mushrooms.

When to Go Ramps are native to several eastern states, first emerging in early April in the Appalachian Mountains, and in June in more northerly states, such as Michigan.

Planning Ramps are found in deciduous forests. Foraging is prohibited in national parks so harvest ramps on private land with the owner's permission. Or try them at a wild leek festival. West Virginia and North Carolina are home to the best of the bunch. Two West Virginia cities hold festivals in April: Richwood's Feast of the Ramson and Elkin's International Ramp Festival.

Websites theforagerpress.com, www.cosbyrampfestival.org, www.richwooders.com

MARYLAND

Soft-shell Crabs

Crustacean-lovers head for Maryland to catch the
seasonal harvest brought in by Chesapeake Bay watermen.

Shrieking gulls wheel over the blue waters of the Chesapeake Bay as they follow the crab boats, whose decks brim with soft-shell crabs, to the waterfront at Crisfield, on the bay's eastern side. Watch the handsome catch being hauled onto the docks by commercial watermen. Then hurry to the nearby J. Millard Tawes Historical Museum to view the exhibits and join a walking tour of this community nicknamed the "crab capital of the world." Soft-shell crabs are Atlantic blue crabs caught in the soft-shell stage after molting. Your tour guide will explain how they are harvested before leading you through a seafood processing plant, where you can watch crabs being prepared for market. The tour ends in time for you to catch the passenger ferry to Smith Island, the largest inhabited offshore island in the bay and a 40-minute cruise from Crisfield. With a population of fewer than 500 people, the island was first settled in the late 1600s and has been home to Chesapeake Bay watermen for 15 generations. Chat with these local crabbers as you inspect the crab floats (holding tanks), before popping into one of the island's restaurants to eat your fill of fried or pan-sautéed soft-shells. Finish your meal with a slice of Smith Island cake—eight to ten thin layers of moist cake laced with sugary-sweet icing baked from recipes passed down from generation to generation.

When to Go Although the season for soft-shell crabs lasts from May through September, the best time to go is during May and June for the pleasant weather and greater availability of crabs.

Planning Walking tours of Crisfield are offered at 10 a.m. daily (except Sunday), Memorial Day through Labor Day. The Smith Island Ferry leaves at 12:30 p.m. sharp, returning at 4 p.m., although you may also travel on the freight and mail boats that operate year-round, weather permitting.

Websites www.visitsomerset.com, www.smithisland.org

Soft-shells on the Menu

Soft-shell crabs can be broiled, sautéed, and even grilled, but to eat like a local order them breaded, fried whole, and served on a sandwich made with sticky white bread, or as a fried crab platter with a couple of sides.

Some of the area's best fried crabs can be found at **The Cove** or the **Waterman's Inn** in Crisfield. On Smith Island you can buy an unusual version of a soft-shell crab sandwich, the Soft Shell Po' Boy, at the **Drum Point Market** in Tylerton, year-round population 70. Or dine at **Ruke's Seafood Deck** or the **Bayside Inn** in Ewell, the island's main community. Make sure to reserve a slice of Smith Island cake—referred to on the island as layer cake—for dessert.

Watermen unload a large haul of crabs in Crisfield on the Chesapeake Bay.

CHINA

Hairy-crab Season

Shanghai, the bustling metropolis on China's southeast coast, celebrates the hairy-crab season like no other city on Earth.

Fall is the time of the hairy crab in Shanghai, and the city's winding neighborhoods of lane houses are interspersed with markets and high-end restaurants hawking this popular, small, bushy crustacean. Hairy crabs are prized in Chinese cuisine for their dense white flesh, which is sweeter than regular crabmeat, and the orange-colored roe akin to rich, just-cooked egg yolk. The Chinese believe hairy crabs have a cooling (yin) effect on the body. Most of the specimens served in Shanghai come from Yangcheng or other freshwater lakes within two hours' drive from the city. Preparation is simple: the crabs are steamed, then dressed with a sweetened black rice vinegar and sliced ginger. Eaten hot, two to four crabs per person make for a handsome meal. At Ye Shanghai, an elegant, colonial-style restaurant in the French Concession (southwest Shanghai), diners tuck into little crabs no bigger than a human palm. Drink like a local and wash the little critters down with yellow rice wine. Those bold enough to order an all-crab banquet should save room for side dishes that include stir-fried crabmeat and crab wontons.

When to Go Hairy crabs are in season from September through mid-November, but visit before mid-October for the freshest, plumpest, and most roe-filled crabs.

Planning If you are planning to visit in September or October and want to eat in Shanghai's top restaurants, you should book a few weeks in advance, especially for a crab banquet. Be wary of hairy crabs bearing stamps from Yangcheng Lake, the most prized source, as the stamps are often faked. If you stick to reputable restaurants, such as Ye Shanghai and the Westin Hotel on the Bund waterfront, or other five-star and hotel restaurants, you should get a taste of the real thing. Avoid hairy crabs that vendors claim are wild: most hairy crabs sold in China today are farmed because of pollution, and genuinely wild crabs are now so rare that they can cost up to five times the price of the farmed alternative.

Websites www.elite-concepts.com, www.timeout.com/travel/shanghai

Shanghai Cuisine

■ Known for rich and luscious dishes, Shanghai cuisine makes extensive use of sugar, which adds an extra meaty dimension to savory sauces. "Drunken" dishes, in which shellfish and chicken are lightly cooked and doused with alcohol, are also common on menus.

■ Shanghai boasts **red cooking**, a popular style of braising meat or vegetables with soy sauce and sugar. Try red-cooked pork, a heady dish often accented with cinnamon and star anise. Another popular dish is "lion's head": baseball-sized meatballs stewed with cabbage.

■ A visit to Shanghai would not be complete without sampling **xiaolongbao**, steamed dumplings loaded with soup and meat. Just look for the steaming baskets that line the windows of high-end restaurants and street stalls, filled with dumplings waiting to be relished.

■ Larger dumplings, called **shengjianbao**, are another favorite street snack. These juicy packages of minced meat wrapped in dough are lightly fried until the bottom becomes crisp, while the top remains deliciously soft.

Opposite: Hairy crabs for sale in Shanghai. Above: Each crab is tied in raffia to keep the claws close to the body.

A woman prepares traditional food for the Hanshi festival.

CHINA

COLD FOOD FESTIVAL

For two days of the year, natives of the city of Xiamen in southwest China follow tradition and dine on cold food alone.

The bustling, subtropical city of Xiamen, in Fujian province, is a modern metropolis full of skyscrapers, and on April 4, the townsfolk celebrate Hanshi, the Cold Food Festival, as they have done for generations. According to Chinese legend, the festival, which dates back more than 2,500 years, memorializes a servant named Jie Zhutai, who was accidentally burned to death by the Zhou-dynasty Prince Chong'er. Full of remorse, the prince forbade the setting of fires for three days each year in commemoration of Jie and only cold food could be eaten. Three days are now one, and Xiamen is among the few places in China still to observe the tradition. Along tree-lined alleys, locals tuck into cold vermicelli noodles and spring rolls, usually eaten as appetizers but on this day making up the entire meal. The day following Hanshi is Qingming (Pure Brightness Day)—a national holiday throughout China when families tend the graves of their departed, taking offerings of cold food such as roast pork, chicken with rice, and tea as offerings to deceased relatives. After burning incense, the families eat beside the graves to symbolize being with the deceased, celebrating their ancestors' afterlife.

When to Go Hanshi takes place on the fourth day of the fourth lunar month—April 4 in the Western calendar (April 3 in a leap year). Qingming is on the following day.

Planning Xiamen is a coastal city, easily reached by train or bus from Chinese cities. Plan to stay at least three days, and allow some time to stroll around Gulangyu, an island to the southwest of Xiamen with colonial architecture and lush vegetation. Be sure to visit Xiamen's many teahouses: the region produces renowned tea varieties, like the smokey black Lapsang Souchong and Tieguanyin (Iron Goddess of Mercy).

Website www.whatsonxiamen.com

Fujian Dishes

■ Instead of stir-fried noodles or hot noodle soups, restaurants in Xiamen will dish out **cold vermicelli** topped with scallions, garlic, and chili sauce. The noodles may contain chicken or shrimp, which have usually been cooked the day before.

■ Called *bobin* in the local dialect, Fujian cold **spring rolls** contain bamboo shoots, dried shrimp, bean sprouts, shredded carrots, tofu, and oyster sauce, all wrapped in a thin flour skin.

■ The glutinous rice cakes, covered with black sesame seeds and known as *maci*, have a dense filling made with sweetened peanut powder and more sesame seeds.

■ One of Fujian's most famous dishes, *fo tiao chiang* (Buddha jumps over the wall), is a hot thick soup with more than 20 ingredients, including quails' eggs and several kinds of meat and seafood. It is laborious to prepare and thus tends to be expensive, but it is so tasty that even vegetarian Buddhists (the story goes) are prepared to jump over walls to eat it.

Local people "carve" cold food to look like mice and other creatures.

THAILAND

Phuket Vegetarian Festival

Every year, the residents of this southern Thai island forgo meat in a display of Buddhist devotion.

A curious event takes place every fall on Phuket island: residents go vegan for nine days, consuming no meat, eggs, milk, or fish sauce. Restaurants continue to lure in customers with curries and stir-fries, soups and salads as usual—except that wheat gluten and soy are substituted for meat and fish. Food stalls appear beside most major roads, selling all manner of fried delights—fried dough balls, fried curried corn fritters, fried spring rolls, fried tofu—and glutinous buns and rolls and cubes of wheat gluten. Although it is called a vegetarian festival, the event is not a celebration of food but a purification of society's ills involving rituals of spiritual cleansing and merit-making. The tradition began in about 1825, after a visiting Chinese opera troupe contracted a malady en masse—so goes the legend. The members swore off meat, prayed ritually, and recovered. Every year since, residents of Chinese descent devote nine days to clean living and displays of self-mutilation. Men parade through town sawing their tongues, beating their backs with axes, and piercing their cheeks with sharp objects. Such devotees allegedly acquire supernatural powers as they shift society's evil onto themselves and away from others. They dance and jiggle as firecrackers boom. Then a clairvoyant woman purges the demons and renews the people's spirits. Meanwhile, the streets teem with pure food, clean utensils, and sated bellies—how better to please the gods?

When to Go The first days of the ninth Chinese lunar month, usually early October.

Planning For a full-on festival experience, stay in Phuket town. As per festival etiquette, wear white; buy a cheap T-shirt and pair of cotton pants (sold on the street during festival time) upon arrival. Check a festival schedule for parades, fire-walking, and other events, many of which culminate at the local Chinese temples. Don't miss the fireworks displays, and arrive early to get a good vantage point.

Websites www.tourismthailand.org, www.phuketvegetarian.com, www.phuket.com

Festival Customs

■ Since ancient times, Buddhist vegetarian chefs have employed supreme artifice to craft soy and wheat gluten into elaborate meat-like designs, so as not to alienate non-vegetarian guests.

■ A long list of guidelines steers the festival (no sex, no alcohol, no menstruating women—to name a few). Rule number ten states that participants should not share kitchen utensils, food containers, or meals with non-festival-goers. Keep your food clean and disease will stay away.

■ Although the rituals center around **Phuket town**, vendors sell vegetarian food across the country during festival time. Look for outlets with flapping yellow flags.

At the city's Buddhist temples, Phuket inhabitants place incense sticks among food offerings and statues of gods that they have brought from their homes.

CRAYFISH FESTIVAL

For two months toward the end of summer, the Finns
celebrate Rapujuhlat, a hands-on crayfish feast.

Open season on crayfish is declared on July 21, and until early September, Finns in country and city gather around festive tables to crack, poke, and munch the sweet crustaceans. Netting in local waters has diminished since an algae-fungus infestation in the early 1990s nearly wiped out the native crayfish, *Astacus astacus*. Trapped at night in cold rivers, crayfish are sold at premium prices, so many shoppers rely on imported stock from Spain, Turkey, or the U.S. Preparations for a party include ordering 12 crayfish for each guest and draping a special bib over the back of every chair. The crayfish are cooked in boiling water or brine with heads of crown dill (seeds and fronds), strained, and cooled overnight. To serve, they are piled on a platter to provide the feast's centerpiece alongside dill-sprigged new potatoes. Finland is a bilingual nation, and some traditions vary: for example, Swedish-speaking Finns don pointed party hats and sing schnapps-themed drinking songs with each toast. The way to eat a crayfish is always the same, however: snap it in half, suck the juices out of the head section, and peel the meaty tail out of its crusty case with a special crayfish knife. A squeeze of lemon juice or a dab of *smetana* (tangy sour cream) accent the delicate flavors. Raise a tiny glass of iced vodka to toast the crayfish: *Kippis!*

When to Go The crayfish season runs through August into early September, to savor summer's last nights outdoors (bring a sweater or wrap against the cool evening air). Crayfish often feature on menus in terrace restaurants around Helsinki during August.

Planning Take a week to explore Finland's southern coast, from Turku in the west to the capital, Helsinki, and the picturesque Swedish-speaking port of Porvoo to the east. Join in the toasts: "cheers" in Finnish is *Kippis*, or *Skaal* in Swedish. Drinks include beer and schnapps, vodka, or the clear Finnish spirit known as Koskenkorva, but mineral water or dry white wine can also be enjoyed with crayfish.

Websites www.virtual.finland.fi, www.finnguide.fi, www.crayfishking.com

Rapujuhlat Etiquette

■ A **lakeside sauna** in the Finnish forest often precedes a crayfish feast, marking summer's end before closing up the summer cabin.

■ As an appetizer, some cooks peel crayfish claws to top buttered toast triangles, sprinkled with feathery dill. The season's chanterelles and other **forest mushrooms** also turn up in soups and savory appetizers.

■ The menu may open with crayfish, then feature plank-roasted or poached **salmon** as the main course, and fresh **blueberry tart** or **cloudberries** from Lapland as dessert.

■ This feast is traditionally casual and noisy as everyone slurps tasty juices from the crayfish heads and claws.

Bowls of flame-red crayfish await their destiny as the highlight of summer feasting.

Pairs of cod hang for air-drying on a fish flake—a wooden rack—erected on the shore of a small Norwegian fishing village.

NORWAY

LUTEFISK

Some people consider this infamous national dish—reputedly conceived by the Vikings—to be a major gastronomic challenge.

Unless you are that rare gourmet—a *lutefisk* (or lyefish) aficionado—there is a certain bravado involved in sampling this dish in its place of origin. For centuries, huge shoals of cod have migrated south from the Barents Sea to spawn in the sheltered waters around the Lofoten Islands, near the city of Tromsø in northern Norway, where they are fished from January through May. The sun may barely rise above the horizon in this northerly place, but Lofoten hosts a number of warm and welcoming restaurants that will prepare lutefisk with expertise and authenticity. You could also visit the more southerly city of Ålesund, a center of lutefisk production. The dish starts as stockfish—that is, air-dried cod—which develops a powerful aroma. Soaked first in a solution of caustic soda (derived from the potash salts of wood ash, usually birch), the fish is soaked again to remove most of the chemicals. Then it is ready for cooking. The history of this extraordinary dish is much disputed and, unsurprisingly, the stuff of legend. Was it invented when a Viking longship carrying stockfish was destroyed by fire and its cargo rescued after a soaking in seawater? Or perhaps when a wood-staved drying unit suffered a similar fate and the resulting smoked fish were considered too precious to waste? Whatever its origins, lutefisk has been documented since the Middle Ages and remains a winter staple in these most northerly lands of Europe.

When to Go Lutefisk season officially kicks in around November and continues throughout Christmas, with Christmas Eve being the most traditional occasion for consuming the dish.

Planning Combine a visit to the Lofoten Islands with a cruise to see the Northern Lights. Norway's excellent public transportation leaves you free to take in the spectacular scenery.

Websites www.visitnorway.com, www.norway.com, www.norway.org.uk

Lutefisk

The flavor of lutefisk has provoked fierce reaction, but in truth it is rather delicate. The fish requires precise preparation to be palatable: several days' soaking in daily changes of fresh water, followed by a very few minutes' cooking—in its own juices—until the fish is translucent and jelly-like but not falling apart. Oven-baking in butter is an alternative.

Traditional accompaniments—such as a **smooth white sauce**, **plain-boiled potatoes**, and **grainy mustard**—should provide a range of contrasting textures, if not colors, although people who eat lutefisk regularly tend to add **crisp bacon** and **green peas**.

TOP TEN

SAINT'S DAY FEASTS

Saint's days have been occasions for celebration since the first millennium.
The religious symbolism may be vague nowadays, but the feasting continues.

❶ Blessing of the Fleet, Stonington, Connecticut

The weekend-long celebrations in this New England village include a parade with floats and a statue of the patron of fishermen, St. Peter. On the menu are lobsters, clams, and various Portuguese specialties reflecting many Connecticut fishermen's origins in the Azores.

Planning The festivities normally take up July's last full weekend. www.stoningtonblessing.com

❷ Fête des Cuisinières, Guadeloupe, France

In 1916 the city of Pointe-à-Pitre's *cuisinières* (female cooks) set up a *tontine* (joint fund) to cover members' funeral expenses, but soon spiced up their mission with a vibrant carnival honoring St. Lawrence of Rome, patron of cooks. Flamboyantly dressed chefs carry their finest Creole dishes for blessing at Sts. Peter and Paul Cathedral, then hold a lively parade to the École Amédée Fengarol, where they stage a five-hour banquet and ball.

Planning The festival fills the Saturday nearest August 10. The parade is open to all; the banquet is ticket only. www.lesilesdeguadeloupe.com

❸ Día de Los Santos Reyes, Mexico

Mexicans mark the Three Holy Kings' Day, or Epiphany (January 6), by sharing the *rosca de reyes*—an oval, ring-shaped cake. A small doll inside represents the baby Jesus. Whoever finds it throws a party for all others present on Candlemas (February 2), offering tamales and the hot, grainy drink, *atole*.

Planning Aside from private parties, the rosca de reyes is widely available in restaurants, patisseries, and bars. www.visitmexico.com

❹ St. Martin of Tours, Skåne, Sweden

In Sweden's goose-rich southernmost province of Skåne, this winter-harvest festival falls when geese are plump and prime for slaughter. Traditionally, banquets on St. Martin's Eve (November 10) start with *svartsoppa*, a richly seasoned goose-blood bisque, followed by roast goose stuffed with apples and prunes, then apple pie or *spettkaka*, a cone-shaped meringue cake.

Planning Most locals go to a restaurant; preparing the banquet is time-consuming. Skanör's Gästgifvaregård enjoys renown for its goose. www.skane.com, www.skanorsgastis.se

❺ St. Mark, Venice, Italy

April 25 is St. Mark's Day and the anniversary of Venice's founding in A.D. 421. Venetians once honored the doge (head of state) with a dish of creamy rice and the season's first baby peas in a vegetable broth: *risi e bisi*. The doges have gone but the dish, part soup, part risotto, remains traditional at home and in restaurants.

Planning April 25 is also Liberation Day, a public holiday. Many shops and attractions close. www.turismovenezia.it

❻ Festa di San Lorenzo, Florence, Italy

The focus of Florence's popular Feast Day of St. Lawrence (August 10) is Piazza San Lorenzo. The day comprises several Masses said in the basilica, a parade in historic folk costume, concerts, and at 9 p.m., free lasagna and watermelon for all.

Planning Allow a whole day to enjoy the various events and visit the Museum of the Medici Chapels for free. www.firenzeturismo.it

❼ St. Joseph, Sicily, Italy

The legend goes that medieval Sicilians facing a severe drought beseeched St. Joseph for rain, and he obliged. The islanders repaid him with a lavish feast consisting of the crops that had kept them going through the drought, including fava beans, fritters made of rice and honey, and elaborately sculpted loaves of bread. The menu remains the same today, and is meat-free as it falls during Lent.

Planning St. Joseph's Day is on March 19. Throughout Sicily, communities organize public celebrations, culminating in a feast in town piazzas. All are welcome. www.bestofsicily.com

❽ Sant Antoni Abat, Andorra

In Catalan, *escudella* means a large, decorated, ceramic bowl, and also the winter-busting, meat-and-sausage stew served in it. Nationwide, Andorrans celebrate the feast of St. Anthony the Great (January 17) outdoors with escudella cooked in huge pots over open wood fires, washed down with wine and bread. The feast is free and open to everyone.

Planning The town of La Massana hosts one of the largest feasts. Mass is held at the Chapel of Sant Antoni de la Grella at 11 a.m. www.andorra.ad

❾ St. James, Santiago de Compostela, Spain

Every year, especially in summer, Catholic pilgrims follow the Way of St. James across northern Spain to Santiago de Compostela. The saint's feast day is July 25, and a fine festive dish is the scarce *santiaguiño* (slipper lobster), which has a mark on its back resembling the saint's cross.

Planning Explore the city's market for seafood and other Galician foods. In summer, fried green peppers (*pimientos de padrón*), some sweet, some spicy, are a local specialty. www.pilgrimage-to-santiago.com

❿ St. Patrick, Ireland

The Irish celebrate St. Patrick's Day (March 17) with parades, pub crawls, and Guinness, and many also eat traditional dishes, including bacon and cabbage, soda bread, colcannon, and corned beef and cabbage. If the 17th falls on a Friday, dishes include smoked or fresh salmon with potato cakes.

Planning For traditional Irish food try Country Choice, Nenagh, County Dublin; or The Winding Stair, Dublin. www.stpatricksday.ie

Right: Cuisinières in resplendent carnival colors attend Mass at the cathedral in Guadeloupe's largest city, Pointe-à-Pitre.

This spread of traditional Georgian dishes includes turkey *satsivi* (bottom left) and the dumplings known as *khinkali* (top right).

GEORGIA

A Country Feast

Georgia is famous for its food and wine, which can be enjoyed to their full in the wine-growing region to the east of T'bilisi.

Georgia's wine country lies in the Alazani River Valley in the eastern province of Kakheti, where the Caucasus Mountains rise above hillsides planted with fruit trees and vines. As soon as warm spring weather arrives, Georgians gather for impromptu picnics. Tablecloths are spread with a dazzling array of dishes flaunting vivid colors and flavors, from ruby-red beet puree (*pkhali*) to turkey *satsivi* (enrobed in an earthy, walnut-inflected sauce made golden from dried and ground marigold petals). Georgian food expresses both Mediterranean and Middle Eastern tastes, the result of a rich interplay of culinary ideas carried along the ancient trade routes by merchants and travelers. Creamy water-buffalo yogurt and sharp *suluguni* cheese complement the grilled meats that Georgians claim recall the legend of Prometheus, who is said to have given fire to mankind when chained to a rock on nearby Mount Elbrus. Seasonal fruits—tart lady apples, sugary peaches, pink gooseberries, cherries, apricots, and many varieties of plums—beckon for dessert, along with *churchkhela*, long strings of nuts that have been dipped in fresh grape juice, then dried. Plenty of local wine will wash down the food as Georgians give praise for nature's bounty with toasts and singing.

When to Go Between May and October, as electricity can be unreliable and the winters cold.

Planning Flights arrive in the capital, T'bilisi, from most major European cities and from Istanbul. Outside T'bilisi there is no real restaurant culture, though towns and villages have at least one café offering tasty local food. Be sure to visit T'bilisi's central market for its pyramids of spices and beds of fresh greens. Also not to be missed are the traditional bakeries offering hot bread from a *toné*, the Georgian tandoor oven, and *khinkali*, oversized dumplings that are a specialty in the Caucasus region.

Websites www.caucasustravel.com, www.travel.info-tbilisi.com

A Tradition of Toasts

A Georgian **feast**, or **supra**, is a ritual affair. For centuries, the Georgians have gathered around the table to affirm their culture, even under foreign subjugation. A *tamada*, or toastmaster, orchestrates all but the most informal meals. The best tamadas are renowned for their wit and eloquence as they guide the company through a series of toasts. The toasts are uplifting, so that even a sad occasion becomes an affirmation of life.

Toasting begins with an acknowledgment of God's presence; then the host family is thanked. Georgians do not sip, and drinking at random is not allowed. Wine is drunk each time a toast is pronounced, but if inebriation seems imminent, the tamada slows down. Raise your glasses high with excellent local grape varietals, such as **Saperavi** and **Rkatsiteli**.

Asparagus Festival

Every spring, thousands of visitors descend on southern Germany's Asparagus Triangle to celebrate this culinary treasure.

Every year on the first Saturday in May the sedate town of Schwetzingen, in the southwestern state of Baden-Württemberg, is overrun with people, bands, and asparagus stalls. This is the Spargelfest, or Asparagus Festival—a day of music, dancing, and parades in honor of the *Königliche Gemüse*, or royal vegetable. For this is no ordinary asparagus, but the highly prized white-alabaster-stalked variety—so exclusive it was once eaten only by kings. The Spargelfest marks the peak of the asparagus, or *spargel*, season, which lasts from April to June. It is a period of frenzied activity during which around 70,000 tons of the delicacy are gorged, and restaurants offer a special *Spargelkarte*, or asparagus menu. Asparagus mania is concentrated around the two main growing regions, Baden-Württemberg and Lower Saxony, and many towns hold a festival. The largest takes place in the city of Bruchsal (Baden-Württemberg), but the most famous is the one in Schwetzingen, the self-proclaimed "asparagus capital of the world." It was here that the white-asparagus craze started: the town was the summer residence of the 17th-century elector, Karl Theodor, reputedly the first person to grow the vegetable, in the light, sandy soils of his palace gardens. Today, white asparagus is available to everyone, and there is no better opportunity to enjoy it than at the Spargelfest. Visit the stalls, take part in the grand peel-off, where you can test your asparagus-peeling skills, and watch the festival's king and queen being crowned with asparagus spears.

When to Go The first Saturday in May for the Schwetzingen festival; the third Saturday in May for Bruchsal. Check dates for festivals in other places.

Planning Schwetzingen is in the Asparagus Triangle, which lies between Heidelberg and Mannheim, and there are plenty of "asparagus routes" in the area. Allow a full day at the Spargelfest, especially if you are going to Schwetzingen, as the festival is held outside the town's baroque palace, which is also well worth a visit.

Websites www.cometogermany.com, www.germany-tourism.com

White Asparagus

Softer and sweeter than the green version, white asparagus is grown in sandy soil and—unlike its green counterpart—is protected from direct exposure to the sun. This gives the plant its characteristic milky white color.

When choosing white asparagus, make sure the stalks are plump, as these are the sweetest and tenderest of all. The stalks should also, ideally, be pure white from tip to base. Any purple coloring at the tips indicates exposure to the sun and a loss of flavor.

To cook it, tie peeled asparagus in a bundle and stand it upright in a deep pot, in salted boiling water that comes about three-quarters of the way up the stalks, and boil for 10–20 minutes. Try it in cream of asparagus soup, with hollandaise sauce, or, best of all, with melted butter or an oil and vinegar dressing.

Chefs trim white asparagus ready for sale in Mannheim's market. The highest-grade asparagus has straight, white stems.

ITALY

Slow Food in Turin

Whether you want to shop, eat, or just browse, enjoy some of the best slow food in this north Italian city.

It is a bright April morning in Turin, capital of the Piedmont region, and the daily Mercato di Porta Palazzo—said to be the largest outdoor food market in Europe—is packed with shoppers. Like the nearby cathedral housing the Turin Shroud, this is a place of pilgrimage, and not just for food-lovers, but for home-cooks in search of top-quality ingredients for family meals. It being spring, there are new-crop salads, massed young snails—the symbol of the Slow Food movement—making a bid to escape their display boxes, and, on the butchers' stalls, tender lamb. Italians would not think of eating lamb at any other time of year—they are, after all, the most assiduous observers of the seasons, and each season brings its own foods. Three miles (5 kilometers) to the south lies another pilgrimage site. Since 2007, the converted Carpano (Punt e Mes) vermouth factory in the Turin suburb of Lingotto has housed the food emporium called Eataly, showcase of the Slow Food ethos. If a traditional Italian food shop is like a jewel box, this is the treasury. Whole rooms are devoted to fresh fruits and vegetables, seafood, dried and fresh pasta, cured meats, maturing cheeses, wine, preserves, bread, and coffee. There are tasting counters and specialty eateries, plus rooms for seminars and lectures. This is not just a shop, but a declaration of intent to enshrine and preserve the values of fine food that are exhibited at traditional outlets like the Mercato di Porta Palazzo.

When to Go Any time of year. In winter, feel the freshening chill from the snowcapped Alps to the north; in summer, feel the warmth (July and August can be torrid). The biennial Salone Internationale del Gusto festival is held at Lingotto in October (next in 2010).

Planning The Mercato di Porta Palazzo, in the Piazza della Repubblica, takes place every day except Sunday, 6:30 a.m. to 1:30 p.m., Saturday until 7:30 p.m. Eataly is open daily and is accessible from the city center by bus, tram, train, or car (directions Lingotto Fiere/8 Gallery). The restaurants in Eataly tend to get busy at peak hours, so it is best to eat slightly early or late.

Websites www.eataly.it, www.slowfood.com, www.turismotorino.org

The Slow Food Movement

The concept of Slow Food was forged in the mid-1980s, when McDonald's threatened to open a branch by the Spanish Steps in the heart of Rome. To a group of journalists eating together in the town of Bra, to the south of Turin, this represented the ultimate erosion of all they held dear about good Italian food.

Led by **Carlo Petrini**, the journalists campaigned to reverse this trend, promoting instead values such as the local sourcing of good ingredients, sustainability, artisan (as opposed to factory) production, the careful and respectful preparation of food, and conviviality in the eating of it—Slow Food, as opposed to Fast Food.

The idea caught on, and now the Slow Food movement has more than 180,000 members forming local chapters, called *convivia*, in 120 countries. It is also behind the giant biennial food fair in Turin called the **Salone Internationale del Gusto**, and the school of gastronomy, the **Università di Scienze Gastonomiche**.

Opposite: Piedmont's glorious countryside supplies produce for Turin's markets. Above: Leaf-wrapped figs tempt the taste buds.

NEW YEAR'S FEASTS

December 31 is not the only chance to enjoy New Year's feasts. Although some celebrations are largely family events, tradition dictates hospitality to strangers.

❶ Forget-the-Year Parties, Japan

Bonenkai, or forget-the-year, parties are occasions for workmates or groups of friends to celebrate the previous year's successes and drown its failures. They usually take place in *izakaya*, taverns serving smallish Japanese dishes alongside drinks, or restaurants. Rigid protocol applies, at least until everyone is drunk; empty glasses are taboo.

Planning Bonenkai parties take place throughout December; many people attend several. www.jnto.go.jp

❷ New Year, or Spring Festival, China

On the eve of this 4,000-year-old lunar festival, families gather for a lavish reunion dinner. Common components are a chicken, symbolizing wholeness; black moss, indicating wealth; sticky cake, boding a sweet new year; and "longevity" noodles, eaten uncut. Dinner usually ends with a whole steamed fish, which is left unfinished to augur a new year of plenty.

Planning Chinese New Year falls on varying dates in January and February. Wear red: it's a lucky color. www.chinaodysseytours.com

❸ Feast of the First Morning, Vietnam

An ancestor-worship festival, Tet Nguyen Dan (Feast of the First Morning) is also an occasion to entertain friends and family—and start the year auspiciously. Since even cooks relax for Tet, dishes are prepared ahead and include *kho* (a tangy stew flavored with caramel and fish sauce), *banh chung* (sticky pork-and-mung-bean rice cakes), and *cu kieu* (pickled spring onions).

Planning Tet usually corresponds with Chinese New Year. Shops and markets close for up to three weeks. www.footprintsvietnam.com

❹ White Month, Mongolia

Mongolia's three-day lunar New Year festival, Tsagaan Sar (White Month), is celebrated at the junction of winter and spring. *Bituuleg* (New Year's Eve dinner) stars a cooked sheep's rump, accompanied by steamed meat dumplings, lamb patties, and flat biscuits, washed down with fermented mare's milk and milk vodka.

Planning The date varies from year to year. Mongolians prepare enough food for all-comers. Guests should bring presents. Packaged tours are available. www.mongoliatourism.gov.mn

❺ New Year's Eve, Russia

Feasting lavishly is at the core of Russia's biggest festival as many Russians believe the new year will continue as it started. The evening proceeds with a succession of toasts made with vodka or *Sovetskoye Shampanskoye* (Soviet champagne). Typical dishes include caviar, smoked salmon, goose, and suckling pig. Many Russians also celebrate the Julian Old New Year on January 13-14.

Planning Many restaurants arrange package tours. www.russia-travel.com

❻ New Day, Iran

The 3,000-year-old Noruz (New Day) is a Zoroastrian, pre-Islamic festival that remains Iranians' top holiday. Core to the rituals is the *haft sin* (seven *s*'s) spread—usually chosen from *sabze* (green shoots), *samanu* (wheat pudding), *sib* (apples), *sohan* (honey-and-nut brittle), *senjed* (jujube), *sangak* (flatbread), *siyahdane* (sesame seeds), *sir* (garlic), *somaq* (sumac), and *serke* (vinegar). But it is all display. On the eve itself, Iranians usually eat *sabzi polo mahi*, steamed rice with green herbs and fish.

Planning Noruz corresponds with the vernal equinox (usually March 21). www.tourismiran.ir, www.itto.org

❼ New Year's Eve, Piedmont, Italy

A large dinner (*cenone*) is common throughout northern Italy for New Year's Eve, but few places take it to the same extremes as Piedmont, birthplace of the Slow Food movement. Expect a dozen antipasti, boiled homemade sausages with lentils, at least three other main courses, and several desserts, including panettone and hazelnut cake.

Planning For an authentic rural experience, enjoy home-cooked food in a family atmosphere at a farmhouse. www.piedmont.worldweb.com

❽ New Year's Eve, Spain

Spaniards devour a grape with each midnight chime. Most people celebrate at home, but large public festivities in Barcelona's Plaza Catalunya see people assemble with grapes and cava (sparkling white wine) before a night's clubbing.

Planning Peeled, unseeded grapes are easier to swallow rapidly. www.barcelonaturisme.com

❾ New Year's Eve, the Netherlands

Although restrained in their consumption of pastries for most of the year, Netherlanders abandon all prudence on New Year's Eve, when dinner ends with deep-fried *appelflappen* (apple turnovers), *appelbeignets* (battered apple rings), and *oliebollen* (doughnuts). They usually toast the new year with champagne.

Planning Some restaurants and hotels organize special dinners as part of a package, often including accomodation. www.holland.com

❿ Hogmanay, Scotland

On New Year's Eve, called Hogmanay in Scotland, most rituals, such as first-footing (visiting) friends and neighbors after midnight, are home-based. Key among the food traditions is a Scottish steak pie, often ordered in advance from butchers, alongside black bun and clootie dumpling—both rich fruitcakes—and shortbread.

Planning In Edinburgh, the Hogmanay Food Fair or upscale butchers, such as John Saunderson, are good places to stock up on goodies. www.edinburgh.org, www.edinburghfestivals.co.uk

Right: A table is set with traditional foods and decorations for the Iranian Noruz (New Day) celebrations.

WINTER TREATS

Take time off from the ski slopes to enjoy the hearty, warming, winter fare of the Alps in western Austria.

Snow-clad mountains glisten in the winter sun; wooden chalets sigh under the weight of a blanket of snow, the silence broken only by icicles cracking as they slowly melt. The old-world charm of the Austrian Alps has been preserved here, and peasant food is the cuisine of the region—simple, hearty fare made from ingredients that a farmer can produce in his self-sufficient alp, cut off from civilization by yard-high snow for months on end: satisfying dishes made with a few cups of flour, an egg or two, some butter, milk, and a good measure of cheese that's been ripening in the back of the chalet. Many traditional dishes are variations on a theme, changing slightly from valley to valley: such as the state of Tyrol's dumpling dish, *Kasnock'n*. *Schlickkrapfen*—pasta dough filled with spinach and curd, cooked, then tossed in *beurre noisette*—is Austria's answer to ravioli, hailing from the neighboring state of Carynthia. Salzburg's *Kaspressknödel*, dumplings made from stale bread, eggs, some herbs, and a good helping of cheese, are enjoyed in a clear broth or pan-fried and served with salad. Skiers start the day with goat's milk, home-churned butter, dry-cured ham, and crusty farmer's rye before facing the slopes. They come back at lunchtime to a steaming bowl of *Gulaschsuppe* (goulash soup), a dish said to revive the dead; or spend the afternoon lazing on the sun terrace with a mug of *Lumumba* (hot chocolate laced with rum), and doughnuts fried to order, *Germknödel* (a fluffy cloud of steamed yeast dough smothered in vanilla custard), or an indulgent strudel.

When to Go The skiing season starts at the beginning of December, but the best snow is usually to be had in January–also the least busy month. Glacier skiing is available year-round in some resorts.

Planning Fly into Innsbruck, Salzburg, Klagenfurt, or Friedrichshafen (southern Germany). Most hotels also offer shuttle transfers from the closest airport. Accommodations range from five-star hotels to B&B in small pensions and farms.

Websites www.tiscover.at, www.austria.info

Dumplings with Cheese
Kasnock'n

Serves 2
2 tbsp butter
Pinch of salt
Scant 1½ cups/7 oz/200 g all-purpose (plain) flour
Scant 1 cup/7 fl oz/200 ml milk
2 shallots, thinly sliced
7 oz/200 g Bergkäse (Comté or Gruyère are good substitutes)

Mix two-thirds of the butter with salt, flour, and milk, and form into small dumplings (about 0.5 in/1 cm diameter). Bring a pot of salted water to a boil, then reduce to a gentle simmer. Put dumplings in the water for 2–3 minutes. Lift out and set aside.

In an ovenproof pan, fry shallots in the remaining butter until starting to brown. Remove shallots and reserve. Add dumplings to the pan, cover with grated cheese, and broil until cheese has melted. Sprinkle with the shallots and serve.

Skiers in the Austrian Alps refuel on *krapf'n*, a type of large doughnut that comes with savory or sweet fillings.

Mushrooms of every size, shape, and color are sold in the local markets.

FRANCE

Mushroom Picking

Head for the forests of the Auvergne in central France to enjoy the annual fall bounty of delicious fungi.

Every fall, people across Europe set out on dew-fresh mornings and on weekends to forage for mushrooms in woodlands and forests. Wild fungi are one of nature's most bounteous gifts, offered in all shapes and sizes. You will see them piled up on market stalls, spread on sunny doorsteps to dry, and on menus in every restaurant, where they are turned into soups, coulis, pâtés, casseroles, and risottos, or served simply with omelettes or in salads. One of the best places to head for is the Auvergne region in the Massif Central. This land of forests, rolling hills, and extinct volcanoes is never overrun with tourists. The countryside is moist and green, with rivers and springs, and sprinkled with Gallo-Roman sites, churches, châteaux, and spas. Well-marked trails lead through the Livradois Forest Natural Regional Park in the northern Auvergne and the Tronçais, Europe's largest oak forest, in the south—both good places for *champignon*-hunters. While there, you might hear bellowing deer or catch a glimpse of a wild boar. Game is a popular accompaniment for mushroom feasts. The cuisine of the Auvergne is distinctive and farm-based, featuring charcuterie and—in particular—cheeses such as creamy Bleu d'Auvergne, which goes well with raw mushroom salads, and Saint-Nectare, which has a distinctly earthy flavor.

When to Go The last two weeks in September and the first two in October are the best time, though the season can spread into November. Hunting is best after a rainstorm and around trees that have been felled.

Planning Under French law, mushrooms belong to the owner of the land on which they grow. Each village and region has its own regulations about where you can go, what and how many mushrooms you can pick. Your hotel or the local tourist office will put you on the right track. Many guesthouses and auberges offer mushroom trails. If your accommodation is *table d'hôte*, you can dine with the proprietor and eat your day's haul.

Website www.auvergne-tourisme.info

Mushroom Varieties

There are literally dozens of kinds of **cèpes**, **bolets**, **morels**, and **girolles** to be found on the forest floors of the Auvergne, many of them identified by local names, such as "trumpets of the dead."

Use a basket or paper bags (not plastic bags) for collecting mushrooms. Keep different kinds of mushrooms apart in a basket, or collect different types in different bags, as any poisonous mushrooms will affect the edible ones.

Even if you are using a chart or book to identify fungi, you should get a second opinion about whether your haul is safe to eat. Take the mushrooms to a local pharmacy to have them checked before eating: French pharmacists are trained in mushroom taxonomy and will give you free advice. Around 30 people die every year in France from mushroom poisoning.

The many varieties of dried mushrooms make good edible souvenirs as you cannot bring fresh wild mushrooms home with you.

Wild mushrooms sautéed in butter

The truffle's knobbly, irregular appearance belies its rich aroma and flavor.

FRANCE

TRAVELS IN TRUFFLE COUNTRY

The jewel of the cuisine of the Périgord in southwest France, the black truffle has excited gourmets for more than 4,500 years.

The beautiful region known as the Périgord to the east of the town of Bergerac, in the western part of the Dordogne region, has something for everyone: rich history, ancient buildings, fine food and wines, and truffles—the "black diamonds" of the Périgord. From Bergerac follow the D32 eastward, through farmlands and forests. Pass through the village of Liorac-sur-Louyre with its 11th-century Templar church, on to the ancient market town of Sainte Alvère, the domain of the truffle and location of the largest market of its type in the region. The black truffle grows on limestone slopes, hidden under the roots of oak trees, and as they can sell for up to $1,820 per pound ($4,000 per kilogram), their location is a jealously guarded secret. Truffle-hunters use trained sniffer dogs to locate these gems. The smallest shaving of a truffle is all that is needed to impart its delicate flavor to foie gras, pâtés, and omelet. The Sainte Alvère truffle market, held on Monday mornings, is a commercial and social event. In the market room crowds file past tables bearing the pungent lumps of fungi, as vendors carefully weigh out pieces for customers. While in the area, stroll through the nearby villages of Trémolat and Paunat, past medieval walls, courtyards, and ancient archways. Both towns have excellent restaurants where you can experience traditional Périgordine fare.

When to Go The Ste. Alvère truffle market is held every Monday morning from November to March. Arrive punctually as the truffles sell quickly.

Planning The following restaurants are recommended and booking is essential: Chez Julien in the shadow of magnificent Paunat Abbey; the Michelin-starred Le Vieux Logis or Bistrot d'en Face, both in Trémolat's market square. Most restaurants in rural France are closed on Sunday nights.

Websites www.pays-de-bergerac.com, www.viamichelin.com

French Black Truffles

The winter black truffle found in the Périgord comes from the fungus *Tuber melanosporum*. It grows beneath the roots of oak and hazel trees and is found just below the surface to a depth of 8 in (20 cm).

A fresh truffle is blue-black in color and has a strong, earthy aroma. The outside is covered in lots of little bumps, which should be rounded if viewed under a magnifying glass. The flesh should be deep black with thin, white veins running through it.

Truffles are graded according to size and shape. Extra indicates large, perfect truffles; Category 1, smaller, whole, round truffles; Category 2, irregular-shaped truffles. Fragments, either broken or trimmed, are also offered for sale—make sure that they have no soft spots and that their aroma is still strong.

FRANCE

Burgundy Grape Harvest

Every fall, the Burgundy vineyards of eastern France
fill with teams of pickers racing to bring in the harvest.

In late September, Burgundy is a place of amber sunlight and dry heat. The grapes are ready to pick at the moment when the hills cradling the vineyards look their very best: full of rich, ripe color. For ten days, there is a thrill of excitement in the air as teams of grape-pickers descend on the vineyards to bring in the harvest. Grapes are cut from the vine by hand, not machine, as the human eye is considered the best tool for judging the grapes' ripeness and the hand for ensuring that they are picked intact, without bruising or crushing—the crushing comes later! Many Burgundies are named after the village where they are grown and produced. Look out for Appellation Contrôlée (AC) on the labels. A label reading "Premier Cru" after the village indicates an outstanding vineyard; better still are wines where the name of the vineyard appears after the village name. The most prestigious wines are the Grands Crus, which display just the name of the vineyard on the label. The Côte de Nuits area, in the north of Burgundy, is where you will find the slopes that grow the finest Pinot Noir grapes, and which produce most of the Premiers Crus. Exceptional wine-producing villages, such as Gevrey-Chambertin and Vosne-Romanée, are found in this area. Farther north, the Chablis area produces fine dry white wines, and south of the Côte de Nuits, the Côte de Beaune produces reds and whites.

When to Go Grape-picking usually takes place in the second half of September, depending on weather conditions. If you cannot make it at harvest time, Burgundy has food and wine festivals year-round.

Planning During the harvest, some vineyards cut back on their tasting sessions because everybody is in the fields. Wine cities, such as Dijon and Beaune, are expensive, and you may find a more authentic and enjoyable experience in cheaper accommodations in the villages. When selecting a wine to drink, look out for the 1996 and 2000 vintages, which are considered the best of the last 15 years. 2003 was an exceptionally hot year, with an early harvest, and the vintage is an unusual one with tannic, very fruity reds—flavors you are more likely to find in a New World wine than in a Burgundy.

Websites www.burgundyeye.com, fi.franceguide.com, gastronomy.via-burgundy.com

Burgundian Specialties

■ **Boeuf Bourguignon** is a rich beef dish, stewed gently for several hours in red wine with onions, mushrooms, and lardons (cubes) of bacon.

■ **Oeufs en Meurette** are poached eggs in a deeply savory sauce made from stock, brandy, and wine.

■ **Escargots** (snails) are a local favorite. Try them with breadcrumbs and garlic, or stewed in Chablis.

■ **Jambon persillé** is a jellied ham terrine with parsley, usually served as a first course.

■ **Râble de lièvre à la Piron** is saddle of hare, marinated in wine and eau-de-vie.

Traditional woven straw baskets are used for transporting the harvested grapes.

BIKE TOURS FOR FOODIES

What better way to sample the culinary delights of a region than by peddling along its backroads, enjoying the scenery and working up an appetite for the next meal.

❶ Blue Ridge, Virginia

Tucked away in Virginia's vineyard-dotted farmland awaits a land of gastronomic pleasure. After a gourmet breakfast, head out to the region's wineries, and return to a sumptuous dinner in the evening. Some tours include an evening at the Inn at Little Washington, which invented such signature dishes as veal Shenandoah and timbale of Maryland crabmeat.

Planning Base yourself at the Foster Harris House B&B. www.tourdepicure.com, www.virginia.org, www.fosterharris.com

❷ Sonoma and Napa Valleys, California

Vine-covered hills, redwood groves, and sprawling farmlands provide perfect cycling country. Follow Sonoma's backroads in the Dry Creek, Alexander, and Knights Valleys, stopping to taste the wines and the best of California's farm-to-table cuisine. Then move on to Napa Valley's winery-lined Silverado Trail and stay in St. Helena, sampling locally raised lamb, cheeses, and seafood.

Planning Some tours start from San Francisco; or stay in the area and book tours by the day. www.duvine.com, www.sonomacounty.com

❸ Salta Province, Argentina

Beginning in colonial Salta, visit ancient Cachi, remote Estancia Colome—featuring a private tasting of its high-altitude wines—and picturesque Cafayate, the hub of Salta's wine-making business. Gaucho barbecues and a regional cuisine of corn-based Locro stew, tamales, and lots of desserts, are complemented by the Malbecs and Torrontés of the province's vineyards.

Planning The route involves some hard cycling at high altitudes. www.backroads.com, www.argentina.ar, www.turismosalta.gov.ar

❹ The Golden Triangle, Thailand

Sample the cuisine of northern Thailand, with its liberal use of spices, curries, and noodles prepared with fresh local ingredients, on a tour that starts in Chiang Mai and visits hill-tribe communities en route to the ancient Burmese kingdom of Chiang Saen. Peddle past jungle valleys and boat-dotted rivers, eating in local restaurants, and taking in markets and an optional cooking class.

Planning The route goes along rural roads with some climbing. www.backroads.com, www.tourismthailand.org

❺ Rajasthan, India

Rajasthan's royal kitchens turned the preparation of food into an art form, cooking scarce meats with elaborate curries, dried fruits, and yogurt. Sleep in palaces and feast on some of India's finest cuisine in towns such as Umaid Bhawan, Jodhpur, and Udaipur, sharing lonely roads with camel trains and shepherds en route.

Planning This is an easy route. Bikes can be rented in most towns if you want to devise your own tour. www.butterfield.com, www.rajasthantourism.gov.in

❻ Mediterranean Turkey

For centuries Ottoman chefs crafted dishes for sultans, creating a rich culinary tradition in the process. On this tour of epicurean discovery, you will cycle through the citrus-perfumed countryside and along the Mediterranean coast, exploring the seaside towns of Bodrum and Datça, and ending with a three-day cruise on some of the world's most dazzling blue waters.

Planning A challenging route for intermediate and advanced cyclists. www.experienceplus.com, www.tourismturkey.org

❼ Piedmont, Italy

With robust wines (Barolo, Barbaresco) and singular gastronomy, Piedmont is a gourmet's paradise—a typical meal consists of at least six courses, accented with some of the world's finest truffles. Peddle along quiet but hilly country roads, visiting red-roofed villages, such as Alba, and the five towns of Barolo.

Planning Moderately difficult. www.butterfield.com, www.duvine.com, www.regione.piemonte.it

❽ Burgundy, France

With lazy lanes, picturesque canals, farmland, and vineyards galore, Burgundy is a biker's delight. Discover the abbeys at Cluny and Vézelay and the historic cities of Dijon, Mâcon, Tournus, and Beaune, with architecture funded by wealthy wine merchants. Taste the likes of Vosne-Romanée, Gevrey-Chambertin, and Puligny-Montrachet along the way.

Planning A network of linked cycle routes covers the region, providing services and facilities for cyclists. www.frenchcyclingholidays.com, www.burgundy-tourism.com, www.francetourism.com

❾ Basque Country, Spain

The region's cornucopia of ingredients combine to create some of the best cuisine in Spain: including aged beef grilled over hot coals, and *bacalao* (salted cod)—washed down with Basque cider or Rioja wine. Cycling tours take in fishing villages along the area's rugged coast, the cultural delights of Bilbao, and Haro and the Spanish plateau, where Rioja wines are produced in all their glory.

Planning Tours are available tailored to your interests and fitness level. www.veloclassic.com, www.basquecountry-tourism.com

❿ The Cape & Winelands, South Africa

Beginning in Cape Town, explore the Cape Peninsula coast before heading inland to the Franschhoek Valley, with its French roots and magnificent vineyards, and the Shamwari Game Reserve. On the way, taste a medley of Cape Malay, Indian, Afrikaner, and European culinary delights, such as springbok loin in balsamic broth.

Planning Spring and fall are the best times. www.butterfield.com, www.tourismcapetown.co.za, www.franschhoek.org.za

Right: Italy's Piedmont region offers tranquil roads that wind past vineyard-draped hills and farm-dotted valleys.

WILD CORSICA

The herbs of the maquis fill the air on this rugged
Mediterranean island and contribute to its unique cuisine.

Corsica, southeast of the French mainland and west of Italy, is France's wild west. Corsicans protect their wild island fiercely, and the cuisine reflects their free-ranging, hunter-gatherer character. Completely surrounded by the Mediterranean and Tyrrhenian seas, Corsicans are unmoved by fishing and the fruits of the sea—although fish and shellfish are on the menu in coastal resorts—preferring the safety of the inland and upland refuges of Haute Corse and the natural produce to be found there. The maquis, the thick and aromatic vegetation that covers most of the island, flavors the flesh of Corsica's free-range pigs, sheep, and goats, giving meat a very different flavor to that from farm-raised animals. Its herbs—rosemary, thyme, sage, mint, juniper, and myrtle, among others— and wild mushrooms are used in *soupe Corse* or as spices for roasts and stews, especially the famous *civet de sanglier*, or wild-boar stew. Even the *brocciu*—goat or sheep whey cheese often used with mint to flavor everything from trout to omelet—carries the distinctive flavor of the island's herbs. Part of the island is covered with chestnut forests, and Corsicans have long used chestnut instead of wheat flour as a staple for making bread, polenta, and even beer. And wines from the Patrimonio region in Haute Corse are no longer the rough brews that once accompanied Corsica's predominantly winter cuisine.

When to Go October to December are the best months for Corsica's winter cuisine and the brilliant foliage of the Castagniccia, the chestnut forest east of Corte.

Planning Give yourself at least a week; two would be better. There is one airport on the island, or you can arrive by ferry from Nice or Cannes and sail for Livorno, Italy, from Bastia. Car rental is essential for exploring the island. Corsica's music, film, and wind festivals are worth checking out. Napoleon's birthplace and the Fesch Museum in Ajaccio are key visits, as are the megalithic dolmens and menhirs at Filitosa.

Websites www.corsica.net, www.visit-corsica.com, www.bastia-tourisme.com

Charcuterie, Cheese, & Chestnuts

Corsican free-range pigs, often crossed with wild boar, produce highly esteemed sausages and charcuterie products nearly as lean as venison. ***Salsiccia*** is a peppered sausage. ***Coppa*** is a chest cut of solid meat, and ***figatelli*** are partly dried and smoked liver sausages usually grilled over coals. ***Lonzu*** is a smoked pork loin, while ***prisuttu*** is a smoked ham either eaten raw or grilled.

Many Corsican cheeses are too strong to eat indoors. ***Bastelicaccia*** is a soft, creamy sheep cheese; ***sartenais*** is hard and sharp; ***cuscioni*** is an unctuous sheep cheese with a dark, earthy flavor.

Chestnuts are a key Corsican ingredient, used for a cake called ***Castagna***, panetta bread, dry biscuits, and powdered and sugared ***beignets*** (doughnuts) eaten on special occasions.

Corsica's pigs are allowed to roam free in the interior of the island, feeding on chestnuts and herbs, which give Corsican pork its distinctive flavor.

Fresh, sweet, plump strawberries are the ultimate symbol of the English summer.

ENGLAND

Strawberry Season

Enjoy the king of summer fruit along the backroads
of Kent, in England's southeastern corner.

An English summer would not be summer without strawberries and cream. These sweet, scented berries, relatives of the rose, have somehow lodged themselves in the national consciousness. Cardinal Wolsey, chancellor to Henry VIII, was said to be one of the first people to pair wild strawberries with cream. Jane Austen's Emma heads out on a strawberrying party, "Where strawberries, and only strawberries, could now be thought or spoken of. The best fruit in England—everybody's favourite—always wholesome." And for many visitors to the Wimbledon Championships, the tournament is as much about enjoying strawberries and cream, alongside a glass of champagne, as it is about the tennis. Wimbledon's strawberries come from the county of Kent. Traveling through this rolling landscape, famous for pretty villages, fruit orchards, and hop gardens, you can feast on strawberries to your fill at roadside stalls and pick-your-own (PYO) farms. If you want to sample old varieties, such as Royal Sovereign, look out for them at PYO farms, where you will be given a small cardboard basket, or punnet, to fill and take away—and where you can snack on strawberries straight from the bush as you pick them. You may even be lucky enough to find intensely fragrant, small, wild strawberries along the edges of woods or, sometimes, at local markets.

When to Go The English strawberry season runs from mid-June through August.

Planning If you do not want to pick your own strawberries, try a local farmers' market. Strawberries will be cheaper and fresher here than at supermarkets, and will always be local. Some PYO farms grow their strawberries on platforms at waist-height, which makes picking far more comfortable for adults, but can be awkward for children. Call ahead to find out whether the farm you want to visit does this.

Websites www.farmersmarkets.net, www.pick-your-own.org.uk, www.visitkent.co.uk

Eton Mess

Named for the English school, Eton Mess might first have been made by boys stirring together strawberries and cream.

Serves 6
2 cups/8 oz/225 grams
   strawberries
1 tbsp sugar
2 cups/16 fl oz/475 ml whipping
   cream
6 plain meringues

Rinse the strawberries, remove the stalks, and cut in half or quarters. Put the strawberries into a bowl, sprinkle with sugar, and stir to mix, crushing a few against the sides. Chill.
   Whip the cream until it forms soft peaks. Crumble the meringues and add to the cream, then mix in the strawberries. Pile into a large serving bowl or individual bowls.

4
IN THE KITCHEN

For food-lovers, the heart of the action is always in the kitchen. When they travel, no amount of sightseeing can equal the chance to visit a local cook's workplace or private home, learning the secrets behind classic regional specialties or cherished family recipes. For travelers like this, one of the happiest recent developments in tourism is the emergence of small cookery schools that welcome foreign guests for informal, hands-on classes. Kitchen doors are opening everywhere, from Cuba—where enterprising households welcome tourists to their family dinner tables— to South Africa, for an introduction to the east-meets-west flavors of Cape Malay, one of the world's most interesting fusion cuisines. In Italy, small schools demonstrate the country's proudly regional traditions, while specialist chefs in Beijing share their expertise in crafting perfect Chinese dumplings. A trip to Yucatán in Mexico is an opportunity to learn how local people transform an astonishing array of spices, fruits, and other ingredients into the fabulous sauces and desserts of the peninsula's distinctive cuisine.

Olive oil, eggs, tangled ribbons of freshly made fettuccine, and taste-filled parcels of ravioli are some of the key ingredients of Italian culinary paradise. One of the most satisfying food journeys is learning to create such marvels in your own kitchen.

CHILI LOVE IN SANTA FE

The chili pepper is New Mexico's official vegetable,
and it is chilies that breathe fire into the state's cuisine.

Native American craftspeople sell their wares beneath the arcades of the Spanish Palace of the Governors. Here, in Santa Fe's central plaza, the mix of cultures that gives this southwestern city its special vibrancy swirls around you. A few steps away, the Santa Fe School of Cooking shows how the blend works in the kitchen. Try the hands-on, one-and-a-half-hour *chile amor* (chili love) class, where you will learn how to make red and green chili salsas (sauces), served on piping hot tortillas that you have also prepared yourself. If you have ever faced the vexing question of how to get chili oil off your hands after deseeding and chopping this volatile vegetable, pay attention to the tips on handling chilies. In demonstration classes—which last about three hours and end with a meal—you will learn how to make tamales (corn dough steamed in a corn husk, with or without a filling), *nopales* (grilled or boiled prickly pear pads), and an array of incredible salsas. Classes are taught by resident instructors or visiting chefs from top Santa Fe restaurants, using ingredients from local farmers and artisans. Don't want to cook? Take the school's walking tour of the city, stopping to sample the food at some of Santa Fe's most notable restaurants, such as Amavi, Coyote Café, and La Casa Sena.

When to Go Santa Fe is packed for Indian Market on the third weekend in August, but for lovers of Native American crafts, the chance to buy from 1,200 artists representing 100 tribes is worth braving the crowds. Fall offers fewer tourists and clear, cool weather, while cottonwood trees form glorious yellow borders along river valleys.

Planning Visit Santa Fe's Saturday farmers' market. Try a Navajo taco (made with fry bread) at the city's Pueblo of Tesuque Flea Market. Shop for southwestern ingredients to take back with you, so you can share your newfound knowledge with friends at home. And allow time for a hike in the magnificent New Mexico countryside, famous for inspiring the painter, Georgia O'Keeffe.

Websites www.santafeschoolofcooking.com, www.santafe.org, www.santafefarmersmarket.com

Corn, Tomato, and Black Bean Salsa

½ cup/3½ oz/100 g finely chopped onion
1 tsp garlic, minced
2 tbsp olive oil
3 tbsp cilantro (fresh coriander), coarsely chopped
½ tsp cumin seed, freshly ground and lightly toasted
1 jalapeño, minced
2 tbsp cider vinegar
1 tbsp red chili honey
½ cup/3 oz/85 g fresh (or defrosted frozen) corn kernels
3 large ripe Roma tomatoes, chopped
1 cup/7 oz/200 g black beans, cooked

Lightly sauté the onion and garlic in olive oil. In a bowl, combine the cilantro, cumin seed, jalapeño, vinegar, and honey. Season with salt and add the corn, tomato, black beans, and sautéed ingredients. Stir, and set aside for 30–45 minutes to give the flavors time to blend.

Handle with care: students at the Santa Fe School of Cooking learn the art of roasting hot chilies.

Color abounds in the streets of Havana, including here a red motorcycle outside a blue-painted *panadería* (bakery).

CUBA

Home-eating in Havana

Enjoy authentic local food in a private home in Cuba's capital, and learn the secrets of how it is cooked.

Cuba is no stranger to revolutions. And the most recent, on the culinary front, has been universally toasted. There was a time when visitors to the island's capital, Havana, were restricted to a limited choice of expensive restaurants offering mediocre food. All that changed in 1995, with the legalization of *paladares*—independent, state-sanctioned dining rooms in private family dwellings. Here, amid the crumbling grandeur of this most atmospheric of Cuban cities, you can eat home-cooked food while also contributing much-needed revenue to individual households. The fare may be simple, such as *pollo* (chicken) with *Moros y Cristianos* (literally "Moors and Christians," black beans with white rice) or *puerco* (pork) with rice and fried plantains. More sophisticated dishes include tuna in coconut sauce or red snapper in *beurre blanc* sauce. But even when the food is humble, it is always fresh, wholesome, and cheap. Competition from the highly successful paladares has led Havana's conventional restaurants to improve their standards. Even so, don't miss the chance to try a paladar. In houses that are not normally open to tourists, you will learn how *habaneros* (the city's inhabitants) cook, and you will experience local hospitality first hand, which is what eating in Havana is all about.

When to Go Any time of the year, but November through April is best if you want to avoid excessive heat.

Planning No visit to Havana is complete without going to the two best-known paladares: La Guarida and La Cocina de Lilliam. Both serve excellent food in attractive surroundings. With these and the other more popular paladares, be sure to book ahead. You may also want to visit private eating houses in other parts of the island. The town of Trinidad in central Cuba is exceptionally beautiful and has a wide range of paladares.

Websites www.cuba-junky.com, www.laguarida.com

Bending the Rules

By law, paladares are not allowed to take more than 12 diners, and are only permitted to serve rustic food. Seafood is supposed to be served only in hotels and restaurants, but may be available if you ask.

To find a paladar, ask for recommendations from other tourists, or local barmen or taxi drivers—but not from your hotel, because its restaurant is likely to be in competition. If someone offers to take you to a paladar, rather than just recommending one, decline—this is probably a *jinetero*, or tout, expecting a commission. Paladar owners are heavily taxed, so leave a good tip.

CULINARY SURPRISES

Tuck into Welsh tea cakes in Argentina or Congolese fare in Brussels. Long-established minority communities in foreign lands can offer the best of both worlds when eating.

❶ Solvang, California

First settled by Danes in 1911, Solvang retains a Danish majority. Restaurants offer *frikadeller* (fried meat dumplings), *smørrebrød* (open-sandwich buffet), and *æbleskiver* (pancake balls) with *medisterpølse* (pork-and-clove sausages) and eggs. Bakeries dispense *pandekager* (pancakes), Havarti cheese, and, naturally, Danish pastries.

Planning March brings Solvang's three-day Taste of Solvang Annual Food and Drink Festival. In September, the Danish (or Æbleskiver) Days are a celebration of pancakes and all things Danish. www.solvangusa.com

❷ Diwali, Trinidad and Tobago

Hindus—mostly descendents of indentured Indian laborers—compose 40 percent of the population of Trinidad and Tobago. And for the Diwali Festival of Lights, all islanders are honorary Hindus, feasting at public fairs or at home on vegetarian delicacies like *gulab jamun*, scented doughnuts, and curry-filled flatbread.

Planning Diwali usually falls in October or November. The main day, Lakshmi Puja, is a public holiday. www.divalinagar.com

❸ Suriname

Thanks to this South American country's Dutch colonial history and unusually mixed population, its cuisine fuses Dutch, Indian, Javanese, Chinese, Creole, American, and Jewish influences. Sample the Creole *pastei* (chicken-and-vegetable pie), Indian roti, Chinese dim sum, and Indonesian rijsttafel (rice table).

Planning Explore the many bustling food markets in the capital, Paramaribo. www.suriname-tourism.org

❹ Chubut Valley, Argentina

Welsh people first settled Patagonia's Chubut Valley in 1865, eager to revive their culture and language. After long decline, both have resurged, with teahouses as important social hubs. Homemade cakes and dainty china are all part of the tea ritual. For the most authentic teahouses head for Gaiman and Trevelin.

Planning Andes Celtig, based in Trevelin, specializes in tours of the Chubut Valley (*Wladfa* in Welsh). www.andesceltig.com

❺ Macau, China

Fusion food rarely comes finer than in Macau, where Portuguese colonizers and south Chinese bonded culinarily for nearly 450 years. Results include *bacalhau* (salt cod), *paelha* (paella), *chouriço* (spicy sausage), *galinha portuguesa* (Portuguese chicken), *pudim* (crème caramel), *serradura* ("sawdust" pudding), and *pastéis de nata* (egg tartlets). Macau's favorite pastel de nata is a recent innovation by Lord Stow's Bakery on Macau's southernmost island, Coloane.

Planning Lord Stow's is at 1 Rua da Tassara. Also on Coloane is Fernando's Portuguese restaurant, 9 Praia de Hac Sa. www.macautourism.gov.mo

❻ Puducherry, India

French from 1673 to 1954, Puducherry (Pondicherry, French Pondichéry) zealously retains its Gallic cultural influences. The Alliance Française runs Café de Flore in a colonial building with sea views. Good French restaurants include Satsanga, Le Dupleix, and Rendezvous, while Le Club is a bar also serving French food.

Planning A French food festival, Le Gourmet, happens every August. tourism. pondicherry.gov.in

❼ Matongé, Brussels, Belgium

Belgians colonized Congo. Now Congolese colonize Matongé, a downtown quarter named for an equally bustling part of Kinshasa. The main drag, Rue Longue Vie, pulsates with African bars mixing rum punches, food stores selling yams, and restaurants serving mostly Congolese dishes like *moambé* (meat stew).

Planning The district goes especially wild during the two-day Fête du Quartier Matongé, which is held in late June each year. www.brusselsinternational.be

❽ New Malden, London, England

London's "Koreatown" lies in the southwestern suburbs—not far from Wimbledon of tennis fame. Here, on New Malden High Street, you can sample some of the best *panjeon* (seafood pancake) outside Korea, along with *soon du bu chigae* (a spicy stew with tofu, shellfish, and egg), *bulgogi* (barbecued beef), and small side dishes called *banchan*. It is authentic fare, catering for Europe's largest expatriate South Korean community.

Planning The tiny Hamgipak serves exquisite food, but closes at 10 p.m. The Palace keeps longer hours. www.london-eating.co.uk

❾ Libya

Expulsion of the Fascist Settlers Day—commemorating the deportation of Italian colonists—is a national holiday in Libya, yet Italian influences linger. Pasta (*makaruna*) is so significant some historians suggest that the Arabs originally exported pasta to Italy through China. Popular Italian-inspired dishes include risotto, macaroni in a tomato-based stew (*imbakbaka*), spaghetti bolognese, and Libyan soup—a spicy version of minestrone with lamb.

Planning Italian culinary influences are strongest in Tripolitania, the region around the capital. Libya is most temperate November through March. www.libyan-tourism.org

❿ Oktoberfest, Namibia

Oompah bands, bratwurst guzzling, and copious beer consumption are core components of this former German colony's October festival, just as in the fatherland. All are welcome.

Planning The main festival is at the Sport Klub in the capital, Windhoek, with others nationwide. www.namibiatourism.com.na

Right: It is a far cry from the green valleys of Wales—a *casa de te* (teahouse) advertising itself in the wilds of Patagonia.

Outside Mérida's San Ildefonso Cathedral, street vendors sell *marquesitas*—hot cheese wrapped in waffle-like cylinders.

MEXICO

Cooking Yucatán-style

Jutting from southeastern Mexico, the Yucatán Peninsula is home to some of the most intriguing dishes in the country's cuisine.

Cooking Yucatecan food means building layers of flavor based on ancient indigenous ingredients, such as corn, beans, squash, and chili, with added European, Caribbean, and even Middle Eastern tastes and techniques. Here, in the land of the Maya people, whose food and culture still dominate the peninsula, you will create surprising fusions, such as *queso relleno*. To make the stuffing for this ball of Dutch Edam cheese, you season meat with a combination of native tomatoes and the classic Spanish–Moorish mix of olives, almonds, capers, and spices. You can sign up for one of the well-known schools, like Los Dos in the state capital, Mérida, or take more informal classes at one of Yucatán's beach resorts. Among the dishes you will undoubtedly make is *cochinita pibil*, or slow-roasted pork, named for the technique of cooking meat in a *pib*, or underground oven. For this, you will make marinades using chili paste and bitter Seville orange juice. Toasted and ground pumpkin seeds are the key to other local dishes, including *papadzules*—stuffed tortillas bathed in a pumpkin-seed sauce. You will also learn to make dough for Yucatecan tamales, flavored with the bitter herb *chaya* and wrapped in banana leaves. To round things off, local tropical fruits and native chocolate will be the basis for desserts.

When to Go Late fall and winter are best, since the summer is hot and humid.

Planning Beach lovers can take classes in Playa del Carmen, Cancún, or Cozumel, and history buffs can combine classes with visits to Maya pyramids and colonial churches. Spanish-language schools in Yucatán often offer the option of taking regional cookery lessons. Most classes include visits to local markets.

Websites www.los-dos.com, www.cactuslanguage.com, www.isls.com, www.cookforfun.shawguides.com

Pastes for Every Dish

Fragrant seasoning pastes called **recados** are characteristic of Yucatecan cooking. Most often used to season meat and poultry, they consist of a variety of spices, usually ground with garlic and vinegar or bitter orange juice.

■ **Recado colorado** is a bright red-orange paste, also known as achiote paste, which comes from the seeds, called achiote or annatto seeds, of the bixa orellana tree. The seeds are combined with cumin, cloves, coriander, allspice, and oregano to make a marinade for chicken or pork cooked *pibil*-style, wrapped in banana leaves.

■ **Chilmole**, or **relleno negro**, is made from toasted ancho chilies, which are ground with black pepper and aromatic spices to make a dark paste. The mix is diluted with turkey broth and served with turkey, especially around the Christmas and New Year holidays.

■ **Recado para bistec** is used, as its name suggests, to season beef. Cinnamon and oregano are two of its signature flavors. Perhaps surprisingly, one of the most famous dishes made with this sauce is a chicken dish, **pollo Valladolid**. For this, chicken is first cooked with onion, spices, and chili, then rubbed with the recado and roasted or grilled.

CHINA

Beijing Cookery School

Chinese food tastes its best in China,
especially when you have cooked it yourself.

In China's capital you can sample the full range of the country's finest regional cooking, but when in Beijing you should eat like a Beijinger. Even better, discover what is perhaps the best Chinese takeout of all—not the food itself, but the knowledge of how to make it. Classes at The Peninsula Hotel in the central shopping district of Wangfujing teach you to make the humble but satisfying local dish called *jiaozi*, the northern-style meat-and-vegetable-filled pasta packages whose southern relatives are familiar on *dim sum* menus in Chinatowns worldwide, often wrongly translated as "dumplings." In the spacious open kitchen of the hotel's popular Jing restaurant, chefs help students mix flour and water to make an elastic dough. The students hand-roll the dough into small balls, which they squash and roll into disks of near-translucent thinness. Typical fillings are mixtures of chopped pork, vegetables, and dark, broad-bladed Chinese chives, although The Peninsula's chopper-wielding students follow the more subtle recipe used for the jiaozi served in the hotel's award-winning Cantonese restaurant, Huang Ting. A spoonful of filling is dabbed into the center of each disk, and then the chefs reveal the real secret to making jiaozi, which is the deft pinching motion that seals the disks into neat, rib-edged parcels ready for steaming or boiling.

When to Go Lessons are indoors and the stove is going, so don't be afraid of Beijing's bitter winters. But if you want to browse in food markets, visit in April through early May or September through October for the most comfortable weather.

Planning All cookery classes need to be booked in advance, and some only allow small numbers. So make your reservation first, then plan the rest of your trip around that. Reserve your place directly with the school; cookery tours from standard tour operators add a surcharge.

Websites www.peninsula.com, www.hutongcuisine.com, www.green-t-house.com

Other Options

■ Classes at **The Peninsula** include a dim sum lunch in Huang Ting at which students eat their own handiwork alongside an assortment of tidier items made by the professionals. Recipes for several different items are provided to take home.

■ Located in an old courtyard house tucked away in the *hutong* (alleys) of north Beijing, **Hutong Cuisine** offers classes in Cantonese and Sichuan cooking. Students cook four basic Cantonese or spicy Sichuan dishes and eat them at the concluding meal.

■ To make exotic jiaozi in startling surroundings, take a trip to **Green T. House Living** in the countryside northeast of Beijing. Celebrity chef–designer–musician JinR gives half-day courses in making her famous Green T. fennel dumplings.

Students chop ingredients under the eye of their teacher at the Hutong Cuisine school in northern Beijing.

THAILAND

THAI SECRETS

Thai cookery encompasses an astonishing regional variety,
and there are schools to teach every time-honored tradition.

Laboriously prepared, highly aromatic, and exquisitely presented, Thailand's cuisine is world-famous for good reason, and a plethora of schools, from rustic outfits to long-esteemed institutions, cater for the chefs and connoisseurs who flock to the kingdom to delve into its culinary secrets. Many schools begin with a market tour. Accompanied by your instructor, you pick among an array of exotic fare from the country's four corners: lemongrass stalks, mangoes, Kaffir lime leaves, mouse-dropping chilies (which provide the infamous kick in Thai food), Phuket lobster, and much more. With your basket full of goods, you return to the school, where you grind, chop, stir-fry, deep-fry, stew, mix, and mince. Typically, each school offers a four-dish course. At Bangkok's Blue Elephant, you will learn how to prepare Royal Thai cuisine—dishes such as spicy lemongrass soup with prawns or stir-fried noodles with tamarind sauce. At the garden-enclosed Thai House, just north of Bangkok, you can discover "village secrets"—perhaps coconut beef curry and clear melon soup. At Chiang Mai Cookery School, northern dishes with an extra dose of flavor are the specialty, including Chiang Mai curry with chicken and fried fish with chili and basil. On the paradise island of Ko Samui, your endeavors at the Samui Institute of Thai Culinary Arts will have a southern panache—perhaps *chu chi* curry with seafood or pumpkin coconut milk soup with porkballs. All classes end the same way—with a feast showcasing your new skills.

When to Go Classes are held year-round, but the best time to visit Thailand is in the dry, cool season from November through February, with sun every day and temperatures averaging 85-95°F (30-35°C).

Planning Many schools offer a range of courses—half-day, one-day, two-day, and more extensive programs—so you can add a class to your vacation itinerary, or make your vacation a cookery course.

Websites www.blueelephant.com, www.thaihouse.co.th, www.thaicookeryschool.com, www.sitca.net, www.tourismthailand.org

A Question of Balance

The meticulous balance of flavors—sweet, salty, sour, and spicy—lies at the heart of all Thai cooking.

Sweetness is achieved through the use of ingredients such as coconut milk (especially in curries, stews, and stir-fries), palm and coconut sugar, sweet black soy sauce, sweet pickled garlic, and sometimes honey.

Saltiness generally comes from fish sauce, but also through sea salt, Thai oyster sauce, dried fish or shrimp, salted plums, and salt-preserved vegetables.

Lime juice and tamarind juice add **tartness** to a dish, as do lemongrass, coconut vinegar, and rice vinegar.

Spiciness—the quality most commonly associated with Thai food—is typically achieved by using chili peppers, and sometimes chili paste and peppercorns. Ginger, onions, and garlic also give a kick.

Opposite and above left: Fresh seafood is a staple of Thai cuisine. Above right: An instructor at Bangkok's Four Seasons school

HOME-LEARNING IN SAIGON

Experience local hospitality while exploring Vietnam's rich culinary heritage in the southern city of Saigon.

Vietnamese pork fillet in pepper sauce

The boundaries between restaurants and residences are often blurred in Saigon (Ho Chi Minh City), so it is only natural that some of the best cookery classes in town take place in the kitchens of Saigonese homes. Among the programs you can choose from, a good option is one that brings together travelers seeking a gastronomic adventure off the beaten track and Vietnamese home-cooks passionate about sharing their culture with others. Each lesson begins at the local market early in the morning, when fruit, vegetables, seafood, and meat are at their freshest. The heart and energy of a city is often found within its markets, and this is certainly the case in Saigon. Students are steered around the market by a seasoned cook accompanied by an English-proficient university student, who serves as a language translator and cultural guide. Whether it is ground pork for crispy spring rolls (*cha giò*) or saw-tooth herb to garnish beef noodle soup (*pho bo*), you learn about Vietnam's diversity of foods by helping to select the day's ingredients. With bounty in hand, you travel to the cook's home to prepare lunch. Seeing and experiencing life at this level grants travelers a unique understanding of the customs and rhythms of Saigonese life. Then, after a morning of chopping, measuring, and tasting, you sit down with your teacher to savor the fruits of your labor.

When to Go Saigon is pleasant to visit year-round. During the rainy season, from May through November, there is guaranteed to be a daily dousing, so be sure to pack a poncho. Avoid going during Tet, the Lunar New Year (late January or early February), as stores and restaurants shut down for up to three weeks.

Planning Connections Vietnam organizes cooking classes in private homes. The Vietnam Cookery Center runs courses in a classroom setting, and Saigon's Caravelle Hotel offers a one-day program. You can also take classes in beach resorts, such as those around Nha Trang, northeast of Saigon.

Websites www.connectionsvietnam.com, www.expat-services.com, www.caravellehotel.com

Fish Sauce

Inside the cupboards of any Vietnamese kitchen, there is sure to be a bottle of **nuoc mam** (fish sauce). This salty, caramel-colored, utterly pungent condiment is shaken and stirred into practically every dish, from fresh salads to noodle soups. The best sauce is made from anchovies caught and fermented on the island of Phú Quoc.

Nuoc mam is most commonly used in **nuoc mam cham** (dipping sauce). To make this, pure fish sauce is mixed with water, lime juice, chopped chilies, minced garlic, and sugar. The resulting sour and sweet sauce serves as a dressing for staples such as broken rice (rice in which the kernel has cracked) and vermicelli noodles.

A local woman wearing a conical *non la* straw hat passes by the fishing harbor in Nha Trang—a color symphony of blue and green.

Dishes of fresh Canterbury lamb with seasonal vegetables make a kingly feast at Seagars Cook School.

NEW ZEALAND

SEAGARS ON THE SOUTH ISLAND

Burnish your cookery skills and savor superb produce and fine wines in a scenic region of New Zealand's South Island.

In the words of Jo Seagar, creating a great meal should be "easy-peasy." And so it can be, after a hands-on session at her Seagars Cook School, with an array of outstanding local ingredients on hand. Seagars is in Oxford at the center of the fertile Canterbury Plains on New Zealand's South Island—a rich farming district, famous for its dairy products, with salmon fishing in nearby rivers. The philosophy is "Maximum Effect for Minimum Effort." Participants in the Lunch and Learn sessions are welcomed with coffee and just-baked goodies, then spend the next three hours being guided through recipes by Jo Seagar. They pick up time- and labor-saving tips before enjoying a shared lunch complemented with local wines. Menus move with the seasons, taking advantage of freshly picked raspberries and asparagus in spring, salad greens and vine-sweet tomatoes in summer, and apples and pears in the fall. The school also offers wine-appreciation and specialty courses, with themes such as bread-making, gluten-free cookery, and cheese-making. If you do not have time for a course, at least visit the kitchen store or café. If you have plenty of time, take advantage of the bed and breakfast accommodations to stay overnight.

When to Go Most overseas visitors choose spring and fall. Winters (June–August) are cool but usually clear. The summer months (December–February) are the most popular time for New Zealanders to visit.

Planning Include a weekend in Christchurch to visit the Riccarton House farmers' market on Saturday morning and sample the fine local food and wine on offer in the city. The Alpine Pacific Triangle is a 230-mile (370 km) circuit, starting just north of Christchurch. It takes in Kaikoura, where you can eat lobster and go whale-watching, and the mountain spa town of Hanmer Springs, with a range of stylish eateries.

Websites www.joseagar.com, www.newzealand.com, www.waiparawine.co.nz, www.alpinepacifictourism.co.nz

Clean and Green

The range of fresh, locally produced ingredients is one of Seagars' attractions. **Canterbury lamb**, raised on the alluvial pastures of the Canterbury Plains, is known for its fine-grain sweetness. Also farmed here are deer, especially red deer, for **venison**, which appears on local menus as Cervena.

The South Island scores again with **Pacific king salmon**, prized for its firm moist flesh with a very low fat content–try it with locally grown, grated **wasabi** (Japanese horseradish). The salmon are bred in streams of highly oxygenated meltwater, then sea-farmed.

Kumara (sweet potatoes) arrived in New Zealand with the Maori and today are prepared in a variety of ways, from creamy soups to deep-fried salted chips that often accompany fish. More recent arrivals are **olives**, with varieties developed locally from 19th-century Mediterranean imports. These are cultivated both for eating whole and for making into oil.

The nearby **Waipara Valley**, with more than 80 vineyards, is one of New Zealand's fastest-growing wine regions, where long hot falls result in racy Rieslings and spicy Pinot Noirs. Waipara is also known for its Sauvignon Blancs, Chardonnays, and full-bodied Cabernet Sauvignons.

INDIA

SPICES OF RAJASTHAN

Get the authentic taste of the exotic as you learn to cook the way the people of Rajasthan in northwestern India have done for centuries.

The people of Rajasthan are proud of their rich cultural heritage and especially of their food. To learn more, take lessons at one of the numerous cookery schools in the city of Udaipur in the south of the state, many of them housed in the instructors' homes. Some teachers take you shopping on the backs of their Enfield motorbikes, weaving through streets full of cows and monkeys, past the fabled Lake Palace—once home to the Maharajas of Udaipur, now a luxury hotel—as you pick up ingredients at brightly colored food stalls. Back in the coolness of the teacher's house, you learn to use the seven essential spices of most Indian cooking: red chilies, coriander, turmeric, garam masala, anise seeds, cumin seeds, and salt. For Rajasthani dishes, you also need *aginomoto* (lemon salt) and *kasti methi* (dried fenugreek leaves). Everything is made from scratch. Chapatis are fried in a hot skillet using dough made from brown flour, water, and a pinch of salt. Paneer is like cottage cheese, made with milk and lemon juice and set in a thin cotton cloth. Other dishes include the deliciously oily paneer butter masala, spicy vegetable *khichdi* rice, and Udaipur's specialty—*beson gatta*, dough balls immersed in a tangy lentil sauce. Round off the experience by relaxing on your host's cushions with a steaming cup of masala chai, before departing with a full belly and a pocketful of recipes to take home with you.

When to Go It is best to avoid the peak tourist period, December and January, and the summer monsoon season from June through September.

Planning Rajasthan is such a vast and eclectic state that you could spend a month there and still not feel you have had too much. You will find cooking courses in all the major towns and cities, including Jaipur, Jodhpur, and Jaisalmer, although the smaller the better for intimacy. You can travel around by bus, taxi, or train—the last is the most romantic form of transportation in India.

Websites www.rajasthantourism.gov.in, www.indiabeat.co.uk

Spiced Paneer

On its own, paneer cheese is almost completely tasteless, but combined with more flavorsome ingredients, its soft, creamy texture forms a delicious complement to the stronger tastes of a dish's other components. For spiced paneer, spices and herbs are added while making the cheese, which is then good to eat on its own.

Makes 1¾ cups/11 oz/312 g
9¾ cups/72 fl oz milk/2L
2 tbsp lemon juice
1 tsp cumin seeds
1 tsp dried mint

Add the spices to the milk and bring to a boil in a large, heavy-bottomed pan. Add the lemon juice as soon as the milk starts to boil, then stir until the mixture curdles. If it does not curdle, add more lemon juice.
  Line a colander with a piece of cheesecloth (muslin) and drain. Discard the liquid. Twist the top of the cloth to enclose the soft cheese. Turn the colander upside down over a large plate, then place the cheese on top to drain. Weight with a tin can balanced on a small plate.
  After an hour, remove the weight and unwrap the cheese. It is ready to use, sliced into quarters or crumbled.

Opposite: Cooking chapatis in Jaipur. Above: A *thali* selection of dishes is served in the traditional way on a platter.

PETRA KITCHEN

The ancient hidden city of Petra delights the eyes by day, and by night a little gem of a restaurant delights the taste buds.

After a day exploring the ruins of Petra in southern Jordan, further exertion is the last thing you are likely to want when you get back to the modern town of Wadi Musa. Even so, it is worth stirring again to visit Petra Kitchen, a small backstreet restaurant where smiling women from a local cooperative work under the supervision of a professional chef. Here, they introduce local dishes and invite you to partake in the preparation before sitting down to enjoy your meal. The fare you help cook reflects Jordan's history—mainly Arab in style but with hints of the country's past as a Middle East crossroads, which has seen many a foreign army come and go. It also has the merit of being both nutritious and simple to make. Lamb and chicken feature strongly, as well as salads composed of grains and pulses. Gathered in Petra Kitchen's single, open, green-tiled room, lined with kitchen equipment, you stand at wooden tables, chopping parsley and tomatoes for mixing with bulgar wheat, herbs, and lemon juice in a tabbouleh salad. Or you stir the national dish, *mansaf*—lamb cooked until tender and served on a bed of rice and almonds. All is relaxed, informal, and non-technical, and there is pleasure in the companionship of other visitors involved in the common enterprise. Even small children are invited to join in, filling pastry squares with cheese, then folding them into parcels for baking.

When to Go Summers in Jordan are furnace-like and winters are very cold, so the best time to visit Petra is during the spring or fall.

Planning Book your evening at Petra Kitchen in advance if possible or as soon as you arrive in Wadi Musa. There may be fewer customers on the nights when Petra by Night operates, which offers candlelit access to the ruins, starting at 8:30 p.m. Petra Kitchen also offers courses over five evenings, giving a fuller introduction to Middle Eastern cookery and shopping trips to local markets with the chef.

Websites na.visitjordan.com, www.jordanjubilee.com, www.bedouincamp.net

Relive the Experience

■ Written recipes are provided for all the main-course dishes, along with the small appetizers or side dishes known as meze. You will be able to recreate them in your own kitchen as a reminder of your Jordan visit.

■ Many of the dishes are of bedouin origin. Try them as they were conceived to be eaten: outside a tent, in front of a campfire, and under the stars. You can experience this at the **Ammarin Bedouin Camp**, just outside Little Petra, a short drive from Wadi Musa.

■ After sampling **hummus** in Jordan, you will never eat the shop-bought variety again. Made from mashed chickpeas, sesame-seed paste, garlic, olive oil, and lemon juice, hummus is present at almost every meal.

Petra's ancient Nabataean ruins draw tourists from around the world. In the background is the modern town of Wadi Musa.

Making dolmas (or dolmades) is an art in itself as you carefully wrap each vine leaf around its parcel of savory stuffing.

GREECE

GREEK ISLAND KITCHEN

Enjoy a relaxing vacation on a Greek island while learning how to create the subtle flavors of its traditional dishes.

Fish cooked in wild herbs, phyllo pastry pies, meze (appetizers), meat rubbed with lemon-infused olive oil and cooked on a barbecue … these are the flavors of Greek island cuisine. Among many islands with schools offering cookery classes is unspoilt Ikaría in the eastern Aegean. Here, food writer and restaurateur Diane Kochilas, and her husband, Vassilis, run week-long summer courses in the mountain village of Christós Raches, with pine woods on one side and views of the sea on the other. Classes—given in English— take place in their home, designed and built by Vassilis. Each daily three- or four-hour session is organized around preparing a full meal, either lunch or dinner. You will learn how to make specialties, such as Ikarían bread salad, *soufico* (a vegetable dish in which each vegetable is sautéed individually before being combined in one pot), and Greek meze, including dolmas (stuffed vine leaves) and roasted eggplant salad with feta cheese and herbs. The fruit, herbs, and vegetables all come from the couple's organic vegetable garden. Diane and Vassilis will teach you how to make phyllo pastry and will organize visits to local artisan wine-makers, cheese-makers, and beekeepers. Accommodation is included, and in the evening, when the cooking is over, you can drink a glass of ouzo as you watch the sun slip into the Aegean.

When to Go As well as three week-long courses on Ikaría in July and August, Diane Kochilas also runs separate activities in Athens from mid-September to mid-June.

Planning Although you will have plenty of free time during a course on Ikaría, you may want to allow a few extra days to explore the island further. As well as beautiful villages, there are good mountain walks to do, stunning beaches to enjoy, and interesting archaeological sites to see.

Websites www.dianekochilas.com, www.greekislandactivities.com, www.holidayonthemenu.com

Pasta Gratin with Greens, Chickpeas, and Feta

Hilopites are Greek egg noodles. They are often cut into small squares and used in soups, but for this delicious recipe leave them long. If hilopites are unavailable, you can use fettuccine instead.

Serves 4
1 lb/450 g long Greek hilopites or fettuccine
1 lb/450 g Swiss chard, spinach, amaranth, or beetroot greens, trimmed, washed, and drained
1/2 cup/4 fl oz/125 ml extra-virgin Greek olive oil
2 cups/17 oz/480 g canned chickpeas, drained and rinsed
2 cups/10 oz/300 g crumbled Greek feta

Bring a large pot of salted water to a rolling boil and cook the pasta until slightly underdone. Remove and drain.

Heat 3 tbsp of the olive oil and sauté the greens over high heat in a large, nonstick skillet until just wilted. Drain, reserving 2 or 3 cups (16–24 fl oz/475–750 ml) of the liquid.

Combine the pasta, greens, chickpeas, remaining olive oil, and reserved liquid from the greens in an ovenproof gratin dish. Sprinkle with feta. Cover with aluminum foil and bake for 15 minutes.

Heat the broiler, remove the aluminum foil, and place the gratin under the broiler, about 6 in (15 cm) from the heat source. Broil for a few minutes until the feta browns lightly. Remove and serve.

ITALY

TUSCANY'S NOBLE TRADITION

In settings of aristocratic grace, two Tuscan vine- and olive-growing estates share the secrets of the region's famed culinary heritage.

Tuscany in northern Italy is known and loved for its hilltop towns, its artistic and cultural legacy, its wines … and its food. Local signature dishes include hearty game stews suffused with truffles and wild herbs, *bistecca alla fiorentina* (steak seasoned with oil and rosemary, then cooked over a charcoal fire), and richly flavored vegetable soups, notably *ribollita* (literally, "reboiled")—an unlikely masterpiece of recycling, traditionally made with leftover minestrone and stale bread. In Tuscany bread, more than pasta, is the staple, including the flat focaccia and *schiacciata* breads. And in a landscape studded with olive groves, olive oil is everywhere. Badia a Coltibuono and Tenuta di Capezzana are two family-run estates, where you can immerse yourself in this tradition in spectacular surroundings. High in the forested Chianti hills of central Tuscany, Coltibuono is a former monastery, where Benedictine monks first planted vines nearly a thousand years ago. In the 1980s, cookbook writer Lorenza de' Medici—from the family that once ruled Tuscany and wife of the estate's owner—started offering courses there. Capezzana lies farther north, on the slopes of Montalbano, where vines and olives have been cultivated for 1,200 years. You sense that ancient tradition all around as you learn to cook dishes such as *pappardelle alla lepre* (hare stew) and what wines to serve with them. Make sure to sample Capezzana's *vin santo* (holy wine), a dessert wine matured in cherry-wood, oak, and chestnut barrels in the estate's *vinsantaia*.

When to Go Courses at Badia a Coltibuono run from May through October, lasting one day, three days, or a week. Tenuta di Capezzana offers one- or five-day courses on selected dates from March through October. Be sure to book well ahead for either.

Planning The cities of Florence, Lucca, and Siena are fairly close to both estates. From Badia a Coltibuono, visit the market town of Greve in Chianti and the lovely medieval hilltop towns of Radda and Castellina. From Tenuta di Capezzana, the resort towns of Viareggio and Forte dei Marmi on the Versilia coast are worth a visit.

Websites www.coltibuono.com, www.capezzana.it

Poverty Crostini
Crostini di Povertà

Rich in culture and history, Tuscany was also for centuries a region of comparative material poverty—and evidence of that poverty is still there in its cuisine. Nothing could be wasted, not even stale bread. In this version of the traditional crostini canapés, stale bread soaked in wine is used to make a delicious topping.

Serves 4
2 slices/1 3/4 oz/50 g stale bread, without the crust
1 1/4 cups/10 fl oz/300 ml dry white wine
1/3 cup/1 3/4 oz/50 g capers, rinsed
1 tsp chopped parsley
1 tsp tomato paste (puree)
1/3 cup/3 1/2 fl oz/100 ml extra virgin olive oil
4 slices of ciabatta bread

Put the stale bread and wine in a bowl, and let the bread soak for 5 minutes. Take the soaked bread and gently squeeze out any excess wine. Pour off the wine, and put the bread back in the bowl. Add the capers, and drizzle the olive oil into the mixture, whisking constantly. Add the tomato paste and parsley, and mix thoroughly. Toast the ciabatta slices, and spread the bread mixture over it.

Opposite: Capezzana's chef demonstrates the art of making crostini. Above: A farmhouse in the rolling Tuscan countryside

COOKERY SCHOOLS IN ITALY

The locations are glorious, and the cuisine is exceptionally rich and varied. Up and down the Italian peninsula, schools teach you how to cook traditional dishes the authentic local way.

❶ Villa Giona, Verona, Veneto

Lodged in the splendor of the 16th-century Villa Giona, you learn how to make dishes such as fresh tortelloni filled with Swiss chard and ricotta. Writer Giuliano Hazan gives the cookery instruction, while Marilisa Allegrini of the nearby Allegrini winery teaches you about Italy's wine regions. Also included are tours of dairies producing Parmigiano-Reggiano cheese.

Planning One-week courses are held four to five times a year. www.villagiona.it

❷ Divina Cucina, Florence, Tuscany

A Florentine resident with more than 20 years of professional cookery experience, American Judy Witts Francini gives classes for up to six people, guaranteeing a hands-on experience for all. Menus change with the seasons, inspired by the offerings at Florence's Mercato Centrale, steps away from Francini's apartment.

Planning Classes are offered year-round. www.divinacucina.com

❸ Cucina con Vista, Bagno a Ripoli, Tuscany

After a decade running the kitchen at La Baraonda restaurant in Florence, Elena Mattei opened her school in a farmhouse in the hills southeast of the city. Students learn how to make classic regional fare—"grandmother's cooking"—including chicken-liver pâté on toast and meatballs with tomato sauce. Guided tours of Florence's Sant'Ambrogio market and wine tours through Chianti are popular field trips.

Planning Cucina con Vista (Kitchen with a View) offers one- to four-day programs year-round. www.cucinaconvista.it

❹ Villa San Michele, Fiesole, Tuscany

Housed in a 15th-century former Franciscan monastery, the Villa San Michele School of Cookery offers classes given by professional chefs from Italy's Orient-Express hotels. Sessions cover pastas, risottos, soups, and other Italian staples, with an emphasis on the Tuscan tradition.

Planning Classes are run from April through October. There is a program for children aged 8-14. www.villasanmichele.com

❺ Alla Madonna del Piatto, Assisi, Umbria

Every lesson with the husband and wife duo, Letizia and Ruurd Mattiacci, begins with a shopping trip to the nearby village of Santa Maria degli Angeli. The focus of their classes, given in their farmhouse bed and breakfast north of Assisi, is Umbrian and Sicilian food, such as ravioli, fettuccine, and cantaloupe melon mousse. Seasonal vegetables and herbs come from their garden.

Planning The Mattiaccis run classes twice a week on weekdays, from mid-March through December. www.incampagna.com

❻ Fontana del Papa, Tolfa, Lazio

In their 16th-century farmhouse north of Rome, Assuntina Antonacci and her husband Claudio host courses where you experience Italy through its cuisine in a home setting. As well as teaching you how to prepare pasta, gnocchi, saltimbocca, and calzone, the Antonaccis lead hikes through the countryside so you can sample local edible flora. All courses include wine and olive-oil tastings—the olive oils are produced on the property.

Planning Classes run year-round. www.cookitaly.it

❼ Diane Seed's Roman Kitchen, Rome, Lazio

British-born cookbook author Diane Seed has lived in Rome for 30 years. You will leave her classes—given in her home in the Doria Pamphili Palace—with a wide repertoire of Roman recipes, including deep-fried zucchini flowers in yeast batter, *panna cotta*, and pork with fennel and orange. Trips to the market in the nearby Campo dei Fiori bring seasonality to the menu.

Planning Seed gives classes year-round, except August. She is famous for incorporating Roman history into her talks. www.dianeseed.com

❽ Mamma Agata, Ravello, Campania

Amato "Mamma" Agata teaches cooking in her cliff-side home, situated 1,000 ft (300 m) above the Gulf of Salerno with majestic views along the Amalfi Coast. Day-long courses include a three-hour cookery session, where you learn home-style southern dishes. Mamma's cherished specialties include lemon cake and *limoncello*, using organic lemons from her garden.

Planning Classes are offered year-round. www.mammaagata.com

❾ Savoring Sardinia, Orosei, Sardinia

In the seaside village of Orosei on Sardinia's east coast, chef Maria Chessa teaches you the secrets of island dishes, such as seafood risotto and fish ravioli. You tour vineyards and visit a baker making *pane carasau*—thin, crisp, double-baked bread, traditionally eaten by Sardinian shepherds. Lodging is provided in a family-run bed and breakfast, which also has an outstanding restaurant.

Planning Courses last four or seven days, from September through May. www.ciaolaura.com

❿ Casa Vecchie, Vallelunga, Sicily

On her family's wine estate and farm near Palermo, cookbook author Anna Tasca Lanza teaches you how to prepare Sicilian sauces and specialties, such as caponata and pasta with sardines. You shop at markets in the village of Vallelunga, tour the family winery, and observe shepherds making local cheeses.

Planning One-, two-, three-, and five-day classes are available September-November and March-May. www.absoluteitalia.com

Right: The fruits and products of southern Italy's sun-drenched landscape are on display outside a shop on the spectacular Amalfi Coast, south of Naples.

EATING WITH FLORENTINES

When in Florence, eat where and how the Florentines eat, and discover the delights of the authentic local cuisine.

Lexicographers have never satisfactorily explained how the Italian word for a chubby straw-covered wine bottle—*fiasco*—came also to mean a failure or flop. Food- and wine-lovers can ignore such niceties. After viewing the glories of Florence's Duomo (cathedral) and the ancient Baptistery of San Giovanni, where better to refresh yourself than in a *fiaschetteria* (a wine shop and bar, selling a few warm dishes) in Piazza dell'Olio a block away? Here, in the friendly Fiaschetteria Nuvoli, you can enjoy a steaming plate of *ribollita* (hearty vegetable soup), *pappa al pomodoro* (tomato and bread soup), or *trippa alla fiorentina* (tripe stew), all washed down with hearty red Sangiovese. The experience is typical of the pleasures to be found in numerous unpretentious eating stops in Florence, as in any Italian city. To track down such places, first venture into side streets off the main tourist routes. Look for an establishment where the decor is unassuming and customers eat at a long bar table standing up or sitting on stools. Avoid menu boards announcing "specials" in four languages—instead, look for a scrap of brown paper on the door listing in handwriting four or five rigorously traditional dishes of the day. Want something even faster and more flavorful? Let your nose guide you to the nearest *trippaio*, a tiny shop or street cart serving *trippa*. Besides the great-value food, whose ingredients are often sourced directly from Tuscan farmers, there is another reason to choose these places: you can eat with the locals, from taxi drivers to lawyers, art students to bank clerks, and get a real taste of how Florentines live, cook, and eat.

When to Go Year-round, except August when most local restaurants are closed. Many also shut on Sundays.

Planning Good hunting grounds for small restaurants include Via dei Cimatori, Via dei Macci, Via dei Neri, and around Cappelle Medicee. Prepare for crowds at lunchtime and during *aperitivo* (the Italian "Happy Hour", the two hours after office hours are finished).

Websites www.theflorentine.net, www.firenzeturismo.it, www.faithwillinger.com

Street Tripe

Classic **trippa alla fiorentina** has a stew-like consistency—strips of tripe (the inside lining of a cow's stomach), cooked with onions, celery, carrots, tomatoes, and extra-virgin olive oil.

For centuries Florence and Rome contended for the title of *capitale della trippa*—tripe capital. In the end, Florence took the lead with its one-of-a-kind institution: the *trippaio*. Steel kiosks have mostly replaced the colorful wooden carts of old, but vendors remain jovial and proud of keeping alive this street tradition.

Pair your trippa with a robust red wine. Or try a *lampredotto*, a juicier type of tripe, inside a bun. Add garlic and parsley sauce and have a bite: you are taking part in an authentic Florentine ritual.

Florence's Duomo and Baptistery create an almost theatrical backdrop as diners enjoy the pleasant warmth of a summer's evening.

Attention to detail is a hallmark of Le Cordon Bleu. Here, an instructor scrutinizes the offerings of one of his students.

FRANCE

Le Cordon Bleu de Paris

Anyone, not just would-be master chefs, can enroll at the world's most famous food institution, Le Cordon Bleu Académie d'Art Culinaire.

Housed in a quiet street on Paris's Left Bank, Le Cordon Bleu is to haute cuisine what the fashion houses of the Faubourg Saint-Honoré are to haute couture. And here, in the temple of classic French cookery, some of the world's most highly qualified chefs offer one- to four-day courses for food enthusiasts wanting to improve their skills in a range of areas, from cooking meat to preparing patisserie. Classes—conducted in French, with an assistant giving an English translation—take place in specially equipped kitchens, starting with a demonstration, followed by hands-on practice using top-quality ingredients. During the demonstration, overhead mirrors allow you to observe the chef's techniques more closely. It is all part of Le Cordon Bleu's long-standing mission to share its expertise. Founded in 1895, the school was named for the blue cordon, or ribbon, once worn by knights of the Order of the Holy Spirit, known for their lavish feasts. It was the world's first cooking school to organize public demonstrations, and that tradition continues in its program of short courses. You can take classes in creating appetizers, terrines, or crêpes, or perfect your technique in the art of making sauces, bread, or chocolates. While for professionals Le Cordon Bleu holds out the coveted accolade of its Grand Diplôme, for amateurs it offers the chance of learning to flambé, sauté, or make the perfect soufflé in the world's supreme center of culinary excellence.

When to Go Any time of year. Most classes and demonstrations are on weekdays.

Planning The short courses are restricted to 10-15 participants, so book at least a month in advance. Or opt for a gourmet workshop, lasting two or three hours, where you learn how to make a particular appetizer or a main course and dessert. Le Cordon Bleu International also runs courses in some 20 countries worldwide.

Websites www.cordonbleu.edu, www.epiculinary.com

Ambassadress for French Cuisine

One of Le Cordon Bleu's best-known graduates, cookbook writer and TV chef **Julia Child** (1912-2004) first encountered French cuisine when her husband was assigned to the U.S. Embassy in Paris after World War II. It was the start of a life-long passion—"an opening up of the soul and spirit." She enrolled at Le Cordon Bleu, earning its Grand Diplôme despite differences with the director. Her first TV series, **The French Chef**, opened in 1963. At 6 ft 2 in (1.9 m) tall, Child was a commanding, idiosyncratic presence who went on to win a massive following as she introduced U.S. audiences to French culinary skills, from the basics of how to cook an omelet to the refinements of making fresh lemon sorbet. She died in her native California, aged 91.

THE ORIGINAL AND STILL THE BEST

Many dishes and drinks are of unknown or disputed origin; others wield a birth certificate.
Here are a few that you can savor in the places where they became famous.

❶ Bananas Foster, New Orleans, Louisiana

Prepared at the table, this dish of bananas sautéed in butter, brown sugar, cinnamon, and banana liqueur, then flambéed in rum, and served over vanilla ice cream, is as much theater as dessert. Chef Paul Blangé created it at Brennan's Restaurant in 1951; founder Owen Brennan named it for his friend Richard Foster.

Planning Brennan's is at 417 Royal Street in New Orleans's French Quarter. www.brennansneworleans.com

❷ Singapore Sling, Singapore

The first person to serve this long fruit cocktail was Raffles Hotel barman Ngiam Tong Boon around 1910. The sling fuses gin, cherry brandy, Cointreau, Bénédictine, grenadine, a dash of bitters, and pineapple and lime juice, garnished with a cherry and a pineapple slice. Its rosy hue initially made it a ladies' drink, but gentlemen soon acquiesced. Many consider sling-sipping in Raffles's colonial-era Long Bar crucial to a Singaporean sojourn.

Planning Raffles Hotel is at 1 Beach Road (MRT: City Hall). Singapore Airlines serves Singapore slings free in all classes. www.raffles.com

❸ Darjeeling Tea, Darjeeling, India

Shoulder-high to the Eastern Himalaya, the lush countryside around the colonial-era hill station of Darjeeling is tea-growing—and visual—nirvana. Darjeeling is the champagne of teas, whose delicate black leaves regularly fetch record prices. To understand its production, where better to lodge than luxury accommodations on the working Glenburn Tea Estate?

Planning For the dreamiest approach, travel on the Darjeeling Himalayan Railway. The growing season spans March through November. www.glenburnteaestate.com

❹ Bellini Cocktail, Venice, Italy

Near Venice's Piazza San Marco, perennially popular Harry's Bar gave birth to the Bellini cocktail, a fragrant fusion of prosecco and white-peach puree. Barman Giuseppe Cipriani invented it here in 1934, and Italian restaurants swiftly globalized it.

Planning For a less touristy experience, try Harry's quieter sister bar, Harry's Dolci, on Giudecca Island. www.cipriani.com

❺ Parma Ham, Parma, Italy

Production of dry-cured Parma ham is restricted to a rural pocket around the city of Parma in northern Italy. It requires but four ingredients: legs of specially bred pigs; small amounts of salt to preserve it; air to dry it; and patience—at least 400 days. The ham's slightly nutty taste derives from the whey of Parmesan cheese, another local delicacy, fed to the pigs.

Planning Parma Golosa organizes gourmet tours of producers. www.prosciuttodiparma.com, www.parmagolosa.it

❻ Tarte Tatin, Lamotte-Beuvron, France

Made of caramelized dessert apples tucked into puff pastry, this upside-down tart was the accidental invention of sisters Stéphanie and Caroline Tatin—owners of the Hôtel Tatin in the village of Lamotte-Beuvron, central France. They first made the tart in 1898, its fame spread, and it soon joined the menu at Maxim's in Paris.

Planning The Hôtel-Restaurant Tatin still exists and still serves tarte Tatin. www.france-tourism.chambordcountry.com, www.tarte-tatin.com

❼ Peach Melba, London, England

A Covent Garden performance by soprano Nellie Melba one night in 1892 or 1893 inspired this confection of peach, vanilla ice cream, and raspberry sauce. Her singing so impressed Auguste Escoffier, the illustrious chef at the Thames-side Savoy Hotel, that he fashioned the dessert in her honor.

Planning Customers of the Savoy benefit from a $140-million restoration of the legendary hotel, completed in autumn 2009. www.fairmont.com

❽ Banoffi Pie, Jevington, England

Banoffi's birthplace is the Hungry Monk, a pub lying among the South Downs in southern England. The pub's owner, Nigel Mackenzie, and chef, Ian Dowding, concocted the dessert in 1972. Originally named Banoffee for "banana" and "toffee," it comprises toffee—condensed milk boiled in the can—on a shortcrust flan base, topped with whipped cream, bananas, and ground coffee.

Planning Work up an appetite with a hike along the scenic South Downs Way, which passes through Jevington. www.hungrymonk.co.uk

❾ Cheddar Cheese, Cheddar, England

Mass manufacturers of plasticky horrors wallow in Cheddar's lack of controlled appellation, as the brand is not restricted to one region or recipe. Using traditional methods with unpasteurized milk, the Cheddar Gorge Cheese Company is the only cheese-maker in this Somerset village, beneath England's largest gorge, that still makes the genuine "farmhouse" article.

Planning The plant opens daily, with guided tours from Easter through October. www.cheddargorgecheeseco.co.uk

❿ Eccles Cake, Salford, England

The exact origins of this flat, currant-filled puff-pastry cake—sometimes affectionately known as "dead-fly pie"—are murky, but it first scored commercial success around 1790 at James Birch's shop in Eccles, now part of Salford, northwestern England. Trading briskly, it fast became a favorite British teatime treat.

Planning In Eccles, Martins Bakery sells the cakes and Smiths Restaurant serves them with tea. www.martinsbakery.co.uk, www.smithsrestaurant.net

Right: Cheddar cheese is traditionally sold in cloth-bound "truckles," weighing about 5 lb (2.3 kg), as here at a dairy near Evercreech, Somerset.

Traditional Farmhouse
Cheddar

FRANCE

Flavors of Provence

The Lubéron in central Provence is famous for its hilltop villages, bucolic landscape, and the sun-soaked flavors of its cuisine.

On a summer's afternoon, take a terrace seat at the Café de France in the hilltop village of Lacoste. As you look out over peaceful farms, vineyards, and woods to the neighboring hilltown of Bonnieux, take a sniff of the warm air, heavy with the intoxicating perfumes of Provence: wild herbs intermingled with lavender, rose, and honeysuckle, and perhaps a dash of ripe melons or drying figs. Explore the local markets (*marchés paysans*), and your senses will be overpowered by the aromas of vine-ripe tomatoes (the "apple of love"), pungent basil, clusters of garlic, bouquets of freshly picked wildflowers, *boules* of goat cheese, and containers of olives from local farmers who have harvested their crops at the zenith of ripeness. The many restaurants of the region reflect this bounty. Garlic, olive oil, olives, basil, and the abundant *herbes de Provence*—a varying combination of thyme, fennel, rosemary, chervil, summer savory, and oregano, sometimes with orange peel and lavender added—are used to flavor meat, poultry, game, and vegetable dishes. Depending on the season (and your mood), you might be drawn to omelette with truffles and tomatoes; *pistou*, a vegetable soup garnished with a paste made from basil, garlic, and olive oil; rabbit or chicken sautéed with olives and white wine; or daube, cubed beef braised in red wine with garlic, vegetables, and herbes de Provence. Whatever you choose, you know it will be fresh.

When to Go May and June are best, when tourists are few and temperatures warm. Summer is hot, with lavender blooming late June through late July. September and October feature the *vendange* (grape harvest). Winter can be cool, but offers the olive harvest, from mid-November through early January.

Planning To learn the secrets of the local cuisine, book a Made In Lubéron cookery class with chef and restauranteur Philippe Debord. You can choose between a morning class with lunch or an evening class with dinner. Most towns and villages hold a weekly market. Some of the best are in Apt, Bonnieux, Lacoste, Roussillon, Sault, and Vaison-la-Romaine. Arrive early as the stalls pack up by noon. Most items are grown locally—look for the *du pays* sign.

Websites www.madeinluberon.com, www.visitprovence.com, www.beyond.fr, www.provenceweb.fr

Herb-roasted almonds
Amandes grillées aux herbes

In spring, almond blossom sprinkles the hills of Lubéron, and in fall comes the harvest. Roasted with herbes de Provence, almonds make a delicious aperitif to be enjoyed with, say, a delicate Côtes du Lubéron rosé. Soaking the almonds in water before roasting softens their thin brown skins so that the seasoning is absorbed better.

Serves 8
2 cups/10½ oz/300 g almonds
  in their skins
⅔cup/¾ oz/20 g dried herbes
  de Provence, or mixed herbs,
  such as rosemary, basil, bay
  leaf, and thyme
2 tsp salt and freshly ground
  black pepper

Place the almonds in a large bowl, cover with cold water, and let stand for 20 minutes. Drain the almonds and add the salt, black pepper, and herbes de Provence. Mix well, and let stand for an hour.
  Heat the oven to 400°F/ 180°C/Gas Mark 4. Cover the bottom of a large baking sheet with parchment (baking) paper. Spread the seasoned almonds evenly over the paper. Roast for 15–20 minutes until the almonds are dry and crisp. Take from the oven and let the almonds cool before serving.

Opposite: A food shop in the picturesque village of Les Baux-de-Provence. Above: Eggplants are a staple of Provençal cuisine.

EATING IN ANDALUSIA

Arab influence lingers in the cuisine of Spain's southernmost region, creating unexpected combinations of flavor.

Andalusia's culinary canon draws heavily on the North African and Arabic legacy bequeathed by nearly eight centuries of Muslim Moorish rule (A.D. 711–1492). The Moors were skilled agriculturalists, who introduced rice, spinach, chard, semolina (for couscous), eggplant, sugar, saffron, and citrus fruits into the cuisine of Al-Andalus—the Muslim-ruled parts of the Iberian Peninsula—while cumin seed, coriander, fennel, rosemary, nutmeg, and cinnamon became staple herbs and spices used in the preparation of food. Visiting Andalusia today, you encounter Arabic aromas wherever you eat—in combinations such as garbanzos (chickpeas) and spinach laced with cumin seed and paprika, or in counterpoints of salt and sweet, including partridges with dates and *cordero a la miel* (honeyed roast lamb). In Seville, try *boquerones en adobo* (anchovies with cumin). In Córdoba, you can sample classic *alboronía* (eggplant, zucchini, and peppers), and in Ronda a memorable *ajo blanco* (a cold soup of crushed almonds, garlic, and olive oil). In Granada, Bar Los Diamantes offers nonpareil *calamares* (cuttlefish) deep-fried with a hint of cumin. Casa Bigote in Sanlúcar de Barrameda is known for its bitter orange sauce served with fish from the Guadalquivir estuary. And if you want to make such dishes for yourself, there is a range of cookery schools to teach you.

When to Go October through May are the best months to enjoy Andalusia without the stifling summer heat.

Planning Sam and Jeannie Chesterton run Spanish cookery courses at their Finca Buen Vino, set amid mountain cork and chestnut forests in western Andalusia. Or you can try Casa Ana in Las Alpujarras, a historic mountain region southeast of Granada. Companies offering cookery courses, as well as food and wine tours, include A Taste of Spain and Epicurean Ways.

Websites www.andalucia.com, www.fincabuenvino.com, www.casa-ana.com, www.atasteofspain.com, www.epicureanways.com

Three Courses

The three-course meal has its origins in ninth-century **Córdoba**, then capital of a powerful Muslim emirate. The man credited with inventing it was the emir's chief musician, called **Ziryab** (Blackbird) because of his dark complexion and beautiful singing voice. Trained at the sophisticated court of Baghdad, Ziryab became an arbiter of taste in Córdoba. At the table, he is said to have introduced crystal rather than metal drinking goblets. He also organized the way food was served, devising a sequence in which soups came first, then meat and fish dishes, and finally sweets, fruits, and nuts. From Córdoba, the fashion spread to the rest of Al-Andalus—and Europe.

As well as their culinary heritage, the Moorish rulers of Al-Andalus left such marvels as Granada's Alhambra.

Students at Rick Stein's Seafood School enjoy the fruits of their morning's labors, washed down with white wine.

ENGLAND

SEAFOOD IN PADSTOW

A picturesque fishing port in southwestern England makes the perfect setting for a course in cooking seafood.

One of Britain's best-loved chefs, Rick Stein set up his acclaimed Seafood School in the town of Padstow, Cornwall, to increase people's confidence in cooking fish and seafood in a laid-back atmosphere. Amid tastings and discussions, you learn basic fish preparation and cooking techniques, as well as how to make dishes as diverse as *risotto nero* and Thai seafood curry. The common denominator is sparklingly fresh fish. Classes tend to revolve around lunch, and when the morning's tuition is over you eat what you cooked with a bottle of wine. If this seems too much like hard work, there are three Rick Stein fish restaurants in town to choose from. The Seafood Restaurant, overlooking Padstow's harbor and its fleet of brightly colored fishing boats, offers a range of melt-in-the-mouth fish and seafood combinations, including Stein specialties, such as oysters *charentaise*—a combination of ice-cold raw oysters and hot, spicy sausages. For a more informal setting, Rick Stein's Café serves anything from a snack to a three-course meal, and Stein's Fish & Chips is a superior version of the classic British "chippie," where as well as cod and chips you can eat in or take out squid and monkfish tails.

When to Go Avoid summer weekends and the weekends of public holidays because of the crowds.
Planning Most courses last one or two days, but for serious fish-lovers there is a five-week evening course in the spring. While in the area, visit the village of Rock, lying just across the Camel estuary to the east. Often dubbed "Britain's St-Tropez," Rock has become a playground for the rich, partly due to its glorious sandy beach. Aside from stunning holiday homes to look at, it has chic boutiques and a few upscale restaurants.
Websites www.rickstein.com, www.visitcornwall.com, www.thepicturehouse.eu

Crispy Sea Bass

Rick Stein has inspired young chefs across Britain to create recipes such as this one from The Picture House in Bristol.

Serves 2
2 sea bass fillets, 6 oz/175 g each
2 tbsp corn oil
Salt and pepper
4 tbsp olive oil
Juice of half a lemon
2 tbsp dill, finely chopped
1 tbsp capers

Rinse the fish and pat dry with paper towels. Season with salt and pepper on the flesh side and liberally with salt on the skin side.

Over a medium-high heat, heat the corn oil in a frying pan large enough for both fillets. It should be hot but not smoking.

Place the fillets in the pan skin side down. Cook until the skin is crisp and golden and the top opaque. For thicker fillets, turn when the skin is crisp and cook for 2–3 minutes. Be careful not to burn the skin. Remove to a warmed plate.

Add the olive oil and capers; fry until crisp. Add lemon juice and dill. Swirl and pour over the fish. Serve with new potatoes.

Learn to cook scallops to perfection.

MODERN MOROCCAN

In an exquisite hotel in the central Moroccan city of Marrakech, learn to make classic local dishes with a contemporary twist.

Subtle blends of 30 or more spices and herbs are the key to Moroccan cuisine, and herbs are where your morning's session at the Jnane Tamsna hotel starts. In Arabic, *jnane* means "garden of paradise," which is what it feels like as Bahija, the hotel chef, leads you through Jnane Tamsna's beautiful gardens, where herb and vegetable plots are mingled with flowerbeds, olive and lemon groves, and date palms. Meryanne Loum-Martin, a former Parisian lawyer, created the hotel with her U.S. ethnobotanist husband, Gary Martin. "I love mixing influences in food and taking Moroccan cuisine a little bit further in the exploration of spices and herbs," she explains. Bahija, your teacher, shares this philosophy. From the garden, she takes you to the kitchen—weather permitting, the hotel's outdoor kitchen with a traditional clay bread oven—where she sets you to work with chopping knives. You roast and grind cinnamon, cumin, and other vital ingredients, and Bahija imparts the secrets of how to use them in dishes such as chicken *tagine* (stew) with roasted vegetables, *b'stilla* (a savory pastry), and apple *briouat* (another pastry). But with Bahija, nothing is quite what tradition dictates. The normal filling for b'stilla is young pigeon; she achieves a lighter touch with fish and preserved lemons. She also gives you tips on how to recreate these dishes at home, such as using spring roll dough in place of the thin layers of Moroccan *warka* for pastries. When the class is over, you retire to the garden for drinks before sitting down to the lunch you helped prepare.

When to Go Jnane Tamsna is open year-round, but June through September can be uncomfortably hot.

Planning No food-lover will want to miss the food and spice shops of Marrakech's *medina* (old city) or the market stalls in the Djemaa el-Fna (main square). Located outside the medina, in the oasis-like Palmeraie district, Jnane Tamsna is based on the traditional *ryad* (courtyard house) style. When not cooking or eating, you can swim in one of five pools, enjoy a massage, relax with a yoga or reflexology session, or play tennis.

Websites www.jnane.com, www.visitmorocco.com

Preserved Lemons

Preserved lemons will keep for up to a year. Use their juice to flavor salad dressings, soups, or meat, fish, or chicken sauces.

5 lemons
¹⁄₄ cup/2 oz/55 g salt
1 tbsp olive oil
1 cinnamon stick
3 cloves
6 coriander seeds
4 black peppercorns
2 bay leaves

Quarter the lemons nearly to the bottom, sprinkle salt on the exposed flesh, and reshape the fruit. Pack the lemons into a sterilized jar in layers, with the salt, olive oil, and spices between the layers. Press the lemons to release their juices, adding freshly squeezed lemon juice to cover them. Seal the jar and let stand in a warm place for 30 days, shaking the jar every day.

The snow-clad peaks of the Atlas Mountains form the backdrop for a view across the beautiful Menara gardens, west of Marrakech.

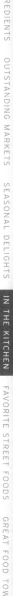

Customers line up to buy fresh ginger and other essential Cape Malay ingredients in a Bo-Kaap spice store.

SOUTH AFRICA

Cape Malay in Bo-Kaap

A historic district of central Cape Town has produced its own distinctive East-meets-West fusion cuisine, Cape Malay.

Walk down cobbled streets as the *muezzin* starts the call to noonday prayer. Men in white robes and fezzes stream past you; shrouded women herd children home from school, and the aroma of spice-rich meals wafts through kitchen windows. This is Bo-Kaap ("on top of the Cape" in Afrikaans), home to Cape Malay cuisine. Freed Malaysian and Indonesian slaves settled here in the 1830s, creating a cooking style that mingles local ingredients and Eastern flavors in a heady mix. Stop at a café on Rose Street for a mug of *faloodah*, a rose-scented milk and tapioca drink. Following the fragrance of cinnamon, cardamom, and ginger may lead you to Atlas Trading, a family-run store where boxes of henna jostle for space with coconut oil and white cardamom. In restaurants such as Biesmiellah or Bo-Kaap Kombuis—with panoramic views of Table Mountain—you dine with locals, sampling classic Cape Malay dishes, including *bobotie*, *denningvleis*, and *smoorsnoek*. And no visit is complete without a *koeksuster* pastry. If this has whetted your appetite and you want to learn more about the local food, operators Anduela offer day tours of the Bo-Kaap that include a Cape Malay cookery demonstration and workshop.

When to Go Flights around Christmas and New Year (mid-summer) are expensive, but you can experience the Cape Minstrel Carnival on January 1 and 2, when hundreds of brightly costumed, banjo-playing minstrels parade through the streets of Bo-Kaap and other parts of Cape Town.

Planning Anduela's day tours start at the Bo-Kaap Museum for an introduction to the area. You then take a guided walk around the neighborhood. As well as the cookery workshop, two meals are included. If you really want to get a feel for the district, Rose Lodge at 28 Rose Street offers bed and breakfast accommodations.

Websites www.cape-town.org, www.andulela.com, www.biesmiellah.co.za, www.rosestreet28.com

Cape Malay Dishes

■ *Denningvleis* is a hearty sweet-sour lamb cutlet stew, flavored with tamarind and served with saffron rice, almonds, and raisins.

■ Minced meat and sultanas are the core ingredients of *bobotie*. This gently spiced but complex dish is baked with a savory custard topping and traditionally served with turmeric rice.

■ Snoek is a full-flavored local game fish, often smoked. It is stewed with potatoes, chopped tomatoes, cloves, and almonds to make *smoorsnoek*.

■ *Koeksusters* are doughnut-like fried pastries, dipped in a cardamom- and ginger-spiced syrup and desiccated coconut.

FAVORITE STREET FOODS

The adventure begins with an alluring aroma of smoke and spices, or the glimpse of unfamiliar delicacies arrayed on a vendor's stall. Exploring the byways of a foreign city or simply playing tourist in your hometown, you come upon a trader doing a roaring business among locals, offering an irresistible choice of traditional dishes and exotic snacks. Certain locations are so famous for their street food that the gourmet traveler scarcely needs another reason to visit. Singapore's clusters of food stalls have become destinations in their own right, luring the grazer with mouthwatering specialties drawn from the range of Asian cuisine—noodles, charcoal-grilled meat, and savory pancakes partnered with curries. Sometimes, a single specialty turns into a symbol of a place: Fish and chips— when deep-fried to golden perfection—are as evocative of a trip to England as a visit to the Tower of London. Chili dogs in Los Angeles, tropical fruit shakes in the Mexican port of Veracruz, jerk pork in Jamaica—the variety of these and many other street offerings tells its own delicious story.

No costly kitchen gear for these Vietnamese street vendors—a pole with a panier hanging at either end to carry ingredients and a few cooking utensils is all they need. Thus armed, they will create *banh khoai* pancakes and other delights.

Hot dog carts are a New York emblem. The dogs and pretzels are hot, the drinks cold.

NEW YORK

New York's Sidewalk Chefs

Who needs smart restaurants when street carts and stands offer some of New York's most exciting and least expensive dining?

The city that never sleeps needs to be able to refuel quickly, so the streets of New York are home to a legion of trucks, vans, stands, and pushcarts all selling food. Most of the vendors are immigrants bringing street versions of the world's multifarious culinary traditions to this already international metropolis. You can snack on Jamaican goat patties, sample Chinese *cheung fun* (broad rice noodles wrapped around a savory meat, seafood, or vegetable filling), take a bite of Egyptian falafel, or enjoy vegan Sri Lankan curry and *dosas* (rice and lentil pancakes). New York takes its street food so seriously that there is an annual award ceremony, the Vendy Awards, for the best sidewalk chefs. Part of the fun is tracking down the best offerings. Trucks and vans often visit different areas of New York on different days; some chefs operate only at certain times of day or only on weekends. Even stalls with regular spots and hours occasionally vanish, as the owner finds a better spot or takes a week off. Follow the crowds, or ask locals for information—hotel doormen and concierges will often let you into the secrets of a neighborhood's best vendors.

When to Go New York's summers are hot and steamy, and its winters can be very cold. The best times to visit the city are in spring and fall, when you can eat your street food without either wilting in the heat or freezing your fingers.

Planning As well as asking people to recommend good street food, you can check the website of the Street Vendor Project for a list of the finalists in last year's Vendy Awards. This tells you where and when they can usually be found.

Websites www.streetvendor.org, www.myspace.com/arepalady, www.halloberlinrestaurant.com

Wurst and Arepas

■ For an authentic German sausage cart, head for 54th Street in Manhattan. Near the Fifth Avenue crosswalk you will find **Hallo Berlin**, offering some of New York's best wurst. Brothers Rolf and Wolfgang Babiel have been running the cart for a quarter of a century. Try the Democracy Special— your choice of wurst with sautéed potatoes, sauerkraut, and homemade sauces. If you want to enjoy your wurst and beer sitting down, the Babiels also operate beer garden restaurants.

■ Crisp, mouth-melting Colombian corn puffs, called *arepas*, are the specialty of the **Arepa Lady**, a regular winner of the Vendy Awards. Based in the borough of Queens, she operates only in the warmer months after 10 p.m. on Fridays and Saturdays ... the Fridays and Saturdays when she feels like it, that is. You would think this was bad for business, but customers flock from Manhattan in arepa-craving droves whenever she is around. Check her MySpace page to find out where she is.

The ever-popular pretzel arrived with 19th-century German immigrants.

PENNSYLVANIA

PHILLY SANDWICHES

Sink your teeth into Philadelphia's famous two-fisted sandwiches in their gritty urban birthplace.

For paradise on a bun—a cheese steak, garlicky roast pork, or a hoagie—ground zero lies in the old Italian row-house neighborhoods of South Philadelphia, where long, crusty rolls brimming with meat come with an extra side of "atty-tude." The cheese steak—essentially, shaved beef grilled with cheese and onions—inspires the most passion, launching long lines from window-service palaces clad in steel and neon. Crowds gather at Ninth Street and Passyunk Avenue, where the sandwich's inventor, Pat's King of Steaks, duels every day with rival, Geno's. But locals have ceded these titans to the tourists, opting for establishments in the deeper reaches of industrial South Philly—such as John's Roast Pork and Tony Luke's, both close to the Delaware River. Here, the sandwiches groan with heftier portions of meat and molten rivers of sharp provolone. John's and Tony Luke's are also prime spots for juice-drenched pork sandwiches, served with garlicky greens and spicy "long hots" (chilies). The hoagie has its roots among 19th-century Italian street vendors called "hokey-pokey" men, who sold "pinafore" rolls filled with antipasto salads. The best can be found in South Philadelphia's corner delis, such as Lombardi's, Cosmi's, and Ricci Bros., where the cold cuts fall directly from the slicer onto rolls fresh from nearby bakeries.

When to Go For weather, the best months are March through May and September through November. The first week of July brings the Philadelphia Freedom Festival, with fireworks, parades, concerts, and other events commemorating the Declaration of Independence, signed in Philadelphia in 1776.

Planning Ninth Street and Washington Avenue also embrace Philadelphia's Mexican and Vietnamese communities. At La Lupe, 1201 South Ninth Street, try the slow-roasted Mexican *barbacoa* lamb wrapped inside freshly pressed tortillas. On Washington, Vietnamese *pho* soup halls vie with restaurants such as Nam Phuong, where you eat off platters laden with spring rolls, "broken" rice, and meat cooked with lemongrass.

Websites www.gophila.com, www.phillyitalianmarket.com

The Italian Market

The awning-fringed sidewalks of **Ninth Street** near **Washington Avenue** are home to South Philadelphia's Italian Market, one of the oldest continuously operating open-air street markets in the U.S. Here, a century-old roster of Italian merchants offers mouthwatering medleys at a variety of food stalls and stores. Make your choice among hundreds of cheeses, salamis, and olive oils at import stores, such as **Di Bruno Bros.** and **Claudio's. Fiorella's, Cappuccio's,** and **D'Angelo's** are old-school butchers, tempting you with sausages and house-cured wild boar prosciutto. For fresh pasta, try **Superior Ravioli** or **Talluto's.** Finish your shopping spree at a pastry shop, such as **Isgro's,** with fresh cannoli piped full of sweetened ricotta cheese.

On East Oregon Avenue, Tony Luke's proclaims itself in multihued neon splendor as home of the real Philly sandwich.

KANSAS CITY BBQ

World capital of barbecue, Kansas City was built on meat, and barbecued meat is still its gastronomic passion.

People wait in line by a gas station on the corner of 47th Avenue and Mission Road. They are not after fuel for their vehicles but fuel for their persons—the kind of fuel that includes a carryout "full slab" of barbecued pork ribs (enough for two or three hungry diners), slices of hot or cold beef brisket by the pound, or a "pig salad" of warm pulled pork. This is Oklahoma Joe's BBQ, one of the most popular of Kansas City's hundred or so barbecue eateries. The phenomenon that is Kansas City barbecue dates to around 1908, when African-American chef Henry Perry started slow-cooking pork ribs over hickory and oak, slapping on a tangy sauce of tomatoes, chilies, and molasses—and serving it all on newsprint for 25 cents a pop. In a city that had grown rich from its railhead, livestock exchange, and meatpacking plants, meat was king—something to be relished in as many different ways as possible, from "burnt ends" (savory tidbits from the end of a smoked beef or pork brisket) to Henry Perry's barbecue magic. Add a touch of jazz and blues glamor—Count Basie, Big Joe Turner, and Charlie Parker were all barbecue enthusiasts—and the Kansas City barbecue was ready for elevation to heavenly status. While chefs since Perry's time have added their own secret ingredients, the basic barbecue sauce and cooking method have remained much the same.

When to Go Fall offers clear skies and moderate temperatures, as well as the American Royal Barbecue competition. Summer brings tornados and triple-digit temperatures, but this is also when numerous barbecue competitions take place, including the Great Lenexa Barbecue Battle and the Laurie Hillbilly BBQ.

Planning The two holy grails of Kansas City barbecue are on Brooklyn Avenue—Arthur Bryant's and Gates & Sons, both direct heirs of Henry Perry's legacy. Among those who have feasted on Bryant's brisket and ribs are U.S. Presidents Truman, Carter, and Reagan. Gates & Sons has other branches around town.

Websites www.visitkc.com, www.kcbs.us, www.americanroyal.com

World Series of Barbecue

In October, barbecue cooks from around the world descend on Kansas City for the **American Royal Barbecue** competition. Launched in 1980, this self-proclaimed "World Series of Barbecue" pits some 600 teams against each other in five categories: **chicken**, **pork ribs**, **beef brisket**, **pork shoulder**, and **sausage**. The four-day cook-off is the climax of KC's barbecue season and the opening blast of the American Royal rodeo, horse show, and livestock extravaganza, held in the city's Kemper Arena. Those aiming for Grand Champion must barbecue in all categories, except sausage. Winners are not always full-time cooks—the first was a psychiatrist. Running alongside the main event are side-dish and dessert competitions. And the best news: members of the public can feast on barbecued delights at vendor stalls.

Racks of slow-cooked pork ribs, chilies, tomatoes, corn, garlic, and a horn-handled knife ... the ingredients are assembled for a real KC barbecue.

The city lights up as dusk falls across downtown L.A. and the San Gabriel Mountains.

CALIFORNIA

L.A. Fast Food Tour

Los Angeles is known for its trendy restaurants with health-conscious menus, but Angelenos enjoy their fast food, too.

Pink's is probably the world's only hot dog stand with a parking attendant. You are in Hollywood, after all, and that limo pulled up alongside may belong to a star—when Aretha Franklin arrived in town for the Grammy Awards in February 2008, her first stop was at Pink's to order eight hot dogs to take back to her hotel. Specialties of the stand, which opened in 1939, include its trademark chili dog (with mustard, chili, and onions), the 10-inch (25 centimeter) stretch chili dog, and the chili cheese dog. Go in, place your order, and watch your dog being built before your eyes. Then top it off with a bottle of YooHoo or Orange Crush soda. Still craving chili? The Original Tommy's World Famous Hamburgers, which started in 1946 as a small walk-up stand on the corner of Beverly and Rampart, has several locations across L.A., all serving chili-slathered hamburgers and cheeseburgers (single-, double-, and triple-burger versions), chili cheese fries, regular fries, tamales, hot dogs, and chili dogs. Want music as you eat? Fatburger, The Last Great Hamburger Stand is now scattered across several U.S. states, but the original Fatburger is in L.A. Jukeboxes blast out everything from rock 'n' roll to soul to R&B as you choose from a classic fast-food menu that includes homemade onion rings.

When to Go October through early June are the best months weather-wise. February brings even more stars than usual for the awards shows—the Academy Awards (Oscars) and the Grammy Awards.

Planning Pink's opens at 9:30 a.m. and stays open until 2 a.m., Sundays through Thursdays, and until 3 a.m. on Fridays and Saturdays. Original Tommy's has most of its restaurants in northern Los Angeles, some open 24 hours. Fatburger has several locations in L.A.—you can order online. Philippe's, a block away from Union Station, is open 6 a.m. to 10 p.m. daily.

Websites www.pinkshollywood.com, www.originaltommys.com, www.fatburger.com, www.philippes.com

Philippe's: Home of the French Dip Sandwich

Philippe's is unique in L.A., a place where patrons share tables with strangers and make use of any available seat. In business for more than 90 years, Philippe's clings to its original ambience with sawdust on the floor, servers that keep the food line moving, and vintage photos and newspaper clippings. Its specialty—**beef, ham, pork,** and **lamb French dip sandwiches**—started with a mistake when the restaurant's founder, Philippe Mathieu, accidentally dropped a French roll into a pan of hot roasting fat. The result was so delicious that customers came back for more. The menu includes other sandwiches, soups and stews, salads, and more esoteric items, such as pickled pigs' feet. Philippe's even has a wine list.

Brilliant tropical colors match the spicy hot seasoning on offer at a "jerk center" on Jamaica's north shore.

JAMAICA

JERK PORK IN BOSTON BAY

The equivalent of about $2 buys you the best meal in Jamaica—a slab of jerk pork wrapped in butcher paper.

Jamaica's biggest waves roll ashore in Boston Bay on the island's northeastern shore, where the scent of sea mingles with the aroma of jerk pork from open-air stalls along the coast road. According to local legend, the jungle-shrouded John Crow Mountains rising to the south are where Jamaican jerk cooking originated among 17th- and 18th-century Maroons (escaped slaves), who roasted wild boar over pimento-wood fires. Nowadays, in Boston Bay they jerk just about anything: pork, chicken, goat, lamb, even fresh fish—poached in aluminum foil over an open flame. Seasoned with allspice (called pimento in Jamaica), Scotch bonnet (a very hot chili pepper), scallions (with a stronger flavor than the ones you buy in the U.S.), thyme, garlic, nutmeg, cinnamon, and whatever else the chef decides to throw in, the meat nearly melts in your mouth. "It was started by the Maroons," says Devon Atkinson, chief cook and *saucier* at Mickey's Jerk Center in Boston Bay. "They used to dig a hole and put it underneath the earth. They put some bushes and pimento wood on top, then covered it." In modern times, the meat or fish is barbecued above ground, but little else has changed. Pimento wood and jerk sauce are still essential. "This is my secret recipe," says Devon, offering a taste on the end of a wooden spoon. "It comes from my grandfather and my great grandfather before that. We jerk the original way."

When to Go Jerk is a year-round treat in Jamaica and so is the tropical weather. Hurricanes occasionally hit the island between August and October, but otherwise the weather along the coast is nearly idyllic.

Planning Take home some bottled jerk sauce, sold at most of Boston Bay's roadside stalls. Although every recipe is slightly different, they are all delightfully piquant. Walkerswood Plantation, near Ocho Rios, bottles different jerk sauces and seasonings, available in hotels, shops, and supermarkets around Jamaica.

Websites www.visitjamaica.com, www.walkerswood.com

Jerk Sauce

2/3 cup/2 oz/55 g allspice berries
2–3 hot chili peppers, seeded
  and chopped
3 tbsp fresh thyme, chopped
5 cloves garlic, crushed
2–3 scallions (spring onions)
1 large bay leaf
1 1/2 tsp brown sugar
1 tsp fresh ginger, grated
1 tsp cinnamon, ground
1 tsp nutmeg, grated
2 tbsp lime juice or rum

Lightly toast the allspice, chilies, thyme, garlic, and scallions in a skillet (without oil), stirring constantly for 5 minutes. Transfer the toasted ingredients to a blender. Add the other ingredients and season with salt and freshly ground black pepper. Blend to a smooth paste, adding some water if necessary. Rub the paste into the meat and let stand for at least an hour before cooking.

AREPAS IN CARACAS

Feeling hungry in Venezuela? An *arepera* serving tasty cornmeal buns with a wealth of fillings is never hard to find.

All across the Venezuelan capital, Caracas, stalls and small restaurants serving piping hot *arepas* stay open throughout the humid tropical nights, catering to local crowds that never seem to dwindle. To Venezuelans, arepas are what bread is to people elsewhere in the world. Looking something like English muffins, they are delicious to eat and easy to make—precooked white cornstarch, water, and salt are the vital ingredients. Venezuelans have arepas for breakfast, as bar or café snacks during the day, with meals, or to fill that hungry hole in the stomach after a night clubbing. And as every good Venezuelan will tell you, arepas can be eaten in all kinds of ways. Once made, the dough is scooped into tennis-ball-sized spheres, then flattened between the palms of the hand into buns, which can be deep-fried, cooked on a *budare* (hot plate), baked, or simply made in an electric arepa-maker. After that, there is the question of the filling. You may just opt for a sliced arepa with butter. Alternatively, try a *reina pepiada*, with a chicken and avocado filling; or a *dominó*, with melted cheese and black beans, so that the inside looks like a domino; or an *arepa de carne mechada* (shredded beef), often served with cheese or a flavorsome tomato and vegetable sauce. If you want something sweet, ask for an *arepa dulce*, made with sugar instead of salt. Arepa in hand, make your way to a park, sit on a palm trunk, and watch a game of *bolas criollas*, the Venezuelan version of boules.

When to Go Venezuela is a year-round destination, but the best time to visit is during the dry season—September through April.

Planning In Caracas's bustling Sabana Grande district, combine shopping with a visit to the funky open-air Arepa 24 Horas on Avenida Casanova—open, like many other areperas, 24 hours a day. Arepas are not confined to the capital—they are popular throughout the country and in neighboring Colombia.

Websites www.venezuelatuya.com, www.southamerica.cl

Tastes of Venezuela

■ Served with everything from arepas to meat, **guasacaca** is Venezuela's version of Mexican guacamole—a spicy salsa made with avocados, chilies, onions, garlic, parsley, and cilantro.

■ Beef is boiled, then shredded—often by hand—and mixed with a black bean sauce to make the national dish, **pabellón criollo**. The meat is served with rice and fried plantain or fried eggs. During Lent, people sometimes use fish instead of beef.

■ **Cachapas** are corn pancakes, folded around a portion of one of the many soft, white, mozzarella-like Venezuelan cheeses. They are often eaten for breakfast.

From olives to cheese to hot chilies, the possible ingredients for arepa fillings are almost endless.

GLORIAS Y RASP
DIABLITOS DE FRUTAS NATURAL

MEXICO

VERACRUZ VARIETY

The street food in this Gulf Coast port city draws on an exotic mix of indigenous, Spanish, and Afro-Caribbean ingredients.

In the sultry climate of Veracruz, the best time to be outdoors is at night, when the air vibrates to the African-inspired rhythms of the ubiquitous *musica tropical*. And as you explore the waterfront or check out the nightlife around the main plaza, what better way to keep yourself going than with mouthwatering cold snacks—*licuados* (fruit shakes), *paletas* (frozen fruit bars), and countless kinds of *helado* (ice cream)? Since its founding by the conquistador, Hernán Cortés, in 1519, Veracruz has been Mexico's main eastern port and a major gastronomic crossroads. Olive oil and a panoply of Mediterranean herbs and spices arrived from the Old World to add new layers of flavor to native Central American ingredients, such as corn, chilies, and different kinds of bean. The local Totonac people were the first to cure vanilla beans for culinary use. Later arrivals included pineapples, sugarcane, peanuts, and the banana's savory cousin, the plantain. Today, this varied legacy is evident all around you. Puff pastry turnovers, called *bolovanes*, filled with a choice of crabmeat, tuna, or pineapple, tempt you from stalls along large thoroughfares. In the morning, freshly boiled shrimps straight from the docks set your taste buds dancing. Sample tamales wrapped in banana leaves, fried *tortitas* made from plantain dough filled with black beans, or thick corn tortillas, called *picaditas*, topped with salsa and cheese. And for a drink that packs a punch, try a *toro*—a milk shake laced with the local *aguardiente*, a potent sugarcane liquor.

When to Go The hot, humid climate makes fall and winter the best times to visit. Carnaval, the city's major celebration, is held during the week before Lent. If traveling in summer, try for July's Festival Internacional Afrocaribeño, a two-week celebration of African music and dance in the Americas.

Planning Spend an afternoon in the town of Boca del Río, south of Veracruz. Its seaside restaurants offer the region's best fish and shellfish, some flavored with the local herb, *acuyo*. Take a day to visit Papantla, north of the city, to see the pre-Hispanic site of El Tajín, buy vanilla beans, and watch the astonishing dance of the *voladores* (flyers), in which four men attached by ropes to a pole fly through the air.

Websites www.planetware.com, www.carnaval.com, www.mexconnect.com

Tropical Fruit Treats

Veracruz and the surrounding area are paradise for lovers of tropical fruit. Whether eaten fresh or enjoyed in the form of cold helados, paletas, or licuados, the fruits include many that are familiar—**mangoes**, **coconuts**, **papayas** (or pawpaws), and **pineapples**. Others may be a new experience.

■ About the size of a grapefruit, the **cherimoya** has a segmented green skin and succulent white flesh. The flavor is fragrant, with hints of strawberry. If you eat a cherimoya fresh, beware of the large black pits.

■ The **guanábana** (or soursop) is recognizable by its spiky green skin. The creamy white flesh is often pulped and used in licuados or helados.

■ The pink or orange flesh of the **mamey** has a sweet pumpkin-like flavor. Try it fresh, with a little lime juice squeezed over it.

■ A favorite in licuados, the **zapote blanco** looks a bit like a large plum. The flavor of its yellowish-white flesh is often compared to a combination of peaches and vanilla.

Opposite: Knock back a *diablito* (little devil), in which chili adds fire to a fruit shake. Above: Tamales in banana leaves

TAKOYAKI IN OSAKA

A spicy octopus mix cooked in batter provides a succulent street snack in the city often called Japan's food capital.

The chef's hand moves rapidly over a well-worn grill, using a chopstick to flick over the doughy contents of each golf-ball-sized *takoyaki*. As the mixture turns, a crispy casing forms on the outside of the balls, while the batter inside—thick with octopus chunks, pickled ginger, and cabbage—remains rich and creamy. Reaching for a thin cardboard tray, the chef piles it high with the freshly cooked takoyaki, adds a generous sprinkling of shaved fish flakes (*katsuobushi*), fine dried seaweed, and savory barbecue-style sauce, and passes it to a waiting patron. Surprisingly perhaps, Osaka's favorite street-side snack was born out of hardship in Japan—caused by food shortages in the aftermath, first, of a devastating earthquake in 1923 and, later, World War II. At these times, batter-based dishes, such as takoyaki, were popular because they were cheap, and by the time the country had recovered, the people of Osaka had developed a lasting fondness for them. These days, you will find stalls, shops, and restaurants serving takoyaki throughout the city, but if you want to enjoy the tasty octopus parcels while taking in the pulsing beat of Japan's second-largest conurbation, visit Dotonbori Street alongside the Dotomborigawa River. Here, flashing neon lights tower above you, while at ground level among a warren of bars and eateries takoyaki vendors ply their trade.

When to Go Year-round. If you go in early April, you will catch some of the cherry blossom festivals that take place around Osaka.

Planning Dotonbori Street is near Namba Station. To experience more of the local atmosphere, visit in the late afternoon or evening—and be prepared for crowds. Japan's street food is generally safe to eat, but go for the busy places with longer lines of Japanese people as these will be selling the best octopus. Also, especially if visiting in summer, check that the octopus is being kept cool and out of the sun.

Websites www.osaka-info.jp, www.japan-guide.com

Make Your Own

■ **Takamasa** in Dotonbori Street offers a "hands-on takoyaki experience," in which you cook your own takoyaki. Takamasa is one of Osaka's best-known takoyaki restaurants, with other branches across the city. Sample the *negi-takoyaki*, with leeks (*negi*) added to the batter mix.

■ *Tamagoyaki* (or *akashiyaki*) is a soggier alternative to takoyaki, in which the octopus balls are dipped in fish broth (*dashi*) before being served.

■ The cult of the takoyaki has earned the dish its own miniature theme park, the **Osaka Takoyaki Museum**. You learn about the history of the takoyaki and sample offerings prepared by some of the city's most popular takoyaki shops.

A headscarfed chef in Dotonbori Street pours the octopus batter over a special grooved grill used for making takoyaki.

Fresh vegetables combined with fish or seafood, then deep-fried, equals a perfect Seoul street snack.

KOREA

Fast Feasts in Korea

In Seoul and other South Korean cities, take your pick from a rich repertoire of street-cooked seafood and other delights.

Evening falls in Seoul, and as food vendors fire up their huge woks in brightly lit stalls, pungent aromas start floating through the city's back streets, transformed by the street chefs' lighting and tent-like canopies into giant walk-in food halls. For an outsider, the tubes, cubes, balls, and other deep-fried concoctions on offer may not seem immediately appetizing, but if you plunge in, the reward can be an outstanding food experience. For a delicious light snack, try *gimbap* (rice wrapped in seaweed) or *dwigim*, the Korean version of Japanese tempura, featuring seafood and vegetables deep-fried in batter. *Mandu* (dumplings) are popular, as are *odaeng* (fish cakes), especially in winter. Or you can sample the ubiquitous *dokbokki* (rice cakes), stir-fried with vegetables and served in a spicy sauce, sometimes wrapped in a sausage. There are several varieties of pancake—including *bindaetteok* (pancakes made with mung-bean flour)—and numerous forms of skewered meat. Dessert items include a Korean version of the waffle and *hotteok*, thick floury pastries with cinnamon fillings. Although most people eat these snacks on the spot, vendors will wrap them for you if requested, so you can take them to a quiet place to enjoy them at leisure.

When to Go Most street stalls set up around dusk and close around 11 p.m., although some stay open later on weekends. There are a few seasonal specialties, such as refreshing iced *bingsu* (concoctions of fruit and other ingredients) in summer and warming soups in Korea's frigid winters.

Planning Jongno, a major east-west thoroughfare, is a prime location for street food in central Seoul. Other good areas include Sinchon (around the university), the Myeong-dong shopping district, and around major railway stations. In the old alleyways of the Insa-dong district, you will find traditional Korean rice cakes (*tteok*) and a wide range of sweet cakes.

Websites www.visitkorea.or.kr, www.foodinkorea.org

Korean Dishes

■ Served with practically everything, Korea's most famous dish, **gimchi** (or *kimchi*) has a salty, spicy, pungent flavor, which can be an acquired taste for Westerners. To make it, cabbage and other vegetables are mixed with garlic, chili, and ginger, then left to ferment in an earthenware pot.

■ Other Korean mainstays include *gimbap* (Korean sushi), numerous varieties of soup (*guk*), *bulgogi* (barbecued beef), and **bi bim bap**—an all-in-one dish that includes boiled rice, gimchi, meat or seafood (or both), all topped with a fried egg and served in a weighty iron bowl.

SINGAPORE

SINGAPORE FUSION

In Singapore's "hawker" centers, you can sample one of the world's most diverse culinary cultures for little more than pocket change.

Three great traditions come together in Singaporean cuisine—Indian, Chinese, and Malay. And in the clusters of hawker stalls, officially called "food centers" or "food courts," that dot the island-state, you can join Singaporeans, from tycoons to taxi drivers, in their quest for the best of this rich diversity. Start with one of the city's most famous dishes—*roti prata* (literally, flatbread), a crisp Indian pancake served with lentil curry. If you are still hungry and in an Indian mood, add a *murtabak*, minced mutton and onions stuffed inside a prata pancake. The national dish, Hainanese chicken rice, is Chinese in origin and found at nearly every hawker stall—you sprinkle it with soy sauce, chilies, and ginger slices, according to taste. Chinese immigrants also brought *char kway teow*, large rice noodles fried in a wok with seafood and pork sausage. Among Malay dishes, *satay* is the best known—tender bits of chicken, mutton, beef, or seafood, cooked on wooden skewers over an open charcoal flame. You can eat the meat unadorned, or relish it with peanut sauce, cucumber, and onion. Fancy a rich seafood soup made with coconut milk and chili? Seek out another Malay offering—*laksa*. *Nasi padang*, a heady blend of curried meat, vegetables, and rice, has its origins in a slightly different direction—the nearby Indonesian island of Sumatra.

When to Go Singapore's balmy tropical climate is ideal for year-round outdoor eating. As nearly every food center is covered, the island's typical afternoon rains will not dampen your appetite. The Singapore Food Festival in July and August includes events at food centers.

Planning As a rule of thumb, you can tell how good a food center is by the number of luxury cars parked nearby. With the sidewalks nearly clean enough to eat off and a government obsessed with rules and regulations, Singapore's street food is as safe as you are likely to find anywhere in the world. Hawker centers are also ideal for watching the lively social intercourse that is an essential part of any Singaporean meal.

Websites www.visitsingapore.com, www.singaporefoodfestival.com.sg, www.laupasat.biz

Fast-food Centers

Singapore's **food centers** were established because of government concerns about the standards of hygiene among street hawkers. Although the centers are found throughout the island, a few are more celebrated than others, some for their food, others because of their outstanding locations.

■ **Newton Circus** is a horseshoe-shaped collection of more than 80 food stalls in the middle of a giant traffic circle on Clemenceau Avenue. Although open throughout the day, Newton is renowned as a late-night gathering place of taxi drivers and after-club eaters. Among its specialties are oyster omelets and popiah spring rolls.

■ Chili crab covered in a tangy red sauce and freshly steamed fish are among the specialties at **East Coast Lagoon Food Village** in the Bedok neighborhood between Changi Airport and downtown Singapore.

■ The multistory **Chinatown Complex Food Centre** on Smith Street may not offer much in the way of romantic ambience, but many locals swear by this place as the best collection of hawker stalls on the island.

■ **Lau Pa Sat Festival Market** offers typical Singapore hawker food in a Victorian-era market setting, beneath a filigree cast-iron roof manufactured in Scotland in 1894.

Opposite: A customer makes his choice at a Newton Circus stall. Above: A satay seller in East Coast Lagoon Food Village

Many of Beijing's most popular *xiao chi* (snack) restaurants have stalls at Jiu Men, so you can take your pick of the best.

CHINA

BEIJING'S BUDGET BITES

Rub elbows with locals, and fill up with a
banquet's worth of flavors for bargain prices.

Wangfujing Xiaochi Jie is Beijing's famous alley of snack stalls. Here, many a Western TV travel-show presenter has grinned bravely for the camera while trying exotic morsels, such as skewered scorpions. But these stalls are now strictly for the tourists. For something more authentic, head just opposite to the Gongmei Dasha Gourmet Food Street in the basement of the Artistic Mansion, where shoppers and office workers elbow each other for access to stalls collectively selling what amounts to a cheap culinary tour of China. To order, all you do is point to the snacks that take your fancy, from steamed stuffed buns and vinegary Shanxi pasta dishes to muttony dishes from China's Muslim northwest. Choose a Qingdao draft beer to wash it down, or perhaps a Taiwan-style fluorescent "bubble" tea, thick with suspended tapioca balls. Then take everything to a central group of long tables abuzz with office gossip, where shoppers scrutinize their neighbor's choices—you might make some local friends. For the best of Beijing's own snacks, visit Jiu Men Xiao Chi ("Nine Gates Snacks")—a rebuilt traditional courtyard house in the Houhai Lake area, where caged mynah birds greet you in Mandarin at the gate. Specialties include dumplings with assorted fillings, stews, noodles, stir-fried tofu, and toothsome sweets, such as candied haws and *ai wo wo*—balls of glutinous rice with a sweet bean paste filling.

When to Go Beijing's weather is best from April through mid-May and in September and October, but food courts are cozy on even the bitterest winter's day.

Planning Most food courts are open throughout the day until 9 or 10 p.m. They are at their busiest around noon and in the early evening on weekdays.

Websites www.shinkong-place.com, www.beijing2008.cn

Food Court Browsing

Food courts are the perfect place to sample dishes that are all too often unknown in Chinese restaurants overseas. If you want to combine shopping with eating, try the food courts located in the basements or top floors of most department stores and shopping malls. Beijing's shiniest food court is in the marble-floored basement of **Shin Kong Place** in the Chaoyang district.

Most food courts operate a stored-value card system, with a minimum payment that includes a small deposit. Head for the cashiers' counter first, hand over at least ¥30 (around US$4), then offer your card to be swiped whenever you make a purchase. If your appetite is bigger than your credit, you can top up the card. Hand over the card when you leave to recover any outstanding balance and your deposit.

THAILAND

STREET CHOICE IN BANGKOK

Wherever you wander in the Thai capital's streets, tantalizing food aromas hijack you and set your taste buds tingling.

A fresh fragrance leads you to a stall selling fruit. Nearby is another stand selling *som tom* (green papaya salad), or skewered cuttlefish, or ice cream—with toppings that include corn, red beans, and candied pumpkin. A recent survey showed that Bangkok has around 20,000 street vendors selling 213 different kinds of food. It is impossible to recommend any specific stall or cart. Few of them have menus, at least in English, so you just have to know what you want (and the Thai name for it) or peer at the ingredients to surmise what is on offer. Want curry on rice? Stir-fried pork? Noodles with beef or seafood in gravy (called *radna*)? Or perhaps something more sophisticated, such as noodles fried with dried shrimp, tofu, bean sprouts, almonds, and herbs (*pad Thai*)? Shuffle up to the cart of your choice, place an order, and watch the cook bend over the wok like the conductor of an orchestra. The ingredients sputter and sizzle in a gossamer of steam, and within minutes you are handed a heaping plate. Pull up a plastic chair and prepare to feast. You will find stands nearly everywhere in the city, but some of the best selections are in clusters off Silom Road, especially along Soi Convent, and on Samsen Road Soi 2, where the stalls stay open all night. The price for a typical plateful is 20 to 50 baht (50 cents to $1.40), and 5 baht (15 cents) gets you an extra *piset* (helping).

When to Go The best time to visit Thailand is November through February, during the dry, cool season, when almost every day is sunny and temperatures average 85–95°F (29–35°C).

Planning There are even more stalls and carts out by night than during the day. If you are concerned about sanitary conditions, Thailand's Department of Health has developed a ten-step code of practice for street vendors, and regular inspections by field officers take place in some areas. In general, frequent stalls where lines are long, because the food is turned over more quickly.

Websites www.tourismthailand.org, www.thaistreetfood.com

Thai noodles on a bed of banana leaves

Noodles & More

■ Noodles are the most common kind of Thai street food, and there are many different kinds to choose from. They include chicken noodles, duck noodles, egg noodles with wanton, and **yen ta four** (noodles in red soy-bean paste with fish balls, squid, and morning glory).

■ Made-to-order food stalls whip up whatever you want, such as **pad kaprao** (stir-fried meat with holy basil leaves), **kai jiaow** (Thai-style omelet), **moo kratium prik Thai** (stir-fried pork in garlic and pepper), and **moo daeng** (red barbecued pork). Rice dishes include **kaao laad kaeng** (curry on rice) and **kaao pad** (fried rice).

With her ingredients and equipment neatly arranged around her, a Bangkok street vendor prepares a feast.

Unusual Food and Drink Festivals

From eels to melons, rattlesnakes to cabbages, no food is too weird or too humble to have a festival in its honor. Many celebrations include parades, cook-offs, competitions, and races.

1 Rattlesnake Roundup, Sweetwater, TX

This rattlesnake rodeo is held every second weekend in March. The four-day festival includes snake-handling demonstrations, a rattlesnake-cooking contest, and a rattlesnake-eating race. Stalls sell fried adder meat, resembling chicken in flavor and alligator in texture, alongside serpentine by-products.

Planning Served by Greyhound bus, Sweetwater is 223 miles (359 km) west of Dallas or 412 miles (663 km) east of El Paso by road. www.rattlesnakeroundup.net, www.sweetwatertexas.org

2 Watermelon Thump, Luling, TX

Originally a frontier cowboy outpost, Luling achieved 19th-century notoriety as "the toughest town in Texas." It is calmer now, but Luling still eschews table manners during this four-day thump, encompassing a seed-spitting contest, with a cash prize for anyone who beats the 1989 world record—68.77 ft (20.96 m)—and a watermelon-scoffing contest.

Planning The thump falls on the last Thursday through Sunday in June. Luling is 59 miles (95 km) northeast of San Antonio by road. Nearby Austin hosts a tongue-in-cheek Spam celebration, the Spamarama, around April Fools' Day. www.watermelonthump.com

3 World Championship BBQ, Memphis, TN

Probably the world's largest hog roast, encompassing some 200 teams, 90,000 spectators, and prize money exceeding $60,000, this three-day cook-off attracts some serious competition; many teams have big-name sponsors. Less seriously, there is also a porcine-themed Ms. Piggie drag show.

Planning Held at Tom Lee Park, the contest occupies a weekend during the Memphis in May International Festival. www.memphisinmay.org

4 Ice Cream Expo, Yokohama, Japan

The Japanese savor unexpected flavors at this two-week annual ice cream celebration. Past ingredients include beef tongue—a 2008 bestseller—caviar, Indian curry, cheese, crab, pit viper, octopus, prawn, raw horse, eel, and oysters.

Planning Held at the Red Brick Warehouse on bay front in Yokohama, south of Tokyo, the annual expo has no fixed dates. www.city.yokohama.jp

5 Cabbage Festival, Vecsés, Hungary

This small town next to Budapest Ferihegy airport lies in the heart of cabbage-growing territory, and its inhabitants enjoy nationwide renown for their purportedly health-giving sauerkraut. Vecsés' brassica bash attracts some 20,000 visitors with cook-offs, food stalls, folk music, and a cabbage-themed pageant.

Planning The one-day festival occurs in October. Vecsés is 25 minutes by train from Budapest Nyugati station. www.hungarytourism.hu

6 Pourcailhade, Trie-sur-Baïse, France

Held in the town of Trie-sur-Baïse in southwest France since 1975, this celebration of everything porcine takes place in one of France's biggest pig-rearing districts, and includes a piglet race, pig-costume contest, a pig-imitation competition, and charcuterie shopping at France's last dedicated pork market.

Planning The festival falls on the second Sunday in August. Trie-sur-Baïse is 20 miles (32 km) northeast of Tarbes, capital of the Haute-Pyrénées department. www.bigorre.org

7 Xicolatada, Palau-de-Cerdagne, France

August 15 has long been a wine-fueled festival in this Pyrenean village near Andorra, and for 300 years villagers in need of a hangover cure next morning have drunk hot chocolate (*xicolatada*) served from giant cauldrons in the village center. Today, the villagers are joined by numerous tourists. The 11 a.m. pick-me-up is made by a guild of master chocolatiers from a secret recipe.

Planning You can reach Palau-de-Cerdagne by the narrow-gauge Train Jaune (Yellow Train) linking La Tour du Carol with Villefranche-de-Conflent; the nearest station is Bourg-Madame. www.midi-france.info

8 Fête des Fromages, Rocamadour, France

This medieval village in the Lot area of southwest France holds a vast annual cheese festival enticing some 50 artisan producers. Attractions include a pungent cheese market, music, and a wine-lubricated dinner dance. Pride of place goes to the village's eponymous cheese, which is made with unpasteurized goat's milk and often eaten very young on toasted walnut bread.

Planning Rocamadour is south of the market town of Brive-la-Gaillarde. The two-day festival spans a weekend in late May. www.rocamadour.net

9 Eel Day, Ely, England

Although eels give rise to its name, this small Cambridgeshire city has but one commercial catcher still in business. Held annually since 2004, the festival starts with a parade led by Ellie the Eel, a giant replica made by local schoolchildren. Chances to sample smoked and jellied eels abound.

Planning The festival is on a Saturday at the end of April/early May. Look out for smoked eel at Ely's farmers' market, held every second and fourth Saturday monthly. www.eastcambs.gov.uk

10 Chili Fiesta, West Dean Gardens, England

Visitors to the fiesta, held in the gardens of West Dean center for arts, crafts, and rural studies, can learn about chili cultivation in the Victorian glasshouses and sample around 300 chili varieties at some 100 stalls.

Planning The ticket-only, two-day festival spans an August weekend. West Dean is north of the city of Chichester. www.westdean.org.uk

Right: A 220-lb (100 kg) ice cream cake decorated with fruit is one of many attractions at the Yokohama ice cream expo.

Vendors in Kota Baharu's night market serve local specialties from pushcarts that operate as portable kitchens.

MALAYSIA

Kota Baharu

Dine under the stars on some of Malaysia's best street food in this small city in the northeast of the country.

Amid steaming woks and smoking charcoal braziers, food hawkers at the *pasar malam* (night market) of Kota Baharu, state capital of Kelantan, quickly boil, baste, grill, and stir-fry a delectable array of ingredients to prepare traditional dishes influenced by the mingling of Indian, Chinese, Thai, and other cultures in the state. A man making *murtabaks*, a type of Indian crepe, flings a piece of dough on a hot grill, spreading it evenly with one hand to the thinness of parchment. Filling it with minced chicken, chopped onions, and eggs, he neatly folds over the sides before flipping and cooking it to a golden brown. Nearby a young girl carefully fans the smoldering coals with a palm leaf as her mother, with a baby balanced on one hip, deftly turns bamboo skewers of sizzling beef satays marinated in a peppery sauce of chilies and fiery spices. At other food stalls in the crowded market, vendors sell *ayam percik* (Malay-style spicy barbecue chicken), beef *rendang* (spiced coconut beef), *sambal udang* (spicy prawns), and fish and lamb curries. A glass of *teh tarik* ("stretched" tea, made with black tea and condensed milk and poured back and forth between two mugs from a height until it cools and froths), tempers the heat of the Kelantanese street food.

When to Go Any time of year, although spring and fall are the wet seasons, with brief daily rains.

Planning There are daily flights to Kota Baharu from Penang and Kuala Lumpur and good road and rail links with other cities. Vendors begin setting up their stalls around 5 p.m. The entire market shuts down at 7 p.m. for about 45 minutes for evening prayers, when everyone must vacate the premises, and then opens again until midnight or later. The market, located just off Jalan Pintu Pong close to Pasar Siti Khatijah (Central Market), is within walking distance of many hotels.

Websites www.tourism.gov.my, www.tic.kelantan.gov.my

Market Etiquette

Supper at a Malaysian street market is a leisurely, social affair and should be tackled one course at a time.

■ Select your first course and then take it to one of the many small tables scattered throughout the marketplace.

■ Although cutlery is usually available, it is customary to eat with your hands, using the teapot of cold water in the center of the table to wash before, during, and after eating. Muslims use only their right hand to eat.

■ When you are ready, wander back through the stalls and pick your next course, returning to a table to eat.

■ Each set of tables is usually attached to a drink stand, so wait for someone to come and take your order. No alcohol is served, but a wide array of fruit juices is available.

VIETNAMESE STREET FOOD

There is no better way to sample Vietnam's diverse cuisine than at the stalls and carts of its many street vendors.

I f you want to know what the Vietnamese eat, look no farther than the street, as cooking and eating in the open is a way of life—shored up by an army of cart-pushing, yoke-carrying, bicycle- and motorcycle-riding vendors selling an unimaginable array of snacks and meals, sweets and drinks. Here a woman serves *bo pia* (spring rolls stuffed with Chinese sausage) to customers seated on low plastic stools; there another stuffs grilled pork, carrot and *daikon* (radish) pickle, and pâté and cilantro sprigs into a crackly-crusted baguette (a holdover from French colonial rule) for *bánh mì*. Amid the displays of fish, meat, and produce in the market in coastal Hôi An, a vendor squats by a charcoal brazier cooking *banh khoai*—crispy pancakes folded around bean sprouts, belly pork, and shrimp—in long-handled crepe pans; another serves *ngo bap* (a breakfast dish of hominy mixed with black beans, chopped peanuts, ground sesame seeds, sugar, and caramelized shallots) from behind a counter. And on Hanoi's streets, holes-in-the-wall offering *bia hoi* (draught beer) sit cheek-by-jowl with others serving Vietnam's national dish, *pho* (beef and noodle soup), and lesser-known northern specialties like *bun rieu*, rice noodles in a rich crab broth, and *bánh cuôn*, steamed rice-flour pancakes rolled around chopped pork and wood ear mushrooms, crowned with sweet caramelized shallots, and served with slivered Thai basil and fish. Faced with such abundance, where do you start? The answer is: anywhere. In Vietnam, if it looks too good to pass up, it probably is.

When to Go December through February are relatively dry in the south, cooler and sometimes rainy in the middle, and damp and chilly in the north. The wet season starts in earnest in June; avoid the flood-prone months of September through November.

Planning Vietnamese street food is a seven-day-a-week, 24-hour-a-day phenomenon, though you will find the most variety from dawn through lunch and in the early after-work hours.

Websites www.spirithouse.com.au, www.luxurytravelvietnam.com, www.vietworldkitchen.typepad.com

A street vendor selling French loaves

Market Tips

Vietnamese **wet (fresh food) markets** offer the best opportunities to try a variety of street foods in one place. All but the tiniest have a food court of permanent stalls selling everything from steaming noodle soups to fruit juices and shaved ice desserts called **che**.

Head for the most crowded stall, or the one that appears to be making the most deliveries to other vendors at the market (watch for women carrying trays of the stall's specialty).

It is acceptable to order by pointing at what someone else is eating. Prices are rarely posted, so ask before sitting down to eat. And if hygiene is a concern, stick to hot dishes like noodle soups.

Some street-food sellers provide low stools so that customers can sit down to eat.

INDIA

Chaat in Mumbai

On the way home from work or school, at the beach or in the park, Mumbaians snack on the city's famous street foods.

The sidewalks of Mumbai, India's largest and busiest city and its financial capital, are captivating places. Pick your way between the pavement dentists, the ear-cleaning men, the shoe-shiners, and street barbers, and you will find a huge variety of sweet and savory nibbles (*chaat*) on sale at roadside stalls and carts. Salty and crunchy, sweet and sour, chaats are made from fried chickpeas, puffed rice, ginger, or potato patties topped with yogurt, onion, and spices. Looking for a quick and tasty meal, some of Bollywood's biggest stars are regularly spotted among the evening crowds that accumulate around the best stalls. Popular ballads have been written about the city's street food—your only challenge is choosing from the hundreds of delicately spiced snacks on offer. *Bhelpuri*—a mixture of crisp puffed rice, spiced potato, *sev* (crunchy gram-flour fragments), onions, fresh herbs, chutney, and lime, all to be scooped into the mouth with your fingers or a piece of flaky bread—is king of Mumbai street snacks, every bite slightly different, and is especially popular at the city's Chowpatty Beach. *Vada*, a highly spiced potato dumpling served on a piece of bread with chutney, is a staple food for the city's workforce. Need to refresh? Try a *lassi*. This yogurt drink is available sweetened or with a pinch of salt—amazingly good at cooling down a mouth on fire from all those chilies!

When to Go If you are planning on eating plenty of street food, avoid the monsoon season between July and September, when there are a lot of flies in the city.

Planning Chaat stalls and houses are dotted all over Mumbai, but the stalls at Chowpatty Beach are famous throughout India. There are clusters of stalls outside railroad stations and the city's colleges. To avoid an upset stomach, eat only from stalls where you can see the food being prepared and cooked in front of you. As always in India, avoid drinks containing ice and water that is not in a sealed bottle, and peel any fruit that you eat.

Website www.mumbai-masala.com/index.html

Mango Yogurt Drink
Mango Lassi

Lassi originated in the Punjab region of India. The traditional version is made with yogurt, water, salt, and spices, but sweetened fruit lassis have become very popular.

Serves 4
1 fresh mango or mango pulp
   (available canned)
3 cups/24 oz/675 g plain
   yogurt
1 cup/8 fl oz/225 g milk
1/2 cup/3 1/2 oz/100 g sugar
Crushed ice to serve
Ground cardamom

If you are using a fresh mango, slice it and remove the pit. Place the mango, yogurt, milk, sugar, and cardamom into a blender and blend until it is smooth, about 2 minutes.

   To serve, fill each glass about halfway with crushed ice and pour in the lassi. Sprinkle a little more cardamom on top.

   The lassi can be refrigerated for up to 24 hours.

Opposite: A vendor wheels his cart into place. Above: Bhelpuri is served with a variety of toppings.

Keep an eye out for wandering salesmen who set up makeshift stalls to sell their puchkas to passersby.

INDIA

PUCHKAS IN CALCUTTA

If you are feeling hungry, fill the gap with a few of these liquid-filled snacks that literally explode in the mouth.

Two disparate experiences collide when you visit the Victoria Memorial Hall and its adjoining gardens in the heart of Calcutta in northeast India. The palatial-looking marble memorial to Queen Victoria, "Empress of India," took 20 years to build and cost 10 million rupees by the time it was inaugurated in 1921. Across the road, the second delight, the *puchka*, holds its own. Unrivaled in its ability to astound the taste buds with its contrast of textures and flavors, this spicy street snack is the Calcutta-dweller's pride and is sold to passersby from stalls, carts, and trolleys all over the city. The vendor takes a crisp, hollow shell of deep-fried dough, or *puri*, makes a hole in it, and fills it with a pungent, sweet and sour, soupy liquid. This rather formidable snack, which should be downed in one mouthful, explodes as you bite into it, a feat that is tricky to perform without mishap, but it is worth the effort as a succession of flavors assault your taste buds. A usual order is five to eight puchkas, and the vendor fills and hands them to you one or two at a time. With practice, devotees find ways to keep pace with the puchka *walla's* (vendor's) quick dip-fill-and-hand-out routine, and contests develop to see who can down the most puchkas without taking a break.

When to Go Calcutta is best in winter—November through March—when the air is crisp and less sultry and humid than in summer.

Planning Flights from most Indian cities and many international destinations come regularly into Netaji Subhash Chandra Bose airport. Local transport is cheap (car rental for half a day costs about 400 rupees/$8). Have some small change on you for paying for street food. And don't miss a ride in the ramshackle trams that clang around the city's crowded streets.

Websites www.indianholiday.com, www.kolkata.org.uk

Puchka Fillings

Called *pani puri* in Mumbai and *gol goppa* in Delhi, puchkas are a favorite taste-bud tickler in many parts of India. The liquid filling is usually spiced with tamarind extract, boiled and strained dates, cumin, ground mint leaves, chili powder, coriander powder, black salt, and cinnamon. The mix differs marginally from region to region.

Once limited to being street food, puchkas have become fashionable and are a constant at wedding buffet tables these days, with iced spiced water, vodka, and other exotic fillings finding favor.

STREET FOOD IN ISRAEL

Among the wealth of street food available in
Jerusalem, drawn from many cuisines, the falafel is king.

Falafel wrapped in flatbread is a
favorite street food.

Thanks to a centuries-old Arab population, and the Jewish state's "ingathering of the exiles" from around the globe, contemporary Israel is where Mediterranean and Middle Eastern cuisines meet. Nowhere is this combination of flavors more easily accessible than in the street food of the city of Jerusalem. The Old City is home to Jaffar's Sweets, a long-established shop on Souk Khan es-Zeit (by the Damascus Gate), where *kanafeh*, neon-orange shreds of phyllo-like dough drenched in syrupy sugar water, and other Arab sweets are made daily. Other indigenous foods include *maqluba*, a casserole made from rice, sliced eggplant, sliced tomato, onion, cauliflower, and mountains of savory lamb or chicken. Hummus, a Middle Eastern staple, is best tasted in the alleyways of the Old City as well as at establishments like Lina and Abu Shukri, although New City blue-collar lunch counters, such as Ta'ami and Pinati, whip up a mean chickpea puree. And everywhere in between kiosks offer the quintessential Jerusalem street food, the deep-fried chickpea balls known the world over as falafel, sold wrapped in flatbread and served with a variety of toppings. Most of the city's falafel recipes yield moist, hot fritters green from cilantro and parsley, but Yemenite-style falafel vendors eschew the herbs for a purer, golden variety.

When to Go The winter festival of Hanukkah, and the harvest-themed Jewish holidays of the midspring and midfall, are magical times in Jerusalem, but the city can be very busy and prices spike. The same can be said of summer, when the weather can be oppressively hot.

Planning Allow a few days to explore the Old City. Other key landmarks in Jerusalem are the Yad Vashem Holocaust memorial, the Mount of Olives, and the Israel Museum. Day trips to the Dead Sea, Bethlehem and the wineries, and the goat-cheese farms and olive-oil presses of the Judean Hills can be arranged.

Websites www.jerusalemite.net, www.jerusalem.com, www.goisrael.com

Falafel Accompaniments

■ Falafel is wrapped in **laffa**. Also called *eish tanur* (oven flame) in Jerusalem, laffa is a large flatbread brought to Israel by Iraqi immigrants.

■ Variously colored cabbage, or **kruv**, is usually pickled and sometimes drenched in mayonnaise.

■ **Amba** is an Iraqi sauce made from cured mangoes with fenugreek and turmeric.

■ A paste of peppers, called **charif,** of Yemenite origin comes in red and green varieties. Its spiciness varies.

Although deep-fried in hot fat, good falafel is not greasy.

The streets of Sarajevo's Old Town are filled with outdoor restaurants, shops, and markets.

Snacking in Sarajevo

Sarajevo is full of shops selling delicious savory pies (**pita**) at all hours of the day. One of the most popular types is **burek**, made of thin layers of flaky pastry stuffed with meat and rolled into a coil, but there are numerous varieties. The range of fillings includes cheese (*sirnica*), cheese and spinach (*zeljanica*), pumpkin (*tikvinica*), and spicy potato (*krompirusa*).

Pies are sold by the slice or by weight. One of the most popular vendors is Bosna, on Bravadziluk Street.

BOSNIA AND HERZEGOVINA

CEVAPI IN SARAJEVO

Cevapi are the national dish of Bosnia, and the best place to enjoy them is in the Bosnian capital's Old Town.

If you wander the narrow, cobbled streets of Sarajevo's 15th-century Baščaršija, or historic Old Town, built during the Ottoman occupation, your senses will be assailed by the aroma coming from the area's many *cevadžnica*, or eateries specializing in *cevapi*. These small, succulent, spicy, mincemeat sausages are grilled over an open coal fire and served inside a soft, pita-like flatbread called *somun*. Cevapi were probably introduced to the region by the Ottomans, and in predominantly Muslim Bosnia they are made with beef or lamb or a mixture of the two. Typically, they are served with chopped raw onions, but you can also enjoy them accompanied with *kajmak*, an unripened cheese similar to clotted cream, or *ajvar*, a spicy sauce made from peppers, eggplants, garlic, and chili, washed down with *ayran*, a thin yogurt drink, or fruit juice. If you enjoy a hotter flavor, try *šis cevap*—sausages made from ground beef mixed with chilies before grilling. Among the best and most popular *cevadžnica* are Željo and its sister branch, Željo II, which are both located on Kundurdzi uk Street, just around the corner from the bazaar and the Gazi Husrev-Beg Mosque.

When to Go Anytime, but the best weather occurs May through September. There is an annual month-long festival in July called Baščaršija Nights, with free outdoor performances showcasing Bosnian music, theater, and dance. The internationally renowned Sarajevo Film Festival takes place every August.

Planning Allow two or three days to explore Sarajevo. It has a compact, easily walkable city center. The Old Town is a short taxi or tram ride from the main bus station, and the airport can be reached direct by taxi, or via tram or bus stations near the airport. You do not need to reserve restaurant tables in advance.

Websites www.sarajevo-tourism.com, www.sarajevo.ba, www.bascarsijskenoci.ba

BELGIUM

FRENCH FRIES IN GHENT

Experience french fries cooked to perfection in one of Europe's most beautiful cities.

Belgium is a nation of food-lovers schooled virtually from birth in the fine arts of good cooking, and they apply this fastidiousness to their street food as well. And the ultimate Belgian street food? Unquestionably it is the humble french fry—*frite* in French, *friet* or *frietje* in Dutch—cooked to perfection: sizzling hot, crispy on the outside, and served with a large dollop of mayonnaise. In the old Flemish university town of Ghent, head for the Vrijdagmarkt, the spacious market square in the historic city center. There you will find Frituur Jozef, a classic wooden *frietkot* (a semipermanent frying van) that has been serving fries since 1898. No corner-cutting here: The husband-and-wife team running the show peel and chop the potatoes themselves each morning. Their frietjes could be a meal in themselves, but Frituur Jozef also offers the traditional range of accompaniments, such as meatballs in tomato sauce, deep-fried sausages, and *stoofvlees* (a rich, sweetened stew of beef cooked in beer, otherwise known as *vlaamse karbonaden*) served with mustard. This is a frietkot to be treasured: traditional *friekoten*, once ubiquitous, are becoming rarer as traders fall to the pressures of commercialism.

When to Go Frituur Jozef is open for business Monday to Friday 11:30 a.m. to 10 p.m., Saturday 11:30 a.m. to 8 p.m., and Sunday 5 p.m. to 10 p.m. Any time of the year is a good time to visit. Ghent is pleasant in summer. In winter, it may be bitingly cold, but the low-angled sunlight gilds the spires, the canals are mirror-still, and the piping hot frietjes bring warmth and comfort.

Planning Ghent is one of the great Flemish cities, easily accessible by train from Brussels, or by motorway links from France, the Netherlands, and Germany. It has interesting churches and a number of good museums and art galleries. The cathedral has one of the great treasures of North European culture, "The Adoration of the Mystic Lamb," a multipaneled painting by Jan and Huybrecht van Eyck from the 15th century.

Websites www.frites.be, www.visitgent.be

The Perfect *Friet*

It has often been said that Belgian fries set the gold standard as the best in the world. Their quality rests on four essential factors, the most important of which is that they are double-fried.

Use an appropriate variety of starchy potato (Belgians prefer the locally produced **Bintje**).

Cut the potatoes to just the right size, about the size of a woman's little finger.

Fry them in clean, hot oil (traditionally, beef dripping was used) until soft, then remove them, and allow them to cool.

Fry them a second time until crisp and golden on the outside and soft inside.

Fries are sold all over Ghent, often in paper cones with a spoonful of mayonnaise.

HERRING IN THE HAGUE

Each spring a festival in the port of Scheveningen heralds the arrival of the new season's herring.

Met of zonder?" is the question. With or without—chopped raw onions. You are standing beneath the flapping awning and Dutch flags of a streetside van that advertises "*nieuwe haring*: new herring." "*Met*," you say, and over the counter comes a fillet of raw herring, complete with tail, laid on a polystyrene platter, along with a large spoonful of chopped onions. The herring is shiny, pearly silver, and pinkish, like a dawn sky over the North Sea. Pick up the herring by the tail, waggle it in the onion, then tip your head back, and lower the fillet straight into your mouth to savor its delicate oily freshness. The Dutch go wild for this snack, especially in summer, when the new season's herrings are young and tender. You can buy raw herrings at any time of the year from the specialist streetside stalls (*haringstalletjes*), found everywhere in the city, and even from the supermarkets, but as the year advances the herrings become fatter, larger, and greasier. Behind their counters, the fishmongers prepare the herrings with astonishing speed, working with short, hyper-sharp knives to skin and fillet the fish (they are gutted onboard the trawlers). They preserve the fillets by storing them in a light brine called *pekel* (from which our word "pickle" is derived). Some street vendors attract passersby with little more than a barrel of nieuwe haring in its pekel, and a container filled with chopped raw onion. "Met of zonder?"

When to Go Early June is best, and you might catch the arrival of the new season's herring; Vlaggetjesdag usually takes place on the second Saturday of June. The new herring season lasts about two months (June–July), but herring can be found year-round, and The Hague is an interesting place to visit in any season.

Planning The Hague is 30 miles (50 km) southeast of Amsterdam and 25 miles (40 km) southeast of Schiphol international airport. The port and seaside resort of Scheveningen is 3 miles (5 km) from the center of The Hague. The Hague is an elegant, vibrant city with good hotels, restaurants, museums, and shopping.

Websites www.denhaag.com, www.vlaggetjesdag.com

New-season Herring

Each year excitement mounts as June approaches. Any day, when the herring have grown to the optimum size and fat content, an official announcement will permit the sale of the first new season's herring—**de eerste vaatje Hollandse Nieuwe**. People flock to The Hague's port of Scheveningen to feast at the herring stalls, and the first barrel brought onshore is auctioned for a colossal sum—more than 50,000 euros (about $68,000 in recent years), which is donated to charity.

On the first Saturday of the season the festival known as **Vlaggetjesdag** (Little Flag, or Pennant, Day) is held in Scheveningen to celebrate the official arrival of the new herring. Boats are bedecked with flags and thousands of people gather to enjoy entertainment, exhibitions of maritime crafts, and seafood.

There is only one way to eat one of the raw herring fillets beloved by the Dutch–lean your head back and lower it in.

Newspaper wrapping is old news; most fish and chips are now served wrapped in plain white paper.

Pie and Mash Shops

Despite the name, the real claim to fame of pie and mash shops is the **eel, either jellied or stewed**. Bright green, jellied eels are served cold. Stewed eels come with mashed potatoes and liquor (parsley sauce) on the side. The less adventurous can enjoy a meat pie—traditionally filled with beef, but other varieties are available, too—with their mashed potato. **M. Manze**—which has three pie, mash, and eel shops—and a few other traditional pie and mash shops can still be found around south and east London. You can recognize them by their wooden benches, marble-topped tables, and tiled walls.

ENGLAND

FISH AND CHIPS

This popular pairing tastes best eaten outdoors in England's coastal towns with a bracing wind coming in off the sea.

Fish fried in a golden, crisp shell of batter and served alongside hand-cut, fried potato wedges has been a favorite meal of English workers since Victorian trawlermen first started bringing in cod from the North Sea, off England's northeast coast. Although this dish is available all over the country, it is often at its best in fish and chip shops (often called "chippies" by locals) in the north of England, where the busiest fishing ports are located and where southern suburban concerns about dietary fat fall by the wayside. The best of the northern chippies prepare their fish and chips in searingly hot beef dripping, the traditional cooking medium, which reaches temperatures so high that the fish cooks in moments, with a shatteringly crisp batter surrounding moist, flaky flesh. Traditionally, fish and chips are served with a cup of sweet, milky tea, a small dish of mushy peas (a savory pease pudding made from split, green marrowfat peas), and plenty of salt and malt vinegar sprinkled on the chips and battered fish. This dish has such powerful symbolism in England that, when he was in power, Prime Minister John Major took the time to advise people of the important fact that the vinegar should always be added before the salt.

When to Go Fish and chips is a year-round dish. The British climate is famously variable, but if you are seeking out northern chippies, the north of the country is often at its most beautiful and dramatic in the cold, glowering weather of winter.

Planning Something about the bracing air by the North Sea works on the appetite. All fish and chip shops offer takeout, usually wrapped in the traditional sheet of paper. Fish and chip shops come and go; to find the best, look up the winners of the Federation of Fish Friers annual Fish & Chip Shop of the Year award.

Websites www.federationoffishfriers.co.uk, www.clickfishandchips.co.uk, www.manze.co.uk

MOROCCO

Evening Food in Marrakech

Each evening the main square in this beautiful city in western Morocco turns into a large, lively, open-air restaurant.

As dusk falls on the busy Djemaa el Fna—the central square in the medina (old quarter) of Marrakech—men and boys laden with makeshift tables, stoves, pots, and pans appear from every direction, and in what seems a matter of minutes, tables and chairs are set up, pots are filled with liquid, braziers are lit, and the air is full of the aromas of spice-infused smoke, kebabs, fried fish, and hot bread … and so it begins. This is the evening food market—the most intense, and spectacular, culinary experience Morocco has to offer. Against a background of beating drums, clanging bells, snake-charmers, storytellers, fire-eaters, and magicians, you can eat some of the cheapest and freshest foods in the city. Walk around the market first; this is an experience in itself and will give you a chance to see what is on offer before deciding if, and where, you want to eat. If you are new to Moroccan food, try a stall offering a little of everything: tagines, couscous, kebabs, vegetables, and salads. If you know what you want, plenty of stalls specialize in one or two foods, such as strips of slow-cooked lamb with cumin and warm bread, *harira* (chickpea and lentil) soup, spicy merguez sausage, or kebabs. Feeling adventurous? You could sample tripe stew or boiled lamb's head. In this rose-colored city, where modern Moroccan cuisine is reaching new peaks of sophistication, the evening market is still the best and most varied eating experience around.

When to Go Any evening after 6 p.m. Morocco is best in the cooler months from September through May.

Planning Allow plenty of time to visit the square and the souks at its north end. It is always busy during the day, with orange-juice stalls, water-sellers in traditional costumes, and snake-charmers, and there are plenty of cafés where you can sit and watch the world go by—try the Café de France with its rooftop terrace overlooking the square. Allow three to four days to see the whole city and sample its fabulous restaurants. Try Riad Tamsna (23 Derb Zanka Daika) for lunch in a chic *riad* (traditional hotel). In the evenings, Le Foundouk (55 rue du Souk des Fassi) offers delicious French-Moroccan food; Dar Moha (81 rue Dar El Bacha) and Dar Yacout (79 rue Sidi Ahmed Soussiare) are two of Marrakech's greatest gourmet restaurants.

Websites www.morocco-travel.com, www.cadoganholidays.com, www.darmoha.ma

Tagine

A traditional Berber dish and a central feature of Moroccan cuisine, the tagine is a slow-cooked, deeply **aromatic stew** containing meat or fish with vegetables, or vegetables on their own.

The stew shares its name with the earthenware cooking vessel with a conical lid that it is normally cooked in. In traditional Moroccan homes, the vessel is placed over a charcoal stove, where the embers are continually added to, to disperse the heat evenly around the base of the dish. The ingredients are therefore cooked gently so that they remain beautifully tender and moist in a flavorful sauce that is slowly reduced.

Tagines are usually chicken- or lamb-based, and traditional versions are distinguished by their cooking fats and spices. Some are cooked in **butter** and **almonds**; some are flavored with **onions**, others with **ginger** and **saffron**. Preserved lemons are added to many versions.

Opposite: A street vendor in the Djemaa el Fna waits for customers. Above: Grilled kebabs are popular in the market.

6 GREAT FOOD TOWNS

What makes a truly great food town? Is it the range and variety of its restaurants? Its inhabitants' passion for their own local specialties? The creativity of its chefs? All of these factors play a part. A place may attract visitors because of its scenery, its historic landmarks, its street life, or the treasures in its museums. But the opportunities for good eating can prove to be as much, if not more, of a draw.

No food-lover needs a more alluring incentive to tour the American South beyond the chance to savor the Cajun delights of New Orleans or Charleston, South Carolina's legendary she-crab soup. Gastronomic pilgrims in search of authenticity will comb the backstreets of Naples for the definitive Italian pizza or tour the medieval cities of southwestern France to assess their rival versions of the mighty cassoulet. Seafood-lovers may be hard-pressed to choose between the glorious crustaceans of Sydney, Australia, and the exuberantly spiced and curried seafoods of Goa, India. On such journeys as these, unfortunately, three meals a day may never be quite enough.

New restaurants have burgeoned all along the south bank of London's River Thames, and many of them provide diners with wonderful views of the city as well as great contemporary cuisine.

QUÉBÉCOIS CUISINE IN MONTREAL

Quebec's continental climate, French roots, and entrepreneurial spirit come together in a perfect storm for gourmets.

The province of Quebec is packed with passionate farmers, sun-drenched market produce, and a Gallic sense of flavor and style. The roots of local cooking lie in Quebec's fur-trapping past, resulting in nourishing, rich food made to keep you warm and content, and in the city of Montreal you can find some outstanding examples, from fine-dining restaurants (or "restos" in the local slang) to smoked-meat joints, where you share Formica-topped tables with other diners. Try *poutine*, a sort of Québécois fast food: French fries topped with a rich gravy and bites of densely textured, squeaky (unaged) cheese curds. Montreal's chefs are known for their close links with the province's farmers, fishermen, and foragers. Look out for the wonderful local cured meats, especially hams and foie gras—some of the world's best foie is prepared in this area. The maple syrup made in Quebec sugarhouses every spring appears here year-round in some world-class desserts, such as *pouding chômeur* (sponge cake doused in maple-syrup sauce) and the achingly sweet *tarte au sucre* (sugar pie). Expect to leave the city several pounds heavier than when you arrived!

When to Go Visit from spring through fall, when fresh foods are in season. Fiddlehead ferns are ready in spring, and a riot of vegetables in summer, but a warm fall, when the maples turn red, can be the best time to visit as wild mushrooms, sweet peppers, eggplants, squashes, and sun-ripened tomatoes match up beautifully with the rich, tasty meats this city loves.

Planning Some of the city's smaller restaurants, especially in the Mount Royal area, do not have a liquor license but allow you to bring your own bottle. Look out for the words "*Apportez Votre Vin*" (bring your own wine) in the restaurant window. Advance booking is essential at most of the best restaurants.

Websites www.montreal.com, www.restomontreal.ca, www.restaurantaupieddecochon.ca, www.restaurant-toque.com, www.schwartzsdeli.com

Pick of the Best

Au Pied de Cochon is uniquely Québécois, and chef Martin Picard is not shy about luxury and flavor. Try duck in a can: a duck breast wrapped around a lobe of foie gras with a head of garlic, sprigs of thyme, and a heartbreakingly rich balsamic maple glaze, all served on a slice of toasted sourdough spread with celeriac puree. Foie gras here is as good as you will find anywhere and stars in almost every dish on the menu.

The award-winning **Toqué!** is considered one of Canada's greatest fine-dining restaurants, and it is here that you will find the area's best fresh produce, cooked with delicacy and flair.

For a low-budget option, try **Schwartz's**. It is the oldest deli in the city and specializes in Montreal smoked meat, a cross between brisket and pastrami. Don't ask for yours to come lean—all the flavor is in the fat.

Place Jacques Cartier in the heart of historic Old Montreal is filled with restaurants, shops, and art galleries.

Hearty gumbos are a mainstay of Lowcountry cooking.

SOUTH CAROLINA

CHARLESTON COOKING

Stroll the narrow cobblestone streets of Charleston's historic district to find a wealth of Southern cuisine and hospitality.

The coastal areas of South Carolina and Georgia are known as the Lowcountry, and the city of Charleston, South Carolina, is the region's culinary capital. Traditionally prepared, fresh, local ingredients predominate in Lowcountry cooking: rice, grits, fresh-from-the-farm vegetables and fruits, plus catches-of-the-day are enhanced by African, Caribbean, French, and other international influences. Start the day with grits—coarsely ground cornmeal cooked in milk and topped with generous helpings of butter—accompanied by fried shrimp. If you want to sample authentic plantation cooking, visit Middleton Place House Museum, a restored 18th-century plantation a half-hour's ride from the center of Charleston. In the restaurant, savor Mary Sheppard's Gumbo, recreated from an authentic plantation recipe. Hearty flavors, including ham hocks, beef ribs, and okra, surround shrimp, onions, tomatoes, baby lima beans, and more in this thickly delicious dish. Finally, no trip to Charleston is complete without a taste of she-crab soup, named for the female blue crabs that are an essential ingredient. Similar to robust chowders, she-crab soup features blue-crab meat with bright orange crab roe in a creamy base flavored with a splash of dry sherry.

When to Go Early spring and late fall are great times to visit, with average temperatures between 60°F and 80°F (15-26°C). The BB&T Charleston Food and Wine Festival, an annual four-day event in early March, includes demonstrations by local chefs and wine tastings.

Planning Spend at least five days in Charleston to enjoy its cuisine, museums, and restored plantations. In addition, you can explore the natural wonders of the coastline and its barrier islands by kayak, ferry, or eco-tour boat.

Websites www.charlestoncvb.com, www.middletonplace.org, www.mavericksouthernkitchens.com, www.charlestonfoodandwine.com, www.culinarytoursofcharleston.com

Sample the Lowcountry

■ Learn to cook Lowcountry food from top area chefs. Regular demonstrations and classes at **Charleston Cooks!** include Taste of the Lowcountry, with a changing menu and a chance to taste the results.

■ Visit the historic district's **Farmers' Market**, open every Saturday from March through November, for local produce, fresh flowers, jewelry, and crafts against a backdrop of live music.

■ Taste your way around Charleston with a guided **culinary walking tour**. Culinary Tours of Charleston organizes walks and bus trips that combine the city's cultural history with visits to restaurant kitchens and artisan food producers.

TRAVELERS' RESTAURANTS

Although most travelers' restaurants are places for people on the go, some are destinations in their own right, offering excellent food in stylish surroundings.

❶ Beaver Club, Montreal, Canada

Founded in 1958, Montreal's grandest hotel, Fairmont The Queen Elizabeth, straddles the main railroad station. Of its three restaurants, the upscale, dinner-only Beaver Club rivals Canada's best. Expect sumptuous contemporary decor, a formidable wine list, impeccable service, and Canadian twists on French classics, like sirloin flambéed in Canadian whiskey.

Planning The restaurant is open Tuesday through Saturday. A dress code applies: no jeans, sneakers, or T-shirts. www.beaverclub.ca

❷ Globe@YVR, Vancouver Airport, Canada

A cut above the usual airport-hotel restaurant, Globe@YVR promises panoramic views of Canada's North Shore Mountains through floor-to-ceiling, soundproofed windows. Those awaiting flights will appreciate the "five-minute lunch," but try to allow more time to savor the top-notch Pacific-Northwest cuisine.

Planning Globe@YVR is above the U.S. departures terminal. www.fairmont.com

❸ Oyster Bar, Grand Central, New York City

Recreating the air of old Manhattan and rail travel's erstwhile glamor, the ornate Oyster Bar has run since 1913, when Grand Central was a spanking-new, beaux-arts wunderkind. Beneath a cavernous vaulted roof, the bar honors its roots by offering almost no non-seafood entrées. The combination pan roast is a signature dish, alongside around 30 raw-oyster varieties.

Planning The restaurant is open daily except Sundays and holidays. www.oysterbarny.com

❹ Indianapolis International Airport

The designers of Indianapolis's replacement terminal aimed to change people's perceptions of airports with local food, live music, and an eco-friendly design. On offer are Indianapolite favorites, including breakfast-vendor Patachou on the Fly, Shapiro's kosher deli, the South Bend Chocolate Company, the speedway-themed Indy 500 Grill, and gourmet popcorn store, Just Pop In!

Planning Some restaurants are in the landside, light-filled Civic Plaza, others airside. www.indianapolisairport.com

❺ El Chepe Railroad, Mexico

One of the world's headiest railroads links Pacific-coast Los Mochis with inland Chihuahua through the Copper Canyon— four times the size of the Grand Canyon. While tableside views are the main draw, the first-class dining car rustles up tasty Mexican fare like enchiladas, chicken quesadillas, nachos, and homemade corn soup alongside exceptionally juicy burgers.

Planning Take the first-class express service for the dining car; the economy-class service just has snack machines. www.chepe.com.mx

❻ Tokyo Station, Japan

Tokyo's railroad station has its own "Kitchen Street" on the first floor, full of restaurants that are popular with locals. If you want more, go across the road to the Maru and Shin Marunouchi Buildings, which also have numerous dining outlets, accessible by an underground passage.

Planning With such a vast selection of restaurants, you will not have to walk far to find somewhere good to eat. www.jnto.go.jp

❼ Colonial Tramcar Restaurant, Melbourne, Australia

Founded in 1983, the world's first traveling streetcar-restaurant company is now a fleet. Elegant burgundy cars from the 1920s to 1940s fitted out in velvet and brass, and modernized with stabilizers and air-conditioning, take diners on a leisurely silver-service tour through Melbourne's downtown and suburbs. The Australian-tinged menu frequently features kangaroo meat.

Planning Depending on when you dine, set menus offer three, four, or five courses with drinks included. Reserve a table months ahead and dress up. www.tramrestaurant.com.au

❽ Le Train Bleu, Gare de Lyon, Paris, France

For dining on the go, few places outclass Le Train Bleu— founded in 1901—for old-world elegance, luxury, and romance. With wood panels, chandeliers, upholstered seats, sculpted angels, vast arched windows, and 41 frescoes depicting landscapes along the Paris-Lyon-Mediterranean route, the restaurant is a palatial Parisian pinnacle of belle-époque architecture. Expect superb service and classic French dishes.

Planning Take a camera or sketchpad. There is a cheaper café with similar decor and elegance next door. www.le-train-bleu.com

❾ Champagne Bar, St. Pancras, London, England

Part of the long-awaited renovation of London's glorious, Victorian St. Pancras station as a Eurostar terminus, Europe's longest champagne bar is a fine place to toast the revival of international rail travel and the regeneration of a long-derelict neighborhood. The food is modern British.

Planning The bar is on the upper concourse. www.stpancras.com

❿ Plane Food, Heathrow Airport, London, England

Owned by Michelin-feted TV chef Gordon Ramsay, this modern-British gourmet restaurant celebrates flying with its aerodynamic design, panoramic runway views, and clever aviation-themed fittings. Dishes are good value, especially the takeout picnic boxes for travelers in a hurry.

Planning The restaurant is in Terminal 5. www.gordonramsay.com

Right: Paris's Le Train Bleu is named for the luxury train service to the French Riviera, whose heydey was in the 1920s and 1930s.

TEX-MEX IN SAN ANTONIO

Aficionados travel a few minutes outside of central San Antonio to seek out the best new tastes or visit longtime favorites.

While you shouldn't miss San Antonio's famous Tex-Mex spots, such as Mi Tierra and Rosario's, if you want to escape the downtown crowds, head north. Start at Cafe Salsita, a tiny indoor-outdoor breakfast and lunch place hidden in a bland strip mall on East Basse Road. All the originality and flavor missing from the decor is packed into the *chili de arbol salsa*: bright orange and creamy, it has a mole-like consistency and sweetness. Try it with "Eric's special," a monster breakfast taco that makes optimum use of bacon—one thick strip complements the scrambled eggs, gooey yellow cheese, and hint of *pico de gallo*. Another five minutes north, on Broadway, is the quirky Taco Garage, where the race-car paraphernalia, photos, and striped driver chairs blend with the neon signs and tropical colors that give San Antonio's Tex-Mex scene its vibrancy. This garage is Tex-Mex heaven. You can choose from a menu of tasty classics, such as *chile con carne* enchiladas, or flip to the back page for the devilishly good *chilaquiles*—a cross between jalapeño nachos and scrambled eggs, rolled into a spongy, hot-from-the-rack tortilla—a perfect combination of cheese, crunchiness, and spice kick, and vegetarian friendly. For a quieter experience head to Teka Molina, the last outpost of a San Antonio institution dating from 1937. Claim a table among Aztec-themed paintings and wait for your corn tortilla stuffed with cheese, vegetables, and your choice of beans, chicken, beef, or guacamole.

When to Go The San Antonio summer is hot, but all the restaurants have air-conditioning.

Planning When you travel outside downtown by taxi, get the service's number for the return trip. You need not make restaurant reservations; most won't take them. Only a few places—such as Rosario's and the famed breakfast taco locations on weekend mornings—draw lines, and these always move quickly.

Websites www.cafesalsita.com, www.centralmarket.com, www.mitierracafe.com, www.tacohaven.info, www.titosrestaurant.com, www.arturosbarbacoa.com

The Adventurous Eater

"Waste not, want not," goes the saying, and in San Antonio you can enjoy every part of the cow. Get started with a tame choice, a **Barbacoa taco** at Arturo's Barbacoa. This is a traditional barbecue from the meat on the head of the cow—soft, juicy, and distinctly smoky.

If you are still hungry try **La Lengua** at Tito's Mexican Restaurant. The tongue comes chopped in chunks and doused in gravy-like sauce. Elsewhere in the city, La Lengua is served in tacos, including at Taco Haven, where the Asada version is served with roasted peppers but without the thick sauce.

And, no matter when you eventually work up the courage, stop at Mi Tierra for a cup of **menudo soup**. Tripe is the main ingredient in this popular traditional breakfast. The good news is that it is rumored to cure margarita hangovers.

Rosario's, located in San Antonio's Southtown arts district, is famous for its margaritas and contemporary Tex-Mex food and draws a large crowd nightly.

The strains of jazz music accompany visitors all over New Orleans's French Quarter.

Cajun in New Orleans

Cajun cooks have combined traditional European dishes and good local ingredients to create new classics.

It was perhaps inevitable that culinary magic should emerge from the kitchens of Louisiana's bayou region given its multicultural roots—the French Arcadians migrated here from Canada in 1755, and the Spanish, Creoles, and Native Americans also called the region home. From early days, Cajun cuisine blended French country cooking methods with local ingredients, in particular seafood, rice, sugarcane, celery, onions, and peppers. Several Cajun dishes are now cherished well beyond the bayou, among them gumbo, jambalaya, and crawfish pie—the three dishes that feature in the classic Hank Williams song "Jambalaya." But there are plenty more where those came from, dishes with names as exotic as they are tasty—hogshead cheese, catfish court-bouillon stew, *maque choux* (sautéed corn and vegetables with seafood or chicken). Cajuns have also transformed the bounty of the swamps into finger-licking dishes, such as frogs' legs with mushrooms and peppers and alligator sauce piquante.

When to Go Spring and fall provide the best weather for eating your way across New Orleans and southern Louisiana.

Planning New Orleans is not the only place for great Cajun cooking. Louisiana's rural food festivals blend great local food, incredible music, and small-town Americana. New Iberia's Cajun Hot Sauce Festival in March includes a jambalaya cook-off and people's choice hot-sauce competition. At the Delcambre Shrimp Festival in August, you can sample shrimp boiled, fried, stuffed, and on a stick as well as gumbo, shrimp po'boys, and shrimp sauce piquante. La Grande Boucherie des Cajuns in St. Martinville is a traditional pig roast that takes place right before Mardi Gras. New Iberia also hosts the World Championship Gumbo Cook-Off in October.

Websites www.louisianatravel.com, www.chefpaul.com, www.emerils.com, www.shrimpfestival.net, www.cajuncountry.org/boucherie

The First Celebrity Chefs

Wolfgang Puck and Anthony Bourdain may beg to differ, but it was a couple of Cajun cooks—**Paul Prudhomme** and **Emeril Lagasse**—who really kicked off the celebrity-chef craze.

Nobody outside of the delta had heard of the gregarious "Chef Paul" (or of blackened redfish) when he opened his **K-Paul's Louisiana Kitchen** in the French Quarter in 1979. Born and bred in the backwoods of St. Landry Parish in southwest Louisiana, Prudhomme later launched a nationwide cooking show and a line of Cajun seasonings. With his distinctive white beret and silver-handled cane, Chef Paul was the first American-born chef to receive the coveted Mérite Agricole from the French government.

Lagasse trekked a different route to Cajun culinary fame. Born of French-Canadian and Portuguese parents in Massachusetts, he didn't set foot in a Louisiana kitchen until 1982, when he was named executive chef at **Commander's Palace** in New Orleans. He later opened his own local eatery (**Emeril's**) and for nearly 20 years has been a stalwart on American television, hosting several food shows and his own NBC sitcom.

A plate of local crawfish

FLORIDA

Nuevo Latino in Miami

Exotic local produce and inspirational Latin-American chefs have put Miami at the forefront of a new style of eating.

Also known as Floribbean and Tropical Fusion, Miami's Nuevo Latino cuisine combines zesty Caribbean and Latin-American flavors with time-honored European cooking techniques. At Ola in South Beach, Cuban roots inspire chef Douglas Rodriguez to create gastronomic surprises. Nibble on a squid-ink empanada filled with lobster, avocado salad, and *salsa rosa*. Then crunch on crispy pork, slow-roasted for 27 hours and served with fried yucca dressed with lemon mojo, black bean broth, and cilantro mojo. Dessert calls for a deconstructed Key lime pie—tart Key lime custard over a bed of toasted-meringue and vanilla-bean ice cream, finished with a toasted-cinnamon walnut tuile. At Yuca, also in South Beach, chef Ramon Medrano entices with yuca ceviche—an intriguing concoction of fresh grouper, shrimp, calamari, octopus, and lobster lightly tossed in a ginger-and-lime marinade. A dash of scotch bonnet pepper adds a punch. Away from the ocean, in the suburb of Doral, Chispa shines with spark-shaped fixtures and energetic Latin music. The cuisine mirrors the high energy. Seared octopus and marinated shrimp rest on a fan of fried plantains paired with a dollop of creamy guacamole and *queso blanco*, while a *relleno*-style mahimahi stuffed with spinach and manchego cheese is accompanied with yucca fries and lemongrass-cilantro mojo.

When to Go Miami is a warm-weather, year-round vacationland where sunny skies reign, although summers can be hot and steamy with afternoon thunderstorms.

Planning The best way to explore Miami is to rent a car. Foodies can opt to visit during one of the many annual food festivals: such as the South Beach Wine & Food Festival (February); Fab Fest–A Taste of the Beach (February); Miami Wine & Food Festival (April); Miami/Bahamas Goombay Fest (May/June); or the International Mango Festival (July). Reservations are advised at Ola, Yuca, and Chispa. Dress is casual chic.

Websites www.miamiandbeaches.com, www.visitflorida.com, www.olamiami.com, www.yuca.com, www.chisparestaurant.com

Plantain Side Dishes

A staple food in tropical climates, the plantain looks similar to a banana but is thicker-skinned, longer, firmer, and lower in sugar content. It is generally cooked as a vegetable, and its mild flavor and texture provide ideal accompaniments to Latino cuisine.

To make **maduros**, overripe (black-skinned) and therefore sweet, plantain is sliced diagonally into pieces about 0.5 in (12 mm) thick. The slices are fried in hot oil for a couple of minutes on each side to a golden brown. Some chefs roll the slices lightly in white or brown sugar before frying them.

Tostones, on the other hand, are fried twice. Underripe, green plantains are cut in pieces and fried, and excess oil is soaked up with a paper towel. The pieces are then squashed flat and fried again. These deep-fried chips are often eaten with a hot sauce for dipping. Sometimes they are served with a cheese topping as an appetizer.

Opposite: Ocean Drive is at the heart of South Beach's restaurant district. Above: Ola's rainbow ceviche

A multitude of traditional and modern restaurants now add to the attractions of Old San Juan, founded by Spanish colonists in 1521 and marvelously preserved.

PUERTO RICO

San Juan's New Cuisine

The city of San Juan, capital of Puerto Rico,
is the center for a bold new fusion cuisine.

Whether you call it Nuevo Latino, New Caribbean, New Puerto Rican, or *exótico criollo* (exotic Creole), this modern culinary style has few signature dishes because it encourages adventurous experimentation. Packing intercontinental fusion twists, it is a playful modern reinterpretation of Latin American dishes—themselves a blend of Amerindian, Spanish, African, and other influences—using French cooking styles. Its undisputed pioneer, Alfredo Ayala, went on a food journey of a lifetime, including training at top restaurants in New York and France. He returned to Puerto Rico in 1981, determined to apply his culinary knowledge to the island's eating scene. At his first restaurant, Ali-Oli, he set about reinventing Puerto Rico's traditional criollo dishes. Initially aghast, islanders were soon coming back for more. Ayala opened new outlets and became an inspiration to other chefs on the island. His most acclaimed disciple, Wilo Benet, is the chef-owner of the hip Pikayo, inside the Museum of Art of Puerto Rico. Other trailblazers include Mario Ferro of the Caribe Hilton, Myrta Pérez of Pasión por el Fogón, and Dayn Smith of Perla. Despite its globe-trotting pedigree, Nuevo Latino cuisine thrives on freshness and typically uses humble local ingredients, such as plantains, yucca, and goat meat, emboldened with zesty marinades, often mango- or citrus-based, and dark rum sauces.

When to Go Puerto Rico is warm year-round, with temperatures of 75°–85°F (23°–29°C).

Planning Public transportation or walking is the best way to get around Old San Juan. Some upscale restaurants have a dress code and require reservations. Expect full-on air-conditioning.

Websites www.gotopuertorico.com, www.restaurantsinpr.com, www.oofrestaurants.com, www.saboreapuertorico.com

Island Specialties

■ Despite growing almost no sugarcane, Puerto Rico is one of the world's largest rum manufacturers, producing 200-plus brands. Two local favorites are **DonQ** and **Barrilito**.

■ The **Oof!** chain is a San Juan culinary highlight. Its restaurants include the Aquaviva, Parrot Club, and Koco for Nuevo Latino, Dragonfly for Asian fusion, and Toro Salao for tapas.

■ The weekend-long **Saborea Culinary Festival** each April is a beachside showcase of Puerto Rico's cuisine, where you can sample food from the island's top restaurants. It also features a demonstration tent with classes from Puerto Rican and international celebrity chefs.

Flavors of Mexico City

Clever combinations of traditional and contemporary
flavors and techniques are transforming an ancient cuisine.

Tostadas—tortillas topped with
shredded turkey from Yucatán

Known by locals as "El DF," for Distrito Federal, Mexico City has more than 15,000 restaurants. With regional food from every state, as well as local specialties and Mexican nouvelle cuisine, there is something for every appetite and budget. Some of the best regional dishes available in the city, including pork *carnitas* from Michoacán (succulent, spicy "bits" or "shreds" of pork), are served by chef Titita Ramirez at El Bajio, a small restaurant in the Axcapotzalco *colonia*, or neighborhood. If you want to sample Oaxacan specialties, try Casa Neri in Colonia Portales, south of the city center, where customers eat outdoors on an attractive colonial patio. And for a wide selection of Puebla's famous moles, (delicious sauces made with chilies, spices, and chocolate) and *pipián* (a similarly piquant sauce often with a base of pumpkin or sesame seeds), go to Ikaro in Colonia Narvarte. The *pibil* (spiced marinated pork) dishes of the Yucatán Peninsula are presented in traditional style at El Habanero in Colonia Napoles, while nouvelle cuisine is best sampled at Izote in Colonia Polanco, north of Chapultepec Park, where the menu borrows cleverly from pre-Hispanic culture with such dishes as squash blossom soup and fragrant shrimp in hibiscus mole sauce. But for the genuine pre-Hispanic cuisine of the Aztecs, visit Fonda Don Chon in Centro, the historic city center, where fried grasshoppers, worms, armadillo in mango sauce, and ant roe are served to adventurous diners.

When to Go Mexico City is a great food destination any time of year.

Planning Be sure to make a reservation and check if the restaurant has a dress code. Mexico has a comprehensive public transportation system and plenty of taxis. Late at night, official secure taxis—*taxi seguro*—operate. Restaurants, bars, and clubs should be able to phone for one or provide a list of numbers.

Websites www.visitmexico.com, www.mexconnect.com

Mealtimes in Mexico

Desayuno is a light breakfast, usually consisting of sweet rolls and coffee. For an authentic Mexican morning meal, try tamales sold at street stands.

Almuerzo is brunch, a mid-morning meal typically consisting of an egg dish such as *huevos rancheros* or *chilaquiles* (fried tortilla strips smothered in salsa and topped with chicken and cheese). Most restaurants serve almuerzo by about 10 a.m.

Comida is the main meal, eaten between 2 and 4 p.m. Look for *comida corrida*, literally "meal on the run," fixed-price specials.

Merienda is a light, early-evening meal, usually consisting of coffee and pastries at a café or cocktails and snacks at a bar.

Cena is a late, light supper eaten at about 9 or 10 p.m.

Fresh, spicy, and wholesome moles—regional sauces and stews—are served in traditional-style restaurants across the city.

BRAZIL

Feijoada in Rio de Janeiro

Brazil's national dish is made in homes and restaurants throughout the country using 1,001 different, hotly debated, traditional recipes.

Brazil's national dish is, by tradition, not on weekly menus. It is served in restaurants only on Saturdays and holidays, at noon, as *o prato do dia* (the special of the day), so seeking out the famed *feijoada* offers the food-loving traveler the opportunity for some real Rio exploration. Feijoada consists of a thick broth produced by slowly cooking black beans and meat together, ideally over a wood fire or in a brick oven. The cuts of meat vary, but traditional feijoada is made from pork trimmings, bacon, sausage, dried beef, and pork loin. Some feijoada chefs, particularly at upscale restaurants, replace the pork trimmings with more succulent cuts of meat, while a few restaurants have also created a vegetarian version. The dish is served with white rice, *farofa* (fried manioc flour), *couve* (finely cut, fried collard greens), and orange slices. The ideal accompaniment is a cold light beer or a *caipirinha*—a traditional drink made with *cachaça* (distilled sugarcane juice) and lime over ice. On public holidays feijoada is everywhere, from Ipanema's five-star restaurants to makeshift firepits in the hillside favelas. Confeitaria Colombo, an establishment famous for its spectacular Art-Nouveau decor, offers one of the best traditional Saturday feijoadas in Rio. But if you really cannot wait for the weekend, visit Casa da Feijoada in Rio's southerly Ipanema district, which serves several variants of the dish seven days a week.

When to Go Rio is warm in winter—July, August, and September—with highs of 75°F (24°C), and hotter in summer, with temperatures around 104°F (40°C). High season starts the week before Christmas and ends after Carnival in February–March. This is the busiest—but most exciting–time to visit.

Planning Accommodations for Carnival and New Year's Eve should be arranged a year or more in advance. At those times excellent feijoada is served in numerous locations, including street parties and *rodas de samba*, the gatherings of music and dance offered by the samba schools.

Websites www.travel.aol.com, www.ipanema.com

Creation Myths

Popular myth holds that feijoada was created by Brazil's African slaves, who used discarded pork trimmings to flavor their bean, dried beef, and manioc rations. However, bean and meat-based stews were—and still are—a common dish in Portugal, and some historians think the dish was introduced to Brazil by the early Portuguese settlers.

Whatever its origins, the indigenous contributions to the dish are unmistakable: The manioc flour used in making farofa—which is essential to any authentic feijoada—has always been a staple part of the diet of Brazilian Indians.

Like many of the world's great dishes, feijoada probably evolved out of a variety of ingredients and preparation techniques from many cultures.

Opposite: A pineapple-seller patrols Ipanema beach. Above: Feijoada with traditional accompaniments

STEAK IN BUENOS AIRES

You can eat beef for breakfast, lunch, and dinner in Buenos Aires, making the city the carnivores' capital of the world.

In this elegant, spirited, Latin-American city there is always an opportunity to stop for steak. Blessed with the best beef in the world, many locals eat it every day, with supersize steak meals available for less than $20. For a perfect Sunday, head to the city's oldest neighborhood, San Telmo, where you can browse the antiques stalls in Plaza Dorrego, which sell everything from swordsticks (canes with a sword concealed inside them) to vintage buttons, watch the tango dancers, and then head to the casual, friendly Desnivel for a perfectly grilled steak washed down with a spicy Malbec. In Palermo, the colorful shoppers' heaven in the northeast of the city, La Cabrera is the outstanding neighborhood *parilla*, or steakhouse, where delicious, classically cut steaks come with a dazzling array of side dishes. Afterwards, profit from the whole cow by buying beautifully crafted handbags or shoes and relaxing over ice cream at one of the city's many exceptional ice-cream parlors (try *dulce de leche,* or "sweet milk" ice cream, an Argentinian specialty with a caramel flavor). Downtown, grab a taste of café culture with pre-dinner drinks in Café Tortoni on Avenida de Mayo before heading over to happening riverside Puerto Madero, where upscale and pricey Cabaña Las Lilas serves beef raised on its own ranch. Other food specialties to try include empanadas—tiny pastries with a wealth of savory meat fillings, and *locro*—a corn, meat, and vegetable stew. Argentinian sparkling wine is also excellent and a bargain.

When to Go Buenos Aires is quiet from Christmas through February as *porteños* (B.A. natives) head to the mountains for their summer holidays. Visit at any other time of year for the true spirit of the town.

Planning Book into one of the boutique hotels in Palermo Viejo or Recoleta and use the Subte (metro) to get around town, remembering that it closes around 10:20 p.m. Buenos Aires is relatively safe, but book only licensed radio taxis and stay away from shantytowns.

Websites www.easybuenosairescity.com, www.bue.gov.ar

Cutting It in Argentina

Argentine steak cuts differ from those in America and Europe. The four main cuts are **bife de lomo, bife de cuadril, bife de ancho,** and **bife de chorizo,** which approximate respectively to fillet or tenderloin, rump, rib eye, and sirloin. Other cuts include **tira de asado** (ribs), **vacio** (flank steak), and **bife de costilla** (T-bone). Steaks are cooked flat on an open barbecue pit or on a vertical spit over the barbecue.

Cheaper cuts are sometimes marinated in **chimichurri**, a sauce of chili, peppers, herbs, garlic, salt, onions, olive oil, and vinegar, which can also be served as an accompaniment.

At a typical barbecue you may also get the chance to sample kidneys and sweetbreads (the thymus gland).

From Café Tortoni, stroll west along the Avenida de Mayo to admire the Palacio Barolo (completed in 1923), whose design is inspired by Dante's *Divina Commedia*.

Workers end the day with drinks and a selection of dishes at an izakaya in Tokyo's Asakusa district.

JAPAN

Tokyo's Izakaya

Diverse and delicious foods make the city's bars some of the best destinations for diners.

The three characters representing *izakaya* mean "store," "alcohol," and "room." Serving a comprehensive selection of beer, sake, and *shochu* (spirits made from grain, fruit, or vegetables), a typical izakaya has all the bustle and buzz of a Western bar or pub. But the Japanese like to eat when they drink, and izakaya also serve excellent food. The dishes are often compared to Spanish *tapas*, but tend to come in larger portions, although no dish is a meal in itself. Izakaya pride themselves on a little exoticism, and however tangy the vinegar-drenched daikon salad or fresh the sushi, foods such as baked potato with cheese or miniature pizza are usually on the menu—familiar to Westerners, but more exotic for Japanese. At the big franchises, such as Tengu, some tables are large enough for groups to share while smaller ones are crowded together, so you will inevitably meet local people. The more dignified Katakura has been on the same site since 1848, and its fare is superior to that of the big chains. "Any food that goes with alcohol is good," says the jovial owner, but a tofu with the consistency of cream cheese (*zarudoufu*), tiny grapes of seaweed dipped in a sweet fruit vinegar, and the potato with salmon and basil are all excellent.

When to Go Late spring (also offering cherry-blossom sightings) and mid-fall (when the leaves turn) are best. Tokyo summers are hot and humid.

Planning Hotel concierges will call the nearest branch of an izakaya and ask them to fax over a map. With Japan's resistance to street names, and its habit of numbering buildings according to the date of their construction, this is essential. Most izakaya are small, loud, and busy, and booking ahead (again, get the assistance of your concierge) is wise and often essential.

Websites www.japantravelinfo.com, www.ramla.net/casual_restaurant/tofuro

Izakaya Know-how

There is no language barrier in an izikaya: whether you are ordering **gyoza** (pan-fried stuffed pasta parcels) or garlic bread, just smile and point at a picture menu, ordering drinks and dishes whenever you please.

Cooked and raw dishes are served. Beef tongue stew, grilled eggplant, squid liver, oysters, and sushi are just some of the dishes that appear on izakaya menus.

For a local drink, try a **grapefruit sour**, whose Japanese name, conveniently, is "grapefruit sour" pronounced with a strong Japanese accent. It is served in a large mug and consists of watered-down *shochu* with ice and the juice of half a grapefruit, giving a pleasant long drink with a kick.

Tengu and **Tofuro** are izikaya chains with multiple outlets across Tokyo and beyond. Tofuro satisfies the growing preference for quieter and more private izakaya, offering cubicles with sliding doors floored with traditional tatami matting. You use the bell push to call for service as needed.

EXTREME RESTAURANTS

Take dining out to a whole new level of experience with this
eccentric selection of eateries worldwide.

❶ Royal Dragon, Bangkok, Thailand

Listed by the *Guinness Book of Records* as the world's largest restaurant in the 1990s, the Royal Dragon has more than 1,000 staff, 5,000 seats, and serves up to 10,000 customers a day. Diners can eat in intimate pagodas, karaoke banqueting halls, or in the Ten Thousand Years Tower with views over Bangkok. Outside, waiting staff wear roller skates to speed up the service around a 3.9-acre (1.5 hectare) dining area.

Planning The restaurant is situated on the Bangna-Trad Highway in the city's southeast and is open daily. www.royal-dragon.com

❷ Titanic Theatre Restaurant, Melbourne, Australia

Billed as "the only place where your night is guaranteed to be a disaster," this venue recreates the final dinner aboard RMS *Titanic*. Appropriately attired passengers join steerage, first class, or the captain's table for a modern international set menu. Performers and musicians keep up morale.

Planning Normally open only on Saturdays, the restaurant is in Williamstown, 30 minutes by train from Flinders Street station. Costume rental is available. www.titanic.com.au

❸ Ithaa, Conrad Maldives Rangali Island

Restaurant fish tanks are no novelty, but Ithaa stretches the concept to oceanic proportions. Based on aquarium technology, it occupies an acrylic tunnel with 270° underwater views. As sharks, stingrays, and other fish peer in, it is unclear who is observing whom. The food is Maldivian-Western fusion.

Planning Guests will almost certainly be staying at the resort. Dinner reservations are advisable. Dress formally. www.hiltonworldresorts.com

❹ SnowCastle, Kemi, Finland

Anyone seeking vodka served perfectly will drink contentedly here: Shots come in ice glasses in this veritable snow citadel. Rebuilt annually, Lapland's SnowCastle assumes a different look each year. One thing is constant: The 23°F (−5°C) temperature. Dress for an Arctic expedition and expect local specialties, such as cream of smoked reindeer soup.

Planning Opens late January through mid-April, weather permitting. Reservations are mandatory. www.snowcastle.net

❺ Witold Budryk Chamber, Wieliczka, Poland

Until it was flooded in 1996, Wieliczka was the world's only salt mine with seven centuries' continuous excavation. Nowadays, tourists have replaced miners. Let the saline air whet your appetite for Polish delicacies, such as *barszcz* (borscht) with ravioli dumplings, at this unique underground restaurant.

Planning Tours last around three hours. Book at least two weeks ahead. Dress for a steady 57°F (14°C). www.kopalnia.pl

❻ Grotta Palazzese, Polignano a Mare, Italy

For romance, few locations beat this natural grotto in Polignano a Mare, a medieval fishing village just north of Italy's heel. From a mezzanine platform inside a massive karst sea cave, diners enjoy seafood and other Apulian delicacies with the backdrop of Adriatic waves crashing onto rocks below.

Planning The grotto is open from May through October. Polignano is 30 minutes by train from Bari. www.grottapalazzese.it

❼ Fortezza Medicea, Volterra, Italy

Imposing forts—one 14th-century, the other 15th—protect a most exclusive restaurant within a high-security prison, open once a month. Customers face security screening, sit at simple wooden benches, and use plastic cutlery, yet the venue is always booked up months ahead. With top Tuscan chefs directing prisoners, diners come expecting not only novelty but also international haute cuisine. Several former inmates now work in dining establishments outside.

Planning Volterra is 90 minutes to two hours by train from Pisa. For reservations email Volterra tourist office. Diners need a clean criminal record. www.volterratur.it

❽ Dans le Noir, London, England

Eating mystery food served by blind waiters in pitch darkness may seem unenticingly gimmicky, but this popular restaurant has a serious side, too. It aims to overturn diners' views of disability as the blind guide the sighted. The darkness also enhances one's sensitivity to taste and texture—and intimacy toward strangers. The menu is modern international.

Planning Open daily except Sundays for dinner only, 30-31 Clerkenwell Green, near Farringdon tube station. www.danslenoir.com

❾ The Treehouse, Alnwick Garden, England

Alnwick's châtelaine, the Duchess of Northumberland, has set out to transform a once-derelict enclosure into a world-class garden. But this is her most ambitious achievement. One of the world's largest wooden treehouses, the creaky 6,000-sq-ft (557 sq m) complex hugs 16 living lime trees linked by suspended walkways. Expect locally sourced dishes, such as venison.

Planning The nearest train station is Alnmouth. www.alnwickgarden.com

❿ Perlan, Reykjavík, Iceland

A ring of six water tanks seems a downright eccentric location for a romantic dinner, but the revolving glass dome added on top of the tanks in 1991 has made this one of Reykjavík's most modish luxury restaurants. Try salt cod, whale, or guillemot.

Planning The restaurant takes two hours to revolve. Open only for dinner. www.perlan.is

Right: For the best view of the Maldives' sharks, rays, turtles, groupers, and a whole host of tropical fish, visit Ithaa during daylight hours.

Spit-Roasted Pig in Manila

Lechon is the spectacular dish of choice in the Philippine capital. Try it takeout, in markets, and in specialty restaurants.

For non-Muslim Filipinos (about 90 percent of the country's population is Christian) pork is king, and the version that reigns supreme is lechon, or whole spit-roast pig. Seasonings and accompaniments vary, but north to south there is little disagreement about what makes a superior version: The skin should be smooth, caramel colored, and exquisitely crispy; The meat should pull away from the bones in succulent, tender shreds. And whether seasoned only with salt and pepper, as in Manila and the northern island group of Luzon, or with lemongrass, scallions, and other seasonings, as in the southern island groups of Visayas and Mindanao, a lechon should taste utterly, extravagantly porcine. La Loma, Manila's lechon district, is chock-full of restaurants and takeouts displaying row after row of bronzed specimens—beautiful to look at, although this is not necessarily the best place to sample them. Try the original branch of Kamayan, an endearingly kitschy Filipino restaurant where pigs are roasted behind glass in full view of the entrance. The milk-basted *lechon de leche* (suckling pig) is served with sweet, sour, and spicy dipping sauces. Lydia's, a down-to-earth chain with a number of branches, made its name with its tremendously moist lechon made from pigs raised on the owner's ranch in Batangas. And the Saturdays-only Salcedo Community Market offers an appropriately boisterous atmosphere in which to sample lechon—and the opportunity to compare the different regional versions of the dish.

When to Go Lechon is available year-round. Try to avoid the flood-prone monsoon season from June through October.

Planning La Loma lies west of Quezon City—the old capital—that now forms the northeast sector of Manila's vast urban sprawl. Here, entire blocks are devoted to roasting and selling pigs for family celebrations. Restaurants serving lechon are found throughout Manila.

Websites www.lydias-lechon.com, www.manila.gov.ph

Eating Etiquette

Lechon is something to be shared joyfully with friends and family, but a certain etiquette is nevertheless required. It is customary for everyone to gather around the table to await the lechon's arrival, whereupon you all dig in at once, aiming first for the highly prized crackly skin, and then for the ears, tail, ribs, and fatty neck meat.

Eating with your hands is allowed—cutlery is out of place with a dish such as this—and cements camaraderie among those sharing the meal. But don't be greedy—Filipinos look poorly upon the guest who captures more than his or her fair share.

A pig vendor arranges his wares in Manila's lechon district. The pigs are roasted over huge troughs for around three hours and then sold on the spit.

Coconut palms grow along the island city's waterfront, with sleek modern skyscrapers rising beyond.

Peranakan Cuisine

The Peranakans of Singapore are the descendants of Chinese merchants, who settled in Singapore in the 18th and 19th centuries, and indigenous Malays. Over the years, the respective cultures merged into a unique hybrid of language, dress, customs, and—most importantly—food.

The epicenter of Peranakan culture is along the East Coast quarter, especially **East Coast Road**. Here, it is possible to lose entire afternoons wandering from stall to stall tasting spicy *laksa* soup studded with sliced fish cakes, rice dumplings filled with pork and gingko nuts, and *pandan*-scented cakes coated with coconut flakes.

Peranakan restaurants in the quarter serve dishes such as chili *sambal*, chicken with black nuts, pork and crab meatballs, and aromatic fish cakes. Among the delicious choice of sweets are sago pudding with palm sugar and tapioca cubes in sweet coconut milk.

SINGAPORE

DINING SINGAPORE STYLE

From fluffy Indian crepes to fragrant spring rolls, Singapore's cuisine is a flavorsome kaleidoscope of cultures.

If there is one trait that defines Singaporeans, it would be their fanatical love of food. When the traditional local greeting is not "Hello," but rather "Have you eaten?," you know gastronomy is a passion. The real joy of a gastronomic tour of Singapore comes from seeing how the island nation has made the cuisines of many cultures its own. Begin with a morning stroll through Tekka Market in Little India, a lively warren of stalls stacked with tiny brinjals (eggplants), coconuts, pungent bunches of cilantro and lemongrass, plump tomatoes, and fat chilies alongside trays of mackerel, river fish, and pink prawns. The neighborhood around the market is jammed with little eateries giving off the aromas of fish-head curries spiked with cumin and pineapple chunks, fluffy naans, and buttery chicken stews. A few train-stops away in Tanjong Pagar, Chinatown tempts the taste buds with silky noodles and seafood cooked in clay pots, while the Arab Quarter presents an exotic mix of multihued cakes and saffron-tinged rice served with fragrant *rendangs*—beef cooked in fresh coconut milk. If you are short of time, you can dip into this dizzying blend of cuisines in one of the 120-odd alfresco hawker centers that dot the island, selling everything from oyster omelets to fried spring rolls.

When to Go Blessed with year-round tropical weather, Singapore can be visited any time. The average temperature hovers around 86°F (30°C) all year, with very slight dips during the December-January monsoons.

Planning A week is an ideal length of time to spend in Singapore. Most of the better hotels are clustered along either Orchard Road or Marina Bay—from here, it is an easy hop to major tourist destinations by the underground trains or taxis. Tipping is not expected anywhere.

Website www.visitsingapore.com

BEIJING ROAST DUCK

Crispy duck roasted in fragrant wood-fired ovens is a triumph
of culinary simplicity—and one of China's greatest dishes.

The presence of a large, yellow-billed, concrete duck in the street indicates the location of a branch of the ubiquitous Quanjude, the best-known name in Beijing roast duck. Founded in 1864, the original restaurant was one of very few to survive the suppression of private enterprise during the first few decades of communist rule. Now franchised city-wide, Quanjude's greeters beckon to tourists, who can also choose from a wealth of other options. Available throughout the city as everything from a polystyrene-boxed, backstreet takeout to part of a multiple-course gourmet banquet, Beijing duck is still usually roasted using the Quanjude method, the birds hung in ovens that are fired with the stumps of apple, *jujube* (a small date), pear, and persimmon trees. First, water is injected between the duck's skin and flesh, then the duck is cooked at a high temperature to crisp the skin and bring the meat to a tender softness. The sliced bird is served with dishes of shredded green onion, strips of cucumber, plum sauce, and a pile of small pancakes. Diners smear the pancake with a little sauce and place a few greens near one edge, then pile pieces of duck on top before rolling the pancake up. The meal is usually followed by duck soup and can be accompanied by dishes involving almost every other part of the duck, including roasted hearts, webs (feet) in mustard sauce, and fried tongues.

When to Go Spring or fall—winters are frigid and summers hot, humid, and often wet. September and October are best, followed by April and early May, although spring sometimes brings sandstorms.

Planning Practice your chopstick technique before leaving home as few restaurants outside Westernized hotels provide knives and forks. Have your hotel write down the name of your destination in Chinese characters so you can show it to taxi drivers. Take the restaurant's telephone number so the taxi driver can use his cell phone to call for further directions if necessary.

Websites www.quanjude.com.cn, www.meiguoxing.com, www.thebeijingguide.com, www.thebeijinger.com/blog/2009/01/14/Dine-Like-a-Local-with-Beijing-Eats

Seeking Duck

■ The new, low-fat duck at either branch of **Da Dong Kaoya** is currently thought the capital's best, especially when accompanied by some of the chef-owner's imaginative new-style Chinese dishes. Choose your selections from a bilingual picture menu.

■ Expat lovers of Beijing *hutong* (alley) atmosphere take their duck in the battered traditional courtyard residence that has become the **Li Qun Kaoyadian**, a duck restaurant lost in the rapidly disappearing labyrinth southeast of the ancient Qian Men towers. The route to the tiny dining rooms is via the kitchen, where you may see your duck in preparation.

The flames blaze in a traditional wood-fired oven used for roasting duck.

A street-side restaurant in Kowloon sells piping hot dim sum to take out.

CHINA

DIM SUM IN HONG KONG

Assemble a custom-made banquet from a seemingly
limitless menu of steamed snacks and delicacies.

I f non-Chinese know any words of Cantonese at all they are likely to be *dim* and *sum*,
which together refer to small steamed morsels of chicken, fish, and assorted stuffed rice
pancakes, pastries, noodles, desserts, and soups, taken with cup after cup of Chinese
tea. Hong Kong claims to have the best dim sum in the world, from street level basics to
pricey rarities and fusion versions served in high-rise restaurants. The classic menu items by
which any dim sum restaurant can be judged are *har gau*, prawns in a bite-sized, rice-noodle
wrapper, and *siu mai*, steamed minced pork bound into a small round parcel with tofu skin,
topped with crab roe. Dishes such as jelly-like beef balls served with Worcestershire sauce
and steamed squid in curry sauce reveal the influence of the 150 years of British colonial
rule that ended in 1997. Smaller items come three or four to a bamboo steamer, while more
exotic items, such as little pasta bags of steamed hairy crab, can be ordered at a price per
item that would buy a whole plate of pan-fried pork dumplings. Most restaurants group
dishes into small, medium, and large categories, referring to price rather than portion size.
Mayhem often breaks out at neighboring tables as Chinese etiquette leads customers to
fight over the bill: Not to avoid it, but for the right to pay it.

When to Go November through January provides warm, dry, comfortable weather. Summers are hot
and very humid, although air-conditioning in much of the city makes the season bearable.

Planning Dim sum is served from early morning but is more commonly eaten from mid-morning to
mid-afternoon. After 11:30 a.m. long lines form even at the vast dim sum restaurants in the New
Territories, where reception has to communicate with waiters by walkie-talkie.

Websites www.discoverhongkong.com, www.hkstreet.com

Dining on Dim Sum

Dim sum is found wherever a
visitor might want to go: the cool
old-world interior of **Shu Zhai** at
Stanley Market; the **Easterngate
Seafood Restaurant** at the ultramodern Citygate shopping mall
at Tung Chung; and outlying
islands, such as **Lamma**, where
harbor-front restaurants offer
cheap dim sum with views.

In some restaurants, towers of
bamboo steamers containing the
dim sum are wheeled around on
carts. Waitresses lift the lids to
reveal the piping-hot contents,
and ordering is simply a matter
of pointing.

CHINA

SICHUAN COOKING

Visit what the Chinese call the heavenly kingdom—Sichuan, in the southwest—to sample divine dishes, some of which are hellishly hot.

Heat is the keynote of Sichuan cooking—and it is imparted by the tiny Sichuan pepper which, despite the name, is related neither to the black pepper nor to the chili pepper. These tongue-numbing delights, fruit of the prickly ash, have a lemony aroma. In China, food is medicine as well as sustenance, so the heating properties of the food are said to combat the effects of a humid climate and its many overcast days. But heat is not the only thing going for Sichuan food. Skillfully blending the full range of flavors—hot, sweet, sour, salty—local chefs use dozens of cooking techniques to make the most of the province's abundant ingredients. The provincial capital, Chengdu, is the best place to sample the most famous dishes: *mapo dofu* (the so-called "pock-marked woman's bean curd," bean curd cooked over a low heat in a chili sauce), fish-fragrant eggplant (a vegetarian dish made with a spice mixture usually used for fish), tea-smoked duck, dry-fried beef shreds, *gong bao ji dong* (spicy chicken and peanuts), and an army of pickles. Hotpots, a kind of casserole, are another Sichuan specialty. Other dishes, such as duck tongues, braised turtle, tendons, tripe, and offal of every variety, are eaten with gusto by the locals but are a step too far for many Westerners. Snack foods, available from street vendors, noodle shops, and restaurants, tempt the taste buds in every corner of Chengdu with the promise of hot pork-stuffed *zhong* dumplings or slippery, spicy *dan dan* noodles with a topping of minced beef and preserved vegetables.

When to Go April, May, September, and October are the most pleasant months to visit Chengdu. Winters are cold and wet, summers hot and steamy.

Planning Two days will be sufficient to visit the Chengdu Panda Breeding Research Center, stroll around the city's antique market, drink a cup of green tea at one of the teahouses along the Funan River or at the People's Park, and taste the hot and spicy flavors of Sichuan cuisine. Be sure to visit the Sichuan Opera.

Websites www.hiasgourmet.com, www.panda.org.cn

A Haven for Tea Drinkers

A visit to a teahouse can be an all-day affair with snacks, visits from a fingernail-cutter or ear-cleaner, a card game, and a never-ending supply of jasmine, green, or oolong tea. As soon as you have drained your cup, a waiter, known locally as a "tea doctor," will replenish it by pouring water from a long-spouted copper pot over the leaves remaining in the bottom. In a show of skill, some waiters pour tea into tiny cups from across the room.

Sadly, teahouses, where young and old mingle in a relaxed yet lively atmosphere, are vanishing from China, pushed aside in the rush to modernity. In Chengdu, however, they can still be found throughout the city, often in parks or Buddhist temples.

If you are lucky, you may witness the ritual of ear-cleaning. Using an array of prongs, scoops, and feather brushes, the cleaner probes the customer's ear with astonishing delicacy. You may want to experience it yourself.

Opposite: Bars and restaurants line a street in downtown Chengdu. Above: The Anlan Suspension Bridge, west of Chengdu

Office workers eat lunch at the Ban-Klang-Nam restaurant on the banks of the Chao Phraya River (River of Kings).

THAILAND

Sensational Bangkok

For aficionados of Thai cuisine, the vast and vibrant
city of Bangkok is the culinary capital of the world.

Maneuvering past a thousand motorcycles and meat skewers, weaving through the noise and the noodle stands, sensory overload sets in long before you set foot in the restaurant. This is Bangkok, where the atmosphere is electric and so is the food. With a little guidance, one can eat shockingly well here. The human tongue can supposedly detect just five categories of flavor—sweet, salty, sour, bitter, and umami (meaty or savory)—but real Thai food makes one wonder why such a conservative estimate has been so widely accepted. Soup is a safe bet—*tom yum pla* (hot and sour fish soup) sings both of those notes loud and clear, while stepping out a little with something like fish viscera soup might yield the fieriest dish you have ever fallen in love with. If you are looking for something more solid, consider the impossibly plump river prawns or indulge in the Thai spin on fried chicken—dusted with pungent slivers of crispy fried garlic. Salads offer further adventures in taste and texture as rare fruits combine with seeds, vegetables, and exotic additions, such as shredded banana blossom. It is difficult to pass up all the street food on the way to dinner, but when you are heading for one of the city's hundreds of restaurants you need to save room for culinary exploration.

When to Go Depending on the time of year, Bangkok's climate is either hot and wet or hot and dry. The latter is preferable for most people, in which case November through February is best.

Planning Public transportation is prolific and the city is easily navigable, so when booking a hotel, focus more on cost and amenities than on location. Restaurant reservations are rarely necessary. Just follow your nose and your stomach. If the seats around you are full of smiling diners, you have found the right place.

Websites www.bangkoktourist.com, www.chotechitr.net, www.alifewortheating.com

Bangkok's Best

■ "What do you feel like eating today?" This is the question the kindly woman greets you with when you sit down for lunch at a tiny, long-established restaurant on the edge of **Ko Ratanakosin**, the old island center of the city. She will then return to the kitchen and loudly whip up a meal so good you won't know whether you owe the thanks to your own well-judged requests or to her thoughtful recommendations. This is **Chote Chitr**, a restaurant with a name that is difficult to pronounce but easy to love (146 Prang Pu Thorn, Tanao Road).

■ On Sukhumvit Soi 36, just off Bangkok's lengthy and vibrant shopping street, Sukhumvit Road, **My Choice** is a no-frills restaurant that dazzles with the harmonious complexity of its food. The 1970s'-hotel-lobby-esque decor may not appeal to everyone, but the chef keeps the focus where it belongs—on the plate.

SEAFOOD IN SYDNEY

With an abundance of ingredients at their fingertips, Sydney's chefs have taken seafood cooking to new heights.

Sydney is a foodie's paradise. With a population of five million it is Australia's largest city, and a diverse multiculturalism ensures that its restaurants offer an ever-changing array of "Mediterr-asian" cuisines. Chefs select from some of the world's finest ingredients, including grain- and grass-fed beef, succulent lamb, free-range poultry, and the more exotic kangaroo and crocodile. But seafood is Sydney's real specialty. Chef Neil Perry's flagship restaurant, Rockpool, in The Rocks district around Sydney Harbour Bridge, has set the standard for seafood in central Sydney for more than 20 years, while Pier—Greg Doyle's restaurant at Rose Bay overlooking a pretty stretch of Sydney Harbour—serves fresh fish, scallops, oysters, and crab with imagination and respect. Dishes such as pot-roasted lobster with kaffir lime and basil, accompanied by a crisp Australian white wine, offer a quintessential Sydney experience. For "Australian modern," Tetsuya's on Kent Street near Darling Harbour is renowned for its marriage of Japanese seasonal ingredients prepared in the French tradition—confit of Petuna ocean trout served with *konbu* (kelp) and fennel is an outstanding signature dish. If all you want is something simple, such as classic fish and chips, go to Frenchmans Beach at Botany Bay in the eastern suburbs, where you can eat a perfect takeout while watching the sun set across the bay.

When to Go Spring (October–November) for seasonal food and fall (March–April) for mild weather. Both are preferable to the busy, hot, humid summer (December–January). Sydney winters can be terrific too, with temperatures around 70°F (21°C), but with chilly evenings. Just pack a sweater.

Planning There are excellent restaurants throughout the capital, though some of the best are found in the central business district, in The Rocks, near Circular Quay, and in the Opera House.

Websites www.rockpool.com.au, www.pierrestaurant.com.au, www.tetsuyas.com, www.sydneyfishmarket.com.au, www.visitnsw.com/sydney.aspx

The Freshest Fish

Sydney Fish Market at Pyrmont sells fresh fish and seafood from all over Australia, including Tasmania, tropical Queensland, and the Northern Territory. Take an early morning tour (every Monday and Thursday, reservations essential) and experience the Dutch auction market, auction floor, and sashimi arcade. Don't miss the Sydney rock oysters, Balmain bugs, snapper, blue swimmer crabs, John Dory, and farmed Atlantic salmon.

The market has simple seafood restaurants and a Chinese restaurant offering **yum cha** (small dishes with tea). It also hosts a cookery school offering sessions by local and international chefs.

Roasted marron tail with artichoke heart and cherry tomato tastes as good as it looks in Sydney's Pier restaurant.

CHINATOWNS

Forget all your troubles, forget all your cares, and go Chinatown. For flavors, aromas, and Oriental escapism nothing beats it. If in doubt where to dine, follow where the Chinese go.

❶ Manhattan, New York City

Housing some 30 percent of the city's Chinese in cramped quarters, Chinatown fills a tiny pocket of lower Manhattan. Hundreds of restaurants, stalls, stores, and pungent seafood markets vend all manner of food from jerky to fried dumplings in one of the world's largest Chinatowns—even the local McDonald's is bilingual.

Planning Organized food tours exist. Canal Street has an Explore Chinatown kiosk. www.explorechinatown.com

❷ Vancouver, Canada

With roughly a third of Vancouverites claiming Asian ancestry, the city's Chinatown is Canada's largest. Dating from the 19th century, attractions include the only full-size Chinese classical garden outside China and a summertime night market selling giant eels, dried fish, and other essentials. On Pender Street East, Foo's Ho Ho is the city's last surviving "village-style" Cantonese restaurant.

Planning The Chinese Cultural Centre provides information. www.vancouverchinatown.ca

❸ San Francisco, California

Many Chinatowns don't look very Chinese in origin as they predate Chinese occupation, but the 1906 earthquake gave residents a chance to rebuild San Francisco's in traditional style. This densely inhabited quarter is North America's largest Chinatown, with a bewildering array of Oriental food and sights. Pick between upscale diners and backstreet holes-in-the-wall.

Planning Chinatown hosts events year-round, from the Night Market Fair to guided food tours. www.sanfranciscochinatown.com

❹ Havana, Cuba

Although at its peak Chinatown covered 44 blocks and Cuba's Chinese numbered around 40,000, the main focus today is the pedestrianized Calle Cuchillo. Behind a huge Chinese arch donated by China, gaily painted restaurants serve an incongruous mix of Cuban-tinged Chinese and Italian dishes.

Planning Tien Tan serves the most authentic Chinese food. www.cuba1847.com, www.cubatravel.cu

❺ Singapore

Although it dates from 1821, modern redevelopments have given Singapore's Chinatown an unusually upscale air. The hub, Smith Street, aka Food Street, has neat rows of stands selling local specialties. Much less tourist-oriented, the renovated Chinatown Complex has some 200 food stalls upstairs.

Planning Many Smith Street stalls open only at dinnertime. The Chinatown Heritage Centre explains Singapore's Chinese heritage. www.chinatown.org.sg

❻ Binondo, Manila, Philippines

Founded in 1594, the world's oldest Chinatown fuses Spanish colonial architecture with more than four centuries of Chinese occupation. A curious mix of Spanish churches, Buddhist temples, and shining temples of commerce and finance, it is also one of Manila's top dining quarters. Restaurants, noodle houses, and stalls dispense everything from suckling pig to Chinese pizza.

Planning A traditional, atmospheric way to explore Binondo is by *calesa* (horse-drawn trap). www.tourism.gov.ph, www.islandsphilippines.com

❼ Jakarta, Indonesia

Jakarta's densely populated Glodok is probably the most alluring of Indonesia's many Chinatowns. With Dutch colonial as well as Indonesian elements thrown into the wok, it offers fusion food at its finest. Vegans tired of tofu dishes elsewhere will find taste-bud-tingling temptations in Gloduk, while carnivores can enjoy freshwater-turtle soup and pig-offal stews.

Planning Glodok can be seedy at night. www.jakarta-tourism.go.id

❽ Brisbane, Australia

There are larger, older Chinese enclaves elsewhere, but for a taste of China—and the Orient generally—few promise such variety and quality in such a confined space. Cantonese, Beijing, Hunan, and Sichuan cuisines are all here—in both restaurants and some truly pan-Asian stores—alongside Japanese, Thai, Singaporean, Malaysian, Vietnamese, Cambodian, and Laotian.

Planning Many restaurants offer good-value lunchtime menus. www.ourbrisbane.com, www.visitbrisbane.com.au

❾ London, England

London's original Limehouse Chinatown suffered heavy bombing during World War II, and its inhabitants moved to Soho. Although few people live in the Soho Chinatown—Europe's largest—it remains a rendezvous for the city's widespread Chinese. Some of the best restaurants are on Lisle Street, such as Mr. Kong and bargain-basement, noodle-soup purveyor Hing Loon.

Planning Chinese New Year celebrations are huge, filling much of London's West End. www.chinatownlondon.org

❿ Manchester, England

Behind the first true Chinese imperial arch built in Europe, Manchester's Chinatown, started in the 1970s, has contributed to this once gritty industrial city's regeneration, long vying with London's for innovative, high-quality fare. Its most acclaimed restaurant, Yang Sing, combines top-class dim sum, a 1930s' Shanghai theme, and tailor-made banquets.

Planning Visit on Sundays, when Chinese from throughout northern England congregate here. www.visitmanchester.com

Right: Restaurants are packed cheek-by-jowl in San Francisco's Chinatown, along with bakeries and tearooms.

INDIA

Goan Melting Pot

Famous for having some of the world's most beautiful beaches, India's smallest state also offers a richly diverse cuisine.

Drenched in spices, often fiery and red in color, the dishes you savor in Goa are quite different from the food elsewhere in India. Here, coconut, tangy *kokum* (the dried skin of the mangosteen fruit), and red chilies brought in from Kashmir are among the dominant flavors. Seafood is the Goans' first love, but they also relish pork—introduced by the Portuguese, who ruled the enclave until 1961—and chicken. The varied local cuisine is the result of a blending of traditions—indigenous, Iranian (via the medieval Muslim sultanate of Bahamani), and Portuguese, as well as influences from East Africa and other regions that had trade links with Goa. As you travel along the spectacular coastline, you can sample some of the best of this fare in numerous small seaside restaurants. At Anjuna Beach in the north, Xaviers behind the flea market is famous locally for its seafood "catch of the day," cooked Goan style with coconut, curry leaves, and other spices. Souza Lobo on Calangute Beach serves outstanding fried mackerel; Florentine in Saligao has what many say is Goa's best *cafreal* (an African-inspired spicy chicken dish), while at Teama in Murod Vaddo near Candolim Beach, the fish and seafood curries are a must. In the south, don't miss Zee Bop, a shack offering authentic Goan cooking in a great ambience on Utorda Beach, or Martins Corner on Betalbatim Beach. Watch the setting sun as a delicious meal is served on small platters, accompanied by *feni*, the local alcoholic brew.

When to Go October through March are best. April through June can be searingly hot and humid, and the monsoon rains are relentless from June through August. Goa has a large Catholic population, and February is the month of the pre-Lenten Carnival, with parades of floats, dancers, and musicians.

Planning Make sure to include Goa's small and charming state capital, Panaji (Panjim), in your itinerary, particularly the Fontainhas quarter with its narrow streets and brightly painted Portuguese colonial houses. Good restaurants in Panaji are Mum's Kitchen, Viva Panjim, and the stylish Portuguese-Goan Horse Shoe.

Websites www.goahub.com, www.gogoa.com, goagovt.nic.in

Liquor, Sausages, and Sweets

■ Goa's local drink, **feni**, is a double-distilled spirit made from coconut or cashew nuts. You can drink it straight or on the rocks, but it is usually more pleasant mixed with pineapple juice. Be warned: feni is fearfully potent.

■ Every Goan home has a supply of spicy homemade **sausages** in the kitchen cupboard. Made from diced pork seasoned with a fiery mix of spices called Goan **piri-piri**, the sausages were a way, before refrigeration, of keeping meat edible during the terrible heat of summer. A side order of sausages with the local *pao* bread makes a perfect snack.

■ Among local sweet dishes, **keli halwa** (bananas in sugar syrup) is Indian-inspired, as are the sweet rice dishes. But for those with a sweet tooth, the most typically Goan offering is the Portuguese-inspired **bibinca**, made from layer upon layer of coconut pancakes.

■ The most colorful showcase for Goan food is the **Friday bazaar** in **Mapusa** in the north. The name Mapusa means to "fill a measure"—or make a sale—and this is where anybody with anything to sell comes to trade. Browse among stalls laden with Goan sausages, huge tins of locally grown cashew nuts, or bottles of feni. Look out for delicious homemade currant, ginger, or beetroot wine.

Opposite: Visitors stroll along Vagator Beach in north Goa. Above: A cow stands outside a restaurant near Calangute Beach.

Thali in Bangalore

In the South Indian city of Bangalore, a traditional *thali* meal, with its mouthwatering variety of dishes, is yours for two dollars.

W ord of mouth keeps the Mavalli Tiffin Room filled with hungry clients from the moment it opens until it runs out of food. Popularly known as MTR, the restaurant occupies a former home near Bangalore's Lalbagh Botanical Garden, with the hall as the main serving area. The utilitarian look of the place is quite forgotten when the food arrives. Much of the menu must have been devised in 1924, when MTR opened as an eating house … and it is all the better for it. This is South Indian cuisine at its best—aromatic, served in piping hot courses, with even the snacks enjoying their share of delicious accompaniments. The food is cooked in ghee (clarified butter), made on the premises, and the spices are more for taste than mouth-searing pungency. A full thali meal—brought to you on a round metal plate called a thali—typically includes an Indian bread (roti, chapati, or *parantha*), rice, a *sambar* (a lentil-based brew) or similar curry-like preparation, *rasam* (a clear spicy soup flavored with tomatoes), cooked vegetables, a salad of freshly sliced cucumber, and yogurt or buttermilk. Around you, elderly *dhoti*-clad gentlemen wandering in for breakfast mingle with joggers in running suits and sneakers—reminders of Bangalore's status as India's Silicon Valley. At lunchtime, the line of would-be eaters is serpentine. Parking problems are part of the package, but nothing deters those who have tasted the fare or been impressed by accounts of it.

When to Go Bangalore's climate is pleasant year-round.

Planning MTR uses a coupon system to allot customers a time and space to eat. Avoid holidays and weekends, when the chances are that the food will run out before you reach the front of the line. The left hand is considered unclean, and Brahmin establishments like this one would prefer customers to eat with the right hand. MTR also owns stores, called Namo MTR, which sell mixed spices and frozen snacks.

Websites www.mtrfoods.com, www.karnatakatourism.org

Tiffin Time

By a quirk of etymological and former imperial fate, a Scottish dialect word, "tiff," meaning "sip," has evolved into a widely used South Asian term for a snack or light meal. A "**tiffin room**" is where you buy such snacks or meals.

Classic South Indian tiffin snacks, eaten for breakfast or in the late afternoon ("tiffin time"), include **idlis** and **dosas**, made from ground parboiled rice and white lentils, mixed into a paste and left to ferment overnight. For idlis, the paste is steamed in special containers. For dosas, it is griddled to make crisp brown pancakes.

Wadas, another local snack, are small dumplings made of yellow or white lentils ground to a paste, seasoned with green chilies and diced ginger, then fried in hot oil. Like idlis and dosas, wadas are served with coconut chutney and sambar.

Two *wadas* are served in the traditional way, placed on a banana leaf on a *thali* (metal plate), with their accompanying sauces and a drink of *chai*.

The Parthenon stands atop Athens's Acropolis, the kind of view that gives added piquancy to any meal.

GREECE

Athenian Tavernas

Discover the Greek capital's authentic flavors—meat and seafood grilled to perfection and served with the freshest of vegetables.

Old photos and murals of local bon vivants adorn the walls of Taverna tou Psiri. Situated in the Psiri district, north of the world-famous landmarks of the Acropolis, the restaurant has been a favorite with Athenians since World War II. Here, you can feast on superb *paidakia* (lamb chops) or other grilled meats, *keftedes* (meatballs), *kolokithia keftedes* (deep-fried zucchini balls), *horta* (boiled greens), and salads. East of the Acropolis, on the edge of the tourist-thronged Plaka district, you could wander past Paradosiako Cafeneon without giving it a second glance. Paradosiako occupies a space on the corner of Nikodimos and Voulis streets that might be more suitable for a barbershop. But it includes a kitchen where Kyria Euginia cooks, and her husband Dimitris serves, some of the best home cooking in Athens. The menu is simple, with specials that change daily. If you order grilled seafood, it will be fresh, especially the whole *thrapsala* and calamari (different kinds of squid). The fish is usually the inexpensive kind you eat on the Greek islands—grilled sardines or *kolios* (mackerel), or fried *gavros* (anchovies). Sausage-lovers should ask for *souzouki*. Around the corner on Apollonos, Euginia's and Dimitris's children run Oinomagerio Paradosiako. Euginia oversees the cooking there, too, so expect similar delights.

When to Go The best months in Athens are May–June and September–October. It is warm enough to dine outdoors, and there are fewer tourists than in high summer.

Planning Other good tavernas include Triantafilo Tis Nostimias on Lekka, near Paradosiako, and Steki tou Ilias on Eptahalkou in the Thission district. For a no-frills neighborhood taverna, try Kalamia near the intersection of Kypselis and Skyrou streets in northern Athens.

Websites www.greecetravel.com, www.greecefoods.com, www.athensguide.com

Basement Restaurants

Athens's basement restaurants are one good reason to visit outside the main tourist season. Often shut during the summer, at other times of the year they are among the coziest places to enjoy a good meal.

Try **Taverna Saita**, a former *bakaliaro* (fried salted cod) restaurant on Kydatheneon Street, which serves fish, grilled meats, and oven dishes. For lunch, where better than **Diopoto** (Two Doors) in the Central Market on Socratous? You sit down, and the owner-cook puts down a paper tablecloth and a pitcher of wine. There may be three things to choose from: a fish, a stew, and a salad. By 2 a.m., Diopoto is a party in full swing, and when the local Albanian accordion player appears, the room breaks into singing and dancing. Don't look for a sign—there is none.

SEA VIEWS TO DINE FOR

Blissful vistas, the crash of waves on the shore, and fresh, salty air to whet
the appetite make these oceanside eateries a treat for all the senses.

❶ Wickaninnish Inn, Tofino, B.C., Canada

Storm-watchers gather, especially in winter, at this rustic
retreat perched at the very edge of Vancouver Island's rain-
battered west coast. Savor top-notch West-Coast food in the
Pointe Restaurant, which has 240° views of the Pacific Ocean.

Planning Ferries to Vancouver Island run from several mainland British
Columbia and Washington State points. The nearest airport is Tofino
Long Beach. www.wickinn.com

❷ Boathouse, Breach Inlet, Isle of Palms, South Carolina

Dolphins often feature on the menu, but only as entertainers
at this nautically themed restaurant occupying the "breach"
between the Intracoastal Waterway and the Atlantic. Choose
from the pine-and-mahogany indoor area, the outdoor deck, or
the rooftop bar. All promise superb sunset views and fresh seafood
dishes, including Boathouse crab cakes and raw oysters.

Planning The Boathouse is at 101 Palm Boulevard.
www.boathouserestaurants.com

❸ Nepenthe, Big Sur, California

Perched high above the rugged California coastline and facing
the setting sun, this family-run business enchants Big Sur
visitors with sweeping views of the Pacific—and occasional
glimpses of migrating gray whales. The food is fresh, local, and
delicious, the California wine sublime.

Planning Reserve a table or visit at off-peak hours for the best views.
Crowds often throng Nepenthe at sunset. www.nepenthebigsur.com

❹ The Baths, Sorrento, Victoria, Australia

Nudging Sorrento's bayside beach, these former sea baths offer
glorious views over Port Phillip Bay. In summer, diners spill
out onto a large decked balcony, while on colder days there are
open fires inside. Modern Australian seafood and other dishes
are served with laid-back Aussie hospitality.

Planning The restaurant is at 3278 Point Nepean Road, near the
Queenscliff–Sorrento car-ferry terminal. Queenscliff is 20 miles
(32 km) southeast of Geelong by road. www.thebaths.com.au

❺ Apsley Gorge Vineyard Café, Bicheno, Tasmania, Australia

Savor divine oysters or scallops washed down with glasses of
chilled Chardonnay as you overlook the crashing Tasman Sea
on the east coast. The ramshackle open-air tables and wooden
knives and forks are all part of the charm. The vineyard produces
some of Australia's most-prized Pinot Noir and Chardonnay.

Planning The café is just outside the small town of Bicheno.
www.apsleygorgevineyard.com.au

❻ Unawatuna, Sri Lanka

This secluded tropical paradise on the south coast is Sri Lanka's
prettiest beach resort and has some of its finest alfresco dining.
With Dutch, Indian, Malay, Arab, British, Moorish, and
Portuguese influences, Sri Lankan food is generally spicier than
in other parts of the Indian subcontinent. A typical dish is fish
curry, which you can enjoy at beach cafés, such as Kingfisher or
Lucky Tuna, while gazing out on palm-fringed ocean vistas.

Planning Unawatuna is just south of Galle and 76 miles (122 km) by
road from Colombo. www.srilankatourism.org

❼ Club 55, St.-Tropez, France

Ever since 1955, when Brigitte Bardot was filming *And God Created
Woman* in this fishing village on the Côte d'Azur, Club 55 has
been at the heart of the St.-Tropez beach scene—with the rich
and famous arriving by private yacht. The club's restaurant on
Pampelonne beach offers fresh local produce and gorgeous views
of the Mediterranean. A large catch of the day for an entire table is
a lunchtime favorite, with the house rosé almost mandatory.

Planning For non-members, lunchtime tables get booked weeks or
months ahead, especially on weekends. www.ot-saint-tropez.com

❽ Reial Club Marítim, Barcelona, Spain

Normally members-only, Barcelona's royal yacht club, founded
in 1881, also runs a restaurant open to all, drawing Spain's
beautiful people with its harbor views and extensive first-class
seafood menu. Highlights include seafood paella.

Planning The club is on the Espanya wharf. Non-members enter the
restaurant through the side door. www.barcelonaturisme.com

❾ Café del Mar, San Antonio, Ibiza, Spain

In a location chosen for its twilight outlook over Conejera
Island, this baroque fantasy—the birthplace of chill-out
music—is the world's most-celebrated sunset bar. Thanks
to its sublime fusion of music, vistas, decor, and climate, it
remains the island's leading pre-party venue. As the sun sets,
a hush descends over customers, followed by clapping.

Planning At sunset the café, open summer only, is packed. Afterwards
enjoy fire-jugglers at Mambo next door. www.cafedelmarmusic.com

❿ Muisbosskerm, Western Cape, South Africa

On the beach just outside Lambert's Bay, this open-air restaurant
offers a sand-between-your-toes setting and fixed-price menu
featuring local seafood prepared in nearly any way you like,
including baked in a clay oven. Despite much competition,
Muisbosskerm remains a South African culinary highlight.

Planning Meals last about three hours. When available, it is worth
splurging on the crayfish supplement. www.muisbosskerm.co.za

Right: Overlooking 50 miles (80 km) of rugged coastline, Nepenthe is one of the most scenic spots to eat in California.

This is Naples, after all, so expect your pizza to be prepared, cooked, and served with theatrical panache.

ITALY

Pizzas in Naples

Luscious tomatoes and vibrantly aromatic basil are two key ingredients in pizzas made in their southern Italian birthplace.

Something is always boiling in Naples, and it isn't lava from nearby Mount Vesuvius towering on the horizon. Instead, in pizzerias around the city, *mozzarella di bufala* (mozzarella made from the milk of the domestic water buffalo) bubbles and blisters in the volcanic heat of wood-fired ovens. It is destined for the queen of pizzas, the Margherita—literally regal, since this gastronomic gift was invented in 1889 for Queen Margherita, consort of Umberto I of Italy. To create a Margherita, the mozzarella is combined with vibrant basil and locally grown San Marzano tomatoes—white, green, and red, the colors of the Italian flag. Also found on the menu of every Neapolitan pizzeria is the marinara, topped with deep-red tomato puree and wildly fragrant oregano. Non-purists may gild the lily with an unmistakably pungent touch of garlic or a few leaves of basil, but if anyone goes beyond that, politely say "Ciao" and follow your nose to the next place down the block. Wherever you stop and whichever pizza you choose, the crust will be distinctly Neapolitan, with a chewy rim, a crisp bottom, irregular pockets of air, and smoky charred patches. The pizza bakes for just 90 seconds, and is often devoured just as quickly.

When to Go Avoid July and August, when temperatures can top 104°F (40°C). Winters are mild, and spring and fall a delight.

Planning For a proper pizza pilgrimage, the unmissable shrine is Da Michele, where Margherita and marinara "pies"—the only two varieties they serve here—fly out of the ovens to satisfy hungry crowds. Going at lunchtime is best, so you can later cancel your dinner plans and come back for more. It is just a short walk from Da Michele to R.M. Attanasio, which turns out warm *sfogliatelle* pastries all day.

Websites www.damichele.net, www.alifewortheating.com/italy/a-pizza-tour-of-naples

Sfogliatelle Napoletane

After Margherita and marinara, the two most important words to learn before traveling to Naples may be **riccia** and **frolla**. They specify the two different kinds of **sfogliatella** (plural: *sfogliatelle*), the ubiquitous sweet treat found in cafés and pastry shops around the city.

These clam-shaped pockets of multilayered pastry pleasure are filled with egg custard flavored with sweetened ricotta cheese, vanilla, and tiny pieces of colorful candied fruits, such as orange and lemon.

Riccia means "curly," which describes this version's scalloped, crunchy exterior. Bite into a sfogliatella riccia and prepare for the shower of flakes that will inevitably cascade down your front. The frolla ("tender") variety is softer, doughier, and often sports a beautiful golden-brown sheen.

Timing is key with sfogliatelle. Go mid-morning to the pastry shop of your choice to have them just as they emerge piping hot from the oven.

ITALY

BOLOGNA

Italy's gastronomic capital, Bologna is known for the richness of its cuisine, earning it the nickname "La Grassa" (the Fat One).

The red-roofed city of Bologna in northern Italy is known for its medieval arcaded walkways, its ancient university, and its love of food. The city is the birthplace of the world's most famous ragu sauce (eaten here with handmade fresh fettuccine, not dried spaghetti), but its range of foods is far more diverse. Stroll down the tangle of narrow lanes east of Piazza Maggiore around Via Clavature and Via Drapperie. This corner of Old Bologna is the site of the city's original medieval markets, today replaced by dozens of *botteghe* (little stores)—*fruttivendoli* (fruit sellers), *pescherie* (fish dealers), *pastifici* (pasta stores), and *latterie* (cheese stores), where goods spill out of open storefronts creating a street market feel. Best of all are the *salumerie*, or delicatessens—try Tamburini or Bruno e Franco—where you will find scores of cheese varieties, fresh tortellini with numerous stuffings, truffles, wild mushrooms, and golden olive oils. The stars of the show are cured meats, such as mortadella (a large smoked pork sausage flavored with peppercorns, pistachios, and olives), *culatello, zampone*, and prosciutto. To savor the potential of such ingredients, step into one of the city's many outstanding restaurants—Ristorante Diana and the less expensive trattorias, Da Gianni and Anna Maria, are all nearby. Order a local favorite, such as lasagne (made from green-spinach flavored pasta), *bollito misto* (a soup made from several kinds of meat and vegetables), or *cotoletta alla Bolognese*, a pork cutlet covered with prosciutto and cheese.

When to Go With hot summers and rainy winters, Bologna is best in spring, the season of new vegetables, and fall, when truffles and wild mushrooms are on hand in the city's kitchens.

Planning Allow three days to explore. Then visit Bologna's two most famous food-loving neighbors: Parma (birthplace of the famous ham and Parmesan cheese) and Modena (world famous for its balsamic vinegar).

Websites www.italytraveller.com, www.eurodestination.com, www.citalia.com, www.deliciousitaly.com

When in Bologna...

Sample the handmade yellow egg pasta known as **sfoglia** (or sheet) because it is rolled to paper-thinness. Melt-in-the mouth and silky in texture, it is made from soft flour rather than the more usual durum wheat. The sheets are cut into fettuccine or shaped into parcels. Tortellini is stuffed with pork or prosciutto, spices, and Parmesan cheese, and traditionally served in a clear broth (*in brodo*), while the larger tortelloni is filled with spinach and ricotta and eaten with butter and sage.

Munch on the local breads: **crescente** (a square bread made with pork fat, with the addition of prosciutto or pancetta); **crescentine** (a light puffy dough served hot with cold meats and cheese); and **piadina** (a flat round bread served like a toasted ham and cheese sandwich).

Enjoy the north Italian sunshine in Piazza Maggiore, flanked on one side by the San Petronio Basilica, the world's fifth largest church.

Danish Smørrebrød

In Copenhagen, eat your fill of truly wonderful open-face sandwiches with a multitude of tasty toppings.

With friendly, English-speaking people and centuries-old buildings rising alongside smart hotels and boutiques constructed in modern Danish design, Denmark's capital is also home to excellent cuisine. Its *smørrebrød*—pronounced something like "smer-er-bruth"—translates as "butter and bread" and describes the city's famous open-face sandwiches. As the name suggests, each smørrebrød starts with a piece of bread—usually *rugbrød*, Denmark's deep brown, sourdough rye—spread with a thin layer of butter. A wide variety of ingredients is used to top this base to make a savory snack or light meal. One popular version is bread topped with pork liver paté and served with crunchy pickled cucumber, bacon, and fragrant fried mushrooms. Fish abounds in this harbor city, and seafood lovers will relish a topping of smoked herring adorned with egg yolk, chives, and grated radishes. Alternatively, try smoked salmon, whose robust taste goes well with mushrooms in a creamy white sauce, or shrimp—you may find Danish shrimps smaller than the ones you are used to, but what they lack in size they make up for in succulence and flavor. To sample the fullest range of toppings, from fillet of plaice to excellent Danish cheeses, head for Restaurant Ida Davidsen. The eatery on Store Kongensgade boasts the world's largest sandwich menu, with about 300 varieties of smørrebrød.

When to Go Copenhagen, and Denmark as a whole, are delightful in the spring and fall. Winter is chilly and damp. Summer is pleasant, but the place swells with tourists.

Planning In addition to the top-notch restaurants throughout the city, you can buy good-quality open-face sandwiches at many corner shops. When dining, remember that tips are automatically included in the price, but you can tip extra for exceptionally good service if you wish.

Websites www.idadavidsen.dk, www.visitcopenhagen.com

Smørrebrød Etiquette

■ Danes are very mindful of manners. They eat their open-face sandwiches with knife and fork rather than pick up the bread with their hands.

■ The whimsically named **Veterinarians' Midnight Snack** (Dyrlægens Natmad) is an open-face sandwich that starts with a base of liver paté and includes corned beef and meat aspic topped with onions.

■ As well as being one of the world's oldest amusement parks, Copenhagen's **Tivoli Gardens**, opened in 1843, brims with restaurants and cafés. The colorful harborside area, **Nyhavn**, is another good place for bars and restaurants.

Stop off in a bar on the Nyhavn waterfront to watch the activities of boats and people as you sip Danish beer and enjoy a tasty snack.

The numerous dishes of a rijsttafel are a colorful feast for the eyes as well as for the taste buds.

Rijsttafel Dishes

A rijsttafel may consist of between six and 20 dishes and condiments—sometimes even more. In a classic example of Dutch understatement, the name simply means "rice table" (from the words, *rijst* and *tafel*), because of the central role played by rice.

■ Typical rijsttafel meat dishes include **nasi goreng** (fried rice with meat or seafood), **babi ketjap** (pork with soy sauce), **rendang** (a spicy beef stew), **perkedel** (fried potato-and-meat cakes), **sate** or **satay** (grilled skewers of meat with a peanut sauce), and **sambal goreng** (various stew-like dishes of meat or fish in a hot sauce). **Sambal** is a chili-based relish.

■ Other common dishes are **atjar** (a spicy sweet-and-sour salad of sliced vegetables), **gado gado** (vegetables with a peanut sauce), **pisang goreng** (fried banana), **nasi kuning** (Indonesian yellow rice), and **krupuk** (light-as-air fried prawn crackers).

THE NETHERLANDS

RIJSTTAFEL IN AMSTERDAM

Fiery beef stews, vegetables in peanut sauce, and fried bananas are just some of the dishes making up an Indonesian "rice table."

The rain-soaked cobbled streets and tree-lined canals of the Netherlands' largest city are a world away from the rijsttafel's tropical birthplace, but even in a damp North European metropolis, the multiple dishes of this spice-laden feast are true to their origins. Step inside one of Amsterdam's Indonesian restaurants, such as Tujuh Maret or Sama Sebo, and immediately the decor, the courteous welcome, and above all the scent of exotic flavorings evoke a distant, warmer world. Either presented as a buffet or brought to your table on trays and placed on plate-warmers, every dish is a different taste experience, from mild and fragrant to searingly hot. For 320 years, Indonesia was a Dutch colony, and although it cut most of its ties with the former colonial power after independence in 1949, its food has remained a strong feature of the Netherlands' culinary landscape. In the old colonial days, the rijsttafel signified the grandest of repasts, enjoyed beneath the ceiling fans of large, airy restaurants in Jakarta, Surabaya, or Jogjakarta, each dish borne to the table by a young server in traditional dress. Nowadays, all across the Netherlands, not just in Amsterdam, there are hundreds of *Indonesische eethuizen* (small restaurants and takeouts), where you can sample the kinds of dish that make up a rijsttafel.

When to Go Amsterdam is a city for all seasons, so any time of the year is good.
Planning Sama Sebo is at PC (Pieter Corneliszoon) Hoofstraat 27, close to the world-famous Rijksmuseum art gallery. Tujuh Maret is at Utrechtsestraat 73. Both are popular, so book in advance. Amsterdam's historic center, contained in and around a concentric web of canals, is easy and agreeable to walk (or cycle) around. Accommodations near the center are most convenient.
Websites www.tujuh-maret.com, www.samasebo.nl, www.iamsterdam.com

ENGLAND

LONDON'S RESTAURANTS

Once a culinary joke, the British capital is now home to some of the world's best chefs producing some of its most exciting food.

A block away from London's Smithfield meat market, the Shaker-like austerity of chef Fergus Henderson's St. John Restaurant sets the tone for a menu of nose-to-tail eating, where roasted bone marrow and chitterlings (pigs' intestines) share space in season with roast game birds, such as woodcock and widgeon. St. John is typical of a new breed of restaurant that has emerged in London during the past 30 years, many clustered around the city's historic market centers—no coincidence and an opportunity to try some of the country's freshest food. Even in the plushest enclaves of the West End, the showcasing of Britain's seasonal produce and gastronomic traditions is a priority for chefs such as Philip Howard at The Square or Richard Corrigan at Corrigan's, both in Mayfair. Success breeds success. TV chef Gordon Ramsay earned his fame with an eye for delicacy and detail, and cooks from his stable, including Angela Hartnett and Mark Sargeant, are now names in their own right—Sargeant presides over the kitchens at Claridge's Hotel, time-honored haunt of film stars and foreign royalty. Farther west again is the place many regard as one of London's holiest shrines of consistently good eating: The River Café. Rose Gray and Ruth Rogers opened the Thames-side restaurant in 1987, and they still supervise a menu that changes with the seasons. The dishes are Italian, but the majority of the fresh ingredients are sourced locally from the highest-quality British produce.

When to Go London is a great city to visit at any time of year. Summer is the most attractive season, although the city does fill up with tourists.

Planning Try visiting one of London's food markets to get a feel for the fresh produce on offer—you will find a list on the Urbanpath website. If you come across a stallholder selling a particularly interesting product, start talking to them. Do they supply any restaurants? What eateries do they recommend?

Websites www.urbanpath.com, www.stjohnrestaurant.co.uk, www.squarerestaurant.org, www.corrigansmayfair.com, www.gordonramsay.com, www.rivercafe.co.uk

St. John's Welsh Rarebit

This makes a steadying snack or a splendid savory at the end of a meal, washed down with a glass of port.

Serves 6
A pat of butter
1 tbsp flour
1 tsp English mustard powder
½ tsp cayenne pepper
Generous ¾ cup/7 fl oz/200 ml Guinness
A very long splash of Worcestershire sauce
4 cups/1 lb/450 g grated, sharp Cheddar cheese
4 slices of toast

Melt the butter in a pan, and stir in the flour. Let them cook together until they smell biscuity but are not browning. Add the mustard powder and cayenne pepper. Stir in the Guinness and Worcestershire sauce, then gently melt in the cheese. When it is all of one consistency, remove from the heat, pour out into a shallow container, and let set. Spread ½ in (1 cm) thick on the toast and place under a preheated broiler. Eat when bubbling golden brown.

Opposite: One-time microbiologist Philip Howard prepares a dish at The Square. Above: Big Ben and the Houses of Parliament

Edinburgh Castle (on the left) and the spire of The Hub (a former church) punctuate the skyline view from The Tower.

SCOTLAND

FINE FOOD IN EDINBURGH

In the Scottish capital, relish the country's incomparable culinary resources in a new generation of award-winning restaurants.

Edinburgh is justly regarded as one of Europe's most beautiful cities. Its attractions, including its castle, the elegant 200-year-old "New Town," and the internationally famous arts festivals in August, have long drawn visitors. But until recently the city would never have figured on anybody's list of gourmet destinations. Happily, things have changed, and Scotland has learned to appreciate national produce that includes seafood from crystal-clear northern waters, Europe's finest beef cattle, lamb with a delicacy of flavor that comes only from grazing by the sea or on heather-clad hills, wild mushrooms, game, and luscious soft fruits. With their inspired treatment of these riches, pioneers such as Andrew Radford—founder of The Atrium and its more informal sister establishment, Blue—have transformed Edinburgh's eateries. And the gradual regeneration of the ancient port of Leith, a short taxi-ride from the heart of the city, has led to the emergence of a lively quayside dining quarter, where chef-patrons Martin Wishart and Tom Kitchin have earned Michelin stars for the restaurants that bear their names. Back on the higher ground of the city center, The Tower, on the top floor of the Museum of Scotland in the atmospheric Old Town, offers you some of the best of modern Scottish cuisine, all garnished with spectacular views.

When to Go Edinburgh is busiest—and most exciting—in August, when audiences and performers at the Edinburgh International Festival, Book Festival, and Fringe swell the population several times over.

Planning Advance reservations are essential for the most popular restaurants, especially on weekends and during the August festival period, when tables may be booked up weeks or even months in advance.

Websites www.list.co.uk, www.atriumrestaurant.co.uk, www.thekitchin.com, www.martin-wishart.co.uk, www.tower-restaurant.com

Farmers' Market

Make time to explore the Castle Terrace Farmers' Market, held every Saturday from 9 a.m. to 2 p.m. Here, you can graze on sweet and savory free samples, or sit down for brunch at a cluster of tables among the stalls. Try hot **porridge**—that Scottish breakfast classic—garnished with fresh fruit, preserves, or whiskey and cream. Meat-lovers might prefer a sandwich of hot **roast pork**, reared on a farm in the Scottish Borders, with stuffing, apple sauce, and crisp crackling. You may be lucky enough to find the Scottish seafood specialty called the **Arbroath smokie**—a delicately flavored smoked haddock, prepared in a mobile smokehouse, boned to order, and ready to eat.

BISTROS MODERNES IN PARIS

A "new wave" of Parisian chefs offers fabulous bistro dining, good for both the palate and the wallet.

The *bistro moderne* movement began as a reaction against the fussy cuisine that used to prevail in Paris. Chefs started to look to seasonal market goods, less expensive cuts of meat, and food from local producers to offer customers excellent meals at affordable prices. Spearheading the move was Yves Camdeborde, a classically trained chef who had worked at the Ritz, Maxim's, and La Tour d'Argent. In 1992, he set up his first restaurant, La Régalade, in southern Paris, serving rich gourmet French bistro fare at prices that were unheard of in the city at the time. Other chefs observed his success and quickly cottoned on to the formula, with the result that there is now a plethora of options. On the Left Bank, try Jean-François Debré's Les Racines in Rue Monsieur Le Prince or the Delacourcelle brothers' Le Pré Verre in Rue Thénard—ideal for lunch after viewing the stunning "Dame à la Licorne" (Lady and the Unicorn) tapestries in the nearby Hôtel de Cluny. In eastern Paris, sample the menu at Thomas Dufour's L'Ébauchoir near the Bastille or the Nidhsain brothers' La Boulangerie in Ménilmontant. As for the man who started it all: Chef Camdeborde sold the La Régalade in 2005 and now heads up a tiny bistro called Le Comptoir at the Hotel St.-Germain, also on the Left Bank. There are only 20 tables, and all the diners eat from the same five-course, prix-fixe menu. It is one of Paris's most authentic and delicious meals—and will cost 45 euros (about $60).

When to Go Paris in the springtime may be every lover's fantasy, but Paris in late fall is the gourmet's preference. This is when truffles and foie gras are in season, and cheeses made with the summer's buttery milk are ripening.

Planning For bistro recommendations, strike up a conversation with other customers in a good café. Parisians know their food well and are not as unfriendly as their reputation suggests. Always book in advance.

Websites www.hotel-paris-relais-saint-germain.com, www.lebauchoir.com, www.lepreverre.com

Bistro Fare

■ Terrines, sausages, cured meats, and unusual cuts are the order of the day in a Parisian bistro moderne. Look out for **boudin noir** (blood sausage), plates of **charcuterie**, **riz de veau** (sweetbreads), **pieds de cochon** (pig's feet), and **joue de boeuf**—the cheek of a cow, a rich and delicious cut of meat.

■ Bistros modernes are also great places to sample some of the best of France's cheeses. Ask the waiter to talk you through the cheese cart. Some bistros will have more than a dozen to choose from. A good waiter will help you pick out exactly what you want—and a wine to go with it.

A dizzying choice of French cheeses—served before dessert, not after—will be a high point in any bistro moderne meal.

FRANCE

Secrets of the Cassoulet

In southwestern France, three cities and the regions round them claim to make the best cassoulet. Why not try all three?

In Carcassonne, they insist that the meat of the red-legged partridge is the key to a good cassoulet. In Toulouse, cooks add sausages and *confit de canard* (preserved duck) to enrich the flavors of this hearty dish of beans, pork, onions, and carrots. In Castelnaudary, between the other two cities, the essential "added value" ingredients are pork ribs and *confit d'oie* (preserved goose) from the surrounding Lauragais region. The different traditions are jealously maintained—Carcassonne and Castelnaudary even have *confréries du cassoulet*, brotherhoods pledged to defend their particular interpretations—and they reflect the essentially sociable nature of cassoulet. Traditionally, it was a way of using the ingredients on hand to feed a crowd—a harvest crew, say, or a family gathering. Despite the variations, beans are the basic ingredient—*haricots de Tarbes* or *lingots de Castelnaudary*—and long, slow baking is vital to allow a crusty top to form. In the old days, people would prepare cassoulets at home, then take them to the local baker, who slid them into his oven after the day's baking was done. In Castelnaudary, they still puncture the crust four times while cooking to let it reform and seal in the flavors. Ready to let your taste buds loose? Within the medieval walls of Carcassonne's Cité, head for L'Écu d'Or, where you can choose from five versions of cassoulet. In the center of Toulouse, after a walk along the historic Canal du Midi, Au Gascon offers top-notch cassoulet for a modest price. In Castelnaudary, join aficionados for a cassoulet lunch at the Hôtel de France—you may pick up a cassoulet-maker's secret or two.

When to Go Southwestern France is pleasant year-round. But to immerse yourself in the food and wine of "cassoulet country," the cooler months are best. In winter, black truffles appear on restaurant menus.

Planning Cosmopolitan Toulouse deserves a full weekend to enjoy its museums, concerts, and nightcaps with the late crowd. Northwest of Carcassonne visit Saissac, one of the region's castles left in ruins after the 13th-century Albigensian crusade against the Cathars.

Websites www.carcassonneinfo.com, www.cassoulet.com, www.uk.toulouse-tourisme.com

Cassoulet Country

■ The Carcassonne-based Académie Universelle du Cassoulet (Universal Academy of Cassoulet) has devised a **Route des Cassoulets**, which allows you to explore the different versions of the iconic casserole. Driving past fields of wheat, beans, and sunflowers, and farmyards with noisy ducks and geese, you understand the origins of the dish.

■ In **Toulouse**, visit the main square, the **Place du Capitole**, which becomes an organic farmers' market every Tuesday and Saturday morning. Nearby is the covered **Marché Victor Hugo**, where vendors sell fresh produce daily. In winter, you may find stalls selling black truffles.

■ The Not brothers in **Mas-Saintes-Puelles**, northwest of Castelnaudary, are among the few potters who still produce the broad earthenware dishes called **cassolles**. These give the cassoulet its name—*caçolet* or *lou cassoul* in the Occitan language spoken across southern France. You can see some original cassoles in the **Musée Présidial**, overlooking Castelnaudary.

■ Full-bodied, regionally produced Languedoc wines stand up well to the strong rustic flavors of cassoulet. Try a **Cabardès**, a **Malepère**, or a deep garnet **Corbières**.

Opposite: From Carcassonne's Cité, view the countryside that gave birth to cassoulet. Above: A cassoulet in its *cassolle*

At restaurants like Le Miramar, the fish makes one course, with the broth used for cooking it served separately.

FRANCE

THE REAL BOUILLABAISSE

Once simple fisherman's fare, *bouillabaisse marseillaise* has evolved into one of the world's most delectable seafood concoctions.

When in France's chief Mediterranean seaport, don't order just any bouillabaisse. Marseille's famous herb-flavored seafood stew requires a specific combination of ingredients, all laid down by tradition. In the old days, when Marseille fishermen returned to harbor, they sorted out the best of their catch to sell and took home the unmarketable leftovers to be boiled and served with garlicky bread crusts and *rouille*—a spicy mayonnaise-style sauce. Then, as Marseille rose to prominence as a trading port in the 19th century, the city's upper classes finessed bouillabaisse, creating the extravaganza eaten today. Be warned: There are imposters waiting to take your euros for lesser fare, sometimes labeled *soupes des pêcheurs* or *bouillabaisse à notre façon*. In 1980, a group of chefs signed a charter stating which ingredients should go into a bouillabaisse. To be assured of the truest, finest specimens, meeting the charter's criteria, head for the area around the beautifully renovated Vieux Port. Here, Le Miramar looks out over bobbing yachts and fishing boats and the two forts guarding the port's entrance. Nearby, two other restaurants pride themselves on serving the real thing—Chez Michel on Rue des Catalans and Chez Fonfon on Rue Vallon des Auffes.

When to Go Marseille has hot summers and mild winters. The Festival de Marseille, with a full program of dance, music, theater, and cinema, takes place in June and July. Remember that the French take their summer holiday en masse in August, and many restaurants shut down for the month.

Planning Be sure to go to the Quai des Belges in the morning to see the fishermen bringing in their catch. For fabulous views of the city and Vieux Port, climb up to the immense Byzantine-style Basilica of Notre-Dame de la Garde, built in the mid-19th century atop Marseille's highest hill.

Websites www.marseille-tourisme.com, www.chez-fonfon.com

Authentic Ingredients

Purists insist that bouillabaisse must contain at least four species of indigenous Mediterranean fish, most commonly **scorpionfish** (*rascasse* in French), **conger eel** (*congre*), **red gurnard** (*galinette*), and **John Dory** (*St. Pierre*). If the fish is cooked with fresh tomatoes, potatoes, a hearty measure of fresh fennel, and perhaps some anise-flavored Pernod, it has the makings of an authentic bouillabaisse. Due to overfishing in the Mediterranean, the indigenous species are harder and harder to find. Even so, bouillabaisse with salmon is never the real thing, and with shellfish it is debatable.

Traditionally, bouillabaisse is served up in two courses. First comes a bowl of the broth, which is ladled over garlic-rubbed bread croutons, smothered with rouille. The croutons should never be added afterward to float on top of the broth and never covered with grated cheese. After this, you have the fish, which your waiter will fillet for you as you watch. The perfect wine to accompany bouillabaisse is a dry, white Cassis or Bandol rosé—both, naturally, from near Marseille.

BASQUE COOKING

With more Michelin stars per capita than anywhere in the world, San Sebastián in northern Spain is a top global food destination.

The elegant resort of San Sebastián (Donostia in Basque) is famed for its scallop-shaped bay and stunning belle epoque architecture. It also boasts a stellar triumvirate of chefs, Juan Mari Arzak, Martín Berasategui, and Pedro Subijana, all running restaurants at the cutting edge of culinary innovation. But if you restrict yourself to top-end establishments, you will miss out on other Basque eating experiences. From *asadores* serving roast meats to restaurants offering specialties such as *bacalao al pil-pil* (spicy salted cod), the food is outstanding whatever your tastes and budget. Sample the fare in a *sidrería* (cider house), where you drink cider drawn from oak barrels as you eat, or in a harbor- or beach-side café serving seafood so fresh it still quivers. But for the most authentic Basque experience, head for bars such as La Cepa in the narrow lanes of the Parte Vieja (Old Quarter) to enjoy San Sebastián's best *pintxos*—equivalent to tapas in the rest of Spain. These exquisite bite-sized morsels include potato *tortilla* (omelet), slices of glistening ham, green peppers deep fried and eaten with sea salt, *chorizo* sausage, and cod croquettes—don't forget to look at the blackboard for special items that need on-the-spot cooking. Pile what you want onto a plate and enjoy it with some *txakoli*—the local semi-sparkling white wine, traditionally poured from a height to aerate it. Go from bar to bar like this for an evening as the Basques do, and you will be in exalted company—Michelin-star chefs are said to come here for inspiration.

When to Go Spring and summer are best. Despite San Sebastián's three splendid beaches, this part of the Basque country does not attract huge crowds of tourists. Winters tend to be rainy.

Planning Be sure to visit the underground food market of La Bretxa in the Parte Vieja. And allow time to explore the beautiful Basque coastline, with fishing towns, such as Lekeitio, where you can enjoy freshly caught seafood in harbor-side cafés, or Getaria for seafood cooked on huge charcoal broilers.

Websites www.basquetours.com, www.arzak.info, www.martinberasategui.com, www.akelarre.net

A Culinary Revolution

Owner of San Sebastián's triple-Michelin-starred Restaurant Arzak, **Juan Mari Arzak** is generally regarded as the champion of new Basque cuisine. Inspired, it is said, by hearing French chef Paul Bocuse speak about *nouvelle cuisine* in the 1970s, he was determined to use Bocuse's principles to reinvent Basque cooking. He organized reunions among fellow chefs, in which he presented updated versions of classic Basque dishes along with original creations. His revolution went on to form the basis of new Spanish cooking, **La Nueva Cocina**. Arzak still runs his restaurant with his daughter Elena, and he is still creating imaginatively innovative food based on classic Basque dishes. Try the lobster in white olive oil or fried potato with prawns in a saffron sauce.

San Sebastián's famous beach forms an almost perfect round shell shape—hence its name, Playa de la Concha (the beach of the seashell).

Suckling Pig in Segovia

Just over an hour's drive northwest of Madrid, a 19th-century mesón (inn) offers visual delight combined with epicurean bliss.

Through the latticed windows of the multistoried Mesón de Cándido, you watch the afternoon sunlight stroke the graceful arches of the ancient city of Segovia's 2,000-year-old Roman aqueduct. Beside your table, a waiter is apportioning the crispy roast suckling pig you ordered. This feast, a Segovian specialty, is not for the squeamish. It starts with a carefully selected 21-day-old unweaned piglet. Having passed through the butcher's hands, the suckling pig has its bristles singed off and is rubbed with a mix of garlic, bay leaf, and lard. It is then slow-roasted for two hours over glowing oak coals in the Méson de Cándido's 150-year-old brick oven. The pig is now ready for the table. According to ritual, the waiter divides it into serving portions using the edge of a plate to demonstrate the roast's crisp perfection on the outside and the meat's melt-in-the-mouth tenderness on the inside. After that, the plate is shattered on the stone floor for extra brio. A good red Ribera del Duero wine, from grapes grown in the Duero valley north of Segovia, stands up well to this winter favorite. Take your time and enjoy the repast while, outside, the low slanting sunlight turns the immense aqueduct to deepening hues of gold.

When to Go Suckling pig is available year-round, but hearty local roasts—lamb and partridge as well as piglet—are more suitable for winter weather than the intense, dry heat of the Castilian summer.

Planning Segovia is an easy day trip from Madrid, and there is plenty to see and do as well as eat. In addition to the Roman aqueduct, sights include the cathedral, a late Gothic masterpiece, and the Alcázar (castle), a royal residence of the medieval kings of Castile, which occupies a dramatic location on a high spur of land overlooking the surrounding countryside. Mesón de Cándido has several worthy competitors in Segovia, though none with the exquisite views of the aqueduct.

Websites www.mesondecandido.es, www.turismodesegovia.com

Castilian Hospitality

The family-run Mesón de Cándido is more than a restaurant—it is an institution. Its heyday began in 1931, when **Cándido López Sanz** (1903-92) took over the operation of the mesón from his mother-in-law. His motto was that anyone "who honors this house with their presence, whatever their nationality or condition, deserves the respect and all kinds of attention to which Castilian hospitality is obligated."

During his long lifetime, Don Cándido played host to guests including royalty, the legendary bullfighter El Cordobés, the writer Ernest Hemingway, and numerous film stars, from Orson Welles to Ursula Andress. His children and grandchildren still run the restaurant, which now bears his name, and in 2006 they opened the luxurious Hotel Cándido on the outskirts of Segovia.

Be warned: When your roast suckling pig arrives at the table, you will be in no doubt about what you are eating.

For valencianos one of the best ways of cooking paella is over an open-air fire on a mild, sunny winter day.

SPAIN

Paella in Valencia

The city of Valencia on Spain's Mediterranean coast is the undisputed capital of the country's most famous dish.

People in Valencia have strong opinions about their relationship with Barcelona and Catalonia to the north, their language (which many refuse to call Catalan), and paella. First made by Moorish peasants in the days of Muslim rule in the Iberian peninsula, paella started life as poor man's fare, using short-grain rice cooked with olive oil, saffron, vegetables, and anything else at hand, usually chicken, rabbit, duck, or snails. Short-grain rice is still the key ingredient, which in a perfectly cooked paella should be soft on top, while the layer beneath is crunchy and caramelized—this lower layer, called the *socarrat*, is considered the best part. There are two basic versions: *paella valenciana*, made with meat, and its seafood rival, *paella marinera*. Purists in Valencia do their best to enforce paella-making commandments—thou shalt not add sausage, mix seafood with meat, fail to add green peas, omit broad beans—but in the end, the best thing is just to enjoy the dish. Well-known emporiums in Valencia include Casa Roberto, El Forcat, La Pepica, La Marcelina, and El Rall. The city's Michelin-starred chefs, meanwhile, are busy creating inventive versions of paellas at restaurants such as Ca Sento and La Sucursal.

When to Go Paella is popular year-round. March 15-19 are five days of annual madness when Valencia celebrates the fiesta of Las Fallas, famous for the huge papier-maché and plaster *ninots* (puppets) that are paraded through the streets. Needless to say, paella-eating is involved.

Planning Sights in Valencia include the ancient Barrio del Carmen and the ultramodern Ciutat de les Arts i les Ciències (City of Arts and Sciences), designed by Valencian-born architect Santiago Calatrava. Feeling hungry? Browse in the lovely Mercado de Colón (Columbus Market).

Websites www.gotovalencia.com, www.valencia-on-line.com, www.whatvalencia.com, www.lapepica.com

Pans and Variations

■ Paella is almost literally synonymous with the broad, shallow steel pans that are used to cook it—the word "paella" derives from the Latin *patella*, meaning "pan." Paella-loving Spanish households always have stoves with an extra-large burner on top to accommodate a paella pan.

■ In Barcelona, the dish called *arròs* (literally, "rice") is virtually identical to paella. Its many variations include *arròs a banda* (made with shelled seafood) and *arròs negre* ("black rice," dyed black by squid ink). Another dish, *fideuà*, is made with vermicelli noodles instead of rice, and also cooked in squid ink.

■ Valencian purists never add sausage to paella. But the dish has largely escaped Valencian control, and entire autonomous communities on the Iberian peninsula would never touch a paella if it did not include some spicy *chorizo* sausage.

■ A fast-food version of paella, called **Paellador**, is often offered in tourist traps. It cannot compare with a proper home- or restaurant-cooked paella.

HISTORIC RESTAURANTS

Owing to their age, noble surroundings, or historic menus, these landmark restaurants have become venerable institutions, still drawing in successive generations of diners.

❶ Union Oyster House, Boston, Massachusetts

Established in 1826 and occupying a handsome Georgian building, this is America's oldest restaurant in continual use. Serving New England specialties like clam chowder and crock-of-oyster stew, the restaurant is a popular stop on the Freedom Trail. John F. Kennedy's favorite booth is commemorated with a plaque.

Planning The Oyster House is at 41 Union Street (Subway: Government Center). Sit in the ground floor bar to watch your oysters shucked in front of you. www.unionoysterhouse.com

❷ Owariya, Kyoto, Japan

Close to Kyoto's Imperial Palace, this august institution has been perfecting noodle-making since 1465. Choose between *soba*, thin buckwheat noodles, or *udon*, thick wheatflour noodles, both often accompanied by *dashi*, a broth of dried fish flakes, seaweed, sweet sake, and sugar. The owners maintain Kyoto's mountain water is crucial to dashi—hence branches haven't opened elsewhere.

Planning Open 9 a.m.–7 p.m. daily, except January 1. Owariya is at 322 Kurumayacho-Nijyo. www.honke-owariya.co.jp

❸ Asitane, Istanbul, Turkey

Opened in 1991 in a restored 19th-century mansion, Asitane recreates Ottoman court cuisine, with many dishes based on a banquet given for Süleyman the Magnificent's sons in 1539. In summer, there are tables in a tranquil courtyard in the shadow of the Chora Church.

Planning Asitane is in the Kariye Hotel. www.asitanerestaurant.com

❹ Yar, Moscow, Russia

Founded in 1826 and moved to its present location in the landmark Sovietsky Hotel in 1910, Yar is a playground of Moscow's well-to-do. With marble columns, floor-to-ceiling frescoes, stucco and gilt aplenty, this restored restaurant valiantly recreates the opulence of the turn of the 20th century. While tiger prawns, sturgeon, and lobster loom large alongside French classics, don't overlook treats like borscht, piroshki, and veal Stroganoff.

Planning Yar is at 32/2 Leningradsky Prospekt (Metro: Dynamo). www.sovietskyhotel.com

❺ Olde Hansa, Tallinn, Estonia

Occupying a medieval merchant's house in the old town, this restaurant commemorates Tallinn's Hanseatic heyday. All the ingredients for an authentic medieval banquet are in place: murals and tapestries line walls, lutists strum ballads, wenches ply platters and pitchers, and candles flicker. The meticulously researched menu spans elk fillet, wild hog shank, and bear. Brave the strong beer with herbs.

Planning Olde Hansa is at Vana Turg 1. www.oldehansa.ee

❻ Wierzynek, Kraków, Poland

Poland's most renowned restaurant dates back to 1364, when a banquet was held for visiting European royalty. More recent guests, who have included King Juan Carlos and Emperor Akihito, sample upscale Polish dishes, such as a composition of quail, deer, and wild boar; duck with apples; and filled dumplings.

Planning Reserve a table overlooking the old-town square. www.wierzynek.com.pl

❼ Le Procope, Paris, France

Founded in 1686, Paris's oldest café thrived during the French Revolution, being a favorite meeting place of French—and later American—republicans, including Robespierre, Napoléon, Franklin, and Jefferson, alongside writers like Voltaire. Thanks to a 1989 refurbishment, the salons and dining rooms spread over two floors retain their 18th-century magnificence.

Planning Le Procope is at 13 Rue de l'Ancienne Comédie, St.-Germain-des-Prés (Métro: Odéon). www.procope.com

❽ La Tour d'Argent, Paris, France

Michelin's downgrading of France's erstwhile haute-cuisine showcase from three stars to two—later to one—created a culinary cause célèbre. Yet today reservations remain as coveted as centuries ago, when noblemen dueled for tables. The restaurant enjoys superb riverside views over Notre-Dame, and the house specialty is duck, served rare inside and caramelized outside. Visit the remarkable cellar, which houses around 400,000 bottles from the 1700s onwards.

Planning The restaurant is at 15–17 Quai de la Tournelle (Métro: St.-Michel). www.tourdargent.com

❾ Rules, London, England

London's oldest restaurant opened in 1798 and retains a softly lit, memento-clad Victorian aura thanks to an 1873 refurbishment. The menu features British classics, such as Brown Windsor soup, potted shrimps, and spotted dick (a raisin-studded steamed cake) alongside game treats like jugged rabbit, snipe, and woodcock.

Planning Rules is at 35 Maiden Lane (Tube: Leicester Square). www.rules.co.uk.

❿ Botín, Madrid, Spain

Founded in 1725 in a 16th-century building embedded into Madrid's city walls, this wood-beamed restaurant was a favorite of Ernest Hemingway. Although popular with foreign tourists, Botín still sports uncompromisingly Spanish fare. Specialties include suckling pig and lamb roasted in the restaurant's original oven.

Planning Botín is at Calle Cuchilleros 17 (Metro: La Latina). www.botin.es

Right: Situated in London's Covent Garden, Rules is famous for its game, which is sourced from the restaurant's own Pennine estate.

MADRID'S RESTAURANTS

Spain's culinary traditions are richly varied, and in the capital's eateries you have a perfect "anthology" for sampling them.

King Philip II is best known in the Anglo-Saxon world for his attempt to bring Elizabethan England to heel with the ill-fated Spanish Armada. He was also the man who in 1561 moved Spain's royal court from Toledo to the Iberian peninsula's geometrical center, Madrid, making it the new capital of his far-flung empire. He probably never imagined the magnetic pull that the wealth pouring into the city would have on Spain's four corners. Madrid has long been famed as Spain's first "port," where fish from both the Atlantic and the Mediterranean arrives in pristine condition, better in quality than products left behind on the coasts for locals to consume. Regional Castilian fare stars roasts and stews, best in winter, but in Madrid's restaurants, with the pick of the entire national cuisine to choose from, you will find food for every season—Andalusian gazpacho, Mediterranean rices, Basque fish, Galician seafood, and modern Catalan "molecular" gastronomy. For roasts, go to Asador Frontón I; for *cocido madrileño* (a hearty bean and meat stew, typical of Madrid), try La Bola or Lhardy, while Casa Ciriaco or Casa Lucio are best for other Castilian dishes, such as partridge and broad bean stew. Ranging further afield gastronomically, Casa Benigna and L'Albufera are good for rice dishes, La Trainera and Combarro for fish, Asador Gaztelu and Julian de Tolosa for Basque beef, and La Terraza del Casino and Santceloni for creative contemporary cuisine.

When to Go Lying at the heart of the Iberian landmass at 2,188 ft (667 m) above sea level, Madrid has a fairly extreme climate, with icy winds in winter and hot, dry summers. Spring and fall are best.

Planning Feast your eyes on Madrid's other banquet–its vast trove of paintings. The special "Art Mile" ticket to the three main repositories–the Prado, Centro de Arte Reina Sofia, and Museo Thyssen-Bornemisza–is the basic meal ticket to artistic riches that could take a lifetime to explore properly.

Websites www.esmadrid.com, www.gomadrid.com

Tasty Tapas

Tapas and the itinerant grazing known as the *tapeo* have always been popular in Madrid. Originally morsels served with drinks, tapas in Spain have become miniature culinary art. Look for a crowded space with the boisterous sounds of an open cocktail party. Go in and sample saucer-sized platefuls of **boquerones** (anchovies), **gambas** (shrimps), **queso manchego** (a ewe's milk cheese), grilled **pimientos** (peppers), and other delights. Plaza de Santa Ana and Calle Huertas have dozens of tapas bars, beginning with a famous Hemingway haunt, the Cervecería Alemana. Below the Plaza Mayor in Cava Baja and along Calle el Almendro are a series of popular tapas taverns. The Barrio de Salamanca is another hunting ground.

Customers relax in a café in Madrid's Plaza Mayor (main square), with the prospect of tapas galore in the streets nearby.

The funicular tram called the Elevador da Bica hauls its way up from Lisbon's fish market area to the Bairro Alto.

PORTUGAL

Fish in Lisbon

For seafood, it is hard to do better than the Atlantic-seaboard capital of a nation that is crazy about fish.

Portugal consumes more fish per capita that any other country in Europe, and one of the best places to experience this piscine passion is Lisbon's Bairro Alto—the lively "high town" of narrow streets, set above the grid of the city's central Baixa ("Lower Town") and the Tagus estuary. Up here, the air fills in summer with the smell of sardines being grilled on makeshift barbecues, and dozens of restaurants offer menus crammed with octopus, squid, crab, clams, shrimp, scallops, swordfish, mackerel, hake, and *bacalhau* (salted cod). At heart, Portuguese food is the food of the people. So why not try your luck at the Toma-Lá-dá-Cá, a popular family restaurant just south of the Bairro Alto? Any kind of fish may be served here, but it is likely that bacalhau will be on the menu. In Portugal, bacalhau comes as a starter called *pastéis de bacalhau* (deep-fried fish balls), as *bacalhau à brás* (with onions, potatoes, and eggs), as *bacalhau com pimento e chouriço* (with pepper and sausage), and as *bacalhau com molho de caril* (with curry sauce). In fact, there are said to be 365 different ways to cook bacalhau—one for every day of the year. If you want to enjoy a similar menu in grander surroundings, try the Pap'Açorda—all mirrors, gilt, and crystal chandeliers, even though it is named after a simple soupy dish of bread and seafood.

When to Go Late April and early May are the best time—the air is fresh and the streets are filled with flowers. Lisbon is lively year-round, but temperatures can go above 90°F (32°C) in July and August.

Planning The Bairro Alto is also a center for clubs, nightlife, and plaintive traditional *fado* singing. The Portuguese tend to start their evening meal late, around 10 p.m., and restaurants stay open until 2 a.m. Pap'Açorda is at Rua da Atalaia 57. Toma-Lá-dá-Cá is at Travessa do Sequeiro 38 (no bookings).

Websites www.visitportugal.com, www.golisbon.com

Fish Baked in Sea Salt
Peixe Assado no Sal

Salt baking enhances a fish's delicate taste and texture. It is particularly well suited to meaty fish with delicate, white, lean flesh. In Portugal, robalo (snook) is commonly used to make this dish, but sea bass is a good alternative. The fish, which must be very fresh, is gutted and cleaned but otherwise left whole.

Serves 4-6
1 whole 5 lb/2.3 kg sea bass, gutted and cleaned
7 lb/3 kg coarse sea salt
3 egg whites
1 lemon, sliced into rounds
A handful of fresh herbs, such as thyme, parsley, or wild fennel stems

Preheat the oven to 425°F/ 220°C/Gas Mark 7. Line a large roasting pan with wax paper or aluminum foil. Pat the fish's outside and inner cavity dry. Beat the egg whites until frothy, then add the salt, and mix well— the mixture should resemble lightly packed snow.

Spread about a third of the salt mixture evenly across the lined pan. Lay the fish on its side on top and stuff the cavity with the lemon slices and fresh herbs. Mound the remaining salt mixture over the fish, gently packing it around the fish with your hands. Bake for 40-45 minutes. Remove from the oven and let stand for 10 minutes.

To serve, crack the crust and carefully remove all the salt and skin. Move the fish to a clean plate, fillet, and serve with olive oil and lemon.

Couscous forms the centerpiece of a colorful Tunisian feast, washed down with fresh mint tea.

TUNISIA

FEASTING IN TUNIS

The banging of hammers on brass and the muezzin's call mingle with the scent of spices and grilled meat in the Tunisian capital.

Start your tasting tour of Tunis in North Africa by entering the Medina (old quarter) through Bab el Bahr, one of the gates into the city's medieval heart. Inside you can lose yourself in a maze of narrow alleyways, all of which lead to the souk, or marketplace. Each part of the souk features a different product (perfumes, carpets, clothes, and so on), but everywhere hole-in-the-wall restaurants beckon. Sit inside or at one of the tiny tables that line the narrow alleys and enjoy a snack of *merguez* or *brik* at rock-bottom prices. For a more formal lunch or a delicious dinner, visit La Galette, Tunis's port. Like all ports, this one appears to have seen better days, but it is worth the trip if only to visit one of the neighborhood's fish restaurants. Avenue Franklin Roosevelt is lined with eating places, including Le Café Vert and L'Avenir, both of which serve sparkling fresh fish to an enthusiastic local crowd. At any time of day, you will find Tunisians drinking strong, sweet, cardamon-scented Arabic coffee or enjoying a glass of fresh mint tea. In Sidi Bou Said, a few miles northeast of Tunis, visit Café des Nattes, where the Swiss-born painter Paul Klee found inspiration. A few streets away, sit on whitewashed benches outside Café Sidi Chaabane, drinking in gorgeous views of the sparkling blue Gulf of Tunis along with your tea.

When to Go Hot summers and cool winters make spring and fall the favored times to visit. Even in winter, however, it is warm enough to eat lunch outside on a sunny day.

Planning To escape from Tunis's hustle-bustle atmosphere, stay in nearby Sidi Bou Said. This village of white houses, blue doors, and magenta bougainvillea is only 20 minutes by train from downtown Tunis. When you get your bill, remember that the TGV is a tax, not a service charge. It is unusual for women to travel alone, so lone female travelers should be cautious.

Websites www.darsaid.com.tn, www.tourismtunisia.com

A Tunisian Lexicon

The national dish, *couscous*, is usually eaten for lunch, although tourist restaurants serve it at dinner, too. The grains form a base for a thin, fragrant stew of meat and vegetables. *Mloukia* is a thick lamb or beef stew flavored with bay leaves, usually served with French bread. *Merguez* are thin, spicy lamb sausages, served grilled with a squeeze of lemon. *Brik à l'oeuf* is a flaky pastry parcel with a lightly cooked egg inside. The outside is crisp fried, while the inside is soft and molten, making for a delicious mess when you attempt to eat it. It is served as a starter with a squeeze of lemon. Tunisian *tajine* is a cold egg dish—not to be confused with the famous Moroccan stew of the same name.

SOUTH AFRICA

Dining Out in Cape Town

It is said that you can eat somewhere different
in Cape Town every night of the year.

French pastries for breakfast … fresh local snoek fish for lunch … full English afternoon tea … and you still have to choose among French, Ethiopian, or local Cape Malay for dinner. Such is your delectable dilemma when eating out in Cape Town. Restaurants with sea views abound along the coastline, from stalwart Blues in Camps Bay and Salt perched above the rocks in Bantry Bay to the Mariner's Wharf in Hout Bay. Gourmands will enjoy exploring the funky, varied restaurants of the City Bowl, where you can sample Ethiopian *injera* (sourdough pancake bread) at Addis in Cape Town, Turkish meze at Anatoli, or innovative Afro-European menus in historic properties, such as Aubergine or 95 Keerom. Colonial influences are strong at the Mount Nelson Hotel, while the Victoria and Albert (V&A) Waterfront caters to all tastes and budgets. The surrounding Cape Winelands, meanwhile, offer classic French fine-dining options, including Constantia's La Colombe or Franschhoek's Le Quartier Français. Fresh seafood is always on the menu, whether wrapped in newspaper on the beach at Mariner's Wharf, as sushi in trendy Balducci's, or with a view at Baia. Be sure to try the spicy flavors of Cape Malay food in Biesmiellah, and authentically African dishes, such as *umngqushu* (samp and beans). Above all, don't miss some of the innovative combinations of local ingredients and classic dishes that are surfacing, including Thai green ostrich curry, springbok carpaccio, or *fynbos* honey bavarois.

When to Go Around Christmas (mid-summer), Cape Town is uncomfortably packed with visitors. The weather remains excellent until at least April, so try February or March for the best of all worlds.

Planning Cape Town has little reliable public transportation, so be prepared to rent a car. Restaurant reservations are advisable. Crime is a problem: Don't explore on foot at night (although the V&A Waterfront is fine), don't carry valuables or flash cash, and check with your hotel if a particular place is safe to visit.

Websites www.dining-out.co.za, www.waterfront.co.za

Pumpkin fritters
Pampoenkoekies

These sweet pastries are an easy South African favorite.

Generous ¾ cup/4½ oz/125 g
  all-purpose flour
1 heaped tsp baking powder
Ground cinnamon
A pinch of salt
2 eggs
1½ cups/23 oz/650 g pureed
  cooked pumpkin, well-drained
Sunflower oil for frying
3 tsp granulated sugar

Mix the flour, baking powder, 1 tsp of the cinnamon, and the salt. Beat the eggs well, combine with the pumpkin, and stir into the dry ingredients. Heat enough oil to cover the bottom of a frying pan. Drop spoonfuls of batter into the hot oil and fry until lightly browned on both sides. Drain on paper towels and serve sprinkled with a mix of three parts granulated sugar to one part ground cinnamon.

At Blues restaurant in the smart Cape Town suburb of Camps Bay, beachside eating is brought to a pinnacle of quiet elegance.

ULTIMATE LUXURIES

This selection is, without a doubt, at the extreme end of great dining, and a dedicated food-lover embarking on any one of these quests would be well advised to go prepared. First, patience and persistence are required: For some establishments, it may take months, or even years, to secure a table. Once inside, an ability to live fully in the moment is also an asset, to relax and enjoy a once-in-a-lifetime experience. And finally, once the bill arrives, a strong constitution (and a healthy bank account) are vital. Indulgence on this scale rarely comes cheap. These gastronomic glories take many rich and varied forms. Sometimes luxury comes in the shape of a rare and carefully sourced ingredient, such as the Kobe beef of Japan. It may be the opportunity to experience the artistry of a chef such as Ferran Adrià, whose multisensory experiments draw global gourmets to his elBulli in rural Catalonia. For others, luxury is as much about the setting as about the food—whether from the roof of a Manhattan skyscraper, from alongside Venice's Grand Canal, or from a mountaintop hostelry high in the Alps.

Described as a paradise within a paradise, Le Saint Géran Hotel on the island of Mauritius serves world-class food, which guests can savor in private dining pavilions suspended over the Indian Ocean.

The art-deco Chrysler Building towers over Grand Central Terminal in Manhattan, one of New York's cultural hubs.

NEW YORK

New York Institutions

Indulge yourself with the city's finest cuisine,
drawn from all four corners of the Earth.

The very best places for food can be found both uptown and downtown. Gallery-hopping in Chelsea? Check out the superlative sushi at Morimoto. Headed toward Lincoln Center and crazy about cheese? Step into New York City's luxury Picholine (with a fabulous cheese cave) and try chef Terrance Brennan's light crepe with peeled roast pear on a bed of ricotta cheese and Zinfandel syrup of orange and raspberry concentrate. You'll not find a match for such perfection in texture, color, and taste anywhere. Unless, that is, you head to Brennan's Artisanal Fromagerie, Bistro & Wine Bar on Park Avenue, where some 250 world cheeses feature on the menu. If you are hanging out in Greenwich Village and want the best organic farm-to-table experience, drop in to Blue Hill, or join the crowds and high energy at Lupa Osteria Romana for traditional Italian trattoria fare. If the elegance of a three-star Michelin restaurant appeals to you, make a reservation well ahead of your visit at Le Bernardin, the greatest of them all, whose dining room excels in luxury with museum-quality oil paintings on the walls and ample space between tables permitting conversation during dinner. Union Square Cafe is the most popular top restaurant in New York City and specializes in the perfection of American seasonal cuisine, often paired with California wines.

When to Go Summer in the city can be oppressively hot.

Planning All of the luxury restaurants in New York City require reservations ahead of time, with most tables booked at least two weeks in advance. If you can't get a reservation for your dream cuisine, waltz right into the bar, where all of the above serve the celebrity chef's full menu without reservations.

Websites www.picholinenyc.com, www.le-bernardin.com, www.unionsquarecafe.com, www.wd-50.com

Three of the Best

■ Head for the Lower East Side if you want to experience the most creative and inventive cuisine in the city. At **wd-50**, chef Wylie Dufresne thrills with unusual combinations: How about foie gras, candied olives, green peas, and beet juice? Or beef tongue with fried mayo and tomato molasses?

■ At the midtown **Le Bernardin**, seafood is the passion of celebrity chef Eric Ripert, who divides his fish menu into three categories: Almost Raw, Barely Touched (poached), and Lightly Cooked. Try the thinly sliced conch marinated Peruvian-style in dried corn.

■ At **Picholine** on the Upper East Side, chef-owner Terrance Brennan's fricassee of Maine oysters with leeks, potatoes, and bacon bits in a creamy vermouth sauce with sprigs of baby parsley is absolute ambrosia.

CHICAGO STYLE

Inventive chefs crafting sophisticated contemporary
dishes have turned the city into a great dining destination.

The Windy City is a place where meals featuring layered flavors are a notable part of the landscape. One of the city's most venerated chefs is Charlie Trotter—winner of ten James Beard Foundation awards and author of 14 cookbooks—whose food empire started in an eponymous townhouse in the Lincoln Park neighborhood. His eight-course tasting menus, which are never repeated, showcase seasonal ingredients. Selections from the restaurant's three wine cellars make this an even finer dining experience. And if you can't get a reservation, you can pick up gourmet takeout at Trotter's To Go, a big retail shop several blocks from the flagship restaurant. An evening downtown at Tru feels like being treated to Mediterranean-influenced French food in a contemporary art museum. Sweet is as much the focus as savory on the six-to ten-course tasting menu, which includes pastry chef Gale Gand's decadent concoctions. Sturgeon aficionados will be lured by the Luxury Caviar Staircase, while the candy cart is beyond even Willy Wonka's wildest dreams. If your culinary tastes lean toward foams and gels, make a reservation at Alinea, where the techniques pioneered by Spanish chef Ferran Adrià of elBulli are but a springboard to the innovative dishes here. These dining establishments also have their entertainment value—especially at Charlie Trotter's and Tru, where you can reserve the kitchen table.

When to Go Anytime is fine for these indoor culinary experiences. Go in winter if you like bitter temperatures and bracing winds. Summer can get steamy, but you can generally rely on some cooling breezes near the lake.

Planning Charlie Trotter's is open Tuesday-Saturday; Tru is closed Sunday; Alinea is open Wednesday-Sunday. Make reservations as far ahead as possible; Charlie Trotter's, for example, accepts reservations up to four months in advance. Chicago Restaurant Week is an annual event in February.

Websites www.charlietrotters.com, www.trurestaurant.com, www.alinea-restaurant.com, www.explorechicago.org, www.chicagofoodplanet.com, www.stylechicago.com

Presidential Favorites

■ The Obamas had their first post-election-night dinner out at **Spiaggia**, known for its sophisticated take on Italian cuisine, lake views, and cheese cave.

■ Chef Rick Bayless was mentioned as a serious contender for White House chef. His casual eatery **Frontera Grill** (James Beard Foundation's Outstanding Restaurant of the Year, 2007) and the more upscale **Topolobampo** both honor authentic Mexican culinary traditions.

■ Michelle Obama often dines at **Sepia**, next door to the shop of Maria Pinto, one of her designers of choice.

A Heart of Palm dessert from Alinea: bite-sized slices of heart of palm are hollowed out and stuffed with intensely flavored foams and gels.

NEVADA

LAS VEGAS HOT SPOTS

With the arrival in Vegas of some of the world's superchefs, fine dining has been added to the city's star attractions.

Las Vegas has come a long way since its experiments in building casinos that look like fiberglass castles and circuses. Old-fashioned glamor is back in Sin City, and along with the velvet-lined gaming halls, the world-class spas, and deluxe hotel suites, the allure of Vegas has drawn some of the biggest names in global cuisine. Head to the Bellagio hotel, where Picasso, a love song of a dining room overlooking the casino's famous fountains, is filled with sculpture and paintings by Spanish artist Pablo Picasso. Sample chef Julian Serrano's sublime tasting menu—one of the city's best. Elsewhere, Guy Savoy at Caesars Palace, Joël Robuchon at the MGM Grand, and Alain Ducasse at Mix (in THEhotel at Mandalay Bay), are all worth seeking out for that ultimate Vegas dining experience. Even Thomas Keller of The French Laundry in California—often cited as America's best chef—has an outpost at Bouchon at The Venetian, which serves a startlingly good breakfast. Early birds can tuck into light-as-a-feather French toast, handmade pastries, and perfect omelets. No expense is spared at some of these restaurants. At Wynn's Bartolotta, for example, high rollers can sample fish that have been flown direct to the desert from the Mediterranean and cooked in an authentic Italian style.

When to Go Las Vegas has two low seasons, when room rates are extremely good: The month before Christmas sees the city relatively empty and you will find reservations easy to come by. The height of summer is also quieter as tourists try to avoid the baking sun and extremely dry heat.

Planning It is worth booking your table well in advance, especially around holidays, when the city is very busy. Most restaurants do not have a dress code, but some of the more expensive places do; check the restaurant website before you visit. Traffic in Las Vegas is frequently very bad, so if you plan on driving or taking a taxi, be sure to leave plenty of time.

Websites www.bellagio.com, www.caesarspalace.com, www.venetian.com, www.vegasdiningscene.com, www.lasvegasrestaurants.com

The Best Buffets in Town

Most of Vegas's famous buffets are best avoided by the serious foodie. There are, happily, a few exceptions:

■ The buffets at the **Wynn** and **Bellagio** are a cut above the rest. They also provide a champagne brunch every weekend.

■ Every Sunday, **Bally's** hosts a Sterling Brunch. It is the priciest buffet in town, but you will get value for your money with the bottomless Perrier-Jouët champagne, as much lobster as you can eat, oysters, wild mushrooms, cedar-planked salmon, and an array of beautifully cooked meats and seafood. Caviar also features, although you will have to ask for it at the sushi bar—it is the only buffet offering not on display.

Opposite: Guests enjoy private dining at Wynn's Bartolotta. Above: Roasted Duck and Crab Soup at Bellagio's Sensi

SAN FRANCISCO CHIC EATS

Flower power, Bay Area entrepreneurialism,
and agricultural bounty are all packed into one bowl.

Seared Colorado lamb rack, one of the specialties at Campton Place

California is renowned for a unique cuisine that blends fresh-from-the-farm ingredients, straight-from-the-net seafood, and cutting-edge cooking methods. Chef and cookbook author Alice Waters is credited with creating what is generally known as "California cuisine" when she opened a modest little eatery called Chez Panisse in Berkeley in the early 1970s. With menus based mainly on organic ingredients and sustainable farming, Chez Panisse was soon the leading edge of a whole new trend in food, one that synced perfectly with California's counterculture vibe. The kitchen at Chez Panisse begot a whole new generation of Bay Area chefs dedicated to the same philosophy, maestros like Jeremiah Tower, Mark Miller, and Russell Moore, who would redefine American cooking. While Tower eagerly fused Asian and California ingredients with startling presentation at his landmark Stars restaurant in San Francisco, Miller and Moore went in another direction, reaching back to California's Hispanic past at upscale eateries like the Santa Fe Bar & Grill in Berkeley and Camino in Oakland. Bay Area dishes can be as simple as Dungeness crab with asparagus, and rack of lamb with fried artichokes, or something much more exotic sounding, like whole roasted petrale sole with farro, rapini, and green garlic. Either way, it is a whole new adventure in eating.

When to Go San Francisco is best avoided in summer when thick fog and waves of tourists descend on the city. Winters can be rainy and cold, which leaves spring and (especially) fall as the best seasons to go.

Planning Sample dishes from 50 different Bay Area restaurants at the Fall Fest food and wine festival in early October, staged outdoors at Justin Herman Plaza. October is also "Eat Local Month," with tasting fairs that include dishes with ingredients sourced within 250 miles (400 km) of San Francisco.

Websites www.chezpanisse.com, www.caminorestaurant.com, www.camptonplacesf.com, www.cavallopoint.com, www.ubuntunapa.com, www.sffallfest.com, www.murraycircle.com

Three Stars of California Cuisine

■ **Murray Circle** is located at Cavallo Point, across the bay from San Francisco, in the shadow of the Golden Gate Bridge—one of California's most romantic locations.

■ Named one of America's best new chefs by *Food & Wine* magazine, Jeremy Fox labored for the likes of Gordon Ramsay before opening his own restaurant, **Ubuntu**.

■ At **Campton Place** chef Srijith Gopinath and sommelier Richard Dean have created a nine-course degustation menu to match one of San Francisco's most elegant settings.

Cavallo Point commands impressive views across San Francisco Bay.

Perched on the hillside above Gustavia, the Hotel Carl Gustaf has stunning views of one of the Caribbean's prettiest bays.

CARIBBEAN

EXOTIC ST. BARTH

Darling destination of the rich and famous, the hilly little island of St. Barth is the epitome of trendy relaxation.

After whizzing along the island's narrow, winding roads in a rental car, make sure you have it valet-parked in front of St. Barth's coolest restaurant: Le Ti St.-Barth in Pointe Milou on the island's northwest coast. The restaurant's deep-red walls and the dim glow of chandeliers set a fabulously sexy night scene. Start with the Thai beef salad, and if that brings out your inner carnivore, be sure to order "Le Lion Qui Rit"—a tremendously tasty beef dish—for your entrée. In this popular haunt of the beautiful people, your meal will probably be accompanied by a fashion show of models sashaying between the tables—Le Ti St.-Barth provides some of the best spectator sport on the island. For a quieter dining experience, try The Wall House in the island's capital, Gustavia, where seafood with a French flare is the main fare. Order some of the delectable lobster dishes or the mahi mahi filet, but don't overlook the unexpected treat of duck breast in a red wine sauce. And for the best spot to sip cocktails as you watch the sun go down, sit by the pool in the Hotel Carl Gustaf on the hillside overlooking Gustavia bay. This luxury hotel also serves gourmet French- and Caribbean-inspired cuisine.

When to Go Although it is always fun to play spot the celebrity, this 13-mile (21 km) island can get hideously overcrowded in the fashionable months of the year (from December through January). It is far better to visit from late spring, when there are fewer people and therefore more chance of getting a table.

Planning You can stay in a private villa through WIMCO rentals or at one of the small luxurious hotels on the island. If you are a nervous flyer, you may want to take the 45-minute ferry ride from St. Martin. The tiny plane from St. Martin to St. Barth dives down onto the very small runway in St. Jean. Be sure to have a rental car waiting for you at the airport: Even though St. Barth is small, you will need it to get around.

Websites www.st-barths.com, www.wimco.com, wwwhotelcarlgustaf.com

Creole Almond

This eye-opening after-dinner drink was created by chief bartender Jacky Bertrand of the Hotel Carl Gustaf. The combination of caffeine and alcohol will keep you partying into the small hours.

Serves 2
1/4 cup/2 fl oz/60 ml Old Rhum
1/4 cup/2 fl oz/60 ml Amaretto DiSaronno
1/2 cup/4 fl oz/120 ml freshly made cold coffee
2 tbsp/1 fl oz/30 ml almond syrup
2 tbsp/1 fl oz/30 ml vanilla syrup
Ground cinnamon to garnish
2 freshly roasted coffee beans to garnish

Pour all the ingredients into an ice-filled cocktail shaker. Shake vigorously and strain into two chilled martini glasses. Sprinkle with cinnamon and place a coffee bean on top.

CHEFS THE SUN NEVER SETS ON

This band of superchefs—and the empires they have built up in different parts of the world—are at the forefront of culinary innovation.

❶ Alain Ducasse

The worldwide web of eateries owned by Alain Ducasse embraces London, New York, Tokyo, and Mauritius. His sun-drenched, Provençal cuisine seems designed to please palates everywhere. White (or Alba) truffles are one of Ducasse's favorite ingredients, to be savored in fall.

Planning Ducasse's flagship restaurants are at Paris's exclusive Hôtel Plaza Athénée and Monaco's Hôtel de Paris. www.alain-ducasse.com

❷ Todd English

Massachusetts chef Todd English started out with Olives, his award-winning signature restaurant near Boston, in 1989. Try his take on rustic north Italian classics, such as his herb polenta.

Planning English has Mediterranean-style restaurants across the U.S., including five branches of Olives; Figs, a gourmet pizza chain; and Todd English on the luxury liner, the *Queen Mary 2*. www.toddenglish.com

❸ Peter Gordon

Gordon, a New Zealander, was at the head of the fusion food movement in the 1980s and 1990s, bringing together flavors from Southeast Asian and Western cuisines. His dishes reflect his love of flavor and texture from every corner of the world, and offerings may include lamb on crispy rosemary polenta with buttered kale and minted gooseberry chutney. You might not always recognize what is on your plate, but you are sure to enjoy it.

Planning Gordon has restaurants in Britain, Turkey, and New Zealand. www.peter-gordon.net

❹ Emeril Lagasse

Lagasse, a New Orleans chef familiar to almost everybody with a TV in the U.S., rose to prominence as head chef at New Orleans' sublime Commander's Palace. He calls his Cajun- and Creole-influenced style "New-New Orleans." Don't miss his signature dessert—a monstrously rich banana cream pie made using seven bananas.

Planning Lagasse runs restaurants across the southern U.S., including in Orlando, Atlanta, New Orleans, and Las Vegas. www.emerils.com

❺ Nobuyuki "Nobu" Matsuhisa

Nobu's fusion cuisine, blending Japanese and Peruvian flavors, is a favorite from Australia to Las Vegas. His skill in adapting traditional dishes for Western palates saw Nobu pioneer the tempura shrimp roll and the soft-shelled crab roll, both of which are now ubiquitous in Western sushi restaurants. Nobu's signature miso-marinated black cod also sees many imitators.

Planning Beverly Hills, Nassau, Tokyo, Melbourne, and Milan are among the locations of Nobu's restaurants. www.noburestaurants.com

❻ Michael Mina

With three Michelin stars, Michael Mina's exquisitely complicated cuisine is a magnet for gourmets across the globe. His renowned "trio" approach, which involves using one deluxe ingredient in three different ways on the plate, has won him armfuls of awards. Be sure to ask for the signature lobster pot pie, served at all Mina's restaurants.

Planning Mina has 16 restaurants spread across the U.S. and Mexico; his flagship restaurant is in Cisco. www.michaelmina.net

❼ Wolfgang Puck

Not many chefs have the recognition factor that gets them a slot voicing themselves on *The Simpsons* TV series. A visit to one of his restaurants could be your chance to have one of the most luxurious pizzas ever devised—with a topping of smoked salmon and caviar.

Planning Alongside his fine-dining restaurants, Puck's name appears on successful café, grill, and bistro franchises in the U.S. and Japan and on a host of cooking-related products. www.wolfgangpuck.com

❽ Gordon Ramsay

Ramsay's meticulous French-inspired cooking and head for business have seen him grow an empire of restaurants across the world. At Restaurant Gordon Ramsay in London's chic Chelsea district, you may hit upon such delights as sautéed loin of venison with creamed cabbage and bitter chocolate sauce.

Planning Ramsay's empire reaches right around the globe, taking in Toronto, New York, Tokyo, Singapore, Prague, London, and Cape Town. www.gordonramsay.com

❾ Joël Robuchon

With more than a dozen restaurants spread across the globe from Tokyo to Monaco to New York, Robuchon has a total of 17 Michelin stars to his name: more than any other living chef. Taste even the simplest dish and you will see what all the fuss is about—the mashed potatoes are heavenly, anything with truffles is sublime.

Planning Try a foie gras hamburger at Robuchon's L'Atelier in New York. www.joel-robuchon.com

❿ Jean-Georges Vongerichten

New York magazine heralded Vongerichten as the chef who has the most influence over the way New Yorkers eat and the force behind America's answer to nouvelle cuisine. Intensely flavored, light, clean-tasting dishes are his signature, such as duck with cracked Jordan almonds and honey wine jus.

Planning Vongerichten has restaurants in New York, Las Vegas, Vancouver, Shanghai, Paris, London, and Bora Bora. www.jean-georges.com

Right: At French chef Joël Robuchon's Hong Kong L'Atelier, diners get to watch their food being prepared in the open kitchen.

BEIJING

China's economic boom has led to a proliferation of top-notch restaurants serving delicious local and international dishes.

Not so very long ago, high-end dining in Beijing meant shark's fin, abalone, and bird's nest soup added to multicourse banquets, more to demonstrate wealth or give face to guests than for flavor. The service was also invariably hostile and the surroundings shoddy. Now not only is the best of every Chinese school of cooking served with aplomb, but the capital—once so impenetrable to outsiders—is now seeing an invasion of big-name chefs from around the world. Nor does eating foreign food in Beijing necessarily mean visiting some blandly international hotel. New York's Daniel Boulud has opened Maison Boulud in the original American embassy, a stately neoclassical building whose dignified interior once again plays host to diplomats in search of American-influenced French dishes created around local ingredients. The best of the east is here, too. At Shiro Matsu, found in a smart glass box next door, *fugu* master Yakuwa Kazuaki demonstrates his years of training in the preparation of this Japanese fish delicacy. Outsiders are also updating local cuisine. Jereme Leung has arrived from Singapore to open Whampoa Club and serves complex, irresistible updates of the capital's classics. The arresting lobby features myriad lightbulbs in birdcages, while the main dining room is buried beneath a traditional courtyard house with light filtered through an overhead goldfish pond.

When to Go September and October are the best months to visit, followed by April and early May.

Planning Restaurant reservations are recommended. Lunch menus tend to be significantly cheaper than evening ones. For a serial indulgence, sample classic French cuisine in elegant surroundings at Le Pré Lenôtre (Sofitel Wanda) one night, then dine on the most refined Cantonese at Horizon the next night.

Websites www.legationquarter.com, www.sofitel.com

A Cornucopia of Flavors

Chinese food overseas is typically a bland and adulterated version of Cantonese highlights. Menus ignore hot and numbing Sichuan, fiery Hunan, delicate Huaiyang dishes from Hangzhou, sweet and oily Shanghai, sour Guangxi, vinegary Shanxi, and fruity Yunnan dishes.

Luckily for modern visitors, regional food is currently in vogue with Beijingers, with the city attracting the finest culinary talent from around the country. Not to be missed is **shuizhuyu**, Sichuan-style sliced catfish in a bath of pepper-and-numb-spice-filled oil; Dai minority **zhutong zhurou**, steamed pork and coriander served in a bamboo tube, or **mizhi zhibao luyu**, the "secret" paper-wrapped fish of the Kejia minority from the mountains of the southeast.

Located in the heart of Beijing, the Forbidden City was the imperial palace for almost five centuries.

Gold leaf makes a Japanese dessert of sweet dumplings shimmer.

JAPAN

Best of Japan

With a total of 191 Michelin stars awarded to its restaurants, the Japanese capital has more stars than any city in the world.

Tokyo's *ryotei*, the traditional, upscale restaurants that are found throughout the city, are the best places to try the distinctively marbled Wagyu beef that has gained global culinary fame. This tender, richly flavored meat comes from a group of cattle breeds that are predisposed to produce a high level of unsaturated fat—hence the marbling. Several areas of the country are famous for their Wagyu cattle, including Kobe in the Hyogo Prefecture. The Japanese do not cut corners; in order for beef to carry the Kobe label, the cattle must be raised in a traditional way—being fed on grain and beer, and even receiving a regular brushing and massage. Try Wagyu beef in *sukiyaki* or *shabu shabu*, in which thinly sliced beef and vegetables are simmered in broth at the table and served with dipping sauces. Another Japanese specialty, *fugu*, or blowfish, is poisonous if not prepared correctly, and fugu chefs have to be licensed by the government. It is served either raw as sashimi (sliced so thinly that it is transparent), simmered with vegetables, or in salads. To add a taste of luxury, literally, some upscale restaurants decorate dishes with flecks or sheets of gold leaf.

When to Go The Japanese take great pride in seasonal cooking, and each season brings new menus. If you favor root vegetables and hearty warm meals, visit in winter. In summer, lighter, cooling dishes are on offer. Some restaurants close during Obon, the Japanese Buddhist holiday during which families honor their ancestors (mid-August), and Golden Week (beginning of May).

Planning Book a few days in advance for popular restaurants. Fugu is served in specialist restaurants, often indicated by a blowfish lantern hanging over the door.

Websites www.bento.com, www.tsukiji-market.or.jp, www.kahala.in, www.fuchabon.co.jp

Temple Food

Seasonal ingredients are key to good Japanese cooking, and one of the best ways to savor the delicate flavor of vegetables in their prime is **shojin ryori**. This is the traditional vegetarian cuisine of Buddhist temples, with a number of ornate dishes consisting of vegetables, tofu, beans, and fruit served over several courses. An avoidance of meat is one of the central tenets of Buddhism.

Shojin ryori provides a cultural experience to match the gastronomical one, with each meal eaten in a traditional environ, such as a private tatami mat room.

Great emphasis is placed on using seasonal ingredients and shojin ryori cooks take care not to waste any ingredients. The greens and peelings of vegetables such as carrots, for example, are prepared by simmering in a little water or may be added to soups.

Shojin ryori is frequently served in restaurants located near to Zen temples or can be sampled in many of the temples themselves, provided that a reservation is made in advance.

Fugu, or blowfish, is a Japanese delicacy.

JAPAN

KAISEKI FEASTING

This feast has been described as "perfection on a plate,"
and Kyoto is one of the best places to try it.

Originally created by Zen monks, the sumptuous Japanese treat known as *kaiseki* has only recently come to the attention of the outside world. In medieval times, it was a humble repast of Buddhist monks, accompanying the tea ceremony, but over the centuries it has evolved into a 14-course feast incorporating dishes that change with the seasons. Even today the spread is rarely found outside Japan because of a painstaking reliance on fresh ingredients that can be found only in and around the Japanese archipelago. Most of the courses are either vegetable- or seafood-based, although in modern times some of the more leading-edge chefs have started including meat as well. "I try to create a work of art in my dishes," says Yoshihiro Murata, one of Japan's most renowned kaiseki chefs. And indeed, each dish is a miniature work of art, almost too precious to eat if not for the fact that incredible (and often unusual) flavors and textures await the palate. Although the meal can be found at top restaurants around Japan, Kyoto is home to the very best kaiseki eateries. Here diners are treated to an enviable experience in elegant establishments—Murata's Kikunoi restaurant among them—where the exquisitely presented courses are served in private tatami dining suites by geisha-like hostesses wearing silk kimonos.

When to Go Kaiseki ingredients change according to the season, so there is no best time of year to enjoy this Japanese feast. However, weather conditions might influence your decision. Japan's winters are cold and often snowy; summers are hot and humid. Spring (cherry blossoms) and fall (autumn colors) are the best seasons.

Planning Get ready for "sticker shock"–the best kaiseki restaurants charge around $250 for a seven-course lunch and as much as twice that for a full-blown 14-course dinner. Reservations are highly recommended at Kikunoi and other kaiseki icons. Most restaurants include both Western-style dining areas with tables and Japanese, tatami-style dining suites, where patrons recline on traditional floor mats.

Websites www.jnto.go.jp, www.kikunoi.jp

Kaiseki at Kikunoi

Kaiseki incorporates hundreds of unique and often restaurant-specific menus. Each menu consists of different types of food, including appetizers, sashimi, simmered, grilled, and steamed dishes, and others decided on by the chef. Here are a few classic dishes from the Kikunoi restaurant in Kyoto:

■ *Hassun* (an appetizer that sets the seasonal theme of the meal): Three *houzuki* (strawberry tomatoes) stuffed with sea cucumber, mountain peach, and a small freshwater fish called *ayu* from streams in the Japanese Alps.

■ *Mukozuke* (sashimi, or sliced fish): Thinly sliced *onaga* (red snapper) and *hamo* (conger eel) sashimi served on a lotus leaf with *ume* (sour plum sauce) and wasabi mustard.

■ *Noka-choko* **course** (a palate-cleanser): *Ichijiku* (boiled fig) in white miso, served cold.

■ *Shiizakana* (a substantial dish): Hotpot with boiled eggs, roasted eggplant, and fish seasoned with *mitsuba* (Japanese wild parsley) and *sansho* (pepper powder).

■ *Tome-wan* (a palate-cleanser): Steamed rice with hamo wrapped in a lotus leaf, pea soup with sesame jelly, and pickled cucumber with eggplant.

■ *Mizumono* (dessert): Green-tea shaved ice with red beans and jellied rice balls.

Opposite: Fall color frames the Kiyomizu Temple, Kyoto. Above: The serving bowls reflect shapes that are found in nature.

A waitress in 18th-century costume prepares one of the lavish tables at Turandot, Moscow's most luxurious restaurant.

RUSSIA

MOSCOW

Top chefs, the choicest ingredients, and lavish settings make Moscow's restaurants among the very best for opulent dining.

For an authentic slice of pre-Revolutionary Russia, head for the Café Pushkin, with an upstairs dining room that more closely resembles a grand library; Yar, which has remained a decadent haunt of Moscow's elite almost without a break since its foundation in 1826; or CDL at the Central House of Writers, where fine cuisine is served amid a riot of baronial splendor. For a taste of the good old bad old days, Gorki and Politica offer Soviet-style retro chic, but with nothing communist about the food or the service. International cuisine of almost every description is also well represented, with sushi and Asian fusion currently all the rage. Dine on Vietnamese-style frogs' legs wrapped in lily pads alongside oligarchs at Opium in Barvikha Luxury Village, or for pan-Asian cuisine in a setting that pays homage to the Palace of Versailles, try Turandot. As in imperial days, French cuisine is again in vogue, with places such as Mon Plaisir, an 18th-century aristocratic throwback in a classical mansion; Restaurant Villa, resembling a Côte d'Azur villa with Mediterranean dishes to match; or Casual, for mainly Provençal dishes. For the best views in town, reserve a table overlooking the Kremlin and Red Square at upscale Jeroboam in the Ritz-Carlton, or at Yoko, a fine Japanese restaurant with superb views towards Christ the Savior Cathedral.

When to Go Furs and vodka are de rigueur in winter, when temperatures plummet. Summer arrives in June and lasts well into September, with the hottest, most humid weather in July and August.

Planning U.S. and most other citizens require a tourist visa to enter Russia. It is usually easiest to arrange one through a specialist agency.

Websites www.quintessentially.com, www.barvikhahotel.com, www.cafepushkin.ee

Vodka

While vintage champagne is a favorite plutocrat tipple, no trip to Russia is complete without sampling vodka—a clear beverage with an alcohol content of 35–50 percent. To drink it Russian-style, the vodka should be chilled, ideally for several hours in a freezer, and drunk neat in one shot, accompanied by a toast, followed by **zakusky**—bite-size snacks, such as smoked meats, caviar, and crackers. Russians often alternate vodka with soft drinks. It is considered bad form not to finish an opened bottle of vodka, and some bottles come with lids that do not reseal. Banging glasses loudly on the table is appropriate only at wedding parties.

Apart from classics such as Stolichnaya and Moskovskaya, try unusual vodkas, such as Pertsovka—vodka flavored with red and black peppers and other spices. Limonnaya is flavored with lemons, Kerenski with chocolate, Sputnik with horseradish, and Stolichnaya Ohranj is an orange vodka.

SWITZERLAND

KLOSTERS

This sophisticated alpine playground is a wonderful place to relax and enjoy sun, snow, and superb food.

Glistening snowcapped mountains form a magical backdrop to the Michelin-starred Hotel Walserhof in the Swiss village of Klosters—winter playground of European royalty and the world's richest commoners. Inside the chalet-style hotel, age-old carved wood, warm stone, and hints of pine and conifer promise a cozy but elegant dining ambience. Slim candles ensconced in silver candlesticks radiate a golden glow off champagne-colored walls. Subtle aromas waft from the Bündner stone oven, prompting anticipation of freshly prepared creations from chef Armin Amrein. Arouse the taste buds with a foamy potato soup with Serrano ham chips and white Alba truffle. Next, a flawlessly sliced carpaccio of veal fillet bonds with a terrine of artichokes and black truffle. Served as two courses, the chef's signature sea bass in a salt crust with olive oil coulis is complemented by rocket, potatoes, and seasonal market vegetables. To finish, a warm Valrhona chocolate soufflé with caramelized champagne parfait and exotic fruit cocktail gratifies all the senses. A dessert alternative pays homage to Amrein's culinary imagination—a mélange of curd cheese parfait with sesame crisp, grape and mustard ice cream, and a grape mille-feuille.

When to Go This is a winter sports paradise for snowboarders, skiers, and ice skaters, while summer offers a peaceful retreat and idyllic hiking through flower-filled alpine meadows and fresh forests—take your pick.

Planning Hotel Walserhof is a five-minute walk to the train station and to mountain railways. Zurich is 2.5 hours by car or train. Between December and April, a shuttle bus operates between Davos-Klosters and Zurich International Airport. Reservations at the restaurant are recommended. It is closed on Tuesdays during the summer. Other excellent hotel restaurants open to non-residents are The Alpina and Alte Post.

Websites www.walserhof.ch, www.davosklosters.ch, www.myswitzerland.com

Nougat dumplings with sweet fixings from Kloster's Hotel Walserhof

Bündnerfleisch

High in the alpine canton of Graubünden, in southeastern Switzerland, Bündnerfleisch was originally produced as a necessity, but today this **air-dried beef** is considered a delicacy. Pieces of lean beef thigh are seasoned with salt, spices, and alpine herbs and cured at a low temperature for five weeks. A ten- to 15-week drying period follows.

Bündnerfleisch is served thinly sliced—all it needs is a little fresh ground black pepper and maybe some crusty bread and a glass of red wine. It is also served in Graubünden specialties such as *pizokel*–a type of dumpling.

This playground of royalty and the jet set has retained its alpine village character and is as stunning in winter as it is in summer.

RESTAURANTS ON TOP OF THE WORLD

For vertiginous views of cliffs, canyons, and cityscapes, these destinations will take you to new culinary heights in every sense of the word.

❶ 360, Toronto, Canada

Often mislabeled the CN Tower, this seemingly spear-shaped spaceship was built by Canadian National, a railroad company. At an impressive 1,815 ft (553 m), it was once the world's tallest freestanding structure (superseded by the Burj Dubai in 2007). Its revolving restaurant, 360, offers giddy vistas, Canadian-inspired dishes, and the world's highest wine cellar.

Planning It takes 72 minutes for the restaurant to turn one complete revolution. www.cntower.ca

❷ The Rainbow Room, New York City

One of the most recognized buildings in Manhattan, Rockefeller Center's GE Building is a magnificent art deco skyscraper, completed in 1933. Long drawing New York's elite, its 65th-story Rainbow Room offers dinner and dancing with a big band orchestra on selected nights. The revolving dance floor, with impressive views over the city, will transport you to a bygone era of metropolitan glamor.

Planning Jackets are required; no jeans, sneakers, or T-shirts are allowed. www.rainbowroom.com

❸ Top of the World, Las Vegas, Nevada

Even in a city eschewing understatement, this 1,149-ft (350 m) casino-hotel teeters resolutely above all others, with America's highest observation tower—the Stratosphere—and dizzying rooftop thrill rides. Revolving 360 degrees every 80 minutes, its restaurant focuses on steak and seafood.

Planning Stratosphere is at the Strip's north end. For dinner, the dress code is "business casual." www.topoftheworldlv.com

❹ El Tovar Dining Room, Grand Canyon, Arizona

Part Swiss chalet, part Norwegian villa, this lodge is a 1905 confection of stone and Oregon pine. Its rustic restaurant serves spicy Southwestern fare, such as buffalo carpaccio and—for provident diners—breathless views over the Grand Canyon: the canyon's edge is a mere 20 ft (6 m) away.

Planning Hotel guests can reserve dinner six months—other people 30 days—ahead. www.grandcanyonlodges.com

❺ Bella Vista, La Paz, Bolivia

Overlooking San Francisco Cathedral in La Paz, and the Andes mountain range, the Bella Vista restaurant occupies the top floor of the world's highest five-star hotel, the Presidente, in the world's loftiest capital. Grilled meat reigns supreme here, but the trout is also superb.

Planning The hotel is in the heart of downtown La Paz. Beware altitude sickness as La Paz is at 12,000 ft (3,658 m). www.hotelpresidente-bo.com

❻ XEX, Taipei, China/Taiwan

Debate rages as to what actually qualifies as the world's tallest skyscraper; definitions vary. Yet the 1,667-ft (508 m) Taipei 101 is one claimant. When the 86th-floor XEX opens—serving top-notch Italian and Japanese cuisine—its owners aim to make it "the world's best restaurant in the world's tallest building."

Planning XEX is due to launch in 2009. www.taipei-101.com.tw

❼ Sirocco, Bangkok, Thailand

On a sultry Bangkok day, refresh yourself with alfresco dining and live jazz on the city's highest outdoor balcony, at The Dome, atop the 811-ft (247 m) State Tower. The food is Mediterranean with an Asian twist, but most diners come here for the head-spinning, open-air setting.

Planning Check the weather forecast, as high-altitude, dimly lit, alfresco dining is best in fine weather. The Dome also has several covered restaurants and bars. www.thedomebkk.com

❽ Drehrestaurant Allalin, Saas Fee, Switzerland

The world's highest revolving restaurant (11,483 ft/3,500 m) enjoys a spectacular alpine setting on the summit of Mittelallalin above the village of Saas Fee. The restaurant is reached by the world's highest underground funicular railway. Workaday Swiss and Italian dishes refuel skiers, but the crowd-puller is the 360-degree panoramic view toward 13 peaks and—on a clear day—even Milan.

Planning From Saas Fee take the Alpin Express cablecar followed by the Metro-Alpin funicular railway to Mittelallalin. www.myswitzerland.com.

❾ Belgium Taste in the Sky, Brussels, Belgium

Like the Eiffel Tower in Paris, the Atomium in Brussels was originally built as a temporary structure—for the city's Expo '58. This modernist cat's cradle of a building is a massive replica of a crystallized iron molecule. Tubes link its nine spheres; the topmost is a brasserie with Belgian delicacies, such as terrine of *anguille au vert* (eel flavored with herbs), and undisturbed views.

Planning For dinner the normally self-service restaurant runs a *brasserie gastronomique*. The Heysel/Heizel Metro station, on the city's northwest edge, is next door. www.belgiumtaste.be

❿ Jules Verne, Paris, France

For years after its construction in 1889, the Eiffel Tower was so hated by high-class Parisians that writer Guy de Maupassant ate there daily not for the food but to avoid viewing the building. How tastes change. Run by chef Alain Ducasse, the intimate Jules Verne attracts chic gourmets with its contemporary French cuisine, superior panorama—and Michelin star.

Planning Entry is by private elevator. www.lejulesverne-paris.com

Right: The sky-high, open-air Sirocco restaurant at The Dome rewards the intrepid diner with stunning 360-degree views over Bangkok.

A trompe l'oeil of chef Paul Bocuse graces his restaurant in Collonges-au-Mont-d'Or, near Lyon.

FRANCE

FINE DINING IN LYON

At the culinary heart of France, Lyon is a melting pot of cultures and ingredients from all points of the compass.

Located where the Saône River from the north and the Rhône from the east meet and turn south, Lyon connects the traditions of animal-fat cookery from northern France with the olive-oil based cuisine of the Mediterranean, resulting in the best of both worlds. In addition, beef from the Massif Central to the west, butter from Normandy, cheeses from the Alps, and vegetables, seafood, and olive oil from the south provide Lyonnais chefs with an inexhaustible cornucopia of raw materials. This vibrant city, capital of the Rhône-Alpes region, also encompasses traditional French cooking and the lighter nouvelle cuisine introduced by chef Paul Bocuse, among others, half a century ago. Whereas the *mères* and *grand-mères* of the traditional *bouchons* (workers' restaurants) originally established Lyon as France's culinary capital, it was Bocuse and younger chefs, such as Nicolas le Bec, Christian Têtedoie, and Mathieu Viannay, who forged the city's future. With some 60 Michelin stars awarded in the Rhône-Alpes region (19 for Lyon), a swelling list of chefs such as Jean-Christophe Ansanay-Alex, Philippe Gauvreau, Fabien Blanc, Guy Lassausaie, Davy Tissot, and Manuel Viron guarantee that Lyon will not be vacating the forefront of French cuisine anytime soon.

When to Go Lyon is magical during the Festival of Lights in early December, when the city is ablaze with creative and colorful illuminations projected onto its main sites and architectural treasures.

Planning Three to five days are sufficient to get the feel of Lyon, but a week is needed to explore the dining, music, and art options available in this busy and cosmopolitan metropolis. Truffle soup fanatics regularly make the trip to visit Paul Bocuse in Collonges-au-Mont-d'Or just north of the city. The TGV high-speed train service connects Paris with Lyon in two hours.

Websites www.lyon.fr, www.lyonguide.com, www.bocuse.fr

Parisian Haute Cuisine

Take a tour of Michelin three-star restaurants
in the world's undisputed center of haute cuisine.

Tokyo may have more stars, New York and London more variety, but still at the pinnacle of high-end dining is Paris. At the top of this culinary mountain are those establishments that have earned three Michelin stars, of which there were just nine in the captial in 2008. These restaurants vary significantly in style, but are united by a passion to create the very finest dishes the city can offer. At the least formal of the nine, L'Astrance, chef Pascal Barbot creates a new menu each day from whatever is best in the market. Le Meurice near the Louvre has a beautiful belle-epoque dining room, while Ledoyen off the Champs-Élysées and Pré Catelan in the Bois de Boulogne have leafier settings. L'Arpège chef Alain Passard's menu specializes in vegetables grown on his own organic farm southwest of Paris. Influential chef Pierre Gagnaire offers inventive variations on particular ingredients at his eponymous restaurant, and true masters of French cuisine Alain Ducasse and Guy Savoy strive for technical perfection. Of all the restaurants, L'Ambroisie in the beautiful Place des Vosges feels the most artisanal, its chef's passion for food apparent in the care taken to bring out optimum flavor from his ingredients. Whichever you choose, you will experience personal service, the very finest produce France can offer, and the highest level of effort and attention to detail in creating the dishes that you order. Paris may be the world's most romantic city; here the French show passion on your plate.

When to Go Although there is never a bad time of year to visit Paris, most three-star restaurants in Paris close on weekends and for the whole of August.

Planning Reservations are difficult to obtain in the top restaurants, even for lunch, so advance planning is essential. If you are staying in a good hotel, the concierge should be able to help you, but it is vital that you know beforehand where you want to eat. Most three-star venues are very upscale, but not all require formal attire; check with the individual restaurant.

Websites www.andyhayler.com, www.dininginfrance.com

Three-star Menu

Examples of the kinds of dishes you can expect can be seen at **Ledoyen**. You might begin with delicate **langoustines** from Brittany, cooked perfectly and served in their shells with a frothy lemon oil to add just a little acidity. On the side you will find a contrast of langoustine meat deep-fried in a perfectly crisp coating. Perhaps follow with **Parmesan-flavored pasta** presented as a wall inside which ham is enclosed. The earthy flavor of morel mushrooms and their cooking juices are released when the pasta wall is broken down. A selection of five exquisite desserts includes a remarkable **grapefruit confit** topped with additional grapefruit, a delicate crisp, and cylinders of perfect grapefruit sorbet—a refreshing way to end the meal.

The original decor at the restaurant Le Meurice, inspired by the Salon de la Paix at Versailles, has been reinterpreted by designer Philippe Starck.

BANK-BREAKING COCKTAIL BARS

10

Bartenders combine gold, diamonds, vintage champagnes, and expensive,
aged liqueurs to create the world's most luxurious—and costly—libations.

❶ Blue Bar, Algonquin Hotel, New York

The Blue Bar is just as stylish as it was in the 1930s, when the Algonquin Hotel was the center of New York's literary universe. Signature cocktails include the Hot Chili Raspberry Cosmopolitan, the Matilda, and the over-the-top Martini on the Rock, which flaunts a "diamond of your choice." The estimated price of $10,000 varies according to the size and quality of the rock.

Planning Open daily, 11:30 a.m. to 1:30 a.m. www.algonquinhotel.com

❷ Tryst, Wynn Hotel, Las Vegas, Nevada

A Ménage à Trois at Tryst will set you back a cool $3,000. A blend of Hennessy Ellipse cognac, Cristal Rosé champagne, and Grand Marnier, the drink comes with 23-karat gold flakes and a diamond-studded straw. Sip it (very slowly) on the terrace beneath a 90-ft (27 m) waterfall.

Planning Thursday through Saturday, 10 p.m. to 4 a.m. There is a strict dress code, so don't turn up in baggy jeans, sports attire, or baseball cap. www.wynnlasvegas.com

❸ Bar Nineteen 12, Beverly Hills Hotel, Los Angeles, California

Partiers at the Beverly Hills Hotel head for Bar Nineteen 12, where highly innovative house cocktails include a Prickly Pear Margarita as well as mojito jelly shots and martini popsicles. Bottle service runs from a pricey Gran Patron Platinum tequila ($750 per bottle) to an obscenely expensive Hardy Perfection 140-year-old cognac ($23,000 per bottle).

Planning Open daily 5 p.m. to 2 a.m. www.barnineteen12.com

❹ Janbu's Bar, Raffles Resort, Canouan Island, St. Vincent and the Grenadines

Given its pedigree, one expects the Raffles Resort on Canouan Island to make the meanest Singapore Sling in the Caribbean. But the bartenders at beachside Janbu's Bar have created a concoction called the Bushido Martini, which features vodka, dry vermouth, cactaur root—and a miniature 14-karat gold, olive-spearing samurai sword—for a mere $300 per glass.

Planning Bring your swimsuit and take a dip from one of the resort's three stunning private beaches. www.canouan.raffles.com

❺ Astral Bar, Darling Harbour, Sydney, Australia

Perched 17 floors above the Star City Casino, the Astral Bar delivers drop-dead gorgeous views of downtown Sydney and the Harbour Bridge. An extensive selection of straight-up liquors are on offer, but it is the offbeat cocktails—such as the Vanilla Cherry Negroni and the Pear & Ginger Collins—that produce the oohs and aahs.

Planning Open Tuesday through Saturday, 5:30 p.m to late. www.astralrestaurant.com.au

❻ Skyview Bar, Burj Al Arab, Dubai

Perched at the top of the Burj Al Arab, the Skyview Bar hangs 650 ft (200 m) above the Persian Gulf, the floor-to-ceiling windows offering a bird's-eye view of Dubai's skyline and sunset over Qatar in the west. "Mixologists" move from table to table with a mobile bar, creating cocktails with exotic ingredients like camel's milk, saffron, and the best Highland scotch.

Planning Open daily, 12 p.m. to 2 a.m. www.burj-al-arab.com

❼ GQ Bar, Moscow, Russia

Taking its name from the American fashion magazine, Moscow's GQ Bar is indeed the place to see (and be seen) in the Russian capital. Don't let the 17th-century tsarist facade fool you—this is a thoroughly 21st-century bar embellished with chrome, glass, wood, and leather. The drinks menu is peppered with exotic martinis, but if you want to sample the exclusive and pricey Beluga vodka, you will have to ask the bartender as it is off-menu.

Planning The bar is open 24 hours a day, seven days a week. bar.gq.ru

❽ The Bar Hemingway, Hotel Ritz, Paris, France

According to the *Guinness Book of Records*, the world's most expensive house cocktail is the Side Car at The Bar Hemingway. Made with Cointreau, freshly squeezed lemon juice, and 1830 reserve cognac, the tab is more than $500. The bar flaunts leather chairs, rich wood paneling, and black-and-white photos taken by Ernest himself.

Planning Open daily, 10:30 a.m. to 2 a.m. If you go by car, there is a valet parking service. www.ritzparis.com

❾ Donovan Bar, Brown's Hotel, London, England

Donovan is just the sort of place you would expect James Bond to request his martini "shaken, not stirred." This elegant Mayfair establishment blends British tradition and international savoir faire. The signature cocktail, the Space Race, blends vodka, Cointreau, lychee liqueur, cranberry, and guava juice.

Planning Open daily, 11 a.m. to 1 a.m. Monday through Saturday and 12 p.m. to 12 a.m. on Sunday. www.brownshotel.com

❿ The Bar, Merchant Hotel, Belfast, Northern Ireland

Enjoy the Victorian splendor of The Bar, with its antique glass chandeliers and silk damask on the walls as you sip a drink chosen from the 35-page menu. The barman can also shake a $335 daiquiri or mojito (both using 1920s' Bacardi white rum), a $250 whiskey sour (with Old Trimbrook 1937 bourbon), and a $150 cosmo (with Kauffman Inauguration vodka).

Planning Open daily, 12 p.m. to 1 a.m. www.themerchanthotel.com

Right: The Bloody Mary—named for Ernest Hemingway's fourth wife—is said to have originated at The Bar Hemingway in the Hotel Ritz in Paris.

Cafés, galleries, and boutiques line the narrow, cobbled streets of the picturesque medieval town of St.-Paul-de-Vence.

FRANCE

PROVENCE

A bountiful harvest from land and sea makes Provençal cuisine one of the most flavorsome and distinctive in France.

Begin your sybaritic tour of Provence in Avignon, where market stalls inside the historic town walls are loaded with seasonal produce, including Cavaillon's fragrant melons and sun-soaked tomatoes. A natural follow-up to a shopping round of artisanal soaps and olive-wood tools is a tomato-menu lunch at starred restaurant Christian Etienne, a setting steeped in history next to the 14th-century papal palace. The wine menu offers a superb selection of local wines from Châteauneuf-du-Pape. East of Avignon lies the diverse landscape of the Luberon, the popular market town of Apt, and Lourmarin's cluster of gastronomic destinations—among them Edouard Loubet's La Bastide de Capelongue and the inventive cuisine of Reine Samut at Auberge La Fennière. The La Provençale E80/A8 motorway cuts across stunning country all the way to Cannes, where the road turns north to Grasse, famous since the Renaissance for its fine perfumes. Venture east to Vence for a week in art-lovers' heaven and dine amidst 20th-century art at La Colombe d'Or. Between Vence and St.-Paul-de-Vence, the arts have attracted art collectors and gastronomes for more than a century. Panoramas from the rampart walls and beyond to the sea redefine "breathtaking," a reason to pause before the winding road leads south to Nice for a refined Provençal finale on the Côte d'Azur.

When to Go High summer brings heat and crowds, so choose spring or fall for a more tranquil time (and easier reservations). Evenings at higher altitudes in Vence and Grasse can be cool.

Planning From Avignon, take a local train to Arles (for a great view of the Roman bridge) in September during Arles' colorful Rice Festival for a taste of the Camargue. Or rent a convertible to drive to the wine cellars of Châteauneuf-du-Pape, enjoying the open country along the Rhône. The TGV skirts the Côte d'Azur with great mountain and sea vistas en route to Nice; or fly into the bustling airport.

Websites www.beyond.fr, www.lesaintpaul.com

Not To Be Missed

■ **Le Saint Paul** restaurant, located in a 16th-century house on the ramparts of St.-Paul-de-Vence, is a luxurious honeymoon or anniversary hideaway, furnished with Provençal antiques. Enjoy a memorable dinner of chef Olivier Borloo's refined cuisine.

■ In old Nice, the palace Hôtel Negresco's dining room, the **Chantecler**, features tantalizing creations by chef Jean-Denis Rieubland.

■ When in Avignon, look in upscale *épiceries* or the Les Halles market for the unusual chocolate liqueur *papaline*, honey-sweetened with hints of oregano.

ITALY

MILAN

A hub of style, sophistication, and creativity, this most modern of Italian cities is also a bastion of traditional cooking.

It only takes a mouthful to understand why Milan personifies the Italian concept of the *bella figura* ("beautiful figure") like no place else. The idea goes far beyond the chic couture and stylish slippers for which the city is famous. It also implies beauty, quality, and taste, all of which are abundant in Milan's food. And it walks down a shiny runway at innovative chef Carlo Cracco's eponymous restaurant Cracco, just a few paces from the iconic Duomo cathedral. Here a warm chocolate croquette bursts like a liquid bomb in your mouth, while the pile of cool, saline fish eggs squeezed beside it on the spoon does the same in miniature. If chocolate spells indulgence and caviar shouts extravagance, then a dessert that combines them both is surely luxury embodied. Down the street is a gourmet food shop called Peck, where cured hams are worth their weight in gold and the wine bottles in the cellar are older than some countries. Here opulence has been sold since 1883. But fortunately, the treats begin at just a few euros. As you lick a cone of luscious honey gelato and admire the store's display cases, you can be confident that while not everyone is as well heeled as some of the clientele here, it is easy to be as well fed.

When to Go   The best time to visit is during spring, early summer, or fall when the weather is fine. The summer months (July and August) can be too hot for shopping and sightseeing.

Planning   In Italy, many shops and most restaurants are closed on Sundays. Cracco is also shut for Saturday and Monday lunch. Ask to sit at the chef's table in the kitchen, where all of the kitchen is in view through an automatic sliding glass door. The chef will come in and talk to you about what you would like to eat; he might even deliver a course or two. The folks at Peck take a break on Sundays and Monday mornings. Saturday afternoons are when the rest of Milan stocks up on food and wine for the big Sunday family meal, so make the trip on a weekday afternoon instead.

Websites   www.ristorantecracco.it, www.peck.it

Signature Dishes

Milan's food is rustic and refined, classical and contemporary. And both Cracco and Peck reflect that in different ways. A creamy pool of the classic **risotto alla milanese** gets its golden hue from strands of saffron and its characteristic richness from—of all things—bone marrow. Order some to go at Peck or sit down to a plate at Cracco.

Vitello alla milanese, or veal cooked in the style of Milan, is Italy's answer to Wiener schnitzel. At the prepared food counters of Peck you can find it as a traditional thin cutlet of breaded meat fried in olive oil and served with a wedge of lemon. Cracco offers building-block-size cubes of crispy **carne** that come flanked by ingredients that range from tomato and zucchini to Savoy cabbage and pumpkin, depending on the season and the chef's whim.

One of the world's great cathedrals, the magnificent Gothic Duomo—boasting 135 spires—dominates Milan's main square.

ITALY

Hotel Cipriani, Venice

Romance and luxury come together in this famous hotel tucked away from the crowds on the island of Giudecca.

Exquisite Murano-glass chandeliers hang from a series of arches in the hotel's Fortuny dining room, reminiscent of the dome of St. Mark's. Semicircular love seats add to the sense of intimacy created by linen-covered tables haloed by candlelight. Soaring windows face across the lagoon towards the enchantment of Venice's Grand Canal and St. Mark's Square and over the hotel's magnificent gardens. While contemplating the menu of authentic Venetian dishes, sip on a Cipriani cocktail, such as a Rossini (strawberries and Prosecco sparkling wine) or a Bellini (fresh peach juice and Prosecco). Rich, accessible, multilayered flavors are the tenets of chef Renato Piccolotto's traditional Venetian cuisine. In true Italian tradition, pastas and pastries are made fresh every day. At dawn, a short boat ride to the bustling Rialto Fish Market brings back fresh fish—turbot, monkfish, or sea bass, depending on the catch of the day. Whenever the chef needs a fresh herb or vegetable, he simply steps outside to collect them from the hotel's garden. Wine hails from the estate's vineyard, which bears the Casanova Salso label. Appetizers entice with homemade ravioli filled with sea bass and wild fennel, and laced with *quazzetto* (broth). The signature *taglierini verdi* finds fresh thin green noodles with ham au gratin. The memory of the delectable bittersweet chocolate ice cream lingers on after leaving.

When to Go Spring and early fall are probably the best times to visit Venice. Summer can be hot and crowded. The hotel is closed from mid-November to mid-March.

Planning The Hotel Cipriani runs a private launch service to and from St. Mark's Square; the journey takes less than five minutes. Guidecca can also be reached by water taxi and several *vaporetto* (water-bus) routes. Proper attire—jacket and tie for men—is required in the Fortuny Restaurant. Reservations are preferred. The hotel's Cip's Club is a smaller, less formal restaurant beside the lagoon, opposite St. Mark's Square.

Websites www.hotelcipriani.com, www.orient-express.com, www.veneto.to, www.italiantourism.com

Beef Carpaccio

Legend has it that **Giuseppe Cipriani**—founder of Harry's Bar and Hotel Cipriani—invented **beef carpaccio** around 1950. When a countess could only eat raw meat, Cipriani conceived a plate of thinly sliced raw beef served with mustard. He named the dish carpaccio after the late-15th/early-16th century Venetian painter, Vittore Carpaccio, as the reddish and yellow hues of the dish reflect the dominant colors in the painter's work.

Variations abound, but today's carpaccio requires paper-thin slices of prime, low-fat beef arranged on top of arugula (rocket), watercress, or endive and drizzled with a cold vinaigrette of olive oil and lemon juice. A hint of Parmesan cheese joins capers or onions as a topping.

Hotel Cipriani's **classic carpaccio** blends lemon juice, Worcestershire sauce, consommé, mayonnaise, mustard, and a few drops of Tabasco sauce in its dressing. A few artichoke slices, fine shavings of Parmesan cheese, and fresh parsley sprigs round out the garnish.

Opposite: The hotel commands some of the best views in Venice. Above: Guests arrive by private launch.

Head chef at Harrods department store, Guiseppe Silvestri, receives the first grouse of the season.

UNITED KINGDOM

THE GLORIOUS TWELFTH

Halfway through the British summer, gourmets
celebrate the start of the grouse-shooting season.

August 12 is the busiest day in the U.K.'s gamebird calendar. The 1773 Game Act named the date as the opening of the season for red grouse and ptarmigan, and it became known as the Glorious Twelfth. The red grouse, a plump, medium-size bird, is found only in the U.K. and Ireland, where it breeds on heather moors, particularly in Scotland and the north of England. The birds are left to raise their chicks undisturbed every spring, and by the beginning of August the youngsters are fully grown. The day's shoot typically opens with a hearty English breakfast. Those shooting will establish themselves in butts (stone shelters) arranged across the moor before the beaters begin startling any grouse in the heather, making them fly toward the guns. Grouse fly fast and low, providing a challenging target, and gundogs retrieve any grouse that have been hit. Large estates dispatch most of the shot grouse all over the country to be sold to exclusive restaurants and butchers. The classic way of preparing grouse is by roasting, allowing you to relish its tangy flavor. Traditionally, it is served with game chips (wafer-thin slices of potato that have been fried until crisp and golden), game sauce (flavored with red-currant jelly and port), bread sauce, and bread crumbs or slices, which are toasted and fried in the fats (dripping) from the roasting pan.

When to Go The grouse season runs from August 12 to December 10.

Planning You don't need to own an estate to shoot grouse, and you don't need to shoot grouse to eat it. Anyone can shoot it for a price—but spend a day practicing with clay pigeons before joining a shooting party. If you are in Edinburgh in the latter half of August, combine the Festival's cultural attractions with a feast of roast grouse at one of the city's Michelin-starred restaurants, such as The Kitchin in the old port area of Leith.

Websites www.hunting-scotland.com, www.shootingparties.co.uk, www.rules.co.uk

All About Grouse

■ Shot birds are counted and sold in "braces" (pairs). The meat is low in fat, and because grouse cannot be reared in captivity, it is free of artificial additives. The birds will have fed almost entirely on young heather—up to 2 oz (50 g) a day.

■ Traditionally, grouse is "hung" before being plucked and cooked. The birds are suspended by the neck in a cool place, where they used to be left for five days or longer to develop their gamy flavor. Nowadays, they are more likely to be hung for three days, and some people prefer to cook them as fresh as possible off the moor.

■ London's oldest restaurant, **Rules** in Covent Garden, has its own shooting estate in Teesdale and serves grouse every year from the start of the season.

UNITED KINGDOM

LIVE LIKE A LORD

Step into a refined, genteel past with a visit
to one of England's country house hotels.

Tucked between Oxfordshire's rolling hills since Norman times, the manor house that makes up Raymond Blanc's Le Manoir aux Quat'Saisons, with its ancient walled garden, 17th-century pond and orchards, and acres of herb and organic planting, is the epitome of English country luxury. A trip to an English manor house hotel such as this can make you feel like you are living in the pages of a Nancy Mitford novel. In each individually designed, elegant bedroom at Le Manoir, a decanter of fine Madeira awaits, ready for sipping as a nightcap. Alongside the luxurious surroundings, of course, Le Manoir is all about fine food. From the moment you wake up in the morning to the time you slip beneath the covers at night, you will be in foodie heaven—and more than encouraged to indulge in a traditional English breakfast, cream teas in the lounge, the champagne bar, and, to cap it all, one of England's finest restaurants. Awarded two highly prized Michelin stars, Raymond Blanc's cooking is intimate, rich, and elegant; look out for his sophisticated treatments of luxurious ingredients and the perfectly fresh produce from Le Manoir's own beautifully maintained gardens, through which guests are invited to wander (and wonder at the diversity—there are 70 different herbs). Stay here for a couple of nights, and you will leave feeling to the manor born.

When to Go To get the most out of a trip to one of these manors, with their carefully tended gardens, it is worth scheduling your visit for the late spring or early summer, when the kitchen gardens and herbaceous borders are at their very best.

Planning English manors are formal places to stay, and you should make sure that the way you dress is suitable. Many manor houses require jacket and tie for gentleman diners; ladies should also be dressed formally. Be sure to book your meals at the same time you reserve your room.

Websites www.manoir.com, www.lewtrenchard.co.uk, www.georgehotelofstamford.com

Country-house Favorites

Country house hotels with attached restaurants are a wonderful way to sample upper-crust English lifestyle.

■ At the Jacobean **Lewtrenchard Manor** in Devon you can sleep in the bed that used to belong to Charles I's queen, Henrietta Maria. The manor's excellent restaurant also serves food fit for royalty.

■ A hostelry has stood on the site of **The George Hotel** in Stamford, Lincolnshire, for more than 900 years. Today, two gourmet restaurants, ancient walled gardens, inglenook fireplaces to snuggle in front of, and four-poster beds make staying here a luxurious way to experience British history.

Raymond Blanc's English country house, Le Manoir aux Quat'Saisons, remains unrivaled for rural luxury living.

ELBULLI

A small seaside town on Spain's Costa Brava is the unexpected home of one of the world's most innovative chefs.

Named the best restaurant in the world by *Restaurant* magazine in 2006, chef Ferran Adrià's elBulli is one of a kind. The cooking at elBulli has been described as "a language through which all the following properties may be expressed: harmony, creativity, happiness, beauty, poetry, complexity, magic, humor, provocation, and culture." Whether rabbit brains with oysters or begonia flower soup with cashew rocks, amaranth, and Australian finger limes sound like your cup of tea or not, Adrià's imagination routinely keeps diners on the edge of their seats through some three dozen exquisite miniature creations and half a dozen wine selections over five- or six-hour dinners. Beginning with culinary foams and working through even lighter textures, such as frothy "air of carrot" or freeze-fried eggs, Adrià's laboratory will be developing new tastes, textures, temperatures, and techniques by the next season. Far from its humble beginnings in the early 1960s—the name derives from the original owner's toy bulldogs—elBulli today receives up to one million reservation requests a year and has been described as "the most imaginative generator of haute cuisine on the planet."

When to Go elBulli is booked through 2009 and will not begin 2010 reservations before late 2009. When making a reservation, remember that the restaurant season runs from mid-June to mid-December.

Planning The restaurant is in Cala Montjoi, a few miles from the town of Roses and 90 minutes north of Barcelona by car. Given that the five- or six-hour dinner ends well after midnight, a stay at the Almadraba Park Hotel just down the coast is a must. The only way to get to Cala Montjoi is by car (unless you come by boat from Cadaqués). The new elBulli season includes winter cuisine so that Ferran Adrià can work with game and different seasonal products. Once dinner-only, elBulli's opening hours have been extended to include lunch on selected days in summer and most Saturdays in fall.

Websites www.elbulli.com, www.almadrabapark.com

Ferran Adrià

Originally from the working-class Barcelona suburb of L'Hospitalet de Llobregat, **Ferran Adrià** speaks with a blue-collar accent that sounds like Andalusian Catalan. After starting out as dishwasher in a French restaurant, Adrià cooked for an admiral while doing national service in the Spanish navy. During this time he met chef Fermí Puig, now director of Barcelona's Drolma restaurant.

In 1983, Puig convinced Adrià to work as an assistant at elBulli during his summer break, and the following year, at the age of 22, Adrià joined elBulli as a line chef. Eighteen months later, he was head chef.

Adrià began his experiments in molecular gastronomy in the late 1980s. In 1990, the *Michelin Guide* awarded elBulli two stars, and in 1997 the restaurant was awarded three.

The presentation at elBulli is as much a part of the experience as sampling the food itself, as this Icy Truffle of Carrot and Passion Fruit demonstrates.

A snaking gangplank through mangrove trees brings you to the floating tropical paradise of Le Barachois restaurant.

MAURITIUS

TROPICAL GOURMET DINING

Enjoy dining in luxury with menus drawn from the cuisines of three continents on one of the world's most beautiful islands.

You know that the local dining scene must be hot when French chef, Alain Ducasse, opens a signature restaurant, and such is the case on Mauritius, a volcanic island in the southern Indian Ocean that has long been a haunt of the rich and famous and is now an increasingly tasty dining destination. Ducasse's Spoon des Iles restaurant at the Le Saint Géran resort on the northeast coast is a feast for eyes and palate. The open kitchen is crafted from black Zimbabwean granite, the floor made with paving stones from a 17th-century French church. The menu champions local produce cooked with French style—dishes like dorado tuna wrapped in banana leaf, wood-roasted rack of lamb, and creamy guacamole lime soup. Not to be outdone, Le Touessrok, a resort on the east coast, hired London-based chef Vineet Bhatia to create the Safran restaurant. Signature dishes include fresh shrimp with crabmeat risotto and a thoroughly modern version of chicken masala. While Spoon and Safran raised the bar for local foodies, they were not the first gourmet oases on the island. La Flore Mauricienne in downtown Port Louis (the island's capital) opened its doors in 1848 and is universally considered the oldest of all Indian Ocean restaurants. The menu, which ranges from Indian dishes such as roti and curry to French standards such as roast lamb, changes daily.

When to Go Mauritian weather is thoroughly tropical but rarely oppressive—thanks to a steady sea breeze—and almost always conducive to alfresco dining.

Planning One of the most delightful aspects of choosing a restaurant in Mauritius is the stunning location of so many of them. Le Barachois floats on wooden pontoons in the middle of a coastal estuary, while the chic signature restaurant at the Oberoi resort on Turtle Bay is set beneath a soaring palm-thatch roof.

Websites www.mauritius.net, www.spoon.tm.fr, www.letouessrokresort.com, www.oberoi-mauritius.com

Mauritian cuisine

Mauritius was uninhabited until the 16th century, yet subsequent immigration—by Indians and Chinese, British and French, Africans, and Arabs—has spawned a polyglot population that is reflected in the island's eclectic cuisine. While retaining their own unique food cultures, all these groups have borrowed from one another over the years to develop Creole dishes that are unique to the island. In addition to local versions of Indian favorites like biryani rice and curries, inhabitants also relish mango **kutcha** (stir-fried with ginger, garlic, and chilies), fried **faratas** bread (used to scoop up curry), **camarons au palmiste** (grilled shrimp with palm hearts), and **vindaye** (marinated fish or octopus stir-fried with onion, chilies, cloves, and turmeric).

THE BEST WINE, BEER, & MORE

No exploration of the pleasures of the global table would be complete without a visit to the sources of the glorious liquids that fill our glasses, quench our thirsts, and refresh our spirits.

The journeys on these pages will satisfy many different kinds of appetites. For those who appreciate—or seek to learn more about—great wines, there are tours of celebrated wine-growing regions, opening doors into the vineyards and cellars of Champagne in France, California's Sonoma County, Mendoza in Argentina, and South Africa's Western Cape. For whiskey connoisseurs, a pilgrimage to the misty Scottish isle of Islay reveals the scenic and remote locations where the world's great single malts are made. Rum-lovers may prefer the balmier islands of the Caribbean and the rich variety of the region's tipples. And for those who like their beverages served with plenty of tradition, and local color, destinations range from the quirky pubs of rural Ireland to the throbbing conviviality of Munich's Oktoberfest, when millions of visitors indulge their dual passions for robust German cooking and distinctive beers.

Ireland's pubs are at the social heart of their communities, providing a gathering place where locals and visitors can enjoy good conversation, music, food, and, above all, the perfect pint.

BOURBON

The magnificent landscape of the Bluegrass
State provides the backdrop to great distilleries.

The northeast corner of Kentucky—an area roughly bounded by the cities of Louisville, Bardstown, Lexington, and Frankfort—is home to nearly every major bourbon distillery in the world. Driving from the massive Jim Beam operation and the quaint Maker's Mark complex to recently rechristened Buffalo Trace, past rolling wheat fields, fancy bluegrass horse farms, craggy limestone outcroppings, and the knobby foothills of the Appalachian Mountains, visitors can find bourbons that are as varied as the landscape in which they are produced. Straight bourbons are whiskies made from at least 51 percent corn, distilled at no more than 160 proof, and aged for at least four years in brand-new oak barrels with charred interiors that impart color and flavor. Despite these common guidelines, the Bluegrass State's favorite liquor can vary from smooth to spicy to a stinging 120 proof, while aromas and flavors include hints of vanilla, cherries, sweetcorn, and even leather. How does each amber bottle develop its distinct personality? The best way to find out is to visit the distilleries that offer tours to see the bourbon-making process. Most tours end with complementary tastings, making Kentucky bourbon country all the more charming as the day goes on.

When to Go The weather is best from April through October, which is also when the vast majority of attractions are open. The Kentucky Bourbon Festival takes place in Bardstown at the end of September.

Planning An official "Kentucky Bourbon Trail" links the eight major distilleries and can be traveled in a day or two, although you should really devote at least four or five days to visiting Kentucky. Louisville is a convenient starting point and features vibrant and cosmopolitan art, food, and nightlife. There are boutique hotels and bed-and-breakfasts throughout northeastern Kentucky, often with affiliated restaurants serving innovative dishes prepared or paired with bourbon. While you are visiting the distilleries, allow time to explore the food, bluegrass music, horse farms, historic sites, and outdoor activities that await a traveler who chooses to roam rather than rush through the state.

Websites www.kentuckytourism.com, www.kybourbontrail.com, www.heaven-hill.com

Bourbon Cocktails

For the purest experience, order your bourbon straight. Otherwise, you can drink it with water or ice, or both, or try a bourbon-based cocktail.

■ For an **Old-Fashioned**, water, bourbon, bitters, and sugar are served over ice, garnished with an orange slice and one maraschino cherry.

■ A refreshing summer drink, a **Mint Julep** is a combination of bourbon and sugar served over crushed ice and several sprigs of fresh mint. Juleps are traditionally served at the Kentucky Derby in early May.

■ A **Manhattan** consists of bourbon, sweet vermouth, and bitters (optional). They are combined, chilled, strained into a cocktail glass, and garnished with a maraschino cherry.

A distillery worker empties Bourbon barrels at Heaven Hill Distilleries, Bardstown, founded in 1934.

Tranquil Sonoma Valley is ideal vineyard-touring country.

CALIFORNIA

Sonoma Wines

Enjoy world-class wines, beautiful country, and
fine cuisine in the home of California wine-making.

Napa may have kicked off the California wine boom after Prohibition ended, but connoisseurs also relish neighboring Sonoma County, not just for the marvelous quality of its vintage but also for the rustic ambience and personal touches that have nearly disappeared in the Napa Valley. Spanish priests first brought grapes and wine-making to Sonoma when they founded Mission San Francisco Solano in 1823, and in the 1850s Hungarian émigré Count Agoston Haraszthy created the state's first modern winery (Buena Vista Carneros). Haraszthy was also responsible for introducing many of the region's most celebrated grape varieties, including Zinfandel. About 40 miles (65 kilometers) north of San Francisco, Sonoma remains a throwback to a much older, more romantic California—a mosaic of vineyards, orchards, and quiet country towns where it is still possible to combine wine-tasting with biking and hiking. End your day with a dip in a redwood hot tub beneath the stars, and listen to the coyotes howl as you sip your Sonoma Chardonnay.

When to Go Sonoma County is gorgeous in fall, the trees resplendent in their autumn colors, while spring brings out the blossoms and wildflowers but can be a tad rainy. Accommodations can be hard to come by in summer unless you book far ahead.

Planning Other than the historic Sonoma Mission Inn & Spa, the Sonoma Valley does not boast any large hotels. Many of the local accommodations are Victorian-era bed-and-breakfasts, such as the chic Gaige House Inn in Glen Ellen with its sleek Asia-Pacific decor and early-evening wine reception that includes California fusion appetizers. Sonoma's annual culinary bash is the Olive Festival (weekends, December through February), which combines olive- and wine-tasting with other gourmet treats.

Websites www.sonoma.com, www.sonomavalley.com/OliveFestival, www.buenavistacarneros.com, www.kenwoodvineyards.com, www.sebastiani.com, www.valleyofthemoonwinery.com

Sonoma Wineries

■ Count Haraszthy's historic **Buena Vista Carneros** winery has daily tours, a tasting room, and the original 1862 cellar dug by Chinese coolies.

■ **Kenwood Vineyards** is one of the valley's most prestigious names in wine, producing award-winning Cabernet, Merlot, and Sauvignon Blanc among others.

■ The **Sebastiani Vineyards Wine Hospitality Center** in Sonoma town boasts excellent Pinot Noir and Chardonnay.

■ **Valley of the Moon Winery** has been owned over the years by a variety of characters from Oriental scholar Eli Sheppard to mineral king George Hearst.

WINERIES IN WASHINGTON

One of the world's top wine regions, Washington State is proud of its strong, superb quality vintages.

The big, walloping flavors of spice, game, blue fruits, and toasted nuts waltzing with intensity, elegance, and finesse tell the tale of Washington State Syrah. Garnering accolades worldwide and attracting visitors to some of the country's most remote vineyards, this treasure from France's northern Rhône Valley has found another place to call home. While Syrah is the new star here, lushly concentrated, Bordeaux-style blends, such as Cabernet Sauvignon and Merlot, are whispered to represent the best French Pomerol and St. Emilion styles. Do not think you have to slog through the mists and wind-driven downpours of Seattle to the vineyards producing these wines, because they are located on the east side of the Cascade Range, where a different climate prevails. The warm, desert-like regions of the vast Columbia Valley, including the Yakima Valley, Red Mountain, and Walla Walla wine areas within it, are blessed with stunning vistas of orchards, farms, and vineyards. The northern latitude also ensures that the grapes receive up to two hours more sunlight daily without getting too hot.

When to Go Outdoor enthusiasts can enjoy Washington State year-round, but summer and fall are best for wine-lovers.

Planning Visitors based in Seattle should pack picnic lunches and cross the beautiful Cascade Range on a two-and-a-half-hour drive to the sunny vineyards on the other side. The drive from the vineyards in the Puget Sound wine region on the Pacific coast (mostly growing white varieties like Chardonnay and Riesling) to the Walla Walla region in the southeast of the state takes five to six hours, so visitors should plan their trips with these great distances in mind.

Websites www.washingtonwine.org, www.wallawalla.com, www.wineyakimavalley.org, www.adamsbench.com, www.abeja.net

Washington State Towns

■ Less than an hour northeast of Seattle, **Woodinville** in the Sammamish River Valley is a friendly wine town with more than 40 wineries, including the historic and beautiful grounds of Chateau Ste. Michelle and the Victorian mansion of Columbia Winery.

■ Three hours east of Seattle, the **Yakima Valley** is a hub of apple- and hop-growing as well as wineries. The wineries are far apart but worth the visit. Hedges Cellars and Hogue Cellars are recommended.

■ The town of **Walla Walla** has a downtown area dotted with wine-tasting rooms, outdoor cafés, gourmet grocers, and acclaimed restaurants. July's Onion Festival pairs super sweet Walla Walla onions with the region's wines.

Ripe black grapes from Columbia Valley, Washington, are used to produce the region's Cabernet Sauvignon wine.

Widmer Brothers, a celebrated microbrewery in Oregon, produces beers inspired by traditional Bavarian brews.

OREGON

OREGON'S MICROBREWERIES

For more than 30 years, Oregonians have been at the cutting edge of the American microbrewery boom.

While Californians concern themselves with the finer points of Chardonnay, the folks up the coast in Oregon are obsessed with perfecting a different sort of beverage— beer. A number of factors have stoked the trend, including a cool, wet climate ideal for cultivating hops and barley, some of the most pristine water in North America, and people who still think that homegrown and homemade are better than anything that can be bought in a store. It all started with 26-year-old German immigrant Henry Weinhard, who arrived in 1852 with his own copper brewing kettle and a knack for making great beer. By the early 1970s, Weinhard's business was facing intense competition from megabrewers. It produced a brand new beer, "Private Reserve," based on Weinhard's original recipe—the region's first handcrafted or gourmet beer and the spark for many other Oregonians to create their own amber nectar. Portland now has more microbreweries than any other city in the U.S., and many homegrown Oregon suds are now legendary among beer connoisseurs—Widmer Hefeweizen, Hair of the Dog's Adam, and Steelhead's Raging Rhino Red to name a few.

When to Go There is no bad time to drink Oregon's microbeer. The lagers and light ales go down well in the hotter months, the stouts and darker ales when the weather turns cold and gray.

Planning You could combine a gourmet beer safari with winter sports at big-time snow resorts Hoodoo or Mt. Bachelor, or a summer trip that includes good-weather activities like white-water rafting the Rogue River, hiking in Crater Lake National Park, or a paddlewheel-steamer cruise through the Columbia Gorge.

Websites www.traveloregon.com, www.widmer.com, www.steelheadbrewery.com, www.raclodge.com, www.mcmenamins.com, www.rogue.com, www.brewersunion.com

The Oregon Beer Trail

With more brewpubs than anywhere else in the nation— more than 70 in total—Portland is a natural place to start and end your journey along the Oregon Beer Trail. The **Widmer Brothers Gasthaus** on North Russell Street offers all the well-known Widmer brews in an 1890s' Victorian hotel beside the brewery. Another atmospheric spot is the Western-style **Raccoon Lodge & Brewpub** on the Beaverton-Hillsdale Highway, which serves pretty good grub, too.

Next, head over to the Pacific coast, where the **McMenamins Lighthouse Brewpub** perches on the precipitous Cascade Head, overlooking the Pacific Ocean just north of Lincoln City. Farther south, down drop-dead-gorgeous Highway 101, is the **Rogue Brewery** in Newport, with its two-story brewpub, panoramic views of the fishing harbor, and 50 taps.

From there, head southeast through the Coastal Range to the lush Willamette Valley, home to **Steelhead Brewery** in Eugene and the British-style **Brewers Union Local 180** pub in Oakridge (on one of the scenic routes up to Crater Lake). From Eugene or Oakridge, it's an easy drive north on Interstate 5 back to Portland.

A lonely agave tree towers over the spectacular landscape in Mexico's Oaxaca state.

MEXICO

On the Mescal Trail

Produced by a process introduced by the Spanish, mescal's smooth, smoky flavor has won it a worldwide following.

Like tequila but purer, mescal is distilled from the agave (related to the century plant, or maguey) and is made in the arid regions of Mexico, including the southern state of Oaxaca. In Oaxaca City, start in the downtown chocolate district, where the stores offer samples of local mescals not available elsewhere. To see how mescal is made, and for further opportunities to try different varieties, follow the tasting trail from Oaxaca to the village of Santiago Matatlán, where the beverage was originally produced. Santiago Matatlán is known as the "mescal capital," and the route into the village is dotted with *palenques*, or distilleries, most of which provide tours of the mescal-making process. The agave hearts, or *piñas*, are roasted in a pit lined with hot rocks and then crushed to produce a pulp. In many places this is done by machine, but some producers still use a donkey to pull a heavy stone wheel over the roast agave. The pulp is fermented in wooden vats and then double-distilled in copper or ceramic stills. After sampling different mescals at the distilleries, you can buy some to accompany your predinner appetizers back in the city.

When to Go To taste the widest range of mescals, go to the Mescal Fair, held during the Guelaguetza cultural celebration in July (for dates email mezcal@oaxaca.gob.mx).

Planning Santiago Matatlán is 35 miles (56 km) southeast of Oaxaca. Allow enough time for a stop at the Zapotec rug-weaving village of Teotitlán del Valle or the huge Sunday regional market in Tlacolula. Mescal purchased in bulk, sold in unsealed plastic bottles, is not permitted onboard planes, so take home brand names with government seals on the bottles.

Websites www.go-oaxaca.com, www.planeta.com/oaxaca.html

Rock-lined pits are used for roasting the agave hearts before distillation.

Rum Around the Caribbean

This molasses-based drink exploded onto the market in the 16th century, fueling world trade, and is still a global favorite.

As surely as reggae, Rastas, and pirate rogues, rum is an enduring symbol of the Caribbean. More than a drinking phenomenon, it is the region's historic, cultural, and economic raison d'être. Although the distillation of sugarcane juice originated more than a thousand years ago in the old world, it did not reach its peak until the 17th century, when enslaved people in the West Indies ascertained that molasses could be fermented into a tasty alcoholic beverage. The demand for rum in Europe and its North American colonies fueled a sugarcane boom in the Caribbean, which in turn sparked demand for many more slaves and the so-called "triangle trade" that formed the basis of North Atlantic trade for several hundred years. Rum became part of island culture: Now and again it was used as currency in place of precious metal; the British Royal Navy's tradition of a daily ration of rum for all the crew started on ships in the Caribbean and spread around the globe (a tradition ended in 1970); and as in the West Indies song "Dead Man's Chest," rum was the drink of pirates, brigands, and scalawags. Connoisseurs drink it straight or on the rocks, but rum is a good base for any number of cocktails, from the Cuba Libre (rum, cola, and lime) and Mojito to Long Island Iced Tea.

When to Go The Caribbean's climate is tropical throughout the year, although temperatures and humidity are higher in summer; the hurricane season generally runs August through November.

Planning The St. Lucia Food and Rum Festival in January is one of the region's foremost showcases for sugarcane-based alcohol. Rum-makers from around the Caribbean stage tastings and other events, and the festival organizers bring in top bartenders and "mixologists" from around the world to make rum cocktails.

Websites foodandrumfestival.com, www.appletonrum.com, www.casabacardi.org

Caribbean Rum Tours

■ Since 1749, the **Appleton Estate** in Jamaica has produced the reggae island's best rum. Appleton 21 Years is considered one of the Caribbean's best premium rums.

■ **Bacardi**, now based in Puerto Rico, started life in Cuba in 1862. The Cataño factory tour includes an interactive museum and tasting room.

■ Although no one knows for sure, the **Mount Gay** distillery on Barbados claims to be the world's oldest rum producer, with a history spanning 300 years.

■ **St. James** on Martinique produces rum from sugarcane juice rather than molasses, giving a richer taste than regular rum. The distillery includes a tasting room and rum museum.

The Caribbean is famous for its idyllic sandy beaches, such as Soufrière on St. Lucia, as well as its rum.

LITERARY WATERING HOLES

Many writers have used bars, pubs, or cafés as temporary or even permanent offices.
Some remain haunts of writers, while others are merely haunted by their ghosts.

❶ Rose Room, Algonquin Hotel, New York City

Luminaries of stage, screen, and literature have long graced the tables of this watering hole in what is now one of New York's top boutique hotels. But it is probably most celebrated as the place where an intellectual circle later known as the Round Table lunched daily from 1919 to 1929. Members included comedian Harpo Marx, poet Dorothy Parker, and Harold Ross, founder of the *New Yorker*.

Planning The Algonquin is on Club Row, 44th Street, between Fifth and Sixth Avenues. www.algonquinhotel.com

❷ White Horse Tavern, New York City

The White Horse has a room dedicated to poet Dylan Thomas, who reportedly downed 18 whiskey shots here one night in 1953 before going back to the Hotel Chelsea to drop dead. (Medical evidence shows that his demise was from unrelated causes.) This pub has long attracted literary figures, including Jack Kerouac, Norman Mailer, James Baldwin, and Bob Dylan.

Planning On the corner of Hudson and 11th Sts. Try the White Horse whiskey or the excellent ales. www.iloveny.com

❸ Floridita, Havana, Cuba

While the cocktails score more highly than the food, this Regency-style bar-restaurant, which opened in 1817, is an unmissable shrine to Ernest Hemingway and a throwback to the 1930s. Hemingway came here during a Havana trip to research *For Whom the Bell Tolls*. Homages include the dish "Papa & Mary," created here in honor of Hemingway and his fourth wife.

Planning Other restaurants in Havana offer better food at lower prices. Just sip a daiquiri here. www.cubatravel.cu

❹ Literaturnoe Kafe, St. Petersburg, Russia

For lovers of Russian literature, and the poetry of Pushkin in particular, a visit to St. Petersburg is a pilgrimage. This café was the location of Pushkin's last meal, in 1837, after which he went on to lose a duel with his wife's alleged lover. Pushkin's effigy sits at a desk in the entrance hall. Dostoyevsky was also a regular. Occasional poetry readings keep the literary tradition alive.

Planning The café is on Nevskiy Prospekt. There are several other Pushkin-related sites in the city. petersburgcity.com/for-tourists/guides

❺ Brasserie Balzar, Paris, France

Soak up the ambient intelligence at this long-time, Left Bank haunt of intellectuals, artists, and writers. Your fellow diners are likely to be professors and students from the Sorbonne or authors thrashing out deals with publishers.

Planning Expect French classics; try the onion soup. www.brasseriebalzar.com, www.parisinfo.com

❻ Gran Café de Gijón, Chueca, Madrid, Spain

Journalists, writers, artists, and actors—including Federico García Lorca and Rubén Darío—have kept up the creative buzz at this traditional belle-epoque café ever since it opened in 1888. While enjoying coffee or a drink, you can watch the world go by through the large windows or soak up the sun on the café's terrace.

Planning The meat-heavy menu features Spanish and international dishes. Reservations are necessary for dinner. www.turismomadrid.es

❼ Edinburgh Literary Pub Tour, Scotland

Pub crawls have rarely been more educational than this much acclaimed tour. Professional actors guide you through the history of Scottish literature from R.L. Stevenson to J.K. Rowling in the setting of a series of the city's taverns.

Planning The two-hour walking tours start at 7:30 p.m, daily from May through September and less frequently the rest of the year. There is also a shorter bus tour in summer. www.edinburghliterarypubtour.co.uk

❽ Cheshire Cheese, London, England

If walls could talk, this pub would be in a bidding war for its memoirs. Fleet Street, on which it lies, was long the home of much of Britain's national press, and its finest scribes were renowned for their lengthy liquid lunches here. But its literary associations are much older, as it was rebuilt just after the Great Fire of London (1666) and occupies the site of a much older hostelry. Past patrons include Charles Dickens, Voltaire, Mark Twain, and local resident Dr. Samuel Johnson.

Planning Try the excellent Sam Smith's real ales and traditional food, such as fish and chips, and steak and ale pie. www.visitlondon.com

❾ Dylan's Bar, Black Lion Hotel, New Quay, Wales

As much memorial as drinking establishment, Dylan Thomas's favorite pub groans with photographs, mementos, and books related to Wales's most celebrated bard. New Quay may have been the inspiration for the fictional town of Llareggub in Thomas's "Under Milk Wood."

Planning The New Quay tourist office can provide information on the Dylan Thomas Trail. www.blacklionnewquay.co.uk

❿ Winding Stair Bookshop & Café, Dublin, Ireland

Scale a battered wooden staircase above one of Dublin's most eclectic bookstores, an honest-to-goodness venue that has been a favorite haunt of Irish writers and artists since the 1970s. Sit down in the café to enjoy a good read, views over Ha'penny Bridge and the River Liffey, and the company of like-minded literati.

Planning Enjoy superb, unfussy Irish classics, such as seafood chowder and boiled Irish bacon collar. www.winding-stair.com

Right: The White Horse Tavern in Greenwich Village, New York City, is famed for the caliber of its literary clientele.

Tourists and residents from nearby Ica flock to the Huacachina oasis, attracted by its setting and tranquil lake.

PERU

PISCO—PERU'S ESSENTIAL SPIRIT

This pale brandy—foundation of the famed
pisco sour—is the subject of fierce pride in Peru.

One would never expect brandy to bring two nations to the verge of war. But such is the case with pisco, which has been a major bone of contention between Peru and Chile for hundreds of years. With just as much fervor as they take to soccer fields and international boundary disputes, both countries claim the pisco sour cocktail (made with lemon or lime, egg white, and bitters) as their national drink. But there is no disputing the beverage's origin: It was developed by 16th-century Spanish settlers in the coastal valleys of southern Peru and named either after the port of Pisco, from which it was shipped, or the conical pisco pottery, in which the brandy was aged. Nowadays, the lush oasis town of Ica is the focal point of Peruvian pisco production, with more than 80 *bodegas* (cellars) churning out millions of bottles each year. Somewhere between 38 and 46 proof, pisco derives from a single type of grape, most commonly the dark Quebranta grapes imported by the Spanish. There are also aromatic piscos made from Muscat and other green grapes, and potent *acholado* (half-breed) piscos that contain a blend. Grapes are harvested in February and March. After distillation, the liquid is aged for at least three months before it is deemed worthy of imbibing. Old school Peruvians drink it straight up, without ice, and consider the sour cocktail an insult to pisco's good name.

When to Go Ica's climate is hot and dry throughout the year, although winter in the southern hemisphere (June to September) is more moderate. The Fiesta de la Vendimia (Vintage Festival) takes place in March.

Planning Ica lies about 200 miles (320 km) south of Lima on the Pan-American Highway. The family-run Bodega El Catador offers free tours of its vineyard and pisco distillery, as well as a small museum, bar, and restaurant. Vista Alegre—which represents the corporate end of Ica's distillery spectrum—offers daily tours.

Websites www.peru.info, www.vistaalegre.com.pe

Ceviche, Peruvian Style

Peruvians and Chileans argue over who makes the best *ceviche*, a tasty seafood mix that is among South America's most iconic dishes. Although it takes many different forms, Peruvian ceviche in its purest form is raw ***corvina*** (sea bass) marinated in a mixture of lemon, lime, onion, and aji chili for around three hours, a process that pickles the uncooked fish and infuses it with a tangy citrus flavor. Ceviche is normally served with ***cancha*** (roasted maize kernels) and a portion of the leftover marinade in a shot glass.

Nowadays, there are all sorts of variations: ceviche made from shark, octopus, squid, shrimp, scallops, crab, mussels, sea snails, and all sorts of white fish. And there is nothing quite like chasing it with a pisco sour.

BRAZIL

Cachaça in Brazil

This potent distillation forms the basis of the country's national cocktail and is a fine drink in its own right.

Walk into any bar in São Paulo, Brazil, and you will find *cachaça*—the distilled liquor made from sugarcane that is an iconic part of Brazilian culture. It is a "rags to riches" story that began near the town of São Vicente, in the region of São Paulo, in the 16th century, when sugarcane was harvested by enslaved people, who were allowed to let the leftover juice ferment into alcohol. It wasn't long before they hit on the idea of boiling and distilling the juice to produce something altogether more powerful, and cachaça was born. Production has not changed much since then—sugarcane is crushed to extract the juice, which is fermented for 24 hours, then distilled in copper boilers, and either bottled immediately or stored in wooden barrels to achieve a smoother, rounder taste. Once a "poor man's drink," it has now achieved international status as the prime ingredient in *batidos* (fruit juice mixtures) and cocktails—most notably, Brazil's national drink, *caipirinha*—a sublime combination of cachaça, lime, and sugar that has become popular all over the world. Cachaça is mainly produced in the state of São Paulo, in Minas Gerais, and in Rio de Janeiro, but there are *cachaçarias*—bars serving different types of cachaças—across Brazil. Brazilians who drink it *pura* (straight) often deliberately spill a few drops "for the saints" before imbibing. It is certainly something that deserves a healthy respect.

When to Go Visit São Paulo during the Brazilian spring (September through November) or winter (May through October). Avoid summer months (December through March), which can be extremely hot and humid.

Planning There are hundreds of varieties of cachaça; Pirassununga, 125 miles (200 km) from São Paulo, is the production center of the most famous, Caninha 51. The romantically located Cachaça Rochinha estate, set in a mountain valley in the state of Rio de Janeiro, is also worth the three-hour drive from São Paulo.

Websites www.braziltour.com, www.planetware.com

Caipirinha Cocktail

There are many versions of this classic drink, which varies between regions. Optional extras include fruit juices and lemonade.

Serves 1
1 1/2 oz/50 g cachaça
1 lime, cut into eight wedges
2 tsp sugar
Ice cubes or crushed ice

Mash the lime and sugar into a glass. Fill the glass with ice and pour in the cachaça. Keep stirring the contents as you pour to mix in the sugar thoroughly.

Bottles of Brazil's sugarcane alcohol cachaça—some with aromatic herbs to give an extra, unique flavor—line the shelves of a bar.

The cellar of Salentein in the Uco Valley is designed as a theater in the round with barrels set on stepped trancepts.

ARGENTINA

Mendoza's Wineries

Central Argentina's Mendoza Province produces a host of magnificent wines in an equally splendid setting.

In the shadow of the perenially snowcapped Andes, Mendoza Province reigns as Argentina's wine capital, producing three-quarters of the country's total output. Malbec is the name of the game here—a robust, fruity wine with overtones of black currant and prune (ideal with steak). But as the country becomes better known on the world wine circuit—it's already the fifth global wine-seller—its varietals, including Cabernet Sauvignon and Merlot, are fast gaining ground. As you head out on the region's wine roads—glorious, weaving lanes punctuated with tunnels of trees and peek-a-boo views of snow-draped peaks—you will not fail to come across one of the region's 650-plus *bodegas* (cellars). Some are old-fashioned wineries, others state-of-the-art architectural masterpieces. The best place to begin is the High Zone (best known for Malbec), the most convenient to Mendoza, the province's capital (about an hour away). The beautiful Uco Valley, about two hours away, is also worth the drive. Notable bodegas include Luigi Bosca in Luján de Cuyo, whose descendants brought vines from Spain in 1890; ultramodern Bodegas Salentein in Tunuyán, with a spectacular Andean backdrop; and the landmark Bodega Catena Zapata, a fabulous faux pyramid.

When to Go Grape-harvesting takes place in March and April. The Fiesta de la Vendimia (Wine Harvest Festival) in early March is a high-spirited bacchanalia.

Planning Most wineries are free to visit—though tours must be booked in advance. Be sure to pick up the "Caminos de Las Bodegas" collection of maps, available at hotels and at Mendoza's wine shops.

Websites www.descubramendoza.com, www.bodegassalentein.com, www.catenawines.com, www.thegrapevine-argentina.com, www.winemapargentina.com.ar

Argentina's Other Wine Regions

Mendoza may be the self-styled capital of sunshine and good wine, but vineyards extend for more than 1,200 miles (1,930 km) along the country's western border. **Cafayate** in Salta Province is notable for its high-quality Cabernets and fine vintages of fruity Torrontés. Argentina's highest-altitude and oldest surviving winery—**Bodega Colomé**—is here. Founded in 1831, it is 9,849 ft (3,000 m) above sea level.

La Rioja Province, especially in the Chilecito area, is also making distinctive, high-quality wines. Farther south, in the **Rio Negro Valley**, cool-climate varietals like Sauvignon Blanc and Pinot Noir are likewise being acclaimed, as are sparkling wines. It is no wonder Argentina is the world's fifth largest wine-producer, becoming bigger and better every day.

SINGLE MALT IN SAPPORO

World-class, and fast becoming world-famous,
Japanese whiskey is best sampled at the source.

Over the years the Japanese have developed a discerning taste for single-malt whiskey—their distilleries provide a malt for every palette. At Nikka Distillery in Yoichi, Hokkaido, 31 miles (50 kilometers) west of Sapporo city, you will find masculine malts crafted to perfection. Their Taketsuru Pure Malt won the Gold Medal at the International Spirits Challenge in Britain in 2008, and their Nikka Whisky Yoichi 1987 received international acclaim by winning the honor of Best Single Malt Whisky in the World at the 2008 World Whiskies Awards in Glasgow, Scotland. It may be near impossible to get your hands on the limited edition single malt (with just 2,000 bottles released), but seeing where the prize-winning drink was concocted is as simple as joining a tour of the distillery. Yoichi's founder and one of the fathers of Japanese whiskey, Masataka Taketsuru, studied whiskey-making in Glasgow for two years before founding his own distillery in Hokkaido in 1934. His life was dedicated to perfecting the beverage. When sampling his Yoichi distilled single cask, single malt, or pure malt whiskey, you'll see that his talent lives on.

When to Go Time your visit to fit with the annual Sapporo Snow Festival, held for one week in early February. The city swells with tourists who come to see the towering snow sculptures, some around 50 ft (15 m) tall and 80 ft (24 m) wide. Even if you just stick to the whiskey bars in Susukino, you will still be treated to a festive site with 100 ice sculptures being erected in this entertainment area.

Planning The trip to Yoichi takes just under two hours one way from Sapporo by train. Free Japanese tours of the distillery are held every 30 minutes daily (except from December 27 through January 3) from 9 a.m. to 5 p.m. Or you can wander around the production area, shop, and restaurant at your own leisure guided by a map and pamphlet.

Websites www.nikka.com, www.suntory.com, www.japan-guide.com/e/e5311.html, www.welcome.city.sapporo.jp, www.sta.or.jp, www.hyperdia.com.

Whiskey Galore

■ Keep an eye out for Nikka Whisky's namesake bar, **The Nikka**, near Susukino station, in Sapporo's busy nightlife district.

■ Try one of the Suntory bars, such as **Suntory Stylish**, also in the Susukino area. Suntory is the distiller of another one of Japan's highly praised single malts, Yamazaki.

■ Feeling hungry? Forget the wine with dinner. Instead pair a Japanese whiskey with your meal. A stiff whiskey drink is an acceptable dinner accompaniment and is even said to bring out the flavors of Japanese dishes, such as sushi. Cheeses and other seafood dishes are also good single malt matches.

Sapporo's whiskey distilleries are not the only attraction. The massive ice sculptures made for the annual Snow Festival draw visitors from around the world.

JAPAN

SEEKING OUT SAKE

Not really a wine, nor exactly a beer, Japan's celebrated national drink is in a category—and class—of its own.

For thousands of years the Japanese have crafted, refined, and delighted in sake—their unique rice alcohol—and now the rest of the world is joining them in the pleasure. With the country boasting more than 1,600 sake breweries, tourists can sample various kinds while finding out how water and rice are transformed into Japan's top drink. Just like a good wine relies on superb grapes, the rice used in sake is essential to the creation of a good product, and brewers use special sake rice with a high starch content. Turning this rice into rice wine begins with a mechanical process that polishes the grains to the kernel. The kernels are washed, soaked, and steamed, before koji mold and yeast are added to the mix—making sake technically more a beer than a wine. The rigorous process takes more than a month to complete and is followed by the sake settling in storage for around six months. Day-trips to breweries are easy to organize from Tokyo or Osaka. The Ishikawa brewery in Fussa, western Tokyo, first opened in 1881 and still retains its traditional charm. Reminiscent of Japanese temple grounds, it features two 400-year-old zelkova trees enshrining Daikokuten, the god of wealth/good fortune, and Benzaiten, the goddess of water—both essential to the making of sake. Hakutsuru brewery, established in 1743, is situated in Kobe (near Osaka).

When to Go Most breweries are open year-round except for the New Year holiday (from around December 27 through January 3).

Planning Not all of Japan's breweries cater to English-speaking tourists. Check that English tours are available and book in advance. Visit the Hakutsuru brewery museum, which has English information on sake production and history and offers tastings.

Websites www.hakutsuru-sake.com/content/08.html, www.tamajiman.com, www.jal.com/en/sake/visit/index.html, www.sake-world.com

How To Drink Sake

Today, sake is best served chilled, though traditionally it was always served warm as the old brewing process and method of storage created a taste better suited to heating. Warming sake increased the flavor (and the intoxicating effect) of the brew.

Unlike wine, sake does not improve with age. Buy bottles within a year of the date of manufacture, then drink within six to 12 months.

It seems only fitting that sake goes well with seafood—another Japanese favorite. Just like different wine blends, different varieties of sake can be matched to meals.

Opposite: Kegs of sake have been donated to a shrine in thanks for the harvest.   Above: Brewery-workers prepare rice for sake.

Vats of Barossa wine are "pumped over" during fermentation to mix the grape skins and the juice.

AUSTRALIA

BAROSSA VALLEY WINES

With scenic drives from cellar to cellar, South
Australia's Barossa Valley is a top touring destination.

About 40 miles (64 kilometers) northeast of Adelaide, country roads lined with gum trees wind through hillsides striped with the vines of one of Australia's oldest wine-growing regions, famous in particular for big, bright, high-alcohol red wines. The region has names of global distribution, such as Wolf Blass and Penfolds, but in between the big estates lie many smaller, family-run vineyards selling mainly through the cellar door and offering free tastings and advice. Whistler Wines produces about 9,000 cases a year from its own grapes; 70 percent of this modest production from two generations of the Pfeiffer family is sold directly to visitors. Customer-friendly weekend concerts are big draws, but the traditional tin-roof homestead has comfortable sofas at any time, and there is a lawn dotted with umbrellas, tables, and chairs at which to enjoy a glass of potent Reserve Shiraz or a fruity Audrey May Sémillon. Rockford Wines occupies ancient brick farm buildings from 1857, where Robert O'Callaghan makes wine from the fruit of 30 local growers, who use traditional hand-rearing methods in keeping with the basket presses and century-old equipment at the winery. O'Callaghan not only produces one of Australia's best Shiraz but a wine from the obscure Alicante Bouschet grape whose red flesh produces a crisp rosé without the use of skins. It makes perfect summer drinking for the lucky few who come to the cellar door—the only place it is available.

When to Go Cellar doors are open year-round, but a visit in March or April will increase the chances of seeing wine being made. These months offer bright warm days with lightly chilly evenings.

Planning More than half of the Barossa's vineyards can be visited without an appointment. Many cellar doors do not open before 11 a.m., so there is time for a leisurely breakfast and a scenic drive through the hilly countryside before your visit. Weekends tend to have more events but can also be very busy.

Websites www.barossa.com, www.whistlerwines.com, www.rockfordwines.com.au

The Vineyard Experience

■ Getting to and around the **Barossa Valley** is half the fun, as you pass though hamlets of verandaed, low-rise wooden homes with shiny tin roofs, between lines of stately date palms, and wind around hillsides stippled with olives and neatly hatched with vines.

■ At more traditional wineries you can see basket presses at work spewing juice from between their slats, and great lakes of juice and pulp in century-old vats made from local slate.

■ Vineyards are generous with their free tastings and often sell wine by the glass, as well as cheese plates and other accompaniments. Alcohol volumes commonly reach 15 percent, so drivers should take care.

Beer in Bamberg

This UNESCO World Heritage jewel of a town is home to some of Germany's best and most characterful breweries.

Wandering the quiet, cobbled streets to one of Bamberg's many breweries on a warm fall evening, don't be suprised if you think you have stepped into 17th-century Germany. Spared from the bombs of World War II, this picturesque Franconian city has kept its original features, including the 12th-century cathedral and Little Venice's network of bridges, waterwheels, and fishermen's houses along the banks of the Regnitz River. You will have plenty of time to discover the city as you make your way around a nine-brewery tour. Dotted along both sides of the river, the breweries have distinct personalities, and the beers their own characteristics. You can find one of the city's most famous beers at the Schlenkerla brewery, beside the cathedral. The dark, creamy, characterful Aecht Schlenkerla Rauchbier (Original Schlenkerla Smokebeer) has been likened in flavor to smoked bacon and is made by kiln-drying the malt over a beechwood fire. Try this with the classic Franconian dish of *Schäufele*—crispy pork shoulder with dumplings and sauerkraut. If it has all become a little too much, you can even sleep in the Fässla brewery, a block from the north bank of the river, which has rooms available throughout the year.

When to Go As with most European cities, Bamberg becomes busier during the summer. The often hearty beers and food lend themselves well to cold winter nights.

Planning Pick up your self-guided brewery tour pack from Bamberg's central tourist office. The pack includes vouchers for a drink at each destination, a glass, beer mats, and a backpack. Residents of Bamberg and brewery owners are particularly friendly and often speak English, so don't hesitate to ask if you have any questions. Give yourself at least two days to visit all nine breweries—most offer excellent Bavarian fare—and explore the rest of the city.

Websites www.bamberg.info, www.bambergbeerguide.com, www.schlenkerla.de, www.faessla.de

A Fine Brew

For centuries, the purity of German beer was not just a matter of pride and good practice but of law. The *Reinheitsgebot* (Purity Order), dating from 1516, was a ducal decree issued in Bavaria. It dictated that only water, barley, and hops should be used in the production of beer in order to eliminate the use of cheap and often unhealthy additives (yeast, though present, was at that time an unknown constituent in the brew).

The decree, which may have been the first food safety law, was only lifted in 1987, by the European Union, in order to permit the import of foreign beers. German beers still adhere to the traditional standards.

The old town of Bamberg is famed for its traditional architecture and its breweries.

MONASTIC TIPPLES

For centuries monks and nuns have brewed and distilled
their own alcohol—much of rare quality and distinctive flavor.

❶ Ma'loula, Syria

Still largely Aramaic-speaking and Christian, the small mountain town of Ma'loula supports two important Greek Orthodox convents: Mar Sarkis (St. Sergius) and Mar Taqla (St. Tacla). Both produce wine. Mar Sarkis has a shop where the nuns offer a free tasting of their excellent dessert wine while rattling off the Lord's Prayer in Aramaic. Ma'loula also enjoys renown for its arrack.

Planning An hour by bus from Damascus. www.syriatourism.org

❷ Kykkos Monastery, Troodos Mountains, Cyprus

Dating back to the 12th century and originally made by the Knights Hospitaller, this monastery's sweet, amber-colored Commandaria is the world's oldest named wine still in production. But Cypriots prize the monastery most highly for its zivania, a strong spirit distilled from wine-making leftovers.

Planning Kykkos Monastery is open to visitors and has a museum. Other monasteries nearby also produce Commandaria. Travel agencies offer Commandaria Trail tours. www.kykkos-museum.cy.net, www.visitcyprus.com

❸ Strahov Brewery, Prague, Czech Republic

Near Prague Castle, this recently renovated monastery, founded in 1142, has a microbrewery, restaurant, and beer garden. The goulash and St. Norbert Holy Beer—which comes in light and dark varieties—are excellent. The monks also release a special Christmas beer every December 5.

Planning The Christmas beer sells out very quickly. www.klasterni-pivovar.cz

❹ Pannonhalma Archabbey, Hungary

After a hiatus under communism, when the state confiscated their orchards, Pannonhalma's Benedictine monks have recently revived a wine-growing tradition dating back to the monastery's foundation in 996. Since their first post-communist harvest in 2003, annual output has risen to exceed 300,000 bottles. Varietals include Pinot Noir, Merlot, and Cabernet Franc, alongside indigenous types such as Italian Reisling, Sárfehér, and Ezerjó.

Planning The archabbey is on Szent Marton Hill, a steep walk from Pannonhalma, which is 30 minutes by railroad from Gydr. www.bences.hu

❺ Andechs Monastery, Bavaria, Germany

Hospitality has always been core to the Benedictine tradition, and this monastery takes the concept seriously, with a brewery, pub, and restaurant dispensing Bavarian specialties. Much of the fruit for the liqueur comes from the monastery farm. Brace yourself for heady views over the Bavarian Alps.

Planning The distillery tours include tastings. www.andechs.de

❻ Weltenburg Monastery, Bavaria, Germany

On a picturesque bend in the Danube, the world's oldest monastery brewery has been running since 1050. It now uses state-of-the-art technology alongside time-honored recipes to make some of Germany's most acclaimed Dunkel—or dark—beer. Its popular beer garden also serves food.

Planning Closed Mondays and Tuesdays in November and March, and from November 15 through March 15. Travel by riverboat from Kelheim (30 minutes). www.klosterschenke-weltenburg.de

❼ Abbey of St. Sixtus of Westvleteren, Belgium

So popular among connoisseurs is this Trappist abbey's tiny beer output that it strictly rations purchases. Unsurprisingly, a black market has helped feed the demand. The most highly prized beer, the Westvleteren 12—a complex, dark brew packing in 12 percent alcohol—sends beer-lovers into a spin.

Planning Buying the beer requires military-style preparation. Potential customers must phone between specified times to place an order and, if successful, make an appointment to pick it up. Refer to the website for the most up-to-date schedules. www.sintsixtus.be

❽ Chartreuse, Voiron, France

The powerful Green Chartreuse, distilled from 130 plants and flowers, and the slightly sweeter and milder Yellow Chartreuse, are the most celebrated products of Voiron's Carthusian monks—only two of whom ever know the secret recipe. Respectively, the liqueurs measure 55 and 40 percent alcohol.

Planning The cellars are open year-round for free guided tours (weekdays only from November through March). Voiron is in the French Alps, less than 20 minutes by train from Grenoble. www.chartreuse.fr

❾ St. Hugh's Charterhouse, Parkminster, England

The U.K.'s only Carthusian monastery produces apple wine, available commercially through just one outlet, the Union Jack Farm Shop in nearby Cowfold. Visitors who apply in writing can attend services at the monastery and enjoy food and drink there in return for voluntary donations.

Planning The charterhouse is a half-hour drive or 45-minute bus trip (number 17) northwest of Brighton. www.parkminster.org.uk

❿ Kristo Boase Monastery, Brong Ahafo, Ghana

One of Africa's few Benedictine communities, this serenely located monastery, near the central Ghanaian town of Techiman, makes much of its income from the proceeds of its cashew orchard. As well as selling the nuts themselves, the monks use the surrounding fruit to make jam and schnapps.

Planning The monastery offers tranquil accommodations. Cashew schnapps is an acquired taste. www.touringghana.com

Right: The Holy Monastery of the Virgin of Kykkos, Cyprus, is famous for its Commandaria—a sweet, spicy, unfortified dessert wine.

OKTOBERFEST IN MUNICH

The Weis'n, as Munich's annual festival is known to the locals, is a spirited celebration of the glories of German beer.

The atmosphere is electric. Six thousand people have been sitting thirstily at wooden tables in the huge Schottenhamel tent since 10 a.m. Finally, at noon, Munich's mayor taps open the first wooden beer keg with a mallet, and the cry of "*O'zapft is!*—It's tapped" goes up, signalling the start of Oktoberfest—and beer sales. Founded in 1810 to celebrate the marriage of King Ludwig I of Bavaria, Oktoberfest is now one of the world's best-loved festivals, attracting more than six million visitors per year. You can choose between 14 huge tents, each with a different atmosphere ranging from the traditional Schottenhamel (the oldest tent at the festival) to Ochsenbraterei (where whole oxen are spit-roasted). All serve lager-style beers specially brewed for Oktoberfest and supplied by six Munich breweries. The smaller Weinzelt tent serves a good selection of German wines. Make sure you sample the menu of traditional Oktoberfest food, too—like the addictive *Brathendl* (butter-basted roast chicken stuffed with parsley), whose delicious aroma drifts from massive rotisseries in every tent. Other favorites include *Schweinshaxn* (knuckle of pork), *Steckerlfisch* (grilled whole fish on a stick), and *Brezel* (giant pretzels). Waitresses and waiters can carry up to a dozen beer mugs to the long, shared tables, where Bavarians in traditional dress mix with happy tourists from around the world.

When to Go Despite the name, Oktoberfest runs for 16 days at the end of September each year, ending on the first Sunday in October. Weekends are much fuller and more festive than weekdays, but it can be harder to get a table.

Planning Book early. Flights and accommodations get more expensive as the celebration approaches. Public transportation is excellent, so a hotel a little farther from the Weis'n is not a problem. Tables in the tents can be reserved in advance by paying a deposit to the tent's proprietor.

Websites www.oktoberfest.de, www.muenchen.de

Beyond the Wies'n

■ A beer hall, restaurant, and garden in a historic setting in the city center, **Augustiner Keller** serves traditional food in generous portions.

■ The Englischer Garten park in the center of the city is home to **Chinesischer Turm**, an outdoor beer garden with a huge seating area arranged around a pagoda.

■ Probably Munich's best-known beer hall, **Hofbräuhaus** is housed in an elegant building with vaulted ceilings in the old town near the Marienplatz.

■ Just southeast of the Marienplatz is **Viktualienmarkt**, an open-air food market that is a feast for the senses. It is open Monday through Saturday.

Munich's waiters and waitresses deliver large orders of beer to a table with expert skill.

Nebbiolo vines flourish at Carema, on the Alpine slopes of Piedmont's Aosta Valley.

ITALY

THE NOBLE NEBBIOLO

Piedmont is the exclusive home of a very particular grape whose special character is expressed in extraordinary wines.

To know Nebbiolo is to understand the hushed tones and reverential air people use to describe this swirling riot of perfumed blackberry, rose petal, and tar. For this is the haunting grape varietal behind muscular Barolo and brooding Barbaresco—wines seemingly as long-lived as the Piedmontese towns and the snowcapped Alps that rise majestically behind the vineyards. Nebbiolo is a temperamental and fussy grape grown nowhere else on Earth. It flourishes in Piedmont—a special corner of northwest Italy characterized by rolling hills and meticulously kept vineyard estates. Here, the dusty purpled clusters hang amid the early morning fog, or *nebbia*, that cocoons them in late fall when the grapes are picked. The wines take their name from the picturesque villages that lie a few miles apart on either side of the town of Alba, a food- and wine-lover's Shangri-la. The food here is hearty; thick slabs of local beef braised in rich red wine, substantial pastas, roast pheasant and pigeon, fat chunks of artisanal cheeses, thick cured meats, and soulful white truffle. Barolos and Barbarescos can be nothing short of magnificent but here in their culinary home, enjoyed with convivial company, warmed by the glow of a crackling fire, they are positively magical.

When to Go Visit in fall, when the vineyards are a blaze of crimson and the white-truffle hunters bring back the prized delicacy from the surrounding oak forests for your enjoyment.

Planning Plan a stop in Asti, northeast of Alba, for a sparkling sip of Moscato d'Asti. The town of Gavi is home to the fragrant white wine from Cortese grapes, Gavi di Gavi.

Websites www.langheroero.it, www.italiantourism.com/discov5.html, www.italianmade.com/regions/region2.cfm

Beef in Barolo

You can replace pricy Barolo with a full-bodied red wine.

Serves 6–8
3 lb/1.3 kg top round of beef
Salt and black pepper
1 bottle full-bodied red wine
1 bay leaf
2 sprigs fresh thyme
3 tbsp olive oil
1 large onion, chopped
3 carrots, chopped
2 celery stalks, chopped

Season the beef with salt and pepper, and marinate for at least 4 hours or preferably overnight.
  Remove beef from the marinade, reserving the liquid. Preheat the oven to 325°F/170°C/Gas Mark 3.
  Heat 2 tbsp of the oil in a large frying pan and fry the onions, celery, and carrots over a low heat for 10 minutes until golden. Spread over the bottom of a large, ovenproof casserole dish.
  Wipe out the pan, heat the remaining oil, and fry the meat briskly on all sides over a high heat until browned. Place the meat on top of the vegetables. Add the marinade, cover, and cook in the center of the oven for 3 hours.
  Remove the meat and keep warm. Discard the herbs and puree the wine and vegetables. Slice the meat and serve with the sauce.

Chianti's vine-covered hillsides and traditional farmhouses provide the perfect setting for sampling the area's wines.

ITALY

SANGIOVESE IN TUSCANY

Earthy, with flavors of cranberry and cherry, Sangiovese is the grape par excellence of Tuscan sunshine.

There was a time when any mention of Tuscan wines conjured up images of squat, raffia-covered bottles containing sharp-tasting, brown-edged Chiantis. All that has changed. Nowadays, Tuscany offers a glorious choice of wines, from the refinement of a Brunello di Montalcino to the energy of a Chianti Classico, each with its own delicious variations in style. Old-style Chianti was the victim of Italy's Denominazione di Origine Controllata (DOC) legislation governing wine production in Italy, which required that dull white wine grapes be added to Chianti's Sangiovese grapes. Then, in the 1980s and 1990s, a fresh breed of Tuscan wine-makers emerged who blended Sangiovese with non-traditional grapes, such as Cabernet Sauvignon and Merlot, and improved winery techniques. Flamboyant, purple-hued showstoppers, the new blends were barred from a DOC classification, so they took the lower ranking of *vino da tavola* (table wine), but they were awarded their own classification—the Super Tuscans. Recently, DOC requirements have been relaxed, and Chianti can now be made from 100 percent Sangiovese, which has come into its own as an exciting grape, creating wines that shine with exuberance, finesse, and complexity.

When to Go Spring and summer are the seasons for *sagre*—local festivals, held on weekends, generally focused on a single food or dish, and often ending with a communal feast. The wine harvest takes place in August and September and brings another round of sagre.

Planning In Montalcino, wineries to visit include Castello Banfi and Franco Biondi Santi. For Chianti, try Rocca Delle Macie, Castello di Brolio, and Badia a Coltibuono.

Websites www.castellobanfi.com, www.biondisanti.it, www.roccadellemacie.com, www.ricasoli.it, www.coltibuono.com, www.chianticlassico.com

Classico, Brunello, and Rosso

The Chianti DOC region covers a large area, mostly in the provinces of Florence and Siena. For top quality, look out for the *gallo nero* (black rooster) logo of the **Chianti Classico** consortium, whose members include many of the best Chianti wineries. The consortium also produces a good touring map showing you where to find the major vineyards and wineries.

Sitting on a mountaintop under a diaphanous Tuscan sky, the town of **Montalcino** has long produced wines prized for their elegance and nuance. It has fewer vineyards than Chianti to the north, and its wines have always been made solely from Sangiovese grapes. The most renowned among them is **Brunello di Montalcino**—made to last and priced accordingly.

A simpler local wine, also made from 100 percent Sangiovese grapes and giving some idea of what can be done with them, is **Rosso di Montalcino**. Aged for just a year, rather than a minimum of four, a Rosso will cost you about a third of what you have to pay for a Brunello.

ITALY

ENOTECAS IN PARMA

In the north Italian city of Parma, the casual atmosphere of an *enoteca* is the ideal way to enjoy regional wine and food.

Whether rustic country affairs or modern metropolitan bars, *enotecas* hold to one unwritten rule: As well as wine, they feature local food—usually listed on a chalkboard on a wall behind the bar. In Parma, Via Farini is a constant parade of the city's incredibly well-dressed inhabitants, alongside the few tourists wise enough to visit. It is also home to two very different enotecas: Enoteca Fontana and Il Tabarro. The former is an old-style establishment, where at lunchtime students and local workers share long wooden tables as they tuck into the daily special. Fontana features plenty of local wines and even a few from other parts of Italy. Prosecco is always flowing, as is Lambrusco in its true form, sparkling but not sickeningly sweet. Try the excellent pink Pinot Grigio, which is how the smaller local producers make their Grigio. At night, customers sip wines that complement inexpensive antipasti of prosciutto and local cheeses. Farther along Via Farini, near Piazza Garibaldi, Il Tabarro attracts a younger, hipper crowd. The wines—many available by the bottle to take away—change often and are listed on a chalkboard over a case of cured meats and regional cheeses. Along with your wine, browse selected foods from local producers— perfect for learning the fine points of Parmese gastronomy, such as the difference between a Parmigiano Reggiano cheese aged for only 12 months and one aged for 36 months.

When to Go September and October bring a trio of festivities: Parma's ham festival (Festival del Prosciutto di Parma), the Palio (a weekend of races and flag-juggling events in medieval costume), and the Verdi festival, commemorating the works of the province's most famous son.

Planning Enoteca Fontana offers table service both indoors and out. If you want an outside table in the evening, get there early since Via Farini is Parma's busiest socializing street. Il Tabarro's owner, Diego, is very knowledgeable about local wine and food, and he delights in sharing anything new with customers.

Websites www.parmaitaly.it, www.parmaincoming.it

Wine Repositories

Enotecas were originally a way for local wine-producers to get their wares before the public, relieving small wineries of the burden of setting up tasting rooms on site. The word literally means "repository of wines"–a combination of the Greek *oinos* ("wine") and *theke* ("repository")–and in most cases the definition still holds true.

Usually located in historic town centers, enotecas attract more visitors than small-production, artisanal wine-makers could on their own properties, bringing the wines greater exposure. As tourism has evolved and the wine world has become globalized, there is now more diversity in the larger enotecas, including even an occasional French wine.

Wine and good cheer–drinkers toast one another in an enoteca.

The canals that encircle the center of Bruges have won the city the epithet "Venice of the North."

BELGIUM

Beer in Bruges

In medieval Bruges, take your pick from more than 300 Belgian beers in one of the city's atmospheric beerhouses.

Shoppers and tourists throng the cobbled streets of Bruges (Brugge in Flemish) in western Belgium, admiring the church spires, the sleepy canals, and the carillon bells that sing out the hours from the city's medieval bell tower. But step into the quiet alleyway of Kemelstraat, near the cathedral, and duck in under the sign of 't Brugs Beertje. Here, you enter a different world, where drinkers sit around wooden tables, holding up their frothing chalices appreciatively to the light. From behind the bar, the staff help diagnose your thirst if you cannot quite identify the cure. The answer might be a Brugge Tripel, a delicately balanced blond beer, or a Steen Brugge, bearing a picture of St. Arnold. This 11th-century patron of brewers founded the Abbey of Oudenburg, west of Bruges, and championed beer as a remedy against plague and other diseases—it worked to some extent because water needs to be boiled to make beer, killing harmful bacteria. For a truly local beer, go for Brugse Zot (Bruges Fool), a top-fermented ale, produced by De Halve Maan (The Half Moon), the only surviving brewery in central Bruges. Aficionados can visit the brewery, founded in 1856. And real devotees should eat at Den Dyver, an elegant restaurant that specializes in beer haute cuisine. Every dish is matched by carefully selected beers, demonstrating the remarkable range of flavors of Belgium's most celebrated drink.

When to Go There is always plenty to see and do in Bruges, including canal trips and visits to galleries of fabulous late-medieval art. During December, there is a Christmas market.

Planning There are hotels for all budgets, including wonderful boutique hotels in 17th-century town mansions overlooking the canals. 't Brugs Beertje, at Kemelstraat 5, is open from 4 p.m., Thursday through Monday. Den Dyver, at Dijver 5, closes all day Wednesday and for lunch on Thursday.

Websites www.brugsbeertje.be, www.dyver.be, www.halvemaan.be, www.brugge.be

Strong and Varied

Belgian beers are generally strong, between 5 and 12 percent alcohol by volume. Styles include brown ales, blond (honey-colored) ales, and "white" beers (made with wheat). All these are top-fermented—during the brewing process, the yeast is allowed to form a crust, which holds in the flavor. There are also lighter lager or pilsner-style beers, which are bottom-fermented. Flavoring usually comes from hops, but for **Steen Brugge** a medieval mix of herbs and spices, called *gruut*, is used.

Brand names often have monastic origins, "abbey beer" usually signifying high quality. Some abbeys license their name to commercial breweries. Trappist beers, including **Chimay** and **Orval**, are produced by the abbeys themselves.

THE NETHERLANDS

Jenever in Schiedam

Forget the "export gin" used to make a gin and tonic—
jenever is the real Dutch gin, and a very different experience.

Five of the world's tallest traditional windmills stand beside a waterway in the city of Schiedam in the southern Netherlands. Their sails turning against the skyline, high above pretty clusters of old buildings, the windmills share their history with Schiedam's most famous product—gin, or rather the original form of gin, *jenever*. This straw-colored drink, with an attractive scent of malted grain, is named after juniper (*jenever* in Dutch), and a doctor is said to have invented it around 1650 by adding juniper berries to distilled spirit. By the 19th century, a variety of styles had evolved, quaffed for pleasure rather than medicinal purposes. By then, Schiedam was the world capital of gin, with 20 windmills grinding the barley, rye, and corn used to make the spirit and 400 distilleries shipping to destinations around the globe. Want to know more? Head for the city's Jenever Museum, housed in a former distillery, which explains the drink's history and has its own *proeflokaal* ("tasting bar"), where you can sample the different styles. Here, you will learn about the traditional ways of making jenever, the flavorings used, and how the drink is bottled in ceramic containers. In the old days, there was a proeflokaal attached to most distilleries, so customers could sample the wares before buying. There are plenty of such establishments left in Schiedam and elsewhere in the Netherlands. If the museum's proeflokaal has whetted your appetite, try Schiedam's Café-Jeneverie 't Spul, which stocks more than 400 kinds of jenever. *Proost!* (Cheers!)

When to Go In winter, when north or east winds blow, the weather in the Netherlands can be notoriously bitter—and jenever seems particularly warming. The Jenever Museum is closed on Mondays.

Planning Schiedam lies ten minutes by train northwest of Rotterdam. It prides itself on its museums, historic monuments, and windmills. One windmill, De Nieuwe Palmboom (The New Palm Tree), contains a museum of milling. The Jenever Museum is at Lange Haven 74-76. The Café-Jeneverie 't Spul is at Hoogstraat 92.

Websites www.schiedam.nl, www.schiedamsemolens.nl

Pure and Flavored

There are two types of jenever: *oude* (old) and *jonge* (young). This is not a description of aging, but of the method of distillation. The jonge styles, introduced around 1900, have a lighter, less malty finish.

A huge range of flavored jenevers exists, including orange, lemon, apple, chocolate, hazelnut, and vanilla versions.

Jenever is considered a quality spirit, far too good to be spoiled with mixers. It is served in tiny glasses and drunk as an aperitif before a meal, a digestif after a meal, or a "chaser"— known colloquially as a *kopstoot* (head butt)—to accompany pilsner-style beers.

A worker in a jenever distillery shovels coal into the furnace used to heat the stills.

FRANCE

SMALL CHAMPAGNE HOUSES

There is more to champagne than the wines of the most famous houses. Sample the delights offered by smaller producers.

A mosaic of bucolic villages spreads out across the Marne River Valley in northern France. Vineyards dominate slopes and plateaus, where patches of chalk thrust through the soil. Here and only here is where champagne, the nectar of monarchs, is produced. Called "the Pearl of Champagne," the old-world village of Hautvillers is home to Champagne G. Tribaut, a family-owned cellar whose Premier Cru vines, grown on 30 acres (12 hectares) of sunny slopes and chalky terrain, morph into three champagne varieties. The Tribaut wine-maker holds a bottle of their silver-label Grand Cuvée Spéciale. He slices the foil to undo the wire cage (or *muselet*), then adroitly grasps the cork in one hand, and turns the bottle with the other. The Cuvée Spéciale's soul bursts forth as a mature, complex wine with hints of rare spices. A few miles to the south, Pierre Gimonnet et Fils champions Chardonnay-based champagne in the hamlet of Cuis in the Côte des Blancs. A slender flute of Gimonnet Gastronome Blanc de Blancs reveals a soft hue and wonderful depth. Roll the wine around your mouth, noting aromas of honey, toffee, and minerals, a fresh-baked character, and a crisp, nutty finish. In Merfy, north of Reims, the small cellar of Chartogne Taillet belongs to a family that has been making wine since the 16th century. Old vines help intensify blends, particularly the Cuvée Sainte-Anne Brut, an aromatic champagne with delicate bubbles. Apples, pears, and almonds with a nuance of warm caramel encircle the pale straw effervescence, finishing with a touch of mineral.

When to Go May through September is the best time to visit the Champagne region. In September, you may catch Le Cochelet, a festival celebrating the last day of harvest, when growers and pickers feast on *potée champenoise*, a regional dish of meat, cabbage, and other vegetables.

Planning Cellars generally have regular tours during summer months, but double-check before you venture out. To enjoy Champagne fully, rent a car so you can explore its villages and vineyards. In Épernay or Reims, grab a map of the Route du Champagne.

Websites www.champagne.g.tribaut.com, www.chartogne-taillet.fr

Regional Cheeses

The Champagne region produces several cheeses, including Chaource and Langres, that complement the sparkling wines, either as an appetizer or during dinner.

■ **Chaource** has been made since the early 14th century. Similar to camembert, yet creamier in texture, the unpasteurized cow's-milk cheese exudes a rich fruity flavor with a whiff of mushrooms. As it ages, the cheese goes from smooth to creamy. By full maturity, Chaource tastes nutty and a tad salty.

■ Made on the high plains of the Champagne region, **Langres** traces its origins to the 18th century. The cheese is ripened for five weeks in a humid stone cellar, during which time it is regularly washed with an orange pigment. The end result is a dense, slightly crumbly cheese enveloped in a vivid orange rind and with a pungent smell. The depression on top, called a *cuvette* or *fontaine*, encourages partakers to fill it with some champagne.

Opposite: Vines cover the hillside above Cuis. Above: One of the region's labyrinthine cellars

WINE TOURS IN FRANCE

From the vine-covered slopes of Alsace in the northeast to the wind-swept, craggy hills of Corbières in the southwest, the diverse French landscape offers a wine for every palate.

❶ Rhine Valley, Alsace

The Alsace Route des Vins winds south from the town of Marlenheim, known for its rosé wines. After visiting Obernai and Barr, linger in medieval Eguisheim to savor a noble Grand Cru Pfersigberg, made with Gewürztraminer grapes, before wandering through its unusual concentric streets.

Planning At harvest time, August through October, villages celebrate their wines with fêtes—ideal occasions for sampling both wines and local food specialties. www.alsace-route-des-vins.com

❷ Arbois, Franche-Comté

This picturesque medieval town, snug in the Jura Mountains, is best known for its *vin jaune* ("yellow wine"), tasting rather like a fino sherry, and its sweet *vin de paille* ("straw wine"), made from grapes dried on straw mats.

Planning In mid-winter, the festive Percée du Vin Jaune is when people come together to taste vins jaunes that have spent the statutory six years and three months in barrels. www.jura-vins.com

❸ Val de Loire, Centre/Pays de la Loire

The Touraine, the Garden of France, is blanketed with vineyards spread out around historic châteaus. Begin this Loire Valley tour in Vouvray, where Chenin Blanc grapes give a refreshing edge to sparkling wines, then try the rosés of Chinon, and St.-Nicolas-de-Bourgeuil's Cabernet Franc reds. Continue west to Angers for a taste of ten-year-old Savennières.

Planning In Vouvray, walk uphill to the village church—the portal is carved with grapes and harvest images. www.loirevalleywine.com

❹ Gien to Sancerre, Centre

In Gien on the River Loire, enjoy a young Côteaux du Giennois with your lunch, then tour the unusual red-brick Château de Gien. Follow the river south for flinty Pouilly-Fumé and dry Quincy wines. Stop for tastings in Chavignol and Buie near Sancerre, where Sauvignon Blanc underlies crisp white wines.

Planning Perfect with local sausage, salad platters, and picnics are Saint Pourçain *vins de soif* (wines to quench thirst) from farther south. www.vins-centre-loire.com

❺ Côte de Nuits, Burgundy

South of Dijon, known for its mustard, lies the enticing variety of one of the world's most famous wine regions. Begin in Gevrey-Chambertin, at the northern tip of the Côte de Nuits area, home to nine Grand Crus and 27 Premier Crus vineyards. In addition to pricey premiers, Gevrey's skilled village vignerons make reasonably priced wines, best tasted with local fare.

Planning Try *pauchouse* (a freshwater fish stew) paired with an aromatic Hautes Côte de Nuits Chardonnay. www.burgundy-wines.fr

❻ Côtes du Rhône Villages, Provence

South of Bollène, Rhône Valley wines take on the rich, plummy character of Grenache. Taste them on Gigondas' village square, looking out across vineyards running up to cliffs capped with lacy stone, the Dentelles de Montmirail. Travel south to Châteauneuf-du-Pape, whose wines are made from 13 grape varieties.

Planning Allow a week to explore this corner of Provence. The walled town of Vacqueyras has a Fête des Vins in July. www.vins-rhone.com

❼ Corbières, Languedoc-Roussillon

Since the Romans planted grape vines around Narbonne, wines have been central to the life and commerce of the Languedoc. From Durban-Corbières, stop in Tuchan for a tasting of hearty Fitous and Corbières at the Mont Tauch wine cooperative. Drive south to Maury for sweet wines that perfectly complement chocolate desserts.

Planning To avoid summer's intense heat, visit in April and May. Be prepared for stiff Tramontane winds. www.mont-tauch.com

❽ Madiran, Hautes-Pyrénées

The Pyrenees hover on the horizon as you explore the Béarn vineyards around Pau. Madiran wines, a blend of Tannat, Cabernet, and Fer grapes, mellow after ten years in oak. In fall, a Madiran or fruity Tursan complements game birds, veal ragouts, and mushrooms—with an Armagnac to round things off.

Planning Madiran holds a four-day wine fair in mid-August. www.vins-du-sud-ouest.com

❾ Bordeaux, Gironde

Wine-maker Bernard Magrez recently decided to open up some of his châteaus to accommodate, educate, and pamper wine-lovers of all levels. He offers a behind-the-scenes chance to follow the wine-making process, with the possibility to stay at one of four luxury châteaus, visit vineyards and cellars, enjoy wine-tasting sessions, and watch a cooper making an oak wine barrel.

Planning Tours are customizable and you can stay as long or as little as you like. For true luxury, the trip can include transportation by Rolls-Royce, helicopter, or private jet. www.luxurywinetourism.fr

❿ St.-Émilion, Gironde

Troubadours praised the (then white) wines of St.-Émilion. Begin your tour in the 14th-century cloisters of Europe's largest monolithic church—carved out of rock. An uphill drive leads through the satellite vineyards of St.-Georges, Montagne, Lussac, and Puisseguin, where you taste earthy, Merlot-rich vintages.

Planning On the third Sunday in June, watch a procession of red-robed members of the Jurade de St.-Émilion, a medieval body that now promotes St.-Émilion wines. www.saint-emilion-tourisme.com

Right: In Puligny-Montrachet, a village in Burgundy famous for its Grand Cru white wines, workers stand at a conveyor belt sorting the grapes with total concentration.

SWEET WINES OF FRANCE

An aura of magic surrounds the golden glow of a fine *vin liquoreux* (sweet wine) from southwest France. Be enchanted!

The alchemy begins in fall, when ground fog veils the slopes rising from the Ciron River in the hilly Sauternes region, south of Bordeaux. Here, Sémillon grapes are harvested in six successive stages, the ripest being individually handpicked in the final stage. This last crop will have been touched by the fungus *Botrytis cinerea*, the *pourriture noble* (noble rot), essential for a vin liquoreux's distinctive sweetness. After the grapes have been crushed and mixed with the juices of Sauvignon and Muscadelle grapes, the wine begins a long rest of ten years or more, as time transforms it into a complex "nectar," with dense aromas of candied fruit and a voluptuous texture. These Sauternes vintages are the most famous of the southwest's sweet wines, prized at the tables of the rich since the mid-19th century. Having toured the vineyards of Sauternes and Barsac (producing a slightly racier sweet wine), further sweet delights await when you cross the Garonne River at Langon. In the ancient, walled village of Sainte-Croix-du-Mont, taste the vins liquoreux of Loupiac and Sainte-Croix-du-Mont, made on south-facing slopes overlooking Sauternes. Another destination draws you through the enchanting, wine-producing uplands of Entre-deux-Mers, then along the Dordogne River to Bergerac and Monbazillac. At sunset, survey the enchanting panorama of vineyards from the historic Château de Monbazillac, which offers a final taste of noble sweetness, traditionally enjoyed as an aperitif.

When to Go Plum blossoms drift across hillsides in early April—a sunny, if slightly chilly season, ideal for touring and tasting regional specialties. Harvest time, October through early November, is good for stops in colorful farmers' markets, such as the market at Langon.

Planning Allow at least a week for this tour south, then east of Bordeaux. Looking for a packable bottle to tuck in the suitcase? Most wine boutiques stock half-size bottles of sweet wine, the perfect gift.

Websites www.bergerac-tourisme.com, www.chateau-monbazillac.com, www.sauternes-barsac.com

Open Doors to Sweet Delights

■ Enjoy the region's velvety foie gras with a glass of Monbazillac as a first course. Or savor a flaky **tourtière** (layered pastry) with Sauternes at the end of the meal. Vins liquoreux are also well suited to blue cheeses, such as **Roquefort** or **Bleu d'Auvergne**, and freshly shelled walnuts and almonds.

■ The second weekend in November each year is a *portes ouvertes* (open doors) weekend in Sauternes, when wine-makers welcome visitors with open doors. Enjoy a 9-mile (14 km) hike through the vines and a sumptuous on-site lunch before touring the wineries.

■ At Monbazillac, don't miss the displays of old wine-making tools in the château's cellar. The ticket includes a guided wine-tasting in the visitor center.

Vines spread out in front of the Château de Malle, one of Sauternes's best-known estates.

Seville's Plaza de España, built in 1929 in the Moorish style, is an attractive place to stop for a rest or to eat a picnic lunch.

SPAIN

SHERRY AND TAPAS IN SEVILLE

With sherry to quaff and tapas to snack on, Seville in southern Spain offers an outing of rare gastronomic delights.

Andalusia, the birthplace of Spain's tapas tradition, is at its cosmopolitan best in Seville. And as favorite beverages to go with Seville's tapas, two kinds of sherry share honors: Dry sherry, known as *fino*, and *manzanilla*, a sherry from Sanlúcar de Barrameda. To cleanse the palate, cut the heat of summer, and prolong the pleasures of itinerant grazing, a clear, cold, dry fino is hard to beat, whether from Jerez de la Frontera, Puerto de Santa Maria, or Sanlúcar de Barrameda. Manzanilla—so-named for its aromatic resemblance to chamomile tea (*manzanilla* in Spanish)—brings a different zest. Made at the mouth of the Guadalquivir River in Sanlúcar, it has a slight salty tang of the sea. In Seville—or anywhere in Spain—a good *tapeo*, or tapas tour, is confined to a specific area, manageable on foot. In Seville there are four main zones. Centro and El Arenal constitute one of them, with Bar Casablanca and Enrique Becerra as top choices. Another is Barrio de Santa Cruz, where La Giralda is arguably the best tapas emporium in town. In the Barrio de la Macarena and San Lorenzo, Seville's oldest bar, El Rinconcillo, is a classic. And across the Guadalquivir in the traditional sailor, bullfighter, and flamenco enclave of Triana, start at La Albariza, overlooking the river at the end of the Puente de Triana.

When to Go Seville's Feria de Abril, following Semana Santa (Holy Week) by ten days, is the city's annual blowout, starring horses, bulls, and Andalusian beauties dressed in their flamenco finest.

Planning Three days to a week is enough time to explore Seville. For side trips into the surrounding countryside, with Seville as base camp, plan for up to two weeks. Jerez de la Frontera and the other sherry-making towns lie to the south of the city—it takes about an hour and a quarter to drive to Jerez.

Websites www.andalucia.com, www.flamencoshop.com

A Wealth of Ingredients

■ As a result of the cooler temperatures and higher humidity in the area where *manzanilla* is made, it develops a thicker layer of vitamin-B-rich *flor* (yeast) during fermentation. This gives the wine a fresher and more delicate flavor, as well as reputedly curative properties against hangovers.

■ Seafood from the Guadalquivir estuary, Ibérico hams from Huelva, wild mushrooms and cheeses from the Sierra Norte highlands, and fresh farm products from La Campiña all enrich local larders. As a result, breads, pastes, creams, sauces, and puddings are rarely present in Seville tapas. Instead, pure raw materials—fresh fish, ham, cheese, peppers, or vegetables—dominate the miniature cuisine on display in Seville's bars.

■ If you want something a bit more substantial than tapas, *cazuelitas* (small earthenware casseroles) show off some of Seville's best cooking. **La Giralda's** *cazuela Tío Pepe* (shitake mushrooms, shrimp, ham, and dogfish), **Bar Estrella's** *fabas con pringá* (stewed broad beans), and **El Rinconcillo's** *caldereta de venado* (venison stew) are three of the best.

WINES OF LA RIOJA

Enjoy the best of both tradition and innovation
in Spain's most prestigious wine-producing region.

La Rioja has a long history of producing Spain's finest wines. Valdepeñas in central Spain has always made more table wine, but for quality, the oak-aged, vanilla-flavored giants of the province of La Rioja in the north have long been unassailable. A good traditional Rioja—and it is unquestionably one of the world's great wines—comes in one of three categories: *crianza* (aged for at least two years at the winery, including at least a year in oak casks), *reserva* (aged for at least three years, including a year in oak), and *gran reserva* (aged for at least five years, including two years in oak). The resulting smoky counterpoints of oak and fruit are the wines' hallmark flavors, beautifully complementing roast meats and dishes with rich sauces. In recent years, many smaller, local wineries have been bypassing the traditional three classifications. In their vintages, less oak results in wines that, at their best, release the rich fruitiness of the Tempranillo, Graciano, and other grapes used to make a red Rioja, along with a range of spicy undercurrents. The choice is yours. Visit the region and sample all the styles. And don't forget that La Rioja celebrates the gamut of epicurean pleasures—including good food. Begin your tour at Haro, famous for its red wines and superb home-cooking at restaurants such as Terete and Cueva La Recala.

When to Go The fall wine harvest is always a magic time in La Rioja, when the statue of the Virgen de Valvanera is brought down from the Sierra de la Demanda to Logroño, the provincial capital, to bless the grapes and the ritual connections between wine and humanity are most palpable.

Planning Ezcaray, in the Sierra de la Demanda, is the home of the Michelin-starred Echaurren restaurant and inn. Try La Venta de Goyo in the Najerilla valley for game dishes. In Laguardia, the Marixa and Posada Mayor de Migueloa both serve fine cuisine, while the nearby Marqués de Riscal hotel in Elciego has two restaurants directed by Echaurren's Francis Paniego. West of Laguardia is the exquisite Casa Toni.

Websites www.haro.org, www.marquesderiscal.com

Logroño's Tapas Trail

Few pub crawls rival Logroño's *sendero de los elefantes* (elephants' trail) along Calle and Travesía del Laurel—home to two dozen bars, each famed for one specialty or another. The nickname derives from the Spanish *trompas* (trunks), slang for a "snootful." For *champis* (garlic-filled mushrooms topped with shrimp), head for **Bar Soriano**. **Blanco y Negro** specializes in *sepia* (cuttlefish), **Casa Lucio** in *migas de pastor* (breadcrumbs with garlic and chorizo sausage), and **La Travesía** in *tortilla de patatas* (potato omelet). **Bar Alegría** serves a famous *cojonudo* (a quail egg on a toothpick with a sliver of spicy chorizo and hot green pepper), while **El Donosti** makes *embuchados* (deep-fried lamb tripe). Ask for a *crianza Rioja* to go with your food, and out come the crystal glasses.

In La Rioja, traditional summer festivities include a "wine battle" at Riscos de Bilibio near Haro on June 29 each year.

Jacques Faro da Silva, director of the Madeira Wine Company, which owns Blandy's, samples an 1860 Sercial.

PORTUGAL

WINES OF MADEIRA

On the Portuguese Atlantic island of Madeira,
savor wines that are steeped in history.

Entering the tasting room at Old Blandy's Wine Lodge comes as a relief. Lodges are where some of Madeira's finest wines are aged in wooden casks and vats, and after a couple of hours in the bright, buzzy streets of the island's capital, Funchal, their cool, shadowy interiors are wonderfully refreshing. The atmosphere is informal, but there is a respectful hush that is no more than the wines deserve—after all, they are among the world's finest and longest-lived. Like mainland port, Madeira's wines are "fortified" by adding grape spirit (brandy) to stop fermentation and preserve the sweetness of the fruit. Unlike port, the wines are then heated to around 113°F (45°C)—the result of a happy discovery when European sailing ships crossed the equator carrying Madeira wine on their way to and from the East Indies. One effect of this process is that the wine does not deteriorate once a bottle is opened. So without any great risk of wastage, the various lodges—Pereira d'Oliveira and Artur de Barros e Sousa are also worth a visit—can offer some venerable vintages without charging too much. At Blandy's, the youngest wine is a 1977 Verdelho at around $9 a glass. At more than $100 a glass, the lodge's 1908 Bual is not cheap—but for a taste of a wine made in the year that Henry Ford sold his first Model T, who's counting?

When to Go Madeira has been popular as a winter sunshine destination since the 1920s, but sea breezes mean that temperatures are never unbearable, even in summer.

Planning Funchal is a compact city and most of the lodges are within walking distance of the center. The island's interior is a green patchwork, where every square meter flat enough to plant on is pressed into service. Rent a car or take a bus trip around the island to see the vineyards where the grapes are grown.

Websites www.madeira-web.com, www.madeirawinecompany.com

Food Matching

■ **Malvasia** is the sweetest of the four types of wine made in Madeira, all named after the grape varieties used to produce them. Malvasia is a natural partner for rich and creamy desserts. Try it instead of Sauternes with foie gras terrine.

■ Less sweet than Malvasia, **Bual** goes well with pastries and cakes, especially the local *bolo de miel* (honey cake), as well as with hard and blue cheeses.

■ **Verdelho** is a medium-dry wine, delicious as an aperitif with salted almonds or cashews, air-dried hams, and dried fruits.

■ The driest wine, **Sercial** makes a terrific partner for sushi and sashimi dishes, as well as smoked salmon, oysters, and other shellfish.

PORTUGAL

Port Wine in Porto

Visit Portugal's atmospheric second city in the north of
the country and sample one of the nation's finest exports.

Porto, where the River Douro meets the sea, lends its name to one of the world's most famous after-dinner tipples. The story starts in 1689, when—by a happy accident that connoisseurs have been celebrating ever since—the fortified wine that became known as port was invented here. War with France had forced the British to find alternatives to French wines, so they came to Portugal, drawn by the terraced vineyards of the Douro Valley. Casks of wine were brought downriver in sailing boats, called *barcos rabelas*, and unloaded in Porto for export. Traders found that the wines traveled better and tasted better when fortified with brandy, and this chance discovery still defines the taste of the wine. After harvesting, the grapes—from more than 40 different varieties—are taken to *quintas*, or estates, where they are pressed and left to ferment. Adding grape brandy halfway through this stage arrests full fermentation and gives the wine its characteristic sweetness. It is finally matured, in casks for tawny ports and bottles for ruby and vintage ports. You can try this excellent wine in any of the bars in town, ideally accompanied by traditional *fado* music and dancing. But no visit to Porto is complete without a trip across the river to Vila Nova de Gaia on the other side, where the wines are brought to age in a number of port "lodges." The British influence is still very evident here, as you will see from many of the names of the lodges, such as Sandeman's and Taylor's.

When to Go Porto has a mild climate, even through the winter, so any time is fine, but April through May and October through November are best if you want to avoid the tourist crowds.

Planning Allow a few days to soak up the atmosphere. Strolling around is the best way to appreciate Porto's shabby grandeur, including its wealth of baroque architecture, such as the wonderful churches of São Francisco and Santa Clara. If you take your port seriously, be sure to visit the Solar do Vinho do Porto, the official headquarters of the Port Wine Institute, with tastings for visitors.

Websites www.portotours.com, www.cellartours.com

Pass the Port, Please

For a wine to be called port, it must come from one of three designated regions of the Douro Valley: The Baixo Corgo ("Lower Corgo," after the Corgo, a tributary of the Douro); the Cima Corgo ("Upper Corgo"); or the Douro Superiore.

There are many kinds of port, but the main types are **ruby** (fruity rich red ports blended from the produce of different years), **tawny** (amber-colored ports, which are also blended, but less sweet in flavor), and the finest of all—**vintage** ports, produced from a single vintage of exceptional quality.

Serve ruby and tawny ports at room temperature or slightly below. Only vintage ports that have been aged for more than eight years in the bottle need to be decanted. Stand the bottle upright for 24 hours, remove the cork a few hours before serving, then pour into a decanter. Stop pouring if you see sediment appear in the neck of the bottle. To enjoy the aroma, drink port from a good-sized wine glass filled about halfway.

Although often served in France as an aperitif, in Britain port is generally drunk after dinner as a perfect accompaniment to cheese. It is traditionally served clockwise around the table, with guests helping themselves, then passing the port to the person on their left.

Opposite: Traditional *barcos rabelas* are moored in the Douro. Above: Casks for aging tawny port in a Vila Nova de Gaia lodge

Copper pot stills (such as these at Bowmore) are used to heat the spirit, then evaporate it, to increase the alcohol content.

SCOTLAND

ISLAY WHISKEY DISTILLERIES

Follow the flight paths of wild geese and golden eagles to the legendary distilleries on the western Scottish island of Islay.

The "wine of the country" is the nickname bestowed by Scottish devotees on their homeland's most celebrated export—its incomparable array of single malt whiskies. And, like the world's finest wines, each of these possesses unique qualities that embody the essence of the place where it is made and the traditions that inspire its making. For whiskey connoisseurs, a visit to Islay is as enthralling a prospect as a wine-lover's pilgrimage to Bordeaux. Each Islay malt has its own personality, although a degree of peatiness is a common denominator. Some, such as Laphroaig, are intensely flavored, smoky extroverts. Others, including Caol Ila or Bunnahabhain, tell subtler stories, with delicate notes of flowers and fruit. As you travel across the island, with its peat banks, its salt air, and the soft water running off its hills, you begin to understand why the whiskies are as they are. The distilleries, in dramatic coastal locations, complete the picture. Each one has its own particularities, including the shapes and sizes of its stills, its water sources, and the provenance of its malted barleys.

When to Go The distilleries work year-round, but you will have the best chance of good weather—and the widest choice of places to stay—between Easter and mid-September.

Planning Accommodations on Islay are in high demand, especially during the tourist season, so book in advance. Some distilleries—such as Bowmore and Bruichladdich in the north, and Ardbeg, Laphroaig, and Lagavulin in the south—have visitor centers providing guided tours and sample rooms for tasting. Others welcome visitors by prior arrangement. To enjoy your drams with a clear conscience, make sure that there is always one non-drinking driver in your party. Scottish drunk-driving laws are strictly enforced.

Websites www.islayinfo.com, www.calmac.co.uk

Eating and Drinking on Islay

■ Local folk wisdom says the outflow from the distilleries gives the island's oysters their wonderful succulence and depth of flavor. They are often on the menu at the **Port Charlotte Hotel**, in the village of the same name, or at the **Harbour Inn** at Bowmore.

■ If you have a few days to spare, the **Bruichladdich** distillery has its own Whisky Academy, where lovers of single malt can enroll in a hands-on course in the distiller's arts.

■ At **Ardbeg**, located above a small bay near Islay's southern tip, stock up in its Old Kiln Shop and sample the excellent home-cooking at the Old Kiln Café.

■ A short ferry ride from Islay takes you to the wild and rugged **Isle of Jura** to the east. This has its own distillery, whose offerings include the evocatively titled (and award-winning) Superstition.

PUBS IN DINGLE TOWN

Rumor has it that the small seaside town of Dingle in western Ireland has a pub for every week of the year.

Unique and idiosyncratic, Dingle wins over nearly everyone who visits. The town's pubs are part of the secret, full of quirks and prompting the question: How do they fit them all in? The answer is that pubs are pretty much everywhere. Is that a hardware store or a leather shop? It may also be a pub. One of the most alluring of these establishments is Dick Mack's on Green Street. Nicknamed the "Last Pew," because it stands across from the road from the local church, it is where some less devoted locals tend to go instead of church on a Sunday morning. Cozy and warm, Dick Mack's was, indeed, a leather shop until quite recently, when reputedly an issue with health regulations obliged it to focus on the drinking side of its business. The shoes and leather are still there, as a testament to its former trade, while the names of celebrity fans are inscribed in Hollywood-style stars on the pavement outside—including those of Paul Simon and Robert Mitchum. Enjoy a pint of Guinness under a portrait of Charlie Haughey, Ireland's notorious former Taoiseach (Prime Minister) and a local hero. If you don't fancy a Guinness, there is also a fine selection of Irish whiskeys. Sit in the "snug," amid all the decorative paraphernalia, and relish the "craic"—the chat, back chat, and general good company—with the friendly owners and locals.

When to Go Dingle and the surrounding Dingle Peninsula are at their best in the summer. The weather is unpredictable but the craic is mighty. Catch the Dingle Regatta in August or the Dingle Peninsula Food and Wine Festival in October, both lively and full of energy.

Planning Rent a bike and cycle out to Slea Head at the southwestern tip of the Dingle Peninsula. If you are lucky, you will have a sunny day and fabulous views. Or get the ferry to the protected Blasket Islands to see puffins, gannets, kittiwakes, and other seabirds. Dingle's most famous local is Fungi the dolphin—take a boat trip to see the wild dolphin who has made Dingle his home.

Websites www.dingle-peninsula.ie, www.dingle-insight.com, www.blasketislands.ie

Irish Soda Bread

Makes 1 loaf
Generous 2³/4 cup/14 oz/400 g
   all-purpose flour
2 tsp baking soda
¹/2 tsp salt
4 tbsp/2 oz /50 g butter, cut
   into small pieces
1¹/4 cup/10 fl oz/284 ml
   buttermilk
1 tbsp milk

Preheat the oven to 350°F/ 180°C/Gas Mark 4. Lightly grease a baking sheet. Mix flour and baking soda in a large bowl, then rub the butter into the flour with your fingertips. Add buttermilk and mix to a soft dough. Knead gently for about 1 minute. Shape into a ball, and place on the baking sheet. Flatten the loaf slightly, then cut a cross, cutting almost right through the bread. Brush the top with milk and dust with a little extra flour. Bake for 40 minutes until golden brown and well risen. Turn out on a wire rack to cool.

At Dan Foley's, a popular pub at Annascaul, east of Dingle town, you can be sure to find local characters as colorful as its decor.

ENGLISH PUBS

Enjoy the real experience of England—a cozy pub, a pint of good bitter ale to sip, a convivial atmosphere to enjoy, and in more and more cases a plate of wholesome food to tuck into.

❶ The Betjeman Arms, St. Pancras, London

Whether you want a last pint before zooming beneath the Channel to France or Belgium, or a first taste of the best of British ale, hasten along to The Betjeman Arms, a comfortable pub in St. Pancras Station, home of Eurostar. Part "gastro" (good food) and part pub (good beer), this is a highly successful modern take on the railroad pubs of old.

Planning Opening hours: 10 a.m.-11 p.m. www.stpancras.com

❷ The Royal Oak, Borough, London

Situated close to the spot where the Tabard Inn in Chaucer's *The Canterbury Tales* supposedly stood, this pub has its own pilgrims, who come to contemplate the magnificent beers of Sussex brewer, Harveys. Keeping alive the traditions of London pub life, it is a good place for that time-honored pub activity: conversation.

Planning Opening hours: 11 a.m.-11 p.m., weekdays; 12 p.m.-11 p.m., Saturdays; 12-6 p.m., Sundays. www.fancyapint.com

❸ The Bricklayer's Arms, Putney, London

This compact Victorian gem—with wooden floors, old photos on the walls, and a central bar—lies hidden away down a small cul-de-sac not far from the Thames. Run by former actress Becky Newman, it is a showcase for Timothy Taylor's range of pristine Yorkshire ales. There are also guest ales, occasional beer festivals, and delicious food in the evenings.

Planning Opening hours: 12-11 p.m.; 12-10:30 p.m., Sundays. www.bricklayers-arms.co.uk, www.beeralewhatever.com

❹ The Thatchers Arms, Mount Bures, Essex

Sitting atop a ridge, The Thatchers Arms overlooks the Stour and Colne valleys, beloved of the locally born landscape painter John Constable. This is also excellent walking country, and The Thatchers is an ideal place to relax after a ramble. Order a plate of traditional pub food, such as bangers and mash, and wash it down with a pint of local Brewers Gold.

Planning Opening hours: 12-3 p.m., 6-11 p.m., weekdays (closed Mondays); 12-11 p.m., weekends. www.thatchersarms.co.uk

❺ The Anchor, Walberswick, Suffolk

Walberswick is everyone's idea of an English country village, in which The Anchor presents its own distinctive style. A prime example of 1920s' "Tudorbethan" architecture, it has a bright two-roomed bar, while a sea-facing terrace offers space for alfresco eating and drinking. Plump for Adnams' real ales, a tremendous wine list, and a superb menu featuring locally sourced ingredients.

Planning Opening hours: 11 a.m.-4 p.m., 6-11 p.m., weekdays; 11 a.m.-11 p.m., Saturdays; 12-11 p.m., Sundays. www.anchoratwalberswick.com

❻ The Lord Nelson Inn, Southwold, Suffolk

Dedicated students of the local Adnams' ales make a beeline for this cozy coastal pub when visiting the seaside gem of Southwold. The peerless Bitter and more assertive Broadside are brewed around the corner, and time spent studying them inside or in the small back garden is time well spent.

Planning Opening hours: 10:30 a.m.-11 p.m., weekdays; 12-10:30 p.m., Sundays. www.thelordnelsonsouthwold.co.uk

❼ The Cambridge Blue, Cambridge

Located on a street of terraced houses, about a mile from the city center, the two-roomed Cambridge Blue has plain but comfortable decor (stripped wood floorboards), with a light and airy conservatory at the back. More than a dozen real ales add to the delightful atmosphere.

Planning Opening hours: 12-2:30 p.m., 5:30-11 p.m., weekdays; 12-11 p.m., Saturdays; 12-10:30 p.m., Sundays. www.the-cambridgeblue.co.uk

❽ Canal House, Nottingham

This lively city pub is housed in a redbrick former wharf building on a stretch of Nottingham's canal basin. A canal actually passes through its spacious post-industrial interior. Unsurprisingly, this is the only pub in the U.K. where you can see such a thing. Back on dry land, be tempted by real ales from local brewery Castle Rock and hearty helpings of good pub food.

Planning Opening hours: 11 a.m.-11 p.m.; 11 a.m.-10:30 p.m., Sundays. www.viewnottingham.co.uk, www.beeralewhatever.com

❾ The Royal Oak, Prestbury, Cheltenham

It is a short gallop to Cheltenham racecourse from The Royal Oak in Prestbury. This 16th-century, honey-color, Cotswold stone pub hums with activity on race days, but at other times there is plenty to tickle the fancy of the non-sporting type. Sample Taylor's Landlord, along with other local ales. The pub also holds sausage and beer festivals and celebrations of oyster and stout.

Planning Opening hours: 11:30 a.m.-3 p.m., 5:30-11 p.m.; 12-10:30 p.m., Sundays. www.royal-oak-prestbury.co.uk, www.beeralewhatever.com

❿ Old Green Tree, Bath

Bath offers a wonderful selection of pubs but few as comfortable as the Old Green Tree, tucked away on a busy side street in the center of the city. Visit this unspoiled 300-year-old building after a sightseeing or shopping spree. In the trio of wood-paneled rooms off its main bar, you will find a good place to recover from your exertions with a splendid choice of West Country real ales.

Planning Opening hours: 11 a.m.-11 p.m.; 12-10:30 p.m., Sundays. www.viewbath.co.uk, www.beeralewhatever.com

Right: Britain's greatest naval hero would surely approve of the Southwold pub named after him—perfect for a pint after a bracing stroll along the North Sea shore.

Icefiord Bryghus beers include a brown ale brewed with local crowberries (left) and a pale ale brewed with angelica (right).

GREENLAND

GREENLAND GLACIER BEER

Using the world's purest water, Greenland's
beer-makers produce world-beating brews.

The secret to Greenland's fledgling beer industry is water. "Breweries around the world spend so much money on water treatment," says beer-maker Salik Hard. "But we don't have to do that here, because we already have the purest water in the world—our glaciers and ice cap." Hard and other brewers hire fishermen to sail out into the fjords to harvest frozen fragments that have fallen off icebergs. Once the ice is melted, Hard blends the water with Bavarian malt and organic hops from Canada, Germany, or New Zealand to produce beers available in another of Greenland's well-kept secrets—some excellent restaurants, such as Napparsivik, overlooking the old town square in Qaqortoq, near the island's southern tip. Perhaps it is not so surprising, after all, that Hard and his fellows make such fine stout and ale. Greenland has been part of the Kingdom of Denmark—home to Carlsberg and Tuborg beers—for more than 200 years. Hard's Greenland Brewhouse in Narsaq is one of several scattered along the west coast. In the capital, Nuuk, Godthaab Bryghus brews four types of beer. In Ilulissat, the Hotel Icefiord Bryghus makes flavored beers using local ingredients, such as the rhubarb-like angelica plant. On the hotel's terrace, enjoy unobstructed views of icebergs in Disko Bay as you sip your beer, waiting for dishes of smoked halibut, marinated scallops, and musk-ox meatballs ordered from the adjacent restaurant.

When to Go Summer runs from late May through early September. The climate is quite dry, with lots of sunshine, but temperatures are cool even in summer, rarely reaching more than 51°F (10.6°C).

Planning Don't forget to bring some sunscreen. Places such as Ilulissat may be far north, but the summer sun is very intense. And be prepared to shell out. The best brew at Godthaab Bryghus runs to around 95 Danish kroner ($18) per pint.

Websites www.greenland.com, www.bryggeriet.dk, www.hotelicefiord.gl

Polar Cuisine

Greenland's beer goes with the island's culinary delights. Southern Greenland, with warmer temperatures and lush grasslands, is known for free-range sheep and some of the world's best lamb. Meals in the north, with a much cooler climate and shorter summers, revolve around seal meat prepared in various ways, including a rich stew called **suaasat**. Game is popular, particularly reindeer and musk-ox steak.

Seafood favorites include smoked salmon and halibut, dried cod, fresh scallops, and herring-like **ammassat**. Greenland is awarded an annual whale-hunting quota by the International Whaling Commission, so whale meat appears on menus. Greenlanders consider mattak (minke whale blubber) a delicacy, but for outsiders its texture is very rubbery.

SOUTH AFRICA

FRANSCHHOEK VALLEY WINES

In South Africa's Western Cape province, savor a heady blend of fine wines and dramatic scenery in the Franschhoek Valley.

A prison may seem an odd place to start a wine tour, but in this case it is appropriate. Set amid the vine-covered slopes of the Franschhoek Valley, Groot Drakenstein Prison was where Nelson Mandela was transferred in December 1988, 14 months before his final release. Here, he made his "short walk to freedom," heralding the end of apartheid. For his country's wine industry, the new era unleashed a revolution all its own—full access to global markets, an influx of foreign investment, and a spectacular upsurge of local wine-making innovation. Pay your respects to the bronze statue of Mandela outside the prison, then head down the valley to the picturesque village of Franschhoek, heart of one of South Africa's premier wine "wards"—roughly equivalent to a French appellation. Around you, vineyards clothe the valley sides, with old, immaculately white Cape Dutch farmhouses dotted among them. Most of the wineries offer daily wine-tastings. At the Cabrière Estate, sample its flagship white Chardonnay–Pinot Noir blend, a rich red Pinot Noir, and a sparkling Brut Sauvage. High on the side of the Franschhoek Mountains, the smaller, newer Boekenhoutskloof winery makes The Chocolate Box, a fantastic blend of five grape varieties, including Syrah, Grenache Noir, and Cabernet Sauvignon. Farther west lies one of the valley's largest and most famous estates, Boschendal, founded in 1685, growing everything from Chardonnay and Sauvignon Blanc to Cabernet Sauvignon and Merlot.

When to Go Year-round. In February and March (the southern fall), you will catch the grape harvest.

Planning For superb views of the valley, as well as good wines to taste, visit Dieu Donné and La Petite Ferme estates. There is an abundance of good restaurants both in Franschhoek village and attached to the wineries, including Mon Plaisir on the Chamonix estate, also with good views. Browse in the arts, crafts, and antiques shops of Franschhoek village.

Websites www.franschhoek.org.za, www.wine.co.za, www.cape-town.info

French Legacy

■ Visit Franschhoek on the weekend closest to July 14, and you may think you have stumbled into France by mistake. Franschhoek means "French corner" in Afrikaans. The valley was settled by French Huguenots (Protestants) in the late 17th century, and proudly maintains its French links with a **Bastille Festival** each year, where you can sample local wine and food.

■ For festive fizz, try some of the Cap Classique sparklers, bottle-fermented as with French champagnes. They include the Graham Beck Brut NV, made partly with Franschhoek Valley grapes, which was served at President Barack Obama's inauguration dinner in 2009. Franschhoek holds a **Cap Classique and Champagne Festival** on the first weekend in December each year.

On the Cabrière Estate, sip your choice of wines and look out over rosebeds to the mountains rising beyond.

JUST DESSERTS

A little self-indulgence, say the philosophers, can be good for the soul. And despite the challenge to our teeth and waistlines, a great dessert is a surefire way to enhance the sum of human happiness. The craving for sweetness is hardwired into us, and the world's great pastry chefs and confectioners have devised ingenious ways to satisfy this longing—in settings as enticing as the delicacies themselves. American pie, for instance, is more than the name of a song. In their fruit-filled variety, pies embody the places they hail from: Florida's zingy key lime pie from quirky Key West, or the homespun goodness of shoofly and huckleberry pies from tranquil Amish country in Pennsylvania. Lovers of the allied arts of patisserie and architecture will profit from a pilgrimage to Vienna and Budapest to savor glorious constructions of chocolate, fruit, and cream in belle epoque coffeehouses. Press on east to encounter luminous *lokum* (Turkish delight) in its Istanbul home or lick a mango-infused *kulfi*—India's sensuous take on the frozen dessert—on Mumbai's Chowpatty Beach.

Cherries, apples, corn, and garlic, delicately modeled in marzipan and colored with vegetable dyes ... this masterpiece of the pastry chef's art comes from Catania in Sicily, where making such *frutta martorana* is a centuries-old tradition.

SWEET TIME IN NEW YORK

With choices ranging from cookies and cheesecakes to cupcakes and cannoli, your blood sugar need never dip in the Big Apple.

Nowhere else can you indulge your sweet tooth so freely at any time of day or night than in New York City. In midtown Manhattan, fortify yourself for a day of sightseeing with one of Petrossian Café's Bordeaux-style *cannelés*—small molded cakes with caramelized crusts and custard-like centers. Also in Manhattan, conquer a hamburger-size chocolate chip walnut cookie from Levain Bakery, or head for Momofuku Milk Bar near Union Square to guess at the many ingredients in its sweet-and-salty compost cookie. Both treats are served warm and gooey, so be warned: Finger-licking may be necessary. While at Momofuku, grab a slice of candy bar pie—luscious layers of caramel spiked with peanut-butter nougat, shards of peanut brittle, pretzels, and a chocolate glaze—for the road. It takes a strong will to make the pie last even halfway down the block. For exquisite cheesecake, duck into the quiet calm of Lady M Cake Boutique. The *gâteau nuage* ("cloud cake") is your target here—a smooth, sweet, and tangy blend of cream cheese and sour cream on a graham cracker crust, which as its name suggests practically floats on the tongue. While you are sitting comfortably, spring for Lady M's *mille crêpes*, a cake whose name promises a thousand crepes but delivers 20, layered with a fluffy pastry cream. The crowning crepe is dusted with sugar and torched for a caramelized crust like a crème brûlée.

When to Go Avoid the height of summer, when the subways can be as hot as the ovens pumping out sweet treats. New York is much better in the fall, when the chill is just beginning to hit the air.

Planning Levain Bakery is an ideal pause before or after exploring Central Park or the American Museum of Natural History. Petrossian Café and Lady M are a short trot from the shops along Fifth Avenue.

Websites www.petrossian.com, www.levainbakery.com, www.momofuku.com, www.ladymconfections.com, www.roccospastry.com, nymag.com

Cannoli: A Taste of Sicily in New York

The boundaries of Manhattan's Little Italy have been shrinking for years, but New York is still home to the **creamiest, crunchiest cannoli** outside of Sicily. Golden tubes of deep-fried pastry shell are filled with sweetened ricotta cheese. Some bakers gild the lily with chopped pistachios, chocolate chips, or candied citrus. But the key is that the ricotta is piped in fresh to order—and the cannoli devoured in seconds. After a day exploring Greenwich Village, take a sweet break at **Rocco's Pastry Shop & Espresso Café** to savor its sublime cannoli. Or step out of Manhattan to experience New York's real Little Italy in the Bronx, where the **Madonia Brothers Bakery** on Arthur Avenue awaits. You will be amazed by the speed at which they fill the pastries here and by how fast they disappear.

At the Ferrara Bakery and Café in Manhattan's Little Italy, chef Franco Amati squeezes the ricotta filling into cannoli shells.

Amish women traditionally gather together to make quilts, like these ones for sale in Intercourse.

PENNSYLVANIA

PENNSYLVANIA DUTCH PIES

In Pennsylvania Dutch Country, relish shoofly pie and other farmhouse desserts as generations have done before you.

Traveling east from Lancaster along the Old Philadelphia Pike (State Route 340), you hear the clip-clop of a horse-drawn buggy. This is Amish country, with its well-tended farms, one-room schoolhouses, covered bridges, and shops with handmade quilts for sale outside. And all along the route are restaurants, bakeries, and farmers' markets offering food fresh from the farm, including Pennsylvania Dutch pies of all descriptions. Shoofly pie is the regional specialty, but you will also find huckleberry pies and Amish half-moon pies (*schnitz* or dried apple). At the Bird-in-Hand Bake Shop and Bird-in-Hand Bakery, pies have almost every conceivable filling—peach, pumpkin, strawberry and rhubarb, cherry, and sour-cream raisin. Pies sweet and savory are also on the menu at the Plain & Fancy Farm Restaurant, offering family-style, pass-the-platter dining. A few miles along Route 340 is Intercourse, whose parking lots have horse-hitching posts. Visit the Intercourse Canning Company or the Jam and Relish Kitchen at Kitchen Kettle Village to watch Amish and Mennonite women processing hundreds of jams, relishes, butters, salsas, and preserves. Sample pear butter and plum preserve before filling your shopping basket with pumpkin *schmier* (a sweet spread), spiced peaches, and raspberry salsa.

When to Go Year-round, although some of the shops and restaurants are closed during the winter months—usually January and February—and most close on Sunday.

Planning Lancaster County is a 90-minute drive from Philadelphia International Airport. Traffic can be heavy along Route 340, especially in summer and fall when most people visit the region, so allow extra time or travel midweek when it is less crowded. Plan to stay at least a week.

Websites www.padutchcountry.com, www.kitchenkettle.com, www.intercoursecanning.com

Shoofly Pie

This gooey concoction of **molasses** and **brown sugar**, more like a cake than pie, can be found on bakery shelves and restaurant menus throughout Lancaster County. While no one really knows how shoofly pie got its name, the commonly accepted story is that flies had to be "shooed" away from the sugary pies as they were cooling. Pies with a thick layer of molasses under the crumbly brown sugar topping are known as "**wet-bottom**"; "**dry-bottom**" pies have a thinner molasses layer. Some cooks add spices or a layer of chocolate spread on top of the pie, but true connoisseurs eschew anything other than the original-recipe version. Shoofly pie is best served warm, preferably with a scoop of vanilla ice cream.

PLACES TO ENJOY CAFÉ SOCIETY

Good conversation, coffee, cakes, and the chance to linger are
the vital ingredients of café society. Take your pick of places to enjoy it.

❶ Quebec City, Canada

Gallic influences pervade the capital of Canada's mostly Francophone province. The Café de la Paix and Café St.-Malo, both in Vieux-Quebec, superbly recreate Parisian bistros in food, drink, and ambience, as does the Café du Monde, overlooking the St. Lawrence River in Vieux-Port de Québec.

Planning The Café du Monde serves breakfast on weekends and public holidays. www.bonjourquebec.com, www.lecafedumonde.com

❷ Manhattan, New York City

In Manhattan the world is not only your oyster but also your cappuccino, *sachertorte*, and crème brûlée. Pick among the Viennese-style Café Sabarsky, the French-inspired Café Gitane, the Italian Caffe Vivaldi, or the Japanese café at the Kinokuniya bookstore. For something homegrown, try the Theater District's West Bank Café, with contemporary U.S. cuisine, or the Pink Pony.

Planning Caffe Vivaldi has free live music every evening. The Pink Pony holds regular poetry readings. www.iloveny.com

❸ Seattle, Washington

This is the hometown of Starbucks, which opened in Seattle in 1971. But visitors have other options, not least a rival chain, Caffe Ladro (*ladro* is Italian for "thief"), which deliberately opened venues close to its competitors'. Another place, Top Pot, is technically a doughnut store but roasts its own coffee and trounces the competition with its funky atmosphere.

Planning Ladro has outlets throughout Seattle, including two downtown. Its cake and pastry menu changes daily. www.visitseattle.org

❹ Hanoi, Vietnam

A legacy of colonial days, when the French established Vietnam's first coffee plantations, Hanoi's social life revolves around cafés. As places to flee the heat, these are typically dimly lit—and family-owned. In the heart of the old quarter, Café Nhan buzzes with locals and foreign backpackers. More recently established cafés include the hip Highlands at the south end of Hoan Kiem Lake.

Planning Often drunk on ice, ultrasweet espresso is the most popular Hanoian choice. www.tourism.hochiminhcity.gov.vn

❺ Chennai, India

While India is better known for tea, in Tamil Nadu coffee has long reigned alongside it. In Chennai, the Mocha chain attracts a young crowd with its Moroccan-themed decor and eclectic menu. Moving upscale, try Amethyst, a restored colonial bungalow in lush gardens, or the rooftop Casa Piccola next door.

Planning South Indians usually drink filtered coffee boiled with milk, but many cafés cater to international tastes. www.tamilnadutourism.org

❻ Prague, Czech Republic

From art nouveau temples to backstreet cubbyholes, Prague's cafés were hotbeds of resistance under communism. One such meeting place was Café Slavia, but go there also to enjoy art deco splendor and views of Prague Castle. Other noteworthy spots are Café Orient, in one of the world's first cubist houses, and the Café Louvre on Národní, a haunt of Kafka and Einstein.

Planning For a café a short distance from the tourist hordes, try Kaaba in Vinohrady. www.pragueexperience.com

❼ Berlin, Germany

In Berlin, hip multinational youngsters head for Anna Blume, with its splendid breakfasts. Opernpalais has the city's largest cake assortment. To hobnob with high society, try the august Café Einstein, occupying a villa where silent movie star Henny Porten once lived, or its sister café on Unter den Linden.

Planning The best time to see Berliners enjoying café society is Saturday afternoon or Sunday morning. www.berlin-tourist-information.de

❽ Rome, Italy

Sipping coffee at cafés, preferably reached by scooter, is a key part of *la dolce vita*—the sweet life. Founded in 1760, Antico Caffè Greco is Rome's oldest café. Caffè Rosati specializes in Sogni Romani, orange juice mixed with red and yellow liqueurs mimicking the colors of Rome. Caffè Sant'Eustachio sells biscuits filled with coffee cream and coffee beans covered with chocolate.

Planning Romans tend to drink espresso standing at the counter. Sitting down may cost much more. www.turismoroma.it

❾ Paris, France

While tourists have replaced many of the professional thinkers who used to haunt them, Parisian cafés retain their romance. Les Deux Magots is one place for absorbing the city's cultural history—Rimbaud, Verlaine, Picasso, and Jean-Paul Sartre all shaped their ideas here. Ladurée on the Champs-Elysées is renowned for its macaroons and lavish decor.

Planning Parisian cafés are generally open from 7 or 8 a.m. until around midnight or later. www.parisinfo.com

❿ Madrid, Spain

Integral to *madrileño* literary and political circles is the *tertulia*, or discussion forum, typically held in a café. Two places that keep this tradition alive are Café Commercial, a haunt of artists, politicians, and intellectuals since the 1880s, and Café del Círculo de Bellas Artes. For the best pastries in town, try Café La Mallorquina.

Planning Choose among *café con leche* (latte), *cortado* (espresso with a dash of warm milk), and many others. www.esmadrid.com

Right: Views of Prague's Old Town Square with the magnificent Church of Our Lady Before Tyn in the background create a perfect setting for a café.

Jokes aside, Kermit Carpenter of Key West Lime Shoppe is famous for making some of the best key lime pie in town.

FLORIDA

KEY LIME PIE

Smooth yet with a tangy edge, key lime pie encapsulates the very essence of Key West at Florida's sun-drenched tip.

Whenever a trolley train tour passes, Kermit Carpenter, owner of Key West Lime Shoppe, dashes out with a pie generously topped with meringue. Wearing a dark-green cook's hat, he stands poised to throw the pie at startled passengers. But they soon laugh—the pie is a fake. Carpenter is tempting them to try the real thing—key lime pie, the signature dish of the southernmost city in the U.S., where the ghosts of Ernest Hemingway and Tennessee Williams mingle with those of assorted bohemians, pirates, seafarers, and treasure-seekers. The eponymous limes grow throughout the Florida Keys—smaller and tarter than their commercially grown cousins and with yellow juice rather than green. To make the dessert, lime juice is added to egg yolks and sweetened condensed milk, which in the days before refrigeration was much more widely available in the Keys than fresh milk. The mixture is encased in a graham cracker crust, then topped with mounds of meringue beaten from the egg whites. Traditionally, the filling was left to thicken on its own without baking, but today's pie is baked for 10 to 15 minutes. A variation calls for fresh whipped cream on top, garnished with swirls of fresh lime. Key lime pie should be served icy cold—adding green food coloring is considered a faux pas.

When to Go Warm sunshine and balmy breezes cradle Key West throughout the year. Festivals include A Taste of Wine and Music in January and February, followed by the annual Conch Shell Blowing Contest in March. March also brings the annual Original Seafood Festival in Marathon in the middle Keys. The yearly Taste of Key West is in April, and the Key West Lobsterfest takes place in August.

Planning Key West is a three-hour drive from Miami on the Overseas Highway, which connects the necklace of islands with 43 bridges. Air service from Miami, Orlando, Tampa, Atlanta, Georgia, and Charlotte, North Carolina, into Key West International Airport is limited.

Websites www.fla-keys.com, www.keylimeshop.com, www.visitflorida.com

Conch Republic

The islanders were first introduced to **conch meat** in the early 19th century, when **Bahamians** migrated to the Keys. Locals so admired the sea mollusk's tough, hardy nature that they adopted the name to mean a Key West native, while Key West itself came to be known as "Conch Republic."

Harvesting live conch off the U.S. coast is now illegal, but conch meat comes in from the Bahamas. It is used to make deep-fried **conch fritters**, **conch salad**, and spicy **conch chowder**. Although no restaurant uses the same recipe as any other, the more traditional chowder mixes tomatoes, potatoes, lime juice, salt pork, garlic, and onions with conch meat.

CHINA

AFTERNOON TEA IN HONG KONG

In the venerable Peninsula Hotel, savor a sanctuary of colonial splendor, where everything still stops for afternoon tea.

In far-flung tropical places that have long since shaken off the yoke of British rule, one vestige of empire often survives—afternoon tea. Best preserved among expatriate communities, the ritual paraphernalia of sugar tongs, cake stands, doilies, tea strainers, finger sandwiches, dainty scones, and fancy cakes carries on in numerous former colonies. In Hong Kong, despite the 1997 handover to China, this achievement has resulted in an extraordinary trading coup: The British sell tea to the Chinese. At the colonial-era Peninsula Hotel in Kowloon, the experience of taking afternoon tea seems scarcely to have changed since the hotel opened in 1928. You sit in the magnificent neoclassical cream-and-gilt lobby, where the buzz of conversation and the tinkle of spoons against Darjeeling-filled bone china rises above the strains of music coming from a string quartet on the balcony. Sunlight streaming in makes the delicately patterned marble floor glow and bounces off the coppery urns of potted palms. Noël Coward might walk in at any moment in search of cucumber sandwiches or a pot of orange pekoe. If he did, the waiters in snowy white livery, materializing with quiet efficiency, laden with cake stands and teapots, would not even raise an eyebrow.

When to Go Visit November through January to enjoy warm, dry weather. Summers are hot and very humid, although air-conditioning ensures comfort in hotel lobbies, malls, and the aerial and underground passageways that crisscross the busiest areas of both Hong Kong Island and Kowloon.

Planning Afternoon tea at the Peninsula is so popular that it is served from 2 p.m. to 7 p.m. daily. Even so, by 3:30 p.m. there is a long line of people that lasts until late afternoon. Consider skipping lunch and having afternoon tea early, or check in as a guest at the hotel—amongst the world's best—and gain the privilege of jumping the line. Smart casual clothing is recommended—flip-flops, beach sandals, and plastic footwear are frowned upon. After 7 p.m. long trousers and long-sleeved shirts are required for men.

Websites www.peninsula.com, www.discoverhongkong.com

A Proper Cuppa

Queen Victoria's friend, Anna, Duchess of Bedford, is usually credited with inventing afternoon tea. Although tea as a popular drink had held its place in English hearts since the mid-18th century, this **light meal** filled the gap between lunch and a fashionably late dinner. To be worthy of the Duchess's innovation only the highest standards in making tea were—and are—good enough.

Use good-quality **leaf tea**, never teabags. Warm the pot by swilling hot water around inside it. Tip out the hot water and add the tea—traditionally, one teaspoon for each person and another for the pot. Pour on freshly boiled water, then let stand for three to four minutes, depending on the kind of tea. Ideally, use **china cups**—tea tastes better out of china. Add milk and sugar to taste, or drink without milk and add a slice of lemon instead.

Scones with cream and jam ... English country fare has found a refined new home across the globe in the Peninsula Hotel.

INDIA

KULFI AT CHOWPATTY BEACH

On Mumbai's most popular beach, soak up the carnival
nighttime atmosphere as you relish sweet frozen *kulfi*.

By day, all is relatively quiet on Chowpatty Beach, a sandy strip that lies between the Arabian Sea and the busy Marine Drive leading into Mumbai's congested center. Groups of people while away the hours on the sand or shelter from the sun under stunted trees. Then as night falls, the beach comes to life. Lights go on in makeshift foodstalls and the crowds arrive, clamoring for hot snacks, such as fiery *bhelpuri* (rice and potatoes with a tamarind sauce), or a soothing sweet kulfi served on a stick. An Indian version of ice cream with an exquisitely smooth texture, kulfi is made from evaporated milk and sweetened condensed milk. Flavors include cardamom, saffron, pistachio, custard apple, vanilla, rose, chocolate, banana, and mango. Traditionally, kulfi was made in an earthenware pot, called a *matka*, filled with salt and ice; the porous clay helped the milk to freeze. Nowadays, the mixture is more often decanted into molds and frozen in an electric freezer. On the landward side of Marine Drive, a line of people snakes along the sidewalk outside the New Kulfi Centre, which despite its name has been serving the finest kulfi in Mumbai for nearly half a century. Choose from a tantalizing list of flavors, and head back to the beach to enjoy your purchase. As you do so, turn to admire the view of Marine Drive, also known as the Queen's Necklace because of the many lamps that shine like jewels in the night.

When to Go Avoid the monsoon months of June through September. The most comfortable time for sightseeing is October through February.

Planning Sample kulfi, yogurt, and *lassi*—a sweet or salty cold drink made from yogurt—at the Parsi Dairy Farm on the south side of Chowpatty. Approach street food with caution, as standards of hygiene are variable. Fresh sugarcane juice is popular, but bring your own cup.

Websites www.mumbaihub.com, www.mumbai.org.uk

Paan Pulling Power

Across the road from Chowpatty Beach, a stream of sports cars and chauffeur-driven limousines lines up outside an inconspicuous stall off Marine Drive selling *paan*—edible **betel leaves** folded into samosa-like triangles around a filling. The stall has no name and does not need one because the ice-cold paan it offers has a huge following among Mumbai's wealthy executives, producers, and members of the Bollywood glitterati.

Traditionally chewed as a palate cleanser or mouth-freshener, paan can have a variety of fillings, including slivers of areca nut, cardamom, lime paste, and date. Sometimes tobacco is added, or even tiny fragments of silver and gold. The skilled paan-maker, known as a **paanwala**, is considered an artist.

As the setting sun bathes Chowpatty Beach in gold, people start to gather for an evening of kulfi and other delectable snacks.

After a day's sightseeing, take it elegantly easy at Gerbeaud's coffeehouse.

HUNGARY

DELICIOUS BUDAPEST

Sit back to enjoy coffee and cakes in the Hungarian capital's cafés, lavishly restored after years of communist neglect.

Standing on Budapest's Vörösmarty Square, the 150-year-old Gerbeaud is the stately doyen of the city's *kávéházak* (coffeehouses). Here, Hungarian old-timers mingle with tourists to sample cakes and pastries that include Gerbeaud *torta* (chocolate cake spiked with fruit brandy), chocolate-and-caramel Dobos *torta*, and Gerbeaud *szelet*—apricot jam and ground walnuts layered with dough and topped with chocolate. Farther north, the modishly fusty Centrál Kávéház has regained its one-time bohemian atmosphere. Treat yourself to inspired desserts, such as *somlói galuska*—a sponge cake fusing chocolate, vanilla, walnut biscuits, chocolate sauce, and vanilla cream—and Grand Marnier walnut pie. A 20-minute walk from the Centrál, the arcaded interior of the New York Kávéház drips with chandeliers, gilt, and marble, beneath frescoed ceilings. Anyone who still associates Hungarian food with stodgy, unhealthy fare should head to the elegant Lukács Cukrászda, whose owners source the finest artisan ingredients: Quench your thirst with their lemonade, made with freshly squeezed lemons and organic honey. For some of Budapest's best views and finest globetrotting cuisine, dine at the Hilton Castle District's Icon restaurant, overlooking the Danube. Its scrumptious pastries, miniature works of art, valiantly compete for visual attention.

When to Go The most pleasant weather is in May and September, when cafés with terraces are at their liveliest. The Spring Festival in the last two weeks of March is a showcase of Hungarian culture. The hugely popular rock festival on Sziget Island takes place in August.

Planning The Budavári (Buda Castle) district is a dreamily atmospheric place to stay, with some historic cafés. Places tend to close early, especially out of season. In winter, many hotels offer a fourth night free.

Websites www.gerbeaud.hu, www.centralkavehaz.hu, www.boscolohotels.com, www.gundel.hu

Budapest's Restaurants

■ Oozing belle epoque luxury, **Gundel** restaurant, founded in 1894, remains one of Budapest's essential eating stops. The best time to sample its desserts is the Sunday buffet brunch. Not to be missed is the Gundel pancake, filled with rum, raisins, walnuts, and lemon rind, and topped with chocolate sauce.

■ The elegant contemporary **Onyx** restaurant, originally Gerbeaud's takeout, is a winning place to observe how far Hungarian food and wine have evolved since the 1990s. Try its aptly named Hungarian Evolution five-course meal.

A szelet from Gerbeaud

TURKEY

Sweet Treats in Istanbul

Spoil yourself with mouthwatering confectionery in the sweet shops, teahouses, and cafés of Istanbul's Kadıköy district.

Situated on Istanbul's Asian shore, across the Bosporus from such fabled sights as the Topkapı Palace and the Golden Horn, Kadıköy has an almost tangibly different atmosphere from the city's European neighborhoods. For hundreds of years, the port of Kadıköy has been a gateway to Anatolia for people and goods from west, north, and south, and as your ferry from the European shore glides into Kadıköy İskelesi (quay) you immediately sense the difference. The coastline here is marred by modern development and franchise coffee shops, but just a block beyond this unprepossessing facade you enter a district dominated by a vibrant and colorful bazaar. This is where you will find Kadıköy's celebrated patisseries and sweet shops, whose dizzying assortment of confections, pastries, and candies mirrors the variety available in the bazaar. Any time between early morning and 8 p.m., fuel yourself, as Kadıköy's shoppers and vendors do, with coffee, çay (tea), cookies, cakes, and lokum (Turkish delight) from establishments such as Baylan, Beyaz Fırın, Hacı Bekir, and Şekerci Cafer Erol—all of which have been feeding Istanbul's sweet tooth for generations. Thus fortified, wander around the bazaar, where fishmongers peddle catch so fresh that it still seems to be gasping for breath and stalls brimming with seasonal produce stand intermingled with shops selling irresistible arrays of olives, cheeses, dried fruits, herbs, and nuts.

When to Go Year-round, although the weather is most pleasant in the spring and fall. Seker Bayramı (Sugar Festival) is a three-day celebration of all things sweet following Ramadan—dates vary. Museums and other attractions close for the first day, but are usually open and busy on the second and third days.

Planning Ferries ply regularly from Eminönü, Karaköy, and Beşiktaş on the European shore, with less frequent departures from Kabataş—the ride takes 20-25 minutes. Allow two to three hours to explore Kadıköy's sweet shops and cafés, pacing yourself with strolls through the bazaar or a walk south of the port to the smart residential neighborhood of Moda.

Websites www.ido.com.tr, www.hacibekir.com.tr, www.baylanpastanesi.com, www.istanbulcityguide.com

Kadıköy Highlights

■ Founded in 1934, the Greek-owned **Baylan** tea and pastry shop was a favorite haunt of Istanbul's writers, poets, painters, and actors during the 1960s and 1970s. Here, you can join *istanbullus* reliving one of the city's intellectual heydays as they sip their çay and savor sweet delights, including *cup griye*—ice cream, crème chantilly, caramel sauce, pistachios, and almonds.

■ George Stoyanof, a baker from Macedonia (then part of the Ottoman Empire), opened **Beyaz Fırın** more than 170 years ago, in 1836, and it has been in the same family ever since. Specialties at Beyaz Fırın—literally "White Oven"—include delicious dense breads, marzipan, decadent cakes, and macaroons.

■ Large glass candy jars fill the counter at **Şekerci Cafer Erol**, crammed with an assortment of sweetmeats, including *akide şekeri* (hard candies), hand-made chocolates, baklava, sesame-seed halva, and syrup-soaked cookies.

Opposite: The Ortaköy Mosque stands on the Bosporus's European shore. Above: Scooping sweets at Kadıköy's Hacı Bekir

One of Copenhagen's best-known bakeries, Reinh van Hauen, has several shops in the city.

DENMARK

DANISH PASTRIES

An abundance of melt-in-the-mouth pastry treats make the Danish capital an irresistible draw for the sweet-toothed traveler.

Take an early morning stroll through Copenhagen's narrow, winding streets and your olfactory senses will be rewarded with the delicious aromas of freshly made pastries and breads wafting out of the many street-corner bakeries. Step inside and you will be welcomed with a smile and a dazzling array of baked goods. The origin of the Danish pastry can be traced back to the mid-1800s, when a strike by Danish bakers forced bakery owners to hire workers from Vienna, who used their own light, buttery dough recipes. Eventually, the Danish bakers returned to work, but they continued to use the Viennese recipes and the Danish pastry—called *Wienerbrød* or Viennese bread—was born. Today, Copenhagen's bakeries produce a tantalizing array of cream-filled delights, chocolate-glazed buns, tarts, and other luscious desserts. Try a *chokoladebolle*, a puff pastry with cream filling and chocolate icing, or Cinnamon Snails (*kanelsnegle*), which entice with their heady scent of cinnamon and vanilla. Napoleon's Hats (*Napoleonshatte*) resemble the triangular headgear worn by the eponymous emperor—one bite reveals bursts of flavor from the rich, sweet marzipan filling. A *Spandauer* is so-named because the filling of jam or custard is "imprisoned" within the pastry.

When to Go Denmark has a mild, temperate climate. Spring and fall are great times to visit, but bring an umbrella for the frequent rainfalls.

Planning Spend at least a week in Denmark. Visit Copenhagen, the vibrant capital, or take trips to the many outer islands. Reinh van Hauen and Lagkagehuset at Torvegade 45 in Copenhagen are among the best-known bakeries, while Konditori La Glace at Skoubogade 3, which opened in 1870, is one of the best patisseries in the country, famous for its fancy cakes.

Websites www.visitdenmark.us, www.laglace.dk

A traditional *kransekage*, or ring cake

GERMANY

Master Bakers of Bavaria

Join Munich's fashionably dressed denizens for *Kaffee und Kuchen* (coffee and cake), but don't tell your cardiologist.

Rich and delicious cakes and pastries line the windows of bakeries and coffee shops tempting you to grab one to go or to step inside, where you can savor your coffee break in a more leisurely fashion. Sample the *Apfelstrudel*, thin sheets of flaky butter-brushed pastry wrapped around an apple filling. Don't like apples? Have plum, poppy seed, or cheese. And to make it extra-unctuous, order it with vanilla sauce: a thin, vanilla-flavored custard. Munich's sweet treats are not for those with dainty appetites. Try the delicious *Dampfnudel*, a sweet dumpling in a pool of vanilla sauce; or the incredible *Kaiserschmarrn*, literally the Emperor's Omelet, thick yet fluffy pancakes ripped into chunks, fried in butter and caramelized sugar, then served hot topped with apple or plum sauce. If you become exhausted by the calorie-fest, refresh yourself with the view. From a table in Rischart, opposite the town hall, you can sit high above the Marienplatz admiring Munich's lovely central square; in summer, listen to the chimes from the famous moving clock through the open windows. At Conditorei Münchner Freiheit's Schwabing branch, snag a table outside on a tree-lined street in this trendy university district. Year-round on sunny days, well-heeled ladies sit outside in cafés throughout the city spooning up the whipped cream smothering their coffees. Blankets are provided to keep off the winter chill.

When to Go In winter, Munich is snowy and there is good skiing nearby. In summer, sun-worshippers crowd the cafés, the banks of the Iser River, and the English Garden.

Planning Time your visit to Rischart so that you arrive or depart just before 11 a.m., noon, or 5 p.m.–in time to join the crowds admiring the near-life-size figures of jousting knights and dancing peasants as they spin in and out of the chiming clock. In summer, a trip down the Iser on a log raft with a crowd of inebriated Bavarians is not to be missed–ask at the tourist office for details. Or watch the fun from the riverbank.

Websites www.dallmayr.de, www.muenchen.de

Beyond Baked Goods

■ The **Viktualienmarkt**, Munich's central food market, is a grazer's paradise. Try a cool, salty, smoked-fish sandwich or a hot Bavarian specialty, such as *weisswurst* (a white-veal and pork sausage eaten with sweet mustard). Eat at the kiosk or take your snack to the Viktualienmarkt's beer garden, where you can order a foaming tankard of Bavaria's best.

■ Famed throughout Germany for its coffee, **Dallmayr** is an old-world shrine to fine food and drink. There is a department for every foodstuff, including one devoted solely to honey and jam. Enjoy oysters and champagne at the Gourmet Bar, or head upstairs to the restaurant or café. Don't miss the hand-painted ceramic urns from Nymphemburg in the coffee department: The aroma alone will draw you there.

Sit outside Tambosi, at the top of Munich's premier shopping street and just outside the gates of the English Garden, and watch the world go by.

THE CAFÉS OF VIENNA

Join the locals and linger over coffee and cake in the world capital of traditional and elegant coffeehouses.

For centuries the *Kaffeehaus* has been at the hub of Vienna's culture, a place where people from all walks of life have gathered to chat, to exchange ideas, to play chess, to read the newspaper, and above all to linger over their coffee. Stepping into one of the capital's many cafés today is like returning to an earlier age, when everything ran at a slower pace. Opulent decor and high-vaulted ceilings distinguish the most venerable establishments, some dating back to the late 19th century. Parquet flooring and bentwood furniture, or velvet-clad banquettes and marble-topped tables, charming (if sometimes grumpy) waiters in tuxedos, and the clickety-clack of spoons hitting metal trays enhance the timeless atmosphere. Age-old traditions are conserved perfectly here: *Apfelstrudel* (apple strudel) and the famous type of chocolate cake known as *sachertorte* grace the menu, while *Einspänner* and *Melange* are among the coffees of choice. Along with the ubiquitous newspaper, traditional coffeehouse distractions include billiards, musical performances, literary readings, and even political rallies in a back room. The best-known cafés are mostly located in and around the city's historic center (the 1st district), many along the Ringstrasse. The most famous include Griensteidl, Central, Landtmann, Diglas, Prückel, Sperl, and Imperial. For fine patisserie head to Sacher or Demel, and for quirkiness visit Hawelka. Whichever you choose, savor the experience the Viennese way—slowly.

When to Go Summers can be oppressively hot in the capital with temperatures easily reaching 95°F (35°C). Few cafés have air-conditioning.

Planning Coffeehouses are open year-round, usually from the early hours of the morning until late at night. Some offer al fresco seating, although this is a fairly recent trend.

Websites www.aboutvienna.org, www.wiener-kaffeehaus.at

Coffee Compendium

■ Half coffee, half steamed milk, and sometimes served with whipped cream, *Melange* is one of the most popular coffees. *Einspänner* is a long coffee topped with whipped cream.

■ *Eiskaffee* consists of cold *mokka* (similar to espresso) served with a scoop of vanilla ice cream and whipped cream. *Gerührter eiskaffee* is vanilla ice cream blended with a cold mokka.

■ For something stronger, ask for an *Obermayer,* espresso with cream poured onto it over a spoon, or an *Überstürzter Neumann*, an espresso cup filled with whipped cream with espresso slowly poured over it.

■ For an extra kick, try a *Fiaker*–a single-shot espresso laced with hot rum–or a *Maria Theresia*–a double espresso with orange liqueur, generously topped with whipped cream.

A large and tempting display of mouthwatering cakes lures customers into Vienna's Café Demel.

The Spanish Steps, dominated by the church of Trinitá dei Monti, buzz with groups of visitors to Rome.

ITALY

Ice Cream in Rome

What better way to cool off in the Eternal City than with a smooth, throat-soothing scoop of delicious gelato?

Romans hold their ice cream, known as gelato, in high regard. Besides the quality of the ice cream itself, three factors influence the perfect gelato experience: the waffle cone, which should be crunchy; the whipped cream served on top of the gelato, which should be slightly sweet and firm to the right point; and the skill of the *gelataio*, who should use a traditional spatula (never a round spoon) to massage and scoop up the gelato before placing a neat, almond-shaped portion on your cone. The capital's two best gelaterias are in the historic center. At San Crispino, near the Trevi Fountain, the emphasis is on serving gelato in its purest form, so there are no edible cones, only paper cups, and no chocolate sauce or toppings to detract from the flavor. The pistachio ice cream tastes entirely like the nut itself. At the other end of the scale is the sheer exuberance of Gelateria Giolitti, next to the Pantheon, where you can indulge in a mesmerizing selection of flavors—with toppings to your heart's content. Gelato devotees also head to Lanzallotto in the Parioli neighborhood to sample *marron glacé* and *nocciola* (hazelnut) ice creams, and *sorbetti* made from the freshest fruit. Or you can venture into the elegant Prati neighborhood, near the Vatican, and visit Al Settimo Gelo, which is renowned for adventurous flavors, including hot chili-spiced chocolate, honey, and myrtle.

When to Go Although gelaterias are open year-round, the best time to enjoy a gelato in Rome is from April through mid-October. May to September is the best season for sampling granita and *grattachecca*.

Planning Most gelaterias are open 10 a.m.-8 p.m., but a number serve until midnight. There is no wrong time of day to enjoy a frozen snack in Rome—a coffee granita with a brioche is a perfectly acceptable breakfast.

Websites www.romaturismo.it, www.enjoyrome.com, www.ilgelatodisancrispino.it, www.giolitti.it

Granita and Grattachecca

Classical **granita**—similar to sorbet but crunchier—originated in Sicily during the Middle Ages, when it was made by squeezing lemon juice into snow collected from Mount Etna. Today, it is made from flavored water and sugar, spun and lightly frozen until the mixture reaches a semisolid consistency.

On a scorching afternoon, cool off with scoops of coffee, strawberry, and almond granita topped with whipped cream, or sample more unusual flavors, such as mulberry or peanut. You can get good granita in many of Rome's more upmarket coffee bars, such as **Sant'Eustachio**, Sicilian gelaterias, such as **Gelarmony**, and pastry shops, such as **Pasticceria Mizzica**.

Rome's answer to granita is **grattachecca**. Crunchier than granita, it consists of shavings of pure ice infused with fruit syrup. In summer, grattachecca stands are usually open late into the night and draw large crowds of heat-exhausted Romans. One of the best-loved stands is **Sora Maria** in the Prati neighborhood. Try the majestic *grattachecca mista* with cherries and tamarind syrup, topped with chunks of lemon and coconut.

COOL PLACES TO EAT ICE CREAM

Globe-trotters can experience flavors that go far beyond the standard chocolate, vanilla, or strawberry. Experience eel ice cream in Japan or green tea in Florence.

❶ Capogiro Gelato, Philadelphia, Pennsylvania

Made with the freshest ingredients (such as milk from Amish grass-fed cows), the artisan gelatos and sorbettos handcrafted each day at Capogiro Gelato include flavors not seen anywhere else—Madagascar bourbon vanilla, *melograno* (pomegranate), *nocciola Piemonte* (hazelnut), Saigon cinnamon, Thai coconut milk (with a dash of rum), and zucca (long-neck pumpkin).

Planning Capogiro has four cafés in Philadelphia. capogirogelato.com

❷ Ted Drewes Frozen Custard, St. Louis, Missouri

Made from fresh cream, eggs, and sugar, frozen custard is a midwestern dessert that looks, tastes, and acts like its close cousin, ice cream. The stand on Grand Boulevard has been open since 1931, serving frozen custard in cones, shakes, root-beer floats, and house specialties, such as Hawaiian Delight and Crater Copernicus.

Planning Drewes has several locations in St. Louis. www.teddrewes.com

❸ Bombay Ice Creamery, San Francisco, California

Some of the planet's best Indian ice cream can be sampled here, in the Hispanic Mission District. On offer are flavors such as *chiku* (sapodilla), cardamom, chai-tea, saffron, rose, and ginger, rarely found beyond the Indian subcontinent. Traditional *kulfi* (a frozen milk dessert) is also on the menu, plus *lassi* (yogurt drinks).

Planning The opening hours change with the seasons, so check before planning a visit. www.bombayicecream.com

❹ Devon House, Kingston, Jamaica

Built in the late 19th century as the home of Jamaica's first black millionaire, Devon House is a masterpiece of Caribbean Victorian architecture and home to the island's most celebrated ice-cream stand. The 27 flavors run a broad gamut from traditional cherry and pistachio to exotic island treats like mango, coconut, and soursop. There is even an offbeat, beer-based ice cream called Devon Stout. Grab a cone and recline in the sprawling gardens.

Planning Devon House is in central Kingston. Admission includes a tour of the house and access to the gardens. www.devonhousejamaica.com

❺ Helados Scannapieco, Buenos Aires, Argentina

This tiny, no-frills shop seems little changed from 1938, when Italian immigrants Andres and Josefina Scannapieco first opened the doors. Members of the Scannapieco clan still make ice cream the way the family have for 70 years. The menu runs 50 flavors deep, from chocolate and vanilla to other delights, such as *durazno* (peach), *canela* (cinnamon), lemon champagne, and *caipirinha* (a Brazilian cocktail made with cachaça and lime).

Planning Helados Scannapieco is at Avenida Córdoba 4826 in the Palermo district. www.easybuenosairescity.com

❻ Ice Cream City, Tokyo, Japan

With dozens of stands selling more than 300 flavors between them, Tokyo's appropriately named Ice Cream City offers some of the planet's more unusual ice creams, from soy chicken and orchid root to sea-island salt and *unagi* (eel). If you have more conventional tastes, Italian gelato and American ice cream sundaes are also available.

Planning Ice Cream City is part of the food-themed section of the Namja Town amusement park in the Sunshine City shopping complex 15 minutes' walk from Ikebukuro station. www.japan-guide.com, www.sunnypages.jp

❼ Glacé, Sydney, Australia

Glacé is celebrated for its cutting-edge, ice-cream-based desserts, such as bombe Alaska, checkerboard terrines, and chocolate-dipped petit fours. Rose petal, vanilla bean, strawberry pistachio, and Belgian chocolate count among its signature flavors.

Planning Glacé has one retail outlet, at 27 Marion Street in Sydney's Leichhardt district. www.glace.com.au

❽ A'jia Hotel, Istanbul, Turkey

There is nothing more romantic than a summer evening beside the Bosporus, especially when you are having ice cream on the outdoor terrace of the A'jia Hotel. The dessert menu includes fried vanilla ice cream, passionfruit sorbet, and traditional Turkish *dondurma* (ice cream) made from goats' milk.

Planning Located on the western shore of the Bosporus, the A'jia is a 19th-century mansion transformed into a hip new waterfront hangout. www.ajiahotel.com

❾ Vaffelbageriet, Copenhagen, Denmark

Tivoli Gardens amusement park is the venue for this century-old ice-cream outlet. As the name suggests, the specialty is ice cream served in a large waffle cone, called the Amerikaner, which takes up to four scoops plus syrupy topping, whipped cream, and chocolate-covered meringue puff (rather than a maraschino cherry).

Planning Tivoli Gardens is in central Copenhagen, and is open from mid-April through late September. The entertainments include concerts, rides, and 40 restaurants. www.copenhagen.com, www.visitcopenhagen.com, www.tivoli.dk/composite-3351.htm

❿ Perchè No!, Florence, Italy

Going since 1939, Perchè No!—Why not!—sells intensely flavored ice cream produced fresh on the premises each day. The selection varies, but favorites include honey and sesame seed, green tea, and a rich coffee crunch with pieces of chocolate. They also sell a wide assortment of fruit sorbets and granitas.

Planning Perchè No! is in Via dei Tavolini, about two minutes' walk from the Duomo. www.percheno.firenze.it

Right: An ornate fountain and colonnaded facade welcome visitors to Kingston's Devon House, which is famous for its ice cream.

ITALY

Sicilian Marzipan

All around the coast and in the rugged hinterland, marzipan sweets take center stage in the island's *pasticcerias*.

Pastry-shop windows are filled with piles of figs and prickly pears and baskets of luscious strawberries and peaches. The detail is so perfect that they must surely be the real thing. But no—they are, in fact, crafted from sweetened almond paste, or *pasta reale*. The almond paste is said to be of Arabic origin and is one of many culinary legacies from two centuries of Arab influence. All the high days and holy days of the Sicilian calendar are celebrated with a marzipan specialty: Marzipan lambs (*agnello pasquale*) are part of the Easter tradition, while birthdays and other special fêtes are commemorated with *frutta martorana* (realistic fruits). Confectionery fruits are also left in children's shoes by—it is said—their ancestors' ghosts on All Saints' Day in early November. The famous frutta martorana were first made in Palermo's Martorana convent. Long ago, the nuns prepared a festive welcome for an archibishop's visit by crafting marzipan fruits, probably oranges and lemons, which they hung from the branches of trees left bare after the harvest. In Palermo, the Alba and Caflish pastry shops offer finely crafted frutta martorana, and Taormina's Pasticceria Etna is highly recommended, but aficionados travel all the way to Noto—a honey-toned Baroque city set into a hillside to the south of Syracuse—for marzipan creations by Carlo and Corrado Assenza at Caffé Sicilia.

When to Go Avoid winter, when the weather can be cold and wet. Spring weather in southern Sicily can be fickle, so take both umbrellas and sunglasses. Blooming almond trees cover the steep slopes around Noto in early March.

Planning Relax into an easy-going Sicilian pace and allow at least a week to explore the island. Sicily's main towns are linked by train and bus services, but car rental is the best means of reaching more remote places. A train runs from Catania up Mount Etna, stopping at Adrano and Bronte. Don't be surprised if none of the train platforms have a clock set at a time that matches your watch!

Websites www.weather-in-sicily.com, www.thinksicily.com, www.grifasi-sicilia.com/indicedolcigbr.html

A Tasting Tour

■ The evening *passeggiata*, a promenade with friends and family, on **Catania's** Via Etna is best enjoyed with a glass of Castelmonte Frizzante and some *arancine* (fried balls of rice and vegetables) at a sidewalk café.

■ Situated north of Adrano on Mount Etna's western slopes amid 10,000 terraced acres of pistachio trees, **Bronte** is known as *Città del Pistacchio*. The nuts are harvested every two years, an event that is celebrated with a festival in September. For Sicily's best pistachio gelati, *biscotti*, and *fiori di pistacchi* cakes, this is the place to be. Trays groaning with *dolci* (confectionery), towers of *torrone* (an Italian nougat), and even pesto made with pistachios await eager tasters.

■ On Sicily's west coast, a good place for a pastry-shopping stop is **Erice**, a medieval mountaintop town near Palermo, overlooking the sea. Also tucked into Erice's labyrinth of lanes is Ristorante Monte San Giuliano, where you can lunch on seafood and aubergine *involtini* (seafood rolled in slices of eggplant).

■ At **Marsala**, south of Erice, sample some of the dozens of wines that this coastal city has to offer. Many small firms offer fine sweet as well as dry wines, made from Sicilian Zibibbo grapes (a Q seal on a Marsala label assures quality). Sweet Marsala Vergine, aged for five to seven years, complements rich desserts.

Opposite: Acicastello's Norman castle is perched above the sea north of Catania. Above: Marzipan fruits on display in Erice

Chocolate in Brussels

There are hundreds of chocolate emporia dotted throughout the city selling the finest, purest chocolate in the world.

The promise of pure, unadulterated pleasure greets the visitor to Pierre Marcolini's chic boutique on the pretty Place du Grand Sablon. Neatly spaced on trays behind glass cabinets, the jaw-droppingly handsome chocolates are displayed with all the reverence afforded to gems in an expensive jewelry shop. Above all, it is the cool, clean, elegant aroma of the top-notch chocolate that arouses the taste buds. Pierre Marcolini is one of Belgium's most celebrated chocolatiers, and his shop is a showcase for the luxury brand that is now sold worldwide. But he is not alone. Across the square is Wittamer, one of the city's most famous establishments, which opened in 1910 and is still run by members of the Wittamer family. Sample a slice of their divinely light chocolate cake with one of the specialty teas or coffees in the elegant tearoom. Along the Rue Royale is the charming little shop of Mary, chocolate supplier to Belgian royalty. Then there are the larger "chains," selling top-quality chocolates in boutiques dotted around the city and beyond: Leonidas (with 30 boutiques in Brussels alone), Corné Port-Royal, Godiva, and Neuhaus—whose Jean Neuhaus is credited with the invention of the praline in 1912. White-gloved staff fill special boxes known as *ballotins* with liqueur-filled chocolates, white chocolate with fresh-cream fillings, chocolate truffles, almond marzipan, and strips of crystallized orange peel dunked in dark chocolate, to name but a few.

When to Go Brussels is enjoyable year-round, with a calendar of events from January to December. Hotels can be expensive at peak times but may offer remarkably good rates at off-peak times, such as weekends.

Planning Brussels Airport is at Zaventem, just to the northeast of the city, with good links to the center. International rail services arrive at stations located close to the center. The Museum of Cocoa and Chocolate is close to the Grand Place.

Websites www.corne-port-royal.be, www.leonidas.be, www.neuhaus.be, www.godiva.be, www.marcolini.be, www.wittamer.com, www.marychoc.com, www.mucc.be, www.brusselsinternational.be

Pots au chocolat

These puddings can be served in ovenproof pots or ramekins.

Serves 6
2/3 cup/1/4 pt/150 ml milk
1 1/4 cups/1/2 pt/300 ml heavy cream
10 1/2 oz/300 g dark chocolate (70 percent cocoa solids)
4 egg yolks
1/4 cup/2 oz/50 g sugar

Preheat the oven to 275°F/40°C/ Gas Mark 2. Place milk and cream in a pan and heat gently until almost boiling. Remove from heat. Add chocolate and stir until it has melted into the mixture.

Whisk egg yolks and sugar in a bowl until pale and frothy. Slowly whisk in the chocolate mixture.

Pour mixture into 6 ovenproof pots. Place them in a roasting pan filled with boiling water to halfway up the sides of the pots. Bake for 30 minutes, until just set. Let the pots cool, then chill until needed.

Many Belgian chocolates contain fresh-cream fillings and have a shelf life of about four weeks if they are kept cool.

Crowds gather outside the glass pyramid of the Louvre, an ideal place for a patisserie-based picnic.

FRANCE

PARIS PASTRY HUNT

A patisserie pilgrimage around Paris's *quartiers* (neighborhoods) will reward with the most scrumptious pastries on Earth.

For the connoisseur of pastry, the treasures of the City of Light lie not in the Louvre or on the Champs-Élysées, but in the many *pâtisseries* that are dotted throughout each one of the city's 20 *arrondissements*. It is to these shops—many of which have been in the same family for generations—that Parisians return day in and day out to buy cakes and tarts with names that hint at the sweet pleasures to come: *tarte tatin, charlotte aux framboises, Richelieu, mille-feuilles, St.-Honoré,* and *madeleines* to name just a few. Charming paintings on glass dating from the 19th century grace the outside of many of the traditional patisseries. And when you step inside, chandeliers, beautiful tiles, and molded ceilings enhance the feeling of timeless elegance. Here you will find delights such as a *charlenoit*—a hazelnut-almond meringue base spread with a smooth chocolate cream and layered with an inch-thick praline custard cream, decorated on top with a large hazelnut; a *tarte princesse aux poires*—puff pastry layered with fresh stewed pears, covered with meringue cream, and topped with caramelized rosettes; or an *opéra*—fine slices of almond-flavored cake with layers of coffee and chocolate-truffle cream.

When to Go Patisseries are open every month except August, when many proprietors are on their annual holiday. Most open every day, except Monday.

Planning Three highly recommended patisseries are: Le Triomphe (12th arrondissement; closed Sundays and Mondays); Patisserie-Sainte Anne (13th arrondissement; closed Wednesdays and Thursdays, open Mondays); and Vaudron (17th arrondissement; closed Mondays).

Websites europeforvisitors.com/paris/articles/paris-patisserie-tours.htm, chowhound.chow.com/topics/377859

Coffee etiquette

All coffee in France is **espresso** coffee. Order a *café, café express,* or *café noir.* If you would like it diluted with hot water, order *café allongé.* If you want coffee with milk, ask for a *café crème, petit* or *grand,* which is made with steamed milk, not cream.

The French never drink coffee with food. As you are eating your morning *pain aux raisins*—a melt-in-the-mouth golden brioche dough slathered with a light custard-cream—savor it! Never wash it down with coffee, but wait until the pastry is safely in your stomach before having the first hit of strong, black coffee.

In a café, if you stand at the bar to drink your coffee it will cost half as much as it will if you sit at a table, and only a third as much as it would if you sit outside on the *terrasse.*

PLACES TO TRY DEATH BY CHOCOLATE

From all-you-can-eat cocoa-driven buffets to Madrid's favorite late-night pick-me-up, here is our guide to chocoholic heaven.

❶ Chocoholic Buffet, Vancouver, Canada

In a setting reminiscent of a European stately home, Sutton Place Hotel's Fleuri Restaurant plays host to an all-you-can-eat chocolate buffet. The homemade cakes, pastries, and pies, and other goodies are made of premium-quality Schokinag chocolate. Even cocktails and liqueurs are chocolate-themed.

Planning In the heart of downtown Vancouver, the hotel offers two chocolate-buffet seatings every Thursday, Friday, and Saturday evening. www.vancouver.suttonplace.com, www.tourismvancouver.com

❷ Magnolia Bakery, New York City

This cozy little 1950s-style bakery shot to fame when characters from the TV series *Sex and the City* stopped by for a cupcake-fueled sugar rush. As well as red velvet chocolate cupcakes, the bakery dispenses a rainbow of brightly colored cupcakes, plus banana pudding, cookies, cherry cheesecake, and brownies. The German chocolate cake is a high point.

Planning Magnolia has four outlets–including the Bleecker Street branch featured in *Sex and the City*. www.magnoliacupcakes.com

❸ Max Brenner, New York City

Known for its hot chocolate in a specially designed hand-warming "hug mug," the Broadway shop and restaurant offer a mind-boggling array of cacao-based product from chocolate truffle martini and chocolate fondue to Young's chocolate stout.

Planning Max Brenner is at 841 Broadway and 141 Second Avenue. www.maxbrenner.com, www.nycgo.com

❹ Mayan Chocolate, Tabasco, Mexico

Here in the likely birthplace of chocolate—the word itself possibly deriving from the Maya *xocoatl*—taste hot chocolate Maya style: thick, foamy, bittersweet, and flavored with chili peppers. The Spanish conquistadors tempered the bitter brew with sugar, cinnamon, ground almonds, and milk. Try it both ways.

Planning Maya Tabasco organizes Chocolate Route tours. Comalcalco, Tabasco, has a cacao museum and cacao haciendas. www.mayatabasco.com, www.visitmexico.com

❺ Sachertorte, Vienna, Austria

A chocolate sponge cake, thinly coated by hand with apricot jam, and then covered with dark chocolate icing, *sachertorte* is named for its 1832 inventor, Franz Sacher. He created the dessert to impress his employer, Klemens Wenzel, Prince von Metternich, gaining fame and fortune for himself. In 1876 his son Eduard opened Vienna's Hotel Sacher—visit the splendid café or one of Vienna's four Sacher shops.

Planning Top your sachertorte with unsweetened whipped cream and drink it with coffee or champagne. www.sacher.com, www.wien.info

❻ Hot Chocolate, Turin, Italy

In Italy's chocolate capital, sip a *cioccolato caldo*. This winter-buster comes very thick, hot, and agreeably bitter, topped generously with whipped cream. Sample *bicerin*, a layered hot-chocolate-and-espresso drink served in glass cups, available only in Turin, or try *giandujotto*, a foil-wrapped, chocolate-hazelnut candy.

Planning Visit in February for the chocolate festival, Cioccola-Tò. Buy a Choco-Pass at the tourist office and get discounts on sweet treats around the city. www.turismotorino.org, www.cioccola-to.com

❼ Valrhona Chocolate, Tain l'Hermitage, France

In wine-making country, on the Rhône's left bank, visit the home of Valrhona chocolate, favored by many of the world's leading chocolatiers and chefs. Unusually, the chocolate is made only with natural fat from cocoa butter; no vegetable fat is added. Chocoholics will enjoy the chance to sample or buy at the factory shop, while professional chefs can study at Valrhona's École du Grand Chocolat, a chocolate-cookery school.

Planning The factory shop opens daily except Sundays. Explore the medieval city of Tournon, across the river. www.valrhona.com

❽ Chocolate and Churros, Madrid, Spain

Few institutions offer better evidence of Madrid's insomnia than its perennially popular *chocolaterías* (also known as *churrerías*), typically abuzz with late-night revelers from 4 a.m. to breakfast time. Their trademark dish is the *churro*, a long waffle-like stick of savory fried dough, eaten dunked into very thick bittersweet hot chocolate. Stop in at the venerable Chocolatería San Ginés, an 1894 throwback. Expect entertainingly brusque service, bright lights, and a frenzied atmosphere.

Planning Chocolatería San Ginés is downtown on Pasadizo San Ginés. It opens from 9 a.m. to 7 a.m. www.gomadrid.com, www.esmadrid.com

❾ Nemesis, River Café, London, England

One of London's best restaurants and the spawning ground of many a celebrity chef, including Jamie Oliver, the café's signature dessert is the Chocolate Nemesis cake. Gooey with a slight crust on top, it gains its richness from a staggering quantity of chocolate.

Planning Chocoholics can join a Chocolate Ecstasy Tour of London. www.rivercafe.co.uk, www.chocolateecstasytours.com

❿ Chocolate Hotel, Bournemouth, England

To eat, breathe, and sleep chocolate, where better to stay than this chocolate-theme hotel? Chocolate-tasting and chocolate-making classes ensure that chocoholics leave satisfied.

Planning The hotel is on West Cliff, near both beach and downtown. Work up an appetite by walking along the town's magnificent beach. www.thechocolateboutiquehotel.co.uk, www.bournemouth.co.uk

Right: Chocolate, here in a suitably macabre shape, retains an important role in Mexico's religious rituals, such as Oaxaca's Day of the Dead.

Easter Eggs in Paris

Artistic displays of eggs and other chocolate sculptures
herald the arrival of Easter in the French capital.

The shop assistant greets you with "*Joyeux Pâques!*" (Happy Easter) as you walk into the chic little boutique, ducking to avoid the exquisite hand-painted eggshells that are suspended from the rafters like fragile Fabergé creations. Each *oeuf de Pâques* (Easter egg) is a modern-day homage to a French Easter tradition stretching back centuries, when the aristocracy used to spend the last days of winter painstakingly decorating the eggs that were forbidden during Lent in order to present them to each other as Easter gifts. Since the 18th century, when empty eggshells were filled with molten chocolate for Easter, Parisian chocolatiers have been perfecting the art of Easter candy. Stroll down the boulevards and stop to admire the sugary Eastertide delights in the shop windows: a giant Easter egg made of macaroons at Gérard Mulot; pastel-colored eggs and Easter bells (*cloches de Paques*) filled with ganache at Ladurée; a huge egg covered in gold leaf at Pierre Marcolini; or chocolate hens filled with tiny traditional chocolate fish at Jean-Paul Hévin. The ultimate Parisian Easter treat for children is to be let loose in the art deco splendor of Galeries Lafayette on Boulevard Haussmann in search of chocolate eggs in the store's annual Easter-egg hunt. Grown-ups can enjoy a coffee and a slice of *gâteau de Pâques* (a rich chocolate cake often topped with miniature sugar eggs or cherries) under the magnificent glass dome.

When to Go The dates of Easter vary from year to year; if Easter is early (late March), pack for winter; if late (end of April) expect balmier temperatures. April in Paris can be rainy.

Planning Easter Sunday is a holiday, so many shops and restaurants will be closed for the day. Some will remain closed on Easter Monday as well, so be sure to call ahead before arriving at a restaurant. The hour-long egg hunt at Galeries Lafayette is free, but all places must be reserved in advance on the store website—registration closes March 31.

Websites en.parisinfo.com, www.eurostar.com, www2.galerieslafayette.com

Crêpes and *Galettes*

Pancakes, or crêpes, have long been associated with Mardi Gras, when perishable goods were traditionally used up before the 40-day-long fast of Lent. For the best examples, try the **salted butter caramel crepes** at Breizh Café and the savory buckwheat galettes at Crêperie Bretonne.

A galette is also the name of a large, flat cake or tart. Since the Middle Ages, the festival of the Epiphany in January has been celebrated with a Twelfth Night cake known as a *galette des rois*, "kings' cake." The modern cake, a delicious puff-pastry pie filled with frangipane, comes with a paper crown and a special charm or trinket baked into it. The person who gets the slice with the charm is crowned king or queen for the day.

Come Easter, the windows of Paris's chocolatiers and patisseries are decked with *oeufs de Pâques* of every conceivable kind.

The taste of artisanal nougat is a world away from the synthetic nougat fillings in mass-produced candy bars.

FRANCE

MONTÉLIMAR NOUGAT

Eating a slice of freshly made nougat, once a food of the gods, is still a divine experience.

The sound of cicadas and the heady scent of lavender, growing in natural profusion in this corner of Provence, signal your approach to Montélimar, south of Valence, known as the nougat capital of the world. Nougat shops and ateliers line Montélimar's main street, where *nougatiers* like Pierre Bonnieu continue a tradition upheld for centuries. Nougat is an ancient confection based on a whisked mix of egg whites, sugar, and warmed honey enveloping chunks of almonds and pistachios. To be labelled *Nougat de Montélimar*, it must contain 28 percent local aromatic lavender honey, 30 percent almonds, and 2 percent Sicilian pistachios. The ancient Romans offered an early form of nut cake, known as *nux gatum*, to their gods, and the tradition of presenting nougat on special occasions continues to this day. In southern France, the traditional *treize desserts* (the number 13 signifying Jesus and his 12 apostles) eaten on Christmas Eve always include two nougats, one white, the other dark (made of caramelized sugar). On a hot summer's afternoon, opt for a cooling, creamy *glace au nougat* with hints of honey and nuts—a sublime taste of Provence.

When to Go Take at least a week to explore nougat country. From April to the end of June, or from September through October are ideal for travel; avoid the heat and crowds of August.

Planning Travel by TGV (fast train) from Paris to Valence, Montélimar, or Avignon in less than three hours. Many of the ateliers allow visitors to watch nougat being made. Contact the Montélimar tourism office for times. Visits to Boyer in Sault and other nougat-makers are day trips from historic Avignon. *Maître nougatier* André Boyer's shop in Sault merits a detour into the Provence hills.

Websites www.montelimar-tourisme.com, www.beyond.fr

Sweet Provence

■ Created in 1454 for a royal wedding, *calissons* are a specialty of **Aix-en-Provence**. Each *calissonier* has his own secrets for making the lozenge-shaped sweet of almond paste and glazed fruit (most often Cavaillon melon from the town of Cavaillon in Provence) held intact with a sliver of host-wafer paper. On September 1 each year, a special Mass is held in Aix-en-Provence to celebrate the end of a plague in 1630, with calissons replacing host wafers in the Holy Communion. Shop for fine calissons at the Parli boutique in Aix.

■ In March, the hillsides surrounding **Apt** are covered with a profusion of cherry blossom, making this an ideal time to visit this center of **crystallized fruit**. Boutiques and pastry shops sell the finest glazed cherries, pears, melons, and citrus peel. For fresh fruit and divine homemade jams, visit Apt's famous market, which has been held on Saturdays since the 12th century.

■ Made in the shape of a small boat, *navettes* are traditional little pastries, sometimes brushed with orange-flower water, which can be sampled in markets across Provence. In **Marseilles**, where they have been baked since 1781, they are a part of the Candlemas celebrations on February 2. Traditionally, navettes were bought by the dozen, one for each month of the year.

At Bettys, specialty teas and coffees and delicious cakes and breads are served with traditional Yorkshire hospitality.

ENGLAND

Tea at Bettys

One of the jewels in Yorkshire's crown, this family-run business has perfected the tradition of afternoon tea.

The discovery of pungent sulfur-rich springs put Harrogate on the map, but today visitors flock to the genteel spa town in North Yorkshire for a much more palatable kind of refreshment. An ornate wrought-iron canopy bedecked with hanging baskets ushers you into a world that seems hardly to have moved on since the tearoom opened in 1919, the first of a handful of Bettys, all in Yorkshire. Its founder was Frederick Belmont, a Swiss confectioner, which explains why there is Swiss raclette and *rösti* on the menu, alongside the more traditional tarts and tea loaves. When a waitress in a pristine white apron comes to take your order, ask for the afternoon tea with a half-bottle of champagne. Then drift in nostalgic reverie as you nibble your finger sandwiches (fillings like smoked salmon and the local Yorkshire ham are typical) and drool at the exquisite patisseries piled on the cake stand. Other treats include fat rascals, a dense, plump, fruited scone with almonds, citrus peel, and cherries; hot buttered pikelets (small pancakes); sumptuously moist stem-ginger cake; and Bettys fruit cake served with Yorkshire's signature cheese, Wensleydale. And who was Betty? Frederick Belmont never let anybody outside the family know, and nearly a hundred years later, her identity remains a secret.

When to visit The wild, open Yorkshire moors are a stunning location at any time of year, but they are at their very best when the heather blooms and turns them a dusky purple in August and into September.

Planning There is another Bettys at the RHS garden at Harlow Carr in Harrogate, as well as branches in York, Northallerton, and Ilkley. All are extremely popular, so book in advance, especially on weekends. Harrogate is a favorite with antique lovers, who flock to the town's well-stocked antique shops.

Website www.bettys.co.uk

Scones

Every Yorkshire housewife has a recipe for scones, often passed down from her mother. For fruit scones add $1/3$ cup/2 oz/50 g golden raisins with the sugar.

Makes 9 scones
Generous $11/2$ cups/8 oz/225 g
  self-raising flour, sifted
4 tbsp/2 oz/50 g butter
2 tbsp/1 oz/25 g superfine sugar
About $2/3$ cup/5 fl oz/150 ml
  milk, plus extra to glaze

Preheat the oven to 425°F/
220°C/Gas Mark 7.
  Place the flour in a mixing bowl and gently rub in the butter. Stir in the sugar, then mix in enough milk to form a soft dough.
  On a lightly floured surface roll out the dough to $3/4$ in (2 cm) thick and cut out 2 in (5 cm) rounds. Transfer these to a lightly greased baking sheet, and brush the tops with a little extra milk. Bake in the center of the oven for 10 to 12 minutes, until well risen and golden brown.
  Serve warm with plenty of butter and jam.

ENGLAND

DEVONSHIRE CREAM TEA

The West Country is the home of one of England's best-loved afternoon indulgences.

In farms all over the counties of Devon and Cornwall, shallow pans of the finest, freshest unpasteurized milk are heated and carefully watched until a thick, rich cream floats to the top. It is a method that goes back centuries: In the 10th century, Benedictine monks in Tavistock, Devon, handed out the cream to pilgrims helping them to rebuild their abbey. Called clotted cream, this unctuous cream with the consistency of butter is the centerpiece of a Devon cream tea. The other key ingredients are freshly baked scones (two per person) made with butter and either fruited or plain according to your preference, and good homemade strawberry jam—both staples of the traditional farmhouse kitchen. The split scones are generously topped with the clotted cream and jam and the afternoon treat is served with a cup of good strong tea, taken either black or "white" (with milk), but ideally without sugar. These flavors and textures make an irresistible combination. The smooth cream takes the edge off the jam's sweetness, while the scone—halfway between a cookie and a cake—makes a toothsome, crumbly contrast. Traditionally, the hearty scones would have been prepared by the farmer's wife to sustain hungry workers throughout the afternoon, but today a cream tea—served in a farmhouse, tearoom, or pub—is the perfect accompaniment to a relaxing day out in the country.

When to Go Clotted cream–like Devon itself–is best enjoyed in the summer, when the milk is at its richest and the weather is most congenial. Some small farmhouses are open to visitors only during the summer months.

Planning Many farmhouses do not advertise their cream teas. Ask locals where their favorite is– everybody will have an opinion!

Websites www.visitdevon.co.uk, www.devonsfinest.co.uk, www.davidgregory.org/primrose_cottage.htm, www.beautiful-devon.co.uk

Clotted Cream

If you are unable to get to Devon to sample a genuine cream tea, you can try making your own clotted cream at home. You will need access to very fresh, creamy milk. Pour 2 gallons (7.6 liters) of milk straight from the cow into a large, shallow pan and allow it to stand overnight in a cool place, so that the cream rises to the top.

The next day, heat the pan very, very slowly for an hour (the milk should not boil–just shudder very slightly). A thick, wavy layer of yellow cream will gradually appear on the surface. Carefully remove the pan from the heat and allow to cool completely before scooping the clotted cream from the top of the milk. If you don't have any scones, smear the clotted cream over freshly baked bread.

Cows grazing on Devon's lush pasture yield milk with a high enough fat content to produce clotted cream.

INDEX

Acknowledgments

Authors

Jane Adams
Aaron Arizpe
Jaqueline Attwood-Dupont
Matt Barrett
Derek Barton
Katie Cancila
Marolyn Charpentier
Karen Coates
Cathy Danh
Silvija Davidson
Robyn Eckhardt
Alice Feiring
Kay Fernandez
Jacob Field
Ellen Galford
Julie Glenn
Darra Goldstein
Diana Greenwald
Peter Grogan
Ed Habershon
Lisa Halvorsen
Solange Hando
Andy Hayler
Petra Hildebrandt
Paula Hinkel
Jeanne Horak
Sarah Howard
Karen Hursh Graber
Ben Jacobson
Laura Kearney
Andrew Kerr-Jarrett
Diane Kochilas
Diana Kuan
Craig Laban
Tom Le Bas
Ben Ling
Miren Lopategui
Meryanne Loum-Martin
Henrietta Lovell
Margaret McPhee
Glen Martin
Antony Mason
Karryn Miller
Peter Neville-Hadley
Barbara A. Noe
Rose O'Dell King
Katie Parla
John Ralph
Tyler Ralston
Ira de Reuver
Sathya Saran
George Semler
Niamh Shields
Joyce Slayton Mitchell
Barbara Somogyiova
David St Vincent
Barry Stone
Linda Tagliaferro
Adrian Tierney-Jones
Liz Upton
Natalie van der Meer
Johanna-Maria Wagner
Roger Williams
Daven Wu
Joe Yogerst

Recipe Authors

Nick Armitage at The Picture House Restaurant, Bristol, England
Jaqueline Bellefontaine
Katherine Greenwald
Fergus Henderson at St. John Restaurant, London, U.K.
Guido Santi, Convivio Rome, Italy

Toucan Books would like to thank:

Barry & Birgit Blitz
Karin Jones, Hungarian National Tourist Office, London
Doris Lamoso, Puerto Rican Tourism Company, San Juan
Bernard Magrez, Château Pape Clément, Bordeaux
Arne Muncke
Cenk Sonmezsoy
Bethan Wallace, Clementine Communications, London

Picture Credits

T = Top; B = Bottom

1 Left to right: Bruno Morandi/Hemis/Corbis; Hong Kong Tourism Board; Peter Beck/CORBIS; Rawdon Wyatt/Fresh Food Images/Photolibrary; Emilio Suetone/Hemis/Photolibrary; Bob Krist. **2-3** Harald Sund/Getty Images. **4** © Österreich Werbung/Bartl/Austrian National Tourist Office. **5** Tessa Traeger (1); SIME/ Reinhard Schmid /4Corners Images (2); SGM/www.photolibrary.com (3); Caillaut/Photocuisine/www.photolibray.com (4); iCEO/Shutterstock (5); Atlandtide SN.C./age footstock/www.photolibrary.com (6); One&Only Resorts (7); Cuido Cozzi/Atlantide Phototravel/Corbis (8); SIME/Matteo Carassale/4Corners Images (9). **6** Hotel Cipriani, Venice by Orient-Express. **8-9** Tessa Traeger. **10** V.J. Matthew/Shutterstock, T; Ronald Sumners/Shutterstock, B. **11** Brittany Courville/Shutterstock. **13** LOOK Die Bildagentur der Fotografen GmbH/Alamy. **14** Tim Laman/National Geographic/www.photolibrary.com. **15** Traverse City Convention & Visitors Bureau. **16** Catherine Karnow/National Geographic/Getty Images. **17** Thomas Sztanek/Shutterstock, T; Luca Trovato/Foodpix/www.photolibrary.com, B. **19** Fran Gealer/Foodpix/www.photolibrary.com. **20** Peter Gordon/Shutterstock. **21** ©Japan National Tourist Organization. **22** John Noonan, Rare Tea Company. **23** Andy Stewart/Fresh Food Images/www.photolibrary.com. **24** Martin Brigdale/Fresh Food Images/www.photolibrary.com. **25** Iuri/Shutterstock. **26** Stefano Scata/Tips Italia/www.photolibrary.com. **27** Ben Ling, T; newsphotoservice//Shutterstock, B. **28** Roberto Marinello/Shutterstock, **29** ollirg/Shutterstock. **30** David Peevers/Lonely Planet Images. **31** Boath House Hotel. **33** Karl Weatherly/Corbis. **34** SGM/www.photolibrary.com. **35** Ian Shaw/Cephas Picture Library/www.photolibrary.com, T; Pack-Shot/Shutterstock, B. **37** Charles Bowman/Robert Harding Travel/www.photolibrary.com. **38** Turespaña. **39** Philip Lange/Shutterstock. **40** Frederic Courbet/Gallo Images/Getty Images. **41** Olivier Cirendini/Lonely Planet Images. **42-43** SIME/ Reinhard Schmid /4Corners Images. **44** Juan Lopez/©Zabar's & Co, Inc. **45** T.W./Shutterstock, T; Michael Halberstadt, B. **47** Corbis/Franz-Marc Frei. **48** Stephen Saks/Lonely Planet Images. **49** World Pictures/Photoshot, T; Harris Shiffman/Shutterstock, B. **50** Suzanne Wheatley. **51** David Hagerman. **52** Amy Nichole Harris/Shutterstock, T; Juriah Mosin/Shutterstock, B. **53** Teh Eng Koon/AP/Press Association Images. **54** Richard I'Anson/Lonely Planet Images. **55** Martin Roemers/Panos. **57** Jeff Speed/First Light/Getty Images. **58** James Braund/Lonely Planet Images. **59** Alistair Laming/Alamy. **60** Tobik/Shutterstock, T; Japan Travel Bureau Photo/www.photolibrary.com, B. **61** SIME/ Guido Baviera /4Corners Images. **63** Eye Ubiquitous/Robert Harding. **64** Jonathan Smith/Lonely Planet Images. **65** Tibor Bognar/Corbis. **66-67** Ian Armitage. **68** Fortnum and Mason. **69** Andrew McConnell/Robert Harding. **70-71** SGM/www.photolibrary.com. **72** Larry St.Pierre/Shutterstock. **73** Les David Manevitz/ SuperStock. **75** David Loftus. **76** Photo by Timothy Young, Courtesy Food For Thought, Inc. **77** A.Paterson/Shutterstock, T; Paul A.Souders/Corbis, B. **78-79** Peter Charlesworth/OnAsia. **80** ChinaFoto Press/Photocome/Press Association Images. **81** Paul Beinssen/Lonely Planet Images. **82** Franco Figari/Finnish Tourist Board. **83** Gerhard Zwerger-Schoner/imagebroker.net/www.photolibrary.com. **85** Philippe Giraud/Goodlook/Corbis. **86** Hans Rossel. **87** Andrew Cowin/German National Tourist Office. **88** CuboImages/Robert Harding. **89** Gianluca Figliola Fantini/Shutterstock. **91** Christine Osborne/Photos12.com. **92** SIME/Giovanni Simeone/4Corners Images. **93** Alamy/Nicholas Pitt, T; Monkey Business Images Ltd/Stockbroker/www.photolibrary.com, B. **94** Philippe Renault/Hemis/www.photolibrary.com. **95** Owen Franken/Stone/Getty Images. **97** Courtesy of Butterfield & Robinson © Rob Howard. **98** Sami Sarkis/Photodisc/www.photolibrary.com. **99** godrick/Shutterstock. **100-101** Caillaut/Photocuisine/www.photolibray.com. **102** Melissa Brandes/Shutterstock, T; Eric Swanson, B. **103** Hemis.fr/SuperStock, T; rgbspace/Shutterstock, B. **105** Caroline Penn/Panos. **106** Gorm Shakelford/Arcangel Images/www.photolibrary.com, T; Adalberto Rios Lanz/age footstock/www.photolibrary.com, B. **107** Mark Ralston/AFP/Getty. **108** ml-foto/F1 Online/www.photolibrary.com **109** Aaron Arizpe, BL; Four Seasons Hotel, Bangkok, BR. **110** Jean Cazals/Stock Food UK, T; Robert Francis/Robert Harding Travel/www.photolibrary.com, B. **111** Jae Frew. **112-113** Anders Blomqvist/Lonely Planet Images. **114** Ritterbach/F1 Online/www.photolibrary.com. **115** Benjamin F Fink Jr./Foodpix/www.photolibrary.com, T; Greek National Tourism Organization, B. **116** Tenuta di Capezzana. **117** javarman/Shutterstock. **119** Sébastien Boisse/Photononstop/www.photolibrary.com. **120** Barbara Somogyiova, T; Lonely Planet Images/Martin Moos, B. **121** Copyright Le Cordon Bleu International. **123** Neil Phillips/Cephas Picture Library/www.photolibrary.com. **124** Charlotte Hindle/Lonely Planet Images. **125** Vishal Shah/Shutterstock. **126** aniad/Shutterstock, T; JD.Dallet/age footstock/www.photolibrary.com B. **127** Padstow Seafood School. **128** Jean-Pierre Lescourret/Corbis. **129** Hoberman Collection UK/Alamy. **130-131** iCEO/Shutterstock. **132** Bruce Yuan-Yue Bi/ Pictures Colour Library, T; Andrew McDonough/Shutterstock, B. **133** Craig La Ban. **134** Kansas City Convention and Visitors Association. **135** Gunnar Kullenberg/www.photolibrary.com. **136** Debra Cohn-Orbach/Index Stock Imagery/www.photolibrary.com. **137** Gustavo Andrade/Stock Food UK. **138** age footstock/SuperStock. **139** Alan Campbell/Stock Food UK. **140** Jean Chung/OnAsia. **141** dbimages/Alamy. **142** Avril O'Reilly/Alamy. **143** Felix Hug/Lonely Planet. **144** Lou-Foto/Alamy. **145** Tourism Authority of Thailand, T; Ray Laskowitz/Tips Italia/www.photolibrary.com, B. **147** Toru Yamanaka/AFP/Getty Images. **148** Christine Osborne Pictures/Alamy. **149** iCEO/Shutterstock. **150** Julio Etchart/Alamy. **151** Orien Harvey/Lonely Planet Images. **152** Karl Kummels/Superstock/www.photolibrary.com. **153** Annie Griffiths Belt/Corbis, T; State of Israel Ministry of Tourism, B. **154** Ivan Zupic/Alamy. **155** Chris Howes/Wild Places Photography/Alamy. **156** Peter Horree/Alamy. **157** Jackson Vereen/Foodpix/www.photolibrary.com. **158** Bob Krist/Corbis. **159** Isabelle Rozenbaum/Stock Food UK. **160-161** Atlandtide SN.C./age footstock/www.photolibrary.com. **162** Stephen L Saks/Pictures Colour Library. **163** Middleton Place. **165** Jan Kranendonk/Shutterstock. **166** Rosario's Café & Cantina. **167** Philip Gould/Corbis. T; netbritish/Shutterstock, B. **168** Nigel Francis/Robert Harding Travel/www.photolibrary.com. **169** OLA at Sanctuary Hotel, Miami. **170** Richard I'Anson/Lonely Planet Images. **171** Mexico Tourism Board/www.visitmexico.com, T; Danny Lehman/Corbis, B. **172** SIME/Bruno Cossa/4Corners Images. **173** Nico Tondini/Robert Harding Travel/www.photolibrary.com. **174** Krzysztof Dydynski/Lonely Planet Images. **175** Greg Elms/Lonely Planet Images. **177** Conrad Maldives Rangali Island. **178** Jes Aznar/AFP/Getty Images. **179** Regien Paassen/Shutterstock. **180** Gerhard Jörén/OnAsia. **181** Natalie Behring/OnAsia, T; Hong Kong Tourism Board, B. **182** Best View Stock/www.photolibrary.com. **183** Japan Travel Bureau/www.photolibrary.com. **184** Peter Charlesworth/OnAsia. **185** Pier Restaurant, Sydney. **187** Jean Du Boisberranger/www.photolibrary.com. **188** Andrea Pistolesi/Getty Images. **189** Rosemary Behan/Alamy. **190** Aroon Thaewchatturat/OnAsia. **191** Michael Palis/Shutterstock. **193** Ann Cecil/Lonely Planet Images. **194** CuboImages/Robert Harding, T; Aaron Arizpe, B. **195** Atlantide SN.C./age footstock/www.photolibrary.com. **196** CJPhoto/Shutterstock. **197** Claude Vanheye. **198** The Square, London. **199** Horia Bogdan/Shutterstock. **200** The Tower Restaurant, Edinburgh. **201** Gregory Wrona/Pictures Colour Library. **202** Ivars Linards Zolnerovics/Shutterstock. **203** Bernhard Winkelmann/StockFood UK. **204** Corbis/Morton Beebe. **205** Javier Larrea/age footstock/www.photolibrary.com. **206** John Sims/Fresh Food Images/www.photolibrary.com. **207** Michael Jenner/Robert Harding, T; Turespaña, B. **209** Eric Nathan/Pictures Colour Library. **210** Jon Arnold Images/www.photolibrary.com. **211** javarman/Shutterstock. **212** SIME/Reinhard Schmid/4Corners Images. **213** Blues Restaurant and Bar, Cape Town. **214-215** One&Only Resorts **216** Emin Kuliyev/Shutterstock. **217** Photography by Lara Kastner, Courtesy of Alineabook.com. **218** Wynn Las Vegas. **219** Courtesy of MGM MIRAGE. **220** Taj Hotels Resorts and Palaces/Campton Place San Francisco, T; Photograph by Kodiak Greenwood, B. **221** Hotel Carl Gustaf. **223** www.joel-robuchon.com. **224** sunxuejun/Shutterstock. **225** ©Japan National Tourism Organization, T; John Lander/OnAsia, B. **226** Japan Travel Bureau/www.photolibrary.com. **227** ©Japan National Tourism Organization. **228** Robert Wallis/Panos. **229** Hotel Walserhof Klosters, T; Tim Graham Photo Library/Getty Images, B. **231** Lebua Hotels and Resorts. **232** SGM/www.photolibrary.com. **233** Restaurant le Meurice. **235** Ritz Paris. **236** Doug Pearson/Jon Arnold Travel/www.photolibrary.com. **237** Brian Lawrence/Imagestate/www.photolibrary.com. **238** avatra images/Alamy. **239** Hotel Cipriani, Venice by Orient-Express. **240** Jane Mingay/AP/PA Photos. **241** Le Manoir aux Quat'Saisons. **242** Francescu Guillmet/El Bulli. **243** Constance Le Prince Maurice. **244** Cuido Cozzi/Atlantide Phototravel/Corbis. **246** Heaven Hill Distilleries, Inc. **247** Ron Kacmarcik/Shutterstock. **248** Gary Holscher/Getty Images. **249** Widmer Brothers Brewing. **250** Scorpion Mezcal. **251** Yadid Levy/Robert Harding. **253** Bill Wassman/Lonely Planet Images. **254** Andrew Watson/John Warburton-Lee Photography/www.photolibrary.com. **255** Jeff Dunn/Index Stock Imagery/www.photolibrary.com. **256** Andy Christodolo/Cephas Picture Library/www.photolibrary.com, T; Eduardo Longoni/Corbis; B. **257** ©Japan National Tourist Organization/Hokkaido Tourism Association. **258** John Lander/OnAsia. **259** Everett Kennedy Brown/epa/Corbis. **260** South Australia Wine Industry Association Inc. **261** Khirman Vladimir/Shutterstock. **263** Juergen Richter/LOOK-foto/www.photolibrary.com. **264** Norbert Eisele-Hein/imagebroker.net/www.photolibrary.com. **265** Mick Rock/Cephas Picture Library/www.photolibrary.com. **266** Eye Ubiquitous/Photoshot. **267** Holger Leue/Lonely Planet Images. **268** Ian Armitage. **269** photography Zomertijd. **270** Travel Library/Robert Harding. **271** Yvon Monet/Collection CIVC. **273** Ian Shaw/Cephas Picture Library/www.photolibrary.com. **274** Getty Images/Tim Graham Photo Library. **275** Kordcom/age footstock/www.photolibrary.com, T; Natasha Kahn, B. **276** Neil Phillips/Cephas Picture Library/www.photolibrary.com. **277** Fabrizio Bensch/Reuters/Corbis. **278** Tiago Jorge da Silva Estima/Shutterstock. **279** Copyright by Real Companhia Velha. **280** Nigel Blythe/Cephas Picture Library/www.photolibrary.com, T; Igor Terekhov/Shutterstock, B. **281** Richard Cummins/Lonely Planet Images. **283** geogphotos/Alamy. **284** K. Raundrup/T.Kanstrup. **285** Cabrière. **286** SIME/Matteo Carassale/4Corners Images. **288** Mary Altaffer/AP/PA Photos. **289** Sylvain Grandadam/Robert Harding Travel/www.photolibrary.com. **291** Martin Child/Robert Harding. **292** Danita Delimont/Alamy, T; Richard T.Nowitz/Corbis, B. **293** Tim Graham/Getty Images. **294** Hemis.fr/SuperStock. **295** Jean-Luc Bohin/age footstock/www.photolibrary.com, T; Holger Leue/Lonely Planet Images, B. **296** cenap refik ongan/Shutterstock. **297** Steve Outram/Alamy. **298** Christer Fredriksson/Lonely Planet Images, T; Conditori La Glace, B. **299** Barry Blitz. **300** Stephen Saks/Lonely Planet Images. **301** SIME Giovanni Simeone/4Corners Images. **303** Robert Harding Travel/www.photolibrary.com. **304** SIME/Alessandro Saffo/4Corners Images. **305** Paul Harris/John Warburton-Lee Photography/www.photolibrary.com. **306** Regien Paassen/Shutterstock. **307** SIME/Günter Gräfenhan/4Corners Images. **309** Adalberto Rios/age footstock/www.photolibrary.com. **310** Giancarlo Gorassini/ABACA/Press Association Images, T; Joel Saget/AFP/Getty Images, B. **311** J-Charles Gérard/Photononstop/www.photolibrary.com. **312** Harrogate International Centre. **313** Anthony Blake/Fresh Food Images/www.photolibrary.com, T; Stephen Bond/Alamy, B.

Front Cover

Background image: Peter Walton/Index Stock Imagery/Photolibrary.

Picture strip, left to right: Bruno Morandi/Hemis/Corbis; Hong Kong Tourism Board; Peter Beck/CORBIS; Rawdon Wyatt/Fresh Food Images/Photolibrary; Emilio Suetone/Hemis/Photolibrary; Bob Krist.

Back Cover

Background image: Peter Walton/Index Stock Imagery/Photolibrary.

Picture strip, left to right: Aaron Arizpe; Richard T. Nowitz/CORBIS; Floris Sloof/Shutterstock; Catherine Karnow/CORBIS; Gil Giuglio/Hemis/CORBIS; John Warburton-Lee/Photolibrary.

Spine: Nik Wheeler/CORBIS.

Food Journeys of a Lifetime

Published by the National Geographic Society

John M. Fahey, Jr., President and Chief Executive Officer
Gilbert M. Grosvenor, Chairman of the Board
Tim T. Kelly, President, Global Media Group
John Q. Griffin, Executive Vice President;
    President, Publishing
Nina D. Hoffman, Executive Vice President;
    President, Book Publishing Group

Prepared by the Book Division

Barbara Brownell Grogan, Vice President and Editor in Chief
Marianne R. Koszorus, Director of Design
Barbara A. Noe, Senior Editor
Carl Mehler, Director of Maps
Lawrence M. Porges, Project Editor
Carol Farrar Norton, Design Consultant
Bridget A. English, Mary Stephanos, Contributors
R. Gary Colbert, Production Director
Jennifer A. Thornton, Managing Editor
Meredith C. Wilcox, Administrative Director, Illustrations

Manufacturing and Quality Management

Christopher A. Liedel, Chief Financial Officer
Phillip L. Schlosser, Vice President
Chris Brown, Technical Director
Nicole Elliott, Manager
Rachel Faulise, Manager

Created by Toucan Books Ltd

Ellen Dupont, Editorial Director
Helen Douglas-Cooper, Senior Editor
Jo Bourne, Jane Chapman, Andrew Kerr-Jarrett, Anna
    Southgate, Editors
Abigail Keen, Editorial Assistant
Leah Germann, Designer
Christine Vincent, Picture Manager
Sharon Southren, Mia Stewart-Wilson, Picture Researchers
Marion Dent, Proofreader
Michael Dent, Indexer

The information in this book has been carefully checked and is, to the best
of our knowledge, accurate as of press time. It's always advisable to call
ahead, however, as details are subject to change. The National Geographic
Society cannot be responsible for any changes, or for errors or omissions.

The National Geographic Society is one of the world's largest
nonprofit scientific and educational organizations. Founded
in 1888 to "increase and diffuse geographic knowledge," the
Society works to inspire people to care about the planet. It
reaches more than 325 million people worldwide each month
through its official journal, *National Geographic*, and other maga-
zines; National Geographic Channel; television documen-
taries; music; radio; films; books; DVDs; maps; exhibitions;
school publishing programs; interactive media; and mer-
chandise. National Geographic has funded more than 9,000
scientific research, conservation and exploration projects and
supports an education program combating geographic illit-
eracy. For more information, visit nationalgeographic.com.

For more information, please call 1-800-NGS LINE
(647-5463) or write to the following address:

National Geographic Society
1145 17th Street N.W.
Washington, D.C. 20036-4688 U.S.A.

Visit us online at www.nationalgeographic.com

For information about special discounts for bulk purchases,
please contact National Geographic Books Special Sales:
ngspecsales@ngs.org

For rights or permissions inquiries, please contact National
Geographic Books Subsidiary Rights: ngbookrights@ngs.org

LIBRARY OF CONGRESS CATALOGING-IN-PUBLICATION DATA
Food journeys of a lifetime : 500 extraordinary places to eat around the
globe / introduction by Keith Bellows.
    p. cm.
Includes bibliographical references and index.
ISBN 978-1-4262-0507-1 (alk. paper)
1. Food--Anecdotes. 2. Travel--Anecdotes. 3. Food habits. 4.
Restaurants--Guidebooks. I. National Geographic Society (U.S.)
TX357.F646 2009
647.9509--dc22
                    2009019625

Printed in the United States of America

09/RRDW/1